THE ENGLISH LEGAL SYSTEM

A. K. R. KIRALFY, LL.M., PH.D.,
of Gray's Inn, Barrister,
Professor (Emeritus) of Law, University of London

SEVENTH EDITION

LONDON
SWEET & MAXWELL
1984

First Edition	1954
Second Edition	1956
Third Edition	1960
Second Impression	1962
Fourth Edition	1967
Fifth Edition	1973
Sixth Edition	1978
Seventh Edition	1984
Second Impression	1986

Published by
Sweet & Maxwell Ltd. of
11 New Fetter Lane, London,
Computerset by Promenade Graphics Ltd., Cheltenham
and printed in Scotland.

British Library Cataloguing in Publication Data

Kiralfy, A.K.R.
The English Legal System.—7th ed.
1. Law—England   2. Justice, Administration of—
England
I. Title
344.207   KD640

ISBN 0-421-31370-6
ISBN 0-421-31380-3 Pbk

PREFACE

There have been some unusually important changes since the last edition in the field covered by this book. Service of the writ by post has been made general in civil actions and the idea of a notional appearance by the defendant finally eliminated. Here the policy of assimilating High Court and County Court procedure is dominant. The law of contempt of court has been modified in a way which may impose further restrictions on publicity of trial. The role of the Director of Public Prosecutions has also been clarified and the "vetting" of juries formalised. Still newer types of sentence for juvenile offenders are being introduced in an effort to cope with the evergreen problem of the high proportion of crimes committed by the young.

The introduction of the *Mareva* injunction confers on plaintiffs a type of protection long familiar on the Continent of Europe, the securing of judgments against evasion. Charging orders on land add still another to the growing list of forms of enforcement of civil judgments. The House of Lords has explained, but hardly clarified, the question of how far confidential documents are protected from disclosure. The implications of membership of the European Community have been worked out more fully.

There has been a welter of consolidating statutes, but there is much new law as well in the Criminal Justice Act 1982 and some in the Supreme Court Act of 1981. The Arbitration Act 1979 has been taken into account and the Forfeiture Act 1982.

If the current Police and Criminal Evidence Bill passes unchanged it will extend the powers of arrest by police and private individuals and computer print-outs will be admitted in evidence. Other bills may change the distribution of divorce jurisdiction.

The Index has been prepared by Routledge Associates.

King's College London
December 1, 1983   ALBERT KIRALFY

THE ENGLISH LEGAL SYSTEM

AUSTRALIA AND NEW ZEALAND
The Law Book Company Ltd.
Sydney : Melbourne : Perth

CANADA AND U.S.A.
The Carswell Company Ltd.
Agincourt, Ontario

INDIA
N.M. Tripathi Private Ltd.
Bombay
and
Eastern Law House Private Ltd.
Calcutta and Delhi
M.P.P. House
Bangalore

ISRAEL
Steimatzky's Agency Ltd.
Jerusalem : Tel Aviv : Haifa

MALAYSIA : SINGAPORE : BRUNEI
Malayan Law Journal (Pte.) Ltd.
Singapore and Kuala Lumpur

PAKISTAN
Pakistan Law House
Karachi

CONTENTS

TABLE OF CASES

ix

TABLE OF STATUTES

Chapter 1

THE DIVISIONS OF ENGLISH LAW

Case Law and Statute

In many countries legislation is regarded as the normal type of law, and judicial decisions as merely a supplementary or explanatory source, but in England there were few statutes of any great importance until the thirteenth century and even after that time statutes were largely confined to matters of public law. Hence the basic principles of private law were left to be laid down by the courts in the light of common sense and experience under the prevailing feudal conditions.

Even when statutes had become extremely important, as in the nineteenth century, they used language which had acquired a precise meaning in judge-made law, and the courts have the sole right to explain what the legal meaning and effect of a statute is. The courts also developed ground rules as to the interpretation of statute. Unlike the Continental Civil Law systems our statute law has no unifying principles in itself.

It is, therefore, most convenient to deal with "common law" as developed by the courts of common law and then "equity" as developed by the old Court of Chancery, as the basic divisions of English law, modified in their details from time to time by statute, but tending to survive in their fundamentals.

History of the common law of England

The common law is the law of all persons and of all parts of England and Wales. Before the Norman Conquest there were many county customs. There were differences in the law of the various Saxon Kingdoms, and, after the Viking invasions, between the Dane law in the north-eastern half of the country and the Saxon law in the south and west. The unified authority of such Kings as Edgar, Aethelred and Cnut, to legislate for the whole of England did not result in any immediate unification of the rules of law. William the Conqueror undertook to preserve the existing English laws at the time of the Conquest. This was evidently honoured for some time, as lawyers thought it worthwhile to

1

compile "reconstructed" textbooks of Anglo-Saxon law several generations after the Conquest. Seventeenth-century radicals, from Coke to the Levellers still spoke of a restoration of Anglo-Saxon law. But, except where it survived as local custom, as in some boroughs, it had become obsolete soon after the Conquest.

The reasons for the supersession of Anglo-Saxon law by Norman law were practical. The administration of justice and the ownership of land were concentrated in Norman hands. The defeated population were suppressed to a low level of influence and power. The Norman invaders possessed some rudiments of law, since in those days most important men had judicial powers and were acquainted with law and administration. These were adapted to English conditions and underwent a special development here during Angevin times. They may be said to be native rather than English. By the time the English-speaking elements in the population had won a share of power the fabric of the law had become as firm and indestructible as the fabric of the great medieval cathedrals. An occasional writer lamented the passing of the good old laws of Saxon times, often with a very garbled idea of what they had been,[1] but there was no organised attempt to restore the Saxon laws. Most insurgent movements came from within the aristocracy and were designed to preserve the Norman law from alteration. The new rulers themselves soon became nationalistic and drew away from their European legal connections. Thus, in the thirteenth century, the Barons rejected any reference to precedents from Europe in deciding a dispute in England.[2] Succession to land by the eldest son, a rule based on military expediency, became general in England though not in the Norman possessions of the Crown.[3] A special form of tenure of land had come into existence which was called an estate "by the law (or courtesy) of England," to distinguish it from different estates in Normandy.[4] Baronial opposition to foreign law extended to the canon law of the Church and in 1235 the Council of Merton rejected the introduction of the idea of legitimation of an illegitimate child by the subsequent marriage of its parents, because they were unwilling to change the laws of England.

The villeins, in the Peasants' Revolt (1381), wreaked their wrath on the doctors of civil and canon law[5] and in their opposition to all

---

[1] As in Andrew Horn's *Mirror of Justices*, Selden Society Publications, Vol. VII.
[2] Pollock and Maitland, *History of English Law* (2nd ed.), Vol. I, 184.
[3] *Ibid*. Vol. II, 268.
[4] *Ibid*. Vol. II, 415.
[5] Plucknett, *Concise History of the Common Law* (5th ed.), 186.

authority attacked lawyers, and murdered a judge,[6] but not in order to restore the Saxon system. The Pilgrimage of Grace (1536–37), was directed against changes in the law, but these were changes which affected the gentry rather than the commoners.[7] Hence we may say that the Normans had become Englishmen and their law had become distinctively English law. This Norman law was strengthened in the fourteenth century by the growth of the professional Bench and Bar.[8]

In medieval times cities and boroughs had their own customs, confirmed by royal charters, and their own courts. Their urban laws were more commercially oriented than the rather agrarian common law in many respects, e.g. they continued to enforce informal contracts and avoided trial by battle and most features of feudal land-holding. The royal common law tended in time to copy their more progressive rules and adopt urban law, e.g. rights to light and to support by neighbouring buildings.

Bases of the common law

Norman law was at first directed to establish the rights of the new class of Norman landowners, holding as feudal vassals of the Crown, and bringing actions in the royal courts to prove their title to land. The law of "real property" was, therefore, the cornerstone of the medieval common law. Criminal law was also of great importance because the commission of a felony (a particularly serious crime) led to the forfeiture of the criminal's land. "Freehold" and "felony" were, therefore, the two outstanding issues. Other branches of private law gradually developed, especially through the extension of the jurisdiction of the royal courts to matters formerly generally tried in the local courts, such as the recovery of debts and of damages for trespasses.

The declaratory theory of the common law

The common law is a living law. From minute origins it has grown to enormous proportions and is still capable of further growth. This is due to the declaratory theory of the common law. A decision of a court operates retrospectively, declaring what the law is and has been, rather than what it shall be.

In this way it is possible to date the earliest instances of actions at law in various fields, such as trespass and case.[9] It is also

---

[6] Cavendish, C.J. See Foss's *Dictionary of the Judges of England*, 160; Cohen, *History of the English Bar*, 450. The rebels destroyed many legal records and title deeds.
[7] Plucknett, *ubi supra*, 587.
[8] *Ibid.* 237 *et seq.*
[9] *Infra* pp. 35, 40.

possible to date changes in the elements required in such actions. Thus the action of covenant was well known in the time of Henry III, but the rule that the plaintiff must be able to produce a document under seal as proof of the covenant came a century later.[10] The rapid expansion of the Register of Writs from the thirteenth to the seventeenth centuries is a token of the readiness of the courts to allow completely new types of remedy, only a fraction of which had any statutory basis. Maitland said of the Register that "It is a book that grew for three centuries and more. During these three centuries its size increased twenty-fold, thirty-fold, perhaps fifty-fold."[11] At the same time the rules of liability and excuse and other matters also grew in numbers and complexity. A shelf-full of treatises has had to be replaced by large law libraries.

Legal fictions

The common law has always tended to become rigid. Owing to the doctrine of precedent its declarations of law are irrevocable, except by a higher court. Decisions of the highest courts cannot generally be reversed. In order to keep the law in harmony with changing conditions several agencies of law reform have been employed. As Sir Henry Maine pointed out in a classic passage,[12] "These instrumentalities seem to me to be three in number, Legal fictions, Equity, and Legislation." The use of legal fictions was general and salutary, since the judges themselves were in charge of the process. In this way the hereditary entail of land was broken by the fiction known as the "common recovery."[13] The deficiencies of the old and ineffective actions of debt and detinue, for the recovery of money or goods, were overcome by fictitious claims of "indebitatus assumpsit" and "trover." The first rested on an imaginary second promise to pay a debt, and the second on a pretended or supposed accidental loss and finding of goods, which had actually been borrowed or hired.[14] The cumbrous and dilatory remedies for the recovery of land were replaced by a speedy and effective action known as "ejectment" which called upon two imaginary characters, John Doe and Richard Roe, to take part.[15]

---

[10] Pollock and Maitland, *History of English Law* (2nd ed.), Vol. II, 216; Fifoot, *History and Sources of the Common Law*, 257.

[11] History of the Register of Original Writs, in *Select Essays in Anglo-American Legal History*, Vol. II, 549.

[12] *Ancient Law* (Pollock Edition), 29; see also Kiralfy, 10 Amer. Jl. Leg. Hist. (1966), 3; Olivier, P., *Legal Fictions in practice and legal science* (1975).

[13] Potter, *Historical Introduction to English Law* (4th ed.), 533.

[14] *Ibid.* 409, 466.

[15] *Ibid.* 509; cf. *Barnett* v. *French* [1981] 1 W.L.R. 848.

The rigour of the old criminal law, demanding the death sentence for all kinds of felonies, was tempered by a series of fictions, such as benefit of clergy (where a first offender was treated as a priest), assessment of the value of stolen articles at ridiculously low figures, so that the theft could be treated as "petty," and the general power of a jury to acquit in the teeth of a judge's direction to convict the prisoner.[16]

CIVIL AND CRIMINAL LAW

Civil proceedings are taken in order to assist individuals to recover property or enforce obligations made in their favour. Criminal proceedings are taken to suppress crime and punish criminals, and are under the control of the state. In fact many criminal proceedings are also designed to protect the person and property of individuals, and the state may have just as much interest in the stability of civil rights as the individual himself. The real difference between civil and criminal law rests on the form of proceedings and the nature of the courts concerned. (We are not here concerned with "civil law" as indicating modern Roman law as contrasted with English "common law").[17]

History

As the distinction between civil and criminal law is a rationalisation rather than a natural difference, it is to be expected that it would be foreign to early systems of law. Under the Anglo-Saxons a single body of courts existed, in the shires and hundreds, and a single wrong might be redressed by a combination of civil and criminal remedies. Thus a man who wounded another would have to pay compensation to the victim and a penalty to the King. After the Norman Conquest this double jurisdiction survived in the local courts. But the Norman Kings introduced the Pleas of the Crown, reserved for royal courts, mainly "felonies" like robbery and murder. Most other proceedings were civil actions to recover property, including money.

In between the personal actions and the Pleas of the Crown an intermediate group of wrongs were developed by the royal courts known as "trespasses against the King's peace." These all involved some form of violent interference with the person or property of another. The defendant was compelled to pay damages by way of compensation and was also fined for breach of the peace so that

---

[16] *Ibid.* 361; Holdsworth, *History of English Law* (5th ed.), Vol. III, 367, 292.
[17] *Cf.* Milsom, *Historical Foundations of the Common Law* (1969), pp. 353–355.

both civil and criminal elements were present. The civil aspect of trespass developed rapidly and produced the modern law of contract and tort, the criminal aspect developed slowly; some trespasses were tried criminally at the Eyres and Assizes and a number of others were tried by the justices of the peace when these had come into existence. There were very few of these common law crimes "under the degree of felony," but legislation has been responsible for creating a very large number of them over the centuries, known from Tudor times as "misdemeanours," and now as indictable offences. Felonies have now been absorbed in these.

Distinction

Civil law has been largely created in response to pressure from below. Some person has suffered material loss through the act or omission of another and has resorted to the courts for a remedy. Criminal law, on the other hand, is imposed from above. The reasons for the creation of new crimes or the addition of criminal to civil sanctions are various. In some cases no particular individual has any interest in taking the initiative, as in the case of sedition or disclosure of official secrets, as the damage to any one individual caused by an offence against the community is too remote and indirect. In other cases the criminal law is preventive and this requires special public organisations, such as the police force, which do not function in the field of civil law. Public policy requires that the mere counterfeiting of money be an offence even before a single piece of counterfeit money has been passed to a victim. Otherwise counterfeiters could operate their machinery with impunity and be immune from search and arrest. In the same way it is an offence to loiter in certain circumstances, so that the police may arrest a suspect without waiting for a crime to be committed.

Civil wrongs do not generally involve any detective problems. A creditor knows that he has not been repaid by his debtor. A property owner knows that the noxious fumes come from his neighbour's factory. "Hit and run" motorists are uncommon. Disputes as to liability and evidence occur, but seldom problems of identity. In criminal law, on the other hand, detection and identification are important and require a public machinery of investigation. The very fact of the commission of a murder may be unknown until years have elapsed and the body is accidentally recovered. Elaborate frauds may mean that money is embezzled for long periods before detection. Even when it is known that a crime has been committed it is often difficult to identify the criminal and no less difficult to apprehend him. Thus in one case a prisoner admitted over six hundred other unpunished offences. Private actions by the occasional victim who did apprehend the criminal would be futile as a deterrent.

Criminal sanctions punish, to deter other wrongdoers from imitation, and try to correct and reform the criminal, and satisfy public feeling. If all else fails, a criminal sentence can at least keep the criminal from preying on society for a time.

In the modern welfare state many new offences have been created which are really different from the traditional crimes, in that they are not the work of professional or dangerous criminals. But here again there is seldom any private person directly interested in taking action. The private individual may even sympathise with the wrongdoer or dislike the policy of the law. Hence many economic and financial offences must be dealt with by criminal procedure, rather than civil procedure. In order to enforce some social regulations special administrative courts have been set up, which cannot be fitted into any strict division into civil and criminal courts, applying rules which are neither civil nor criminal but administrative. Whether these form part of our "legal system" in the sense of regular judicial machinery will fall to be discussed later.

Courts

Owing to accidents of history, English courts tend to form two distinct hierarchies, one trying civil and the other criminal cases.

Civil cases, including matrimonial cases, are tried by local county courts and by the High Court in London and certain large cities, appeals being taken to the civil division of the Court of Appeal.

Criminal cases triable by jury are tried by Crown Courts, with an appeal to the criminal division of the Court of Appeal.

Summary criminal cases are tried by magistrates' courts with an appeal to a Crown Court or a Divisional Court.

The House of Lords is the final court of appeal for all cases.

Double aspects of wrongs

A single act or omission may at one and the same time constitute a crime and a civil wrong. This generally means that separate proceedings will have to be taken in different courts. The injured party will often have an option. If the defendant is wealthy the victim may prefer to sue for damages; if he is not, he may have the satisfaction of seeing him punished. In one case, that of assault and battery, it is specifically provided by statute that one or other remedy must be pursued and not both.[18]

The burden of proof in a criminal case is more difficult to discharge than in a civil case, although it may approach it in a civil claim based on the commission of a crime.[19]

The rules of evidence in civil and criminal proceedings differ, e.g. an admission is readily accepted in civil cases whereas a confession is rather suspect in criminal cases.

An accused person may plead guilty to a criminal charge and still raise questions of civil liability, e.g. have the amount of damages reduced by reason of the misconduct of the victim.[20]

Where any person is convicted of a crime, there is now a statutory presumption in any later civil action that this decision is correct. It is possible to rebut this presumption only by producing new evidence. The civil court will not of itself dispute the original conviction.[21] The burden of proof on the convicted person is the civil standard and not that of proof of innocence beyond all doubt.[22]

It is specifically provided that a conviction cannot be questioned in libel or slander actions which impute guilt to the convicted person.[23] This does not apply to spent convictions.[24]

The duality of courts does not mean that there is a duality of law. All courts are supposed to take judicial notice of the whole of the law. The civil law may be relevant in a criminal case and criminal law in a civil case. Where a crime requires, for example, that something be taken out of the possession of another person the criminal court may have to decide whether the complainant was in fact in possession, on which there is much authority in civil law. Whether a vehicle is covered by insurance, for the purpose of a highway offence, may depend on the construction of the contract of insurance in civil law. A civil court will not enforce a contract which is designed to offend the criminal law, e.g. a sale at prices in excess of a legal maximum, or compensate a widow whose husband supported her out of the proceeds of crimes.[25] An insurance policy may not lawfully cover certain risks, such as a

[18] Offences against the Person Act 1861, s.45.
[19] *Re Dellow's Will Trusts* [1964] 1 W.L.R. 451. *Cf. Munnich* v. *Godstone R.D.C.* (1965) 63 L.G.R. 506; *R.* v. *Watts and Stack* (1979) 70 Cr.App.R. 187.
[20] *Murphy* v. *Culhane* [1976] 3 W.L.R. 458 (C.A.).
[21] Civil Evidence Act 1968, s.11(1)(2); *Wauchope* v. *Mordecai* [1970] 1 W.L.R. 317 (C.A.); *Re Raphael* [1973] 1 W.L.R. 998; *cf. Hunter* v. *Chief Constable of the West Midlands Police* [1981] 3 W.L.R. 906 (H.L.); *McIlkenny* v. *Chief Constable of the West Midlands* [1980] Q.B. 283.
[22] *Stupple* v. *Royal Insurance Co.* [1971] 1 Q.B. 50.
[23] Civil Evidence Act, s.13; *Levene* v. *Roxham* [1970] 1 W.L.R. 1322 (C.A.).
[24] Rehabilitation of Offenders Act 1974, ss.4, 8.
[25] *Burns* v. *Edman* [1970] 2 Q.B. 541.

deliberate crime by the assured, as this is against public policy.[26] If a crime is committed by "offering" some object for sale, the civil law of contract decides whether an "offer" was made.[27]

Civil actions may not be used to prejudice a pending prosecution in a basically criminal matter.[28]

Statutory torts

A statute imposing a duty or creating an offence may be interpreted by the courts as implying a right to a civil action in favour of persons sought to be protected by the statute. Although statutes are now carefully drafted, the individual still often benefits in this way today. In one case in point the defendant lent his car to an uninsured person whose driving injured the plaintiff. It was a statutory offence to allow your car to be used without insurance cover against third-party risks, because the insurance money would be needed to meet any liability to pay damages.[29] The borrower had no means of his own. The plaintiff was held entitled to recover his damages from the defendant.[30] In a later case a workman injured in a mine as a result of a breach of statutory safety regulations was held entitled to damages.[31]

A house buyer has been allowed to sue a local authority whose inspector passed an improper building plan.[32] On the other hand attempts to bring civil actions for a number of road traffic offences, to obviate the need to prove the defendant's negligence, have been unsuccessful.[33]

Civil and criminal remedies

In principle civil law provides for a complete recovery of losses suffered, including injury to health, shock and loss of earning power, but nothing in the nature of a criminal penalty. It was traditional for damages of an exemplary or punitive nature to be awarded in some civil actions for tort. The House of Lords has however decided that such punitive damages should only be

---

[26] *Haseldine* v. *Hoskin* [1933] 1 K.B. 822; *cf. Ashton* v. *Turner* [1981] Q.B. 137, no civil claim for injuries due to negligent driving of fellow burglar.

[27] *Fisher* v. *Bell* [1961] 1 Q.B. 394 (D.C.), requring the passing of The Restriction of Offensive Weapons Act 1961. *Cf. Mella* v. *Monahan* [1961] Crim.L.R. 175, resulting in Obscene Publications Act 1964; *Partridge* v. *Crittenden* [1968] 1 W.L.R. 1204; *N.C.B.* v. *Thorne* [1976] 1 W.L.R. 543 (D.C.).

[28] *Imperial Tobacco* v. *Att. Gen.* [1981] A.C. 718 (H.L.); *Adams* v. *Commissioner of Police of the Metropolis* [1980] R.T.R. 289.

[29] Now Road Traffic Act 1972, s.143.

[30] *Monk* v. *Warbey* [1935] 1 K.B. 75.

[31] *Grant* v. *N.C.B.* [1956] A.C. 649.

[32] *Dutton* v. *Bognor Regis U.D.C.* [1972] 1 Q.B. 373.

[33] *Coote* v. *Stone* [1971] 1 W.L.R. 279 (C.A.); *Keating* v. *Elvan Reinforced Concrete Co.* [1968] 1 W.L.R. 722. *Scott* v. *Green & Sons* [1969] 1 W.L.R. 301.

awarded in a very few cases (which will be dealt with in Chapter 6).

In principle criminal law punishes the convicted man and does not compensate his victim, but there are some cases in which a kind of civil relief is given in criminal proceedings, to save disproportionate delay and expense. Thus stolen goods may be recovered in a successful criminal prosecution for an ordinary theft.[34] Compensation for material loss or injury to the victim may be ordered by the court which convicts the defendant if there is no real dispute about the civil law position, after hearing representations by the prosecutor and accused.[35] The defendant's means are taken into account.[36] Special provisions exist for the return of stolen property by order of a magistrates' court in straightforward cases.[37] Criminal insolvency orders can be made against offenders required to pay substantial compensation.[38]

A special scheme of *ex gratia* payments for losses over £400 to victims of crime and sufferers in the apprehension of criminals also exists in the form of a Criminal Injuries Compensation Board. Amounts are in line with damages awards in the courts, but technical rules of liability are not followed. Dependants of deceased victims may also apply.[39]

SUBDIVISIONS OF CRIMINAL LAW

Felonies and misdemeanours

The basic historic division of crimes was into felonies and misdemeanours. There are various theories as to the derivation of the word "felony," but there is no doubt that it connoted a heinous and despicable crime, and that the felon, like the outlaw, was disloyal to the Crown and deserving no legal protection. The punishment of death was the only sentence for felonies or for treason. Hence there was a natural reluctance to extend the class of felonies and they remained restricted to crude offences against

---

[34] Theft Act 1968, s.28; it is inappropriate for long-term complicated thefts. (*R. v. Thebith* [1970] Crim. L.R. 298) or where the ownership of the money is not clear (*R. v. Ferguson* (1970) 114 S.J. 472 (C.A.)).

[35] Powers of the Criminal Courts Act 1973, s.35 (amd. 1982); *R. v. Inwood* (1974) 60 Cr.App.R. 70 (C.A.); Magistrates' Courts Act 1980, s.40 (£1,000 limit).

[36] *Ibid.*, s.35(4); *R.. v. Miller (Note)* (1976) 68 Cr.App.R. 56 (C.A.). He should not be burdened with long-term reparations, *R. v. Hunt* (1982) 12 C.L.Y. 333a.

[37] *e.g.* Police Property Act 1897, s.1; *R. v. Chester Justices, ex p. Smith* (1977) 67 Cr.App.R. 133; Police (Disposal of Property) Regs. 1975.

[38] Powers of the Criminal Courts Act 1973, s.39; *R. v. Reilly* [1982] 3 W.L.R. 149 (C.A.); *D.P.P. v. Anderson* [1978] A.C. 964.

[39] See C.I.C.B. 1982 report. (Cmnd. 8752) and (1978) 3 C.L.Y. 60; *R. v. C.I.C.B.* (1983) 1 C.L. 355a.

person and property like murder, arson, robbery and rape. The medieval common law developed a special procedure to deal with these crimes.

New offences were created by statute or by Star Chamber practice and not classed as felonies. They were generally known as trespasses or transgressions, and, since Tudor times, as misdemeanours. A different procedure was also followed in such cases. Misdemeanours were not capital offences, nor did they involve forfeiture of property. Their punishment was by fines or imprisonment.

This division of crimes was sensible so long as felonies remained grave crimes and misdemeanours minor offences. But the penalty of death has been abrogated except in the case of treason and imprisonment substituted, and at the same time the penalties and gravity of misdemeanours have increased. The differences in practice, therefore, had become anomalous and many were removed by statute.

The distinction between felonies and misdemeanours is now abolished, and all matters of law and practice in which there existed a distinction between felonies and misdemeanours are dealt with as for misdemeanours.[40] The present law distinguishes for particular purposes between "arrestable" and "prisonable" offences and other offences.[41]

Indictable and non-indictable offences

The most important and logical distinction today is between indictable and non-indictable offences, since the procedure to be followed differs markedly in the two cases. Procedure on indictment requires a preliminary hearing by magistrates and then trial by jury, whereas summary proceedings are by an immediate trial on the merits by the magistrates without a jury.

Some offences, like murder, can only be prosecuted on indictment. Others, of a minor nature, are solely the subject of summary proceedings. In many cases an offence may be dealt with either summarily or on indictment.

SUBDIVISIONS OF CIVIL LAW

Contract and tort

In medieval times each type of civil action had rules of its own. If you sued for repayment of a debt the method of trial was quite

[40] Criminal Law Act 1967, s.1.
[41] *Ibid*. s.2; Bail Act 1976, Sched. 1.

different from that used in suing to recover possession of land, and that in its turn differed from the procedure used to recover damages for an injury. Many of the older actions became obsolete and were later abolished, but a basic difference still remains between certain main types of action. An action to recover land still differs considerably from all other actions. A suit for a decree of divorce or similar relief aims at a ruling on status. Most other actions are brought to recover payment of a sum of money and these "common law" actions have many common features. Since the reforms of the nineteenth century they have been commenced by an ordinary writ of summons and eventually result, if successful, in judgment for payment of a fixed sum of money.

Within this field an important distinction must be drawn between actions based on tort and actions based on breach of contract. Contracts are concluded by agreements of the participants and are generally enforceable in the absence of various invalidating circumstances. An action in tort (literally "wrong doing") is based on an obligation imposed by law or due to all persons generally. In many cases the parties have never met until the tort occurs, as in the case of a highway collision. The general rule is left to apply. The use of the word "specialty" to describe a contract under seal illustrates this. The making of a contract was considered as the creation of a special law between the parties, apart from which the general law, or law of tort, would apply. There were many historical links between tort and contract, but a general rule developed that an action based on tort could not be combined with one based on breach of contract. Today this is no longer true, but the rule led to a growing separation, and there are important practical consequences even now. A difference over punitive damages has already been mentioned. The jurisdiction of the court to proceed against a defendant who is abroad is also somewhat different. Some details of trial procedure differ. Some tort claims are not provable in the defendant's bankruptcy, and there is no apportionment of damages in contract cases, as there is in some tort actions for negligence.

A curious feature of English law is the possibility of treating the same act or omission as a tort and a breach of contract, e.g. railway accident cases.[42] Alternate claims may now be joined in a single action, but only the single amount of damages is recoverable.

In most cases where alternative remedies in tort and contract exist, the standard of liability is the same. Thus a railway can be sued in tort for negligence resulting in personal injuries to a plaintiff. If the plaintiff sues for breach of a contract to carry him

---

[42] *Lister* v. *Romford Ice & Cold Storage Co.* [1957] A.C. 555.

safely to the destination on his ticket he will find that the liability of the defendant railway is limited to using due care to transport him.[43] On the other hand, pure contract claims like actions to recover loans require no proof of fault on the part of the defendant; it is no defence that he has been robbed, for example, of the money he had set aside to repay the loan.

In some cases it is only possible to sue in tort, even if there is a contract. If B calls in a doctor, C, to treat his child, A, and C is negligent in his treatment, A cannot sue C on the contract made between B and C, but he can sue C in tort.[44]

Where unmerchantable or defective goods are sold by a retailer and the plaintiff is injured, but the retailer was not negligent, an action will lie against the retailer though there is no action against the retailer in tort.[45] An employee may be fully liable to indemnify his employer for liability caused by the employee's negligence, as a matter of implied contract, where the employer is vicariously liable to the victim in tort.[46]

There are also cases in the law of tort where liability is strict, so that the defendant will be liable, except for certain specified defences, quite independently of any fault on his part.[47]

Real property

The English law of property is marked by great variety and complexity. The law of land or "real property" is particularly well developed. English law was formed in feudal times when land was all-important. Even today all activities are carried on upon the land and all material things come from or out of the land. Besides the absolute ownership of land it is possible to construct a series of successive interests in land by means of wills and settlements; the permanence of land making such future provision possible. There are also a number of distinctive interests in and incumbrances on land, such as tenancies or leases, mortgages by which land is made the security for repayment of a debt, rights of way and light vested in neighbouring owners. The ordinary law of tort, on the other hand, governs the actual use and occupation of land. It applies to cases of trespass or nuisance and to cases where persons are injured owing to the unsafe condition of property. It is only where some question of title arises, or some document creating or conveying interests in land is to be construed, that the law of

---

[43] E. Indian Railway Co. v. Kalidas Mukerjee [1901] A.C. 396.
[44] Winfield, Province of the Law of Tort, 69, 73.
[45] Sale of Goods Act 1979, s.14; Grant v. Australian Knitting Mills [1936] A.C. 85.
[46] Lister v. Romford Ice & Cold Storage Co. [1957] A.C. 555.
[47] Rylands v. Fletcher (1866) L.R. 1 Ex. 265; J. & J. Makin Ltd. v. L.N.E.R. [1943] 1 K.B. 467 (C.A.).

property becomes relevant. If your operations on land cause your neighbour's house to collapse, the particular nature of your interest is irrelevant. The margin between tort and property may be very slight. Thus an interference with a natural right of air or light is a tort, but an interference with a specially acquired easement of air or light is a matter of land law. Title to land used to be traced back through a series of different types of conveyances over a number of years. A comprehensive system of registration of title has now been extended to most parts of England, but still reflects the old substantive interests in land.

In medieval times most actions were brought to recover land from intruders. In more settled times we encounter few of these. Actions concerning land title generally take one of three forms. In one a landlord sues a tenant under a lease to recover possession of his land. The tenant cannot dispute the landlord's title but may resist the action on other grounds, whereas as against a squatter in possession, a plaintiff must prove title. The second type of case is a dispute between a vendor and a purchaser, the latter alleging that the vendor's title is defective. The remedy here lies in contract. The third type of case is where a dispute arises as to the meaning of a will or settlement of land. As executors and trustees often have wide powers of sale, this type of case is concerned with equivalent values rather than the actual piece of land settled or devised.

Personal property

All other forms of property are considered to be personal property. These fall into three groups. Tenancies of land and a few other interests are considered to be "chattels real" and are governed by many of the rules of land law. Tangible chattels, such as goods, are termed "choses in possession." Incorporeal rights not connected with land are termed "choses in action," ranging from the interests represented by stocks and shares in limited liability companies to patent privileges and to copyright in plays and films. English law has never developed a uniform law of personal property. Owing to their impermanence and mobility, it is rare to attempt to settle choses in possession on people successively, or to trace title to chattels for any long period. It is unusual to sue for restitution of goods as a matter of property; if A contracts to sell goods to B and fails to deliver them, B will probably sue for breach of contract. If A takes away B's goods without B's consent, B will probably sue A for the tort of taking his goods by trespass. If B finds his goods in A's possession he will sue A for the tort of conversion.

When one passes to the law of choses in action two points stand out. They are so diverse in nature and bewildering in variety that there is little room for common legal principles. Thus disputes as to the extension of the term of a patent for some mechanical device have little in common with a claim to a dividend on a share in a company or to compensation for the goodwill of a business. The rules on assignment differ widely. It is, however, common to make a will of all one's property or to settle all one's property on trusts, or to become bankrupt while owner of a number of these interests. In this field, that of "universal succession," a common financial valuation may be made and common rules of equity applied, since it is the value of the object which is important, and not its peculiar features as an object. The result is that something in the nature of a general law of personal property has developed in equity to deal with beneficial interests, although there is little general law governing the physical objects themselves.

EQUITY

Legal rules have always been subject to modification in particular cases.[48] This is demonstrated by the prerogative of mercy in criminal procedure under which the Crown, on the advice of the Home Secretary, pardons a convicted criminal or reduces his sentence. The Crown has no right, however, to pardon a private debt or excuse the performance of a private obligation. In such cases the suit is not that of the Crown but a subject, and the subject is entitled to his remedy in the courts. Yet general rules often work hardship in civil cases, and the Sovereign was expected to mitigate these hardships.

Origin and nature of equity

In medieval times Parliament met infrequently and was unwilling to concern itself with the intricacies of law. The common law judges hesitated at various critical periods, especially during the fifteenth century, to mould the law as constructively and liberally as they had on other occasions. Hence the law became prematurely rigid, not only in its substantive rules of ownership and liability, but also in its forms of trial and rules of evidence and procedure. The Lord Chancellor, as keeper of the royal conscience, and with the authority of the Sovereign and the Council of State, took it upon himself to satisfy petitions for relief in those cases where the

---

[48] See Coke's view, in 1 Inst. f. 24b. The idea is at least as old as Aristotle's day, Nichomachean Ethics, V.14. See *Equity in the World's Legal Systems* (1973) ed. R.A. Newman.

rules of common law were lacking or worked injustice. The Chancellor, and the formal Court of Chancery which grew up to exercise this jursidiction, never interfered with the rules of law without strong moral grounds, holding that "equity should follow the law." The man who acquired a legal title conscientiously was invulnerable: "Where the equities are equal the law prevails."

It was this moderation which won equity the grudging respect of common lawyers and ensured its survival in spite of the general onslaught on prerogative institutions during the Civil Wars of the seventeenth century. But it was this very limited and piecemeal approach which prevented equity from acquiring any solid foundation of its own. It remained, in Maitland's phrase, "a gloss on the common law," like a commentary on a text. Without the text it would be meaningless. Hence it was for long impossible to compile a treatise on equity which would have any meaning for a reader who was not already a common lawyer. In fact equity practitioners first studied common law, and equity judges were usually masters of common law, so that no difficulties were encountered in practice. No general discussion of equitable rules is therefore possible without a consideration of the common law background, but a few main principles may be usefully discussed.

Equity jurisdiction

Civil claims at common law are said to be due "as of right." There is no option in the court but to satisfy them. Modern statutes have created many cases of judicial discretion to grant or refuse relief through common law forms, but the general principle remains. In equity, on the other hand, two different types of jurisdiction must be clearly distinguished.

Some of the jurisdiction assigned to the modern Chancery Division is of a strictly legal nature. Thus the court is often concerned with the interpretation of a conveyance or contract of sale of land, or with the interpretation of a statute governing the law of real property. Whether or not a sale conferred a particular right is a matter on which no discretion exists. The same is true where the court must decide in whom land has been vested under some statutory provision. In the case of the construction of wills the court's hands are not very firmly tied, but it enjoys no discretion to depart from what it finds to have been the expressed intention of the testator.

On the other hand, there are many cases in which the Chancery Division enjoys a wide discretion, as in the grant or refusal of an injunction, the upsetting of a settlement for undue influence, the approval of a charitable scheme or the granting of additional administrative powers to trustees. Even here it has been the tendency to develop fairly predictable rules as to the exercise of this discretion, since all discretions reposed in judges must be exercised judicially. Large textbooks on such subjects as injunctions and specific performance bear testimony to the way in which the circumstances in which this discretion will be used one way or the other have become almost as rigid as the rules of common law itself.

Among these circumstances are some which differ, however, from any common law analogies. Thus "delay defeats equity," so that an equitable remedy will often be refused where the right to sue for damages will still be open if any material damage can be shown. "He who comes to equity must do equity," and "He who comes to equity must come with clean hands" are maxims which still have some application, as conditions of obtaining equitable relief.

The elevated moral standards required by equity judges are proverbial. On the other hand some of the doctrines of equity, such as the maxim that "Equity looks on that as done which ought to be done," have led to unjust results, in that they create fictitious situations and have been extended beyond their true object, that of enforcing obligations on trustees and other persons in a fiduciary position, to alteration of beneficial rights.

The effect of the Judicature Acts 1873–75 was to eliminate an anomalous conflict between common law and equity. Before 1875 equity also interfered with many common law disputes, such as actions for breach of contract or claims to title to land. Equity recognised certain claims, such as that of a beneficiary under a trust against a trustee, which were unknown to the common law. It also recognised certain defences, such as misrepresentation, in actions for breach of contract, at a time when the common law did not. The result was that it was possible by a suit in equity to override the judgment of a common law court, since the rules of equity had since 1615 enjoyed superiority.

The so-called "fusion" of law and equity took the following form:

(i) Certain institutions completely foreign to the common law, like trusts and equities of redemption of mortgages, were assigned to the Chancery Division;

(ii) Where the common law recognised an institution but did not recognise certain legal aspects, e.g. it enforced contracts but did not recognise a particular defence to an action for breach, such as innocent misrepresentation by the plaintiff, equitable rules were incorporated in the common law, so that the Queen's

Bench Division from that time recognised what had formerly been only equitable defences;

(iii) Where the substantive rules of law and equity were the same but the Chancery offered superior remedies, *e.g.* discovery of documents during proceedings, injunctions as temporary or final remedies, these became available in other courts, and the Chancery Division might also award damages, *e.g.* in lieu of an injunction[49];

(iv) A constructive effort was made to assign to each Division of the High Court topics most conveniently dealt with there, irrespective of their previous history, *e.g.* patent law and the dissolution of companies was assigned to the Chancery Division.

Legal and equitable interests

A striking feature of English equity is the parallel system of legal and equitable interests in property. The legal owner is the outward owner with wide powers of selling and otherwise dealing with the land or other property. The equitable owner has a personal right against the legal owner to have an account of the value of the assets and to apply to the Chancery to restrain him from injudicious action. The equitable owner, even in actual possession, is generally denied the powers of disposition of an owner, and may not use remedies appropriate to an owner against third parties, *e.g.* he cannot distrain on tenants of the property for arrears of rent or serve notice to quit, and he cannot transfer the legal title to the land, no purchaser being required by law to be satisfied with the equitable title.

Equitable rules embodied in statutes

Many rules which originally depended on equitable principles have now been incorporated into statutes, so as to rest on a statutory foundation. Equity once held that even a statute might not be used as a cloak of fraud, but most of the instances in which this occurred have now themselves been embodied in statutes. Thus the doctrine of merger which often led to unintentional loss of valuable rights, by merging a greater in a smaller interest in property, has been modified by equity, and this modification was confirmed by statute.[50] The doctrine of concealed fraud was evolved in equity to defeat a defence based on the statutes of limitation, as it was thought to be unconscionable to allow a man to plead lapse of time as a defence where it was his own fraud

---

[49] *Infra*, p. 222.
[50] Law of Property Act 1925, s.185, re-enacting older legislation.

which prevented the plaintiff knowing of the wrong. Modern legislation has largely adopted this doctrine and made it part of the limitation statute itself.[51] The Statute of Frauds was passed in 1677 in order to prevent fraud, and it required written proof of the conclusion of various contracts, including a contract of sale of land. But in some cases this very provision worked injustice, where a purchaser carried out expensive works on the land without any written contract. Equity, therefore, evolved the doctrine of part performance as an exception to the rule of the statute. This has now been incorporated in the statute as a special exception to the need for a written document.[52]

The doctrine of equitable waste derives in part from common law legislation which prohibited waste or destruction of land, buildings, timber and the like, by owners with limited rights. It became common for the creator of a will or settlement to include an express exemption from liability for waste. It was considered in equity that to allow complete destruction or vicious waste was an abuse of this exemption and that the national interest might also suffer from needless loss of part of the national fortune. Hence, equity severely restricted reliance on it and statute has now made this part of the common law.[53]

The doctrine of "secret trusts" appears to be the sole survival of equity's defiance of statute, since it still rests on no statutory basis. The Statute of Frauds 1677, and the later Wills Act 1837, insisted on all wills being attested with due formality, to ensure that the true intentions of testators were performed. Some testators, however, were ashamed to refer to the persons whom they wished to benefit, and gave legacies outwardly to other persons, but on secret trusts in favour of the real beneficiary. The evidence of a secret trust might be oral or take the form of a separate document. This clearly violated the rules under the Wills Act, unless the document was properly attested as a codicil. At the same time it seemed unjust to allow the apparent legatees to retain property which had only been left to them on the understanding that they would transfer it or hold it on trust for some other person. Equity, therefore, continues to enforce such secret trusts. Should a new Wills Act eventually replace the Act of 1837 some provision may be made for this situation.

---

[51] Now Limitation Act 1980, s.32:
[52] Law of Property Act 1925, s.55.
[53] *Ibid*. s.135, re-enacting older legislation.

CHAPTER 2

HISTORY OF SUBSTANTIVE LAW

PRE-CONQUEST LAW

ANGLO-SAXON law was a much older and cruder form of legal redress than the law imported by the Normans. It exhibited a curious amalgam of barbaric violence and religious piety. Marked by weakening centrifugal tendencies, it comes down to us as a curious overlay of financial and penal details on a sub-stratum of oral tradition, which is now for the most part lost in conjecture.

As it was merely a patchwork of separate customs of Kingdoms, Shires and Hundreds, with the legislation of Saxon and Danish rulers imposed on local traditions, Anglo-Saxon law may be unfavourably contrasted with the Norman "common law" of England.

Since civil, criminal and ecclesiastical cases were all decided by the same courts, held by Shire and Hundred reeves, and bishops' reeves, the distinction between civil and criminal law was undeveloped. The commission of a wrong of any kind led to sanctions some of which were like criminal punishment and were called *wite*, some of which were like a civil award of compensation for tort and were called *bot*, some of which were like an action for a penalty (*cf.* the Roman delict) and were called *wer*.

There were some exclusively criminal offences. These were public law offences,[1] such as desertion from the army and treason, or semi-religious offences like poisoning and witchcraft.[2]

Other rules had the appearance of modern civil law, but were relatively primitive. The law of contract had not evolved far beyond contracts based on the deposit of security, *wed*.[3] There were some sales regulations, reminiscent of the Edict of the Roman Aediles.[4] (For example, publicity of sale was vital, to anticipate any later charge of theft.) Conveyancing of land was oral, but evidenced by written charter, especially where special

---

[1] As opposed to most other wrongs, derived from the composition of private blood feuds.
[2] Robertson, *The Laws of the Kings of England from Edmund to Henry* I, 7, 93, 269.
[3] This survives in our word "wedding," signifying a pledging or plighting of faith (troth).
[4] *Cf.* Robertson, *ubi supra*, 35.

terms were stipulated. Great men could make a will, or *cwide*,[5] but most land descended by popular custom. Such land was known as "folkland" and was governed by the rules of "folkright." Grants of "bookland" were made by the King to great ecclesiastics and others, but these were not so much conveyances of land as charters of liberties, creations of franchises intermediate between the Crown and the subject by which revenues were diverted from the King to the grantees. Special provisions might be made for devolution or inheritance according to the terms of the "book" or charter.

The royal council, or *witan*, which was the legislative and administrative body, would intervene to decide disputes amongst prelates and magnates,[6] but seldom exercised its right to hear appeals from inferior courts in more ordinary cases.

Some forms of feudalism had begun to evolve before the Conquest. There was, for example, the practice of granting a "laen" to a thane or vassal, corresponding to the later grant of a feudal life estate. There is frequent reference in Saxon law to the loyalty owed by men to their "lords." These lords had free tenants as well as serfs, and held their own courts.

Although William the Conqueror professed to confirm the Anglo-Saxon laws, it is difficult in fact to find much trace of them after 1066. Two procedures which did survive and proved obstinate obstacles to law reform were outlawry for contempt of court, and compurgation, whereby witnesses testified to the accused's character, "purging" his guilt. And trial by ordeal, in which guilt or innocence was tried by an irrational test, such as the speed of healing of a wound inflicted on the accused, lingered on until the thirteenth century. The tenure of land by socage, that is, free from burdensome feudal obligations, also survived, and has become universal since the Restoration. Some systems of copyhold land, not abolished until the present century, may go back to Saxon times, while the parts of a conveyance have undergone little change since the Conquest. Local customs lingered on in the walled boroughs, especially in London, which made its separate peace with William, much longer than the feudal countryside. The Kentish custom of gavelkind descent, however, was another notable survivor until the Law of Property Act 1925.

The absence of adequate evidence of everyday Saxon law makes it impossible to go much further in identifying elements of English law with the authentic law of the English people.

---

[5] *Ibid.* 695; *cf.* our word "bequeath."
[6] *Ibid.* 69, 271, 273.

CRIMINAL LAW

Mens rea

Mens rea is the degree of personal fault, or intent, on the part of the accused generally required by the modern law before he can be found guilty of an offence.

Most of the old common law felonies, by their very definition, required some mental element such as malice. Robbery and rape were obviously deliberate, while it was held, in the time of Edward III, that arson could not be committed by accident, but required proof of intention to burn the building.[7] Bracton states in the thirteenth century that larceny had to be committed deliberately and dishonestly and this was no doubt law even before the reported fifteenth-century decision on the point.[8] The position as to mayhem or maiming is less clear.

The main field of doubt was in homicide. The idea of murder, if any explanation is needed for such an obvious concept, may be derived from the Anglo-Saxon "botleas"[9] crime of "foresteal," or premeditated assassination, which was capital before the Conquest. It was associated with the word "murder" because until 1340 surreptitious slaying of a Norman made the hundred liable to the fine known as "murdrum."[10] Such a slaying has obvious analogies with homicide "of malice aforethought." If the murderer of a Norman were apprehended, no fine was payable, so a manslaughter in a public quarrel would not attract any such fine.

In the Middle Ages several factors combined to make the law of murder severe. The death of a human being was most serious. Religious considerations aggravated the position of the slayer, and also, on a secular level, the King lost a useful subject and possible soldier. The circumstances of homicide make it easy to pretend an accident when the only person who could disprove the defence is the victim himself, whose mouth is sealed. Again, it has been emphasised by several writers that strict liability for homicide may be due to the original use of trial by ordeal[11] in which only a simple finding of guilty or not guilty could result from the test, and there was no possibility of adding riders or mitigations.[12]

On the other hand, especially after the abolition of trial by ordeal, a free royal pardon was available for cases of misadventure or self-defence, for it was obviously pointless to destroy another

---

[7] Bracton, f. 146b; Pollock and Maitland, *History of English Law,* Vol. II, 491.
[8] Bracton, f. 150b; Y.B. 13 Edw. IV, P., f. 9, pl. 5.
[9] *i.e.* for which no "bot," or compensation, was payable.
[10] It was abolished by the statute 14 Edw. 3, st. 1, c. 4.
[11] *Supra,* p. 21.
[12] Potter, *Historical Introduction to English Law* (4th ed.) 353.

life where the slayer had not acted in an irreligious or rebellious way.[13] These defences—or more truly mitigations, since they were considered after conviction—could usually be proved by independent testimony, e.g. self-defence in a brawl in a public place. No royal pardon was possible where homicide had been deliberate and designed.[14]

Between these two types of cases were those, such as negligent killing (manslaughter), which were pardoned after a time, or on conditions. The effect in practice was to make a distinction between non-capital involuntary manslaughter and wilful murder. This was underlined in 1531 when the privilege of benefit of clergy was abolished for first offenders in murder cases, but retained for manslaughter.[15]

In more modern times considerations of public policy led to "constructive mens rea," e.g. in the case of killing a policeman in order to resist arrest, or killing A when intending to kill B.[16] Similarly, as society has become more settled, the law has tended once more to treat a slaying in a brawl as murder, unless it is clearly proved to be in self-defence or under provocation.

The idea of an insane person being relieved of liability for his acts has received varying degrees of acceptance at different periods of history. The modern authority as to what constitutes insanity was the M'Naghten Rules.[17] The severity of this test was criticised and consequently the concept of "diminished responsibility" was introduced.[18]

Thus, the doctrine of mens rea has developed in a rather devious fashion in cases of homicide, from the pre-Conquest "botleas" crime through murdrum to the concept of diminished responsibility, so that it is difficult to isolate the particular degree of fault which is an element of each form of killing.

Attempts

It is generally said that the common law failed to provide for the punishment of attempted crimes and that it was left for the Star Chamber[19] in the sixteenth and seventeenth centuries to fill the gap and create a system of preventive law. This is in fact somewhat inaccurate. The common law procedure no doubt proved ineffective, but it did for a long time uphold a line of cases in which "the

---

[13] The Statute of Gloucester 1278 confirmed earlier practice.
[14] Pardon of Offences 1389, 13 Ric. 2 (1389), st. 2, c. 1.
[15] Benefit of Clergy, 1531 23 Hen. 8, c. 1.
[16] R. v. Vickers [1957] 2 Q.B. 664 (C.C.A.); D.P.P. v. Smith [1961] A.C. 290 (H.L.).
[17] These were formulated in 1843 by the judges at the request of the House of Lords.
[18] Homicide Act 1957, s.2; Criminal Procedure (Insanity) Act 1964, s.6.
[19] Infra, p. 26.

will might be taken for the deed" if the accused's intent (will) was proved by an overt act which, however, fell short of the complete felony. The result was very similar to the Star Chamber "attempt." In one common law case in 1353, for example, a robber was hanged although he found nothing on his victim which he wanted to steal.[20] In 1322 a case was cited of a woman executed for wounding her husband with intent to murder him, although he survived.[21] This was a case of petty treason[22]; and the law of treason has always included attempts as if they were completed acts, *e.g.* plots to kill the King, or a conspiracy to aid his enemies.

The rule that an attempt was not a common law felony seems to have been first laid down by dicta in *Hales* v. *Petit* in the sixteenth century,[23] at a time when the Star Chamber was well established. It therefore appears difficult to assign the lack of a common law remedy as a reason for the Star Chamber's punishing criminal attempts.

Punishment of felonies

It is axiomatic that the severity of the criminal law of any society varies inversely with the efficiency of its criminal law enforcement machinery. Early societies, with little police organisation, established severe penalties to offset the weakness of the system of detection and apprehension of criminals. The punishment of common law felonies was therefore capital.

The only alternatives to capital punishment were fines, banishment or remission to pursuing a civil action. There was no effective prison system for punishment in the Middle Ages and terms of imprisonment were not usually imposed, gaols being used only to detain the accused in custody until trial and conviction.

The inadequacy of the law seemed in some cases to shock even contemporary opinion, and consequently a number of expedients were adopted to reduce the scope of felony and limit the death sentence to the elimination of real enemies of society. Some examples of these devices were as follows.

Pardons, as we have seen, mitigated the nominal severity of the law of homicide.

[20] Kiralfy, *Source Book,* 43; Y.B. 27 Ass., f. 137, pl. 38.
[21] Kiralfy, 43; Y.B. 15 Edw. 2, P., f. 463, *per* Spigurnel.
[22] This was a legal fiction by which some crimes were spuriously treated as treasonable, so that the criminal's property was forfeited to the Crown instead of "escheating" to his immediate feudal lord. The Barons complained that their revenues were being depleted in this way and the Statute of Treasons of 1352, therefore, amongst other provisions, prevented the King from forfeiting land in such cases. Curiously, monarchs often re-granted their estates to the heirs of noblemen convicted of treason, after an interval. The treason was often adherence to one side in dynastic disputes.
[23] (1562) Plowd. 253.

Benefit of clergy was used to save a first offender. A man would "plead his clergy," that is, claim to be a clergyman and entitled to trial by an ecclesiastical court, after his conviction by the secular court. The offender forfeited his property to the Crown and was branded to prevent his later "pleading clergy" for another offence, but was spared his life. In theory he was then tried by a church court; in fact this seldom rose above the level of a farce. The privilege was obviously originally intended for the clergy only, but by a legal fiction, it was extended to all persons who could read or recite a well-known verse which was never changed.[24]

Larceny, of a small amount, increasing at various periods from twelve pence to forty shillings, was made a separate offence from grand larceny, apparently to save the really hungry man who stole to stay alive. Kind juries often assessed the value of the goods stolen as less than the maximum amount, to save petty thieves from the death penalty.

The crime of larceny which was, of course, capital was more and more narrowly defined as time went on. First, as already mentioned, some guilty intention was insisted on. Then, it was technically confined to the direct taking possession of goods, so that fraudulent but non-violent cases escaped liability, as where the culprit was lawfully in possession, *e.g.* larceny by a bailee. Again, where the victim voluntarily gave possession to the accused, *e.g.* blackmail, embezzlement, obtaining by false pretences, these cases were not larceny. A number of special statutes, some of them surprisingly late in date, were needed to catch these more skilful crimes, typical of advancing civilisation and the substitution of guile for force. In a few cases the courts themselves eventually extended the law as incidents became commoner, for example, the obtaining of money by verbal threats of a non-violent nature (blackmail) became a crime equated with obtaining money by threats of violence (robbery).[25] By a similar extension in modern times a man to whom a letter was lawfully delivered might be guilty of larceny of the contents if he found, on opening it, that the letter was not meant for him but nevertheless kept it. If the letter was meant for him, however, it was not theft if there was more money in it than he was entitled to and he took it.[26]

The stress on possession has now been dropped, in favour of a broader concept of dishonest dealings.[27]

[24] Psalm 51, v. 1. See Kiralfy, *Source Book*, 12.
[25] 9 Geo. 1 (1722) c. 22.
[26] *R.* v. *Hudson* [1943] 1 K.B. 458; *Moynes* v. *Cooper* [1956] 1 Q.B. 439.
[27] Theft Act 1968 s.1.

Punishment of misdemeanours (indictable offences not felonies)

Until the death penalty was abolished for most felonies in the nineteenth century newly created offences were generally made misdemeanours, to avoid the incidence of capital punishment. The distinction between felony and misdemeanour was abolished in 1967.[28]·

The history of the misdemeanour is interesting but largely unexplored. There are four different sources and jurisdictions which created misdemeanours.

First, from the fourteenth century, justices of the peace have been trying a wide range of offences "under the degree of felony," such as assault, or malicious damage to property, punishable by fines.

The second group of misdemeanours consists of those which were always triable by the royal courts, among them aggravated assault, and contempt of court.

The jurisdiction of the Star Chamber was limited to non-capital cases,[29] so the offences it created, such as perjury or criminal libel, formed the third group of misdemeanours. The Chamber did try other crimes but only by "waiving the felony" and punishing as for a misdemeanour. After the dissolution of the Star Chamber in 1640 this jurisdiction was taken over by royal courts.

The last group of misdemeanours consists of those offences created by statute, which are indictable misdemeanours triable by jury. But those statutory summary offences triable by the magistrates, which are modern creations, are not generally referred to as misdemeanours.

Some new indictable offences, known as "common law misdemeanours," have been added by the superior courts. Examples are escape from prison,[30] and cheating the Revenue.[31] This exercise of power seems historically sound in view of the veteran jurisdiction of the magistrates, but it has been said to be unjust to create new crimes by judicial decision after the event, the modern feeling being that people should not be penalised for something which they could not have known to be illegal. Recent cases, therefore, tend to limit the courts' jurisdiction in this direction to the recognition of new types of conspiracy to circumvent the statute law[32] or to corrupt public morals.[33]

---

[28] Criminal Law Act 1967, s.1(7); *Webley* v. *Buxton* [1977] Q.B. 481.
[29] 25 Edw. 3 (1350), st. 5, c. 4.
[30] *R.* v. *Hinds* (1957) 41 Cr.App.R. 143.
[31] *R.* v. *Hudson* [1956] 2 Q.B. 252.
[32] *R.* v. *Manley* [1933] 1 K.B. 529; *R.* v. *Newland* [1954] 1 Q.B. 158.
[33] *Shaw* v. *D.P.P.* [1962] A.C. 220; *R.* v. *Knuller* [1972] 3 W.L.R. 143 (H.L.); Criminal Law Act 1977, s.5.

Public mischief is a rather vague type of offence. The House of Lords has considered that it is not a distinct offence,[34] but perversion of the course of justice appears still to be indictable.[35]

Criminal procedure at common law

English criminal procedure is worth a little attention in view of its fundamental constitutional importance. It combines features of both medieval and modern practices and preserves the best of both. It is based on the assumption that a criminal trial is a dispute between two litigants, the King (the party making the accusation, from a position of power) and the prisoner (the weaker party, regarded in more modern times as requiring protection from oppression). The unenviable position of the accused was eased from time to time by liberalising forces which sometimes utilised the very procedures designed to ensure trial and conviction, and conversely, measures designed for his protection occasionally proved burdensome. Mention should be made of the following major characteristics of the English criminal trial.

(1) *The equality of the two sides* was rarely more than an ideal, in practice swinging like a pendulum to favour one side or the other. The medieval judge, for example, being a royal official, was not as neutral as his modern counterpart, and took a greater part in the conduct of the trial. The idea of adversary procedure was probably the result of jury trial becoming more independent of the Crown.

(2) *The presumption of innocence* arose in part from the fear of judicial murder of the innocent in a period when almost all crimes were capital. The prosecution must, therefore, prove its case beyond all reasonable doubt. The interpretation of this rule in the past sometimes caused hardship, not to say injustice, to the accused. He was regarded as having no need to defend himself, so for a long period could not give evidence under oath on his own behalf. Before 1688 it was the practice to interrogate the prisoner in court, however, so that he then had an opportunity to testify as to points of fact.[36] From 1688 until the Criminal Evidence Act of 1898[37] he had to remain mute in the face of the charges against him. The position today is that he may give evidence like any other witness but he may elect not to testify at all. The same theory of the impregnable position of the prisoner disqualified him from

---

[34] *D.P.P.* v. *Withers* [1975] A.C. 842.
[35] *R.* v. *Rowell* [1978] 1 W.L.R. 132 (C.A.). *Cf. R.* v. *Dytham* [1979] Q.B. 722, C.A., failure by a police officer to intervene to stop an assault.
[36] Stephen, *History of the Criminal Law*, Vol. I, 440.
[37] s.1.

calling witnesses until 1702[38] and in many cases prevented his representation by counsel. Paradoxically, counsel had always been allowed to appear in trials for misdemeanour. In felony they were given the right of audience on points of law alone in the fifteenth century but were able to argue fact and address the jury only after 1837.[39]

(3) *Trial by jury* is generally regarded as the right of all persons accused of serious crimes. This, like many popular conceptions, is in fact only a half-truth. Whereas in early times an accused man was pressed to death if he refused to accept jury trial (such a refusal would usually be in order to avoid a conviction and subsequent forfeiture of family property to the Crown), in modern times statutes have frequently deprived the accused of the privilege.

(4) *The strict rules of evidence* in criminal cases are the product of centuries of trial by jury, and are designed to avoid prejudicing the minds of lay jurors. Thus hearsay evidence is forbidden, as are leading questions to one's own witnesses, and evidence of similar acts on previous occasions or of previous convictions.[40]

(5) *The right to challenge a juror* belongs to both sides in some degree. Its exercise is on the increase, *e.g.* attempts to get all-women or all-black juries or to achieve a balanced jury including minority representatives.

(6) *Publicity of trial* has always been essential, although rules have sometimes been allowed to survive which have had the effect of obscuring the course of proceedings. In medieval times, for example, the indictment was in Latin and proceedings before the fourteenth century in Norman-French, though the indictment was read to the prisoner and he pleaded to it in English.

(7) *Preliminary examinations* of the facts by lay magistrates have been conducted since 1555,[41] one suspects originally in an effort by the Crown to by-pass the vigilance of the community as represented by the grand jury. Grand juries, nevertheless, continued after the result of the preliminary examination to present their "true bill" of a crime which had been committed in their locality, for trial by a higher court, until 1933.[42] The preliminary examination became first an agency of investigation and later a

---

[38] Anne, st. 2, c. 9.
[39] 6 & 7 Will. 4, c. 114. A proposal has been made to require the accused to testify, subject to certain safeguards; Report on Evidence; Cmnd. 4991 (1972), 215–220.
[40] The Report, 235–250 suggests relaxations of this rule.
[41] 2 & 3 P. & M., c. 10.
[42] Administration of Justice Act 1933, s.1.

brake on frivolous or groundless indictments, and is said now to have outlived its usefulness.

(8) *Compulsory attendance of witnesses* was first effected by the statute of 1555 giving power at the preliminary examination to bind over a witness to testify at the trial. Later by a proceeding analogous to the Chancery subpoena, other witnesses could be summoned to appear at the trial.

(9) *The right of the accused to be released on bail* pending a final decision of his case has always existed in some form but was regulated by statute, from time to time, making it unavailable for many crimes. Bail is now generally available for most offences.[43]

CIVIL LAW

Significance of the forms of action today

English Civil Law has its roots in the medieval period, and it is difficult to understand the modern law of contract, tort or property without some knowledge of the separate forms of action through which they developed.

Under the old system each type of claim was represented by a different writ entailing a distinct procedure. In the nineteenth century these "forms of action" were abolished, and a uniform writ of summons and procedure in the High Court were introduced, but the forms of action have left their mark in many surviving rules of substantive law. For example, there are different degrees of liability in different torts. Thus a plaintiff who sues for assault must prove that the defendant wilfully attacked or threatened him, whereas if he were suing after a motor accident, he would merely have to prove the defendant's negligence, and, in some cases, merely that he caused the damage.

The types of defence which can be pleaded also differ. In an action for assault and battery, the fact that the plaintiff struck the defendant first and forced him to strike back in self-defence would clear the defendant of liability, but it would be no defence to an action for libel to say that the plaintiff first libelled the defendant. On the other hand, it would be a valid defence in libel to show that the defendant acted in good faith in writing the document on a privileged occasion, whereas it is no defence in assault and battery to show that the assailant was actuated by good motives and

---

[43] Bail Act 1976, s.1, Sched. I, Pt. II; The Bill of Rights 1689 prohibits the requiring of excessive bail.

believed that it was in the public interest that the plaintiff receive a beating.

The remedies sought by civil action vary, too. An action to recover possession of land aims at a quite different solution from an action for damages for breach of contract or an action for an injunction to restrain the breach of copyright.

Claims have to be proved in different ways. Some contracts must be in writing to be valid, while others are only enforceable if not only in writing but also under seal.

Procedural differences are many. Cases may be tried by jury or by a judge sitting alone, in one or other of the three divisions of the High Court, in the county court or in the magistrates' court. Even today conflicts may arise between the courts in their jurisdiction over adoption and guardianship.

The same facts may constitute several torts, and alternative claims may be made, an advantage of the modern system. One survival of the old rule is the decision[44] that if the plaintiff elects to base his claim on one tort only, he may fail, even if he could have succeeded if he had pleaded an alternative. The plaintiff must, therefore, seek an alternative basis if the defendant has an obvious defence to one head of a claim; for example, time may have run out under the Statute of Limitations for one claim, but not for another, or it may be too late to apply for an injunction, but not too late to recover damages.

Defects of the forms of action. The old system of forms of action suffered from three major weaknesses which have now been eliminated or modified. These difficulties all arose to a greater or lesser extent from the fact that each form had developed its own distinct procedures, irreversible once set in motion, which in retrospect may seem eccentric but which at the time had a reasonable justification.

In the first place it was possible to lose a meritorious claim because the wrong form of action had been used. If a plaintiff sued by an Action on the Case, but the evidence proved a wrong which amounted to a direct Trespass, the court would have to give judgment for the defendant. The plaintiff had no opportunity of righting this injustice as it was by his own mistake that the wrong action had been chosen. As the law of forms of action was complicated and the evidence often doubtful in advance, it was not necessarily a result of a lawyer's or a plaintiff's stupidity if such a thing happened.[45]

---

[44] *e.g. Esso Petroleum Co.* v. *Southport Corp.* [1956] A.C. 218.

[45] This was admitted by the Parliamentary Commissioners on the Courts of Common Law in their Third Report in 1831, X, 8.

In the same way there were restrictions on the joinder of actions. At one time only one form of action could be used at a time, so that a plaintiff could not escape the danger referred to above by suing in Trespass and Case in the alternative. If a plaintiff had more than one claim against the same defendant he had generally to bring separate actions, sometimes in different courts with each court allowing different remedies, so that repeated actions would be required to conclude a single dispute. It was possible for an unscrupulous defendant in one action to bring, as plaintiff, another action arising out of the same facts but in a different court and deliberately so to manipulate the dates of trial as to make it impossible for the original plaintiff successfully to contest both actions, since he could not be in two courts at once.

The third serious defect in the old system lay in the strict rules of pleading. They required great care to draft, and entailed a real injustice to litigants in many cases. Thus the facts of a case had to be tried and a verdict given before any preliminary legal objection to the claim could be made, as the pleading of any technical point of law automatically excluded any dispute of the facts, which were then taken as admitted.[46] The position as to alternative defences to the facts as pleaded by the plaintiff was curious. In some cases the defendant had to select one point of fact and dispute that at his peril admitting all the other elements of the plaintiff's case; this position remained the same until legislation in 1705.[47] In another line of cases the position was quite the reverse, a defendant being entitled to "plead the general issue," i.e. plead a blank denial without specifying which part of the plaintiff's case he intended to dispute. With this simple refusal to descend into detail the system swung too far the other way, giving the plaintiff no hint of the real nature of the defence before the trial. Sir William Holdsworth illustrates: "If the defendant in an Action of Assumpsit pleaded the general issue Non Assumpsit he put in issue not only the question whether or not the promise had been made, but also any facts which tended to impeach the validity of the promise and any matter of defence which showed that he was not liable; so that though the words Non Assumpsit literally only traversed the promise, the fact, for instance, that the promise had been made and released could be given in evidence under this issue."[48]

The old system of the forms of action in general discouraged legal progress. At the present day any person may issue a writ of summons and deliver a statement of claim which is not covered by the existing law, leaving it to the court to decide whether such a

---

[46] Newis v. Lark (1571) Plowd. 410.
[47] 4 & 5 Anne c. 3.
[48] Holdsworth, History of English Law (3rd ed.), Vol. IX, 322.

new form of liability should be created. Under the old system in these circumstances it was necessary to point out some analogy to one or other of the forms of action and to fit the new case into an already recognised category. This obstacle, however, became less important as the Action on the Case developed, since it was so elastic that an experimental claim could take the form of a special Action on the Case. As that particular type of claim became more common it would acquire a recognised name and become established, but there were always open frontiers for new types of Action on the Case to develop.

Classification of the forms of action

The system of forms of action, it must be remembered, arose in the twelfth and thirteenth centuries at a time when land ownership was very important. The feudal aristocracy was extremely jealous of any radical interference with the land law and considered that no new real actions should be upheld without the consent of the great magnates in the royal council.[49] They were much less interested, however, in the field of personal actions to protect personal property and claims, and the courts were able to develop these with much greater freedom.[50]

The classification of actions is, therefore, of some historical importance. Original writs were used in three types of case, *viz.*, real, mixed and personal actions.

Real actions were concerned with title to land. The actions took their name from the Latin *"res"* (thing), emphasising the physical object rather than the parties to the case. Title to land, however, has never really been absolute, and real actions in fact decided the better right of A and the worse right of B, so as to conclude the matter between A and B. The principal real action was the Writ of Right, which took various special forms. It was a solemn and expensive proceeding, decided by a Grand Assize, *i.e.* a jury of knights.[51]

Mixed actions is a term conveniently used to describe actions concerned with recovering possession of land (called "seisin")

---

[49] Provisions of Oxford, 1258.

[50] Bracton, f. 413b; as to the difference between real and personal property see *supra*, pp. 13, 14.

[51] See XXVII Selden Society xviii, for an example. The word "Assize" was used in medieval times with a confusing variety of meanings. It seems to derive from the holding of a "session" at which something was decided. The decision, such as a decree or law, was called an assize, *e.g.* the Assize of Clarendon. Groups of jurors who arrived at verdicts at sessions were known as Grand and Petty Assizes, and the proceedings in which they took part were also so called. The royal itinerant judges who went around the country to record the verdicts of such jurors were said to "take the Assizes" and were also said to "go on Assize" in the sense of holding sessions at which such verdicts were taken.

rather than the freehold title to it. The principal mixed action was the Assize of Novel Disseisin which was decided by a Petty Assize of twelve freeholders. The plaintiff claimed that the defendant occupier had forcibly evicted ("disseised") him instead of suing him in the courts. The occupier, if he lost the case, was dispossessed but might vindicate his title by bringing a real action afterwards, since the mixed action did not claim to decide title. Another group of mixed actions were known as Writs of Entry. In these the plaintiff claimed specific flaws in the occupier's title, such as the latter's being the heir of a man who had wrongfully seized possession, or his having been entitled to possession only for a fixed term of years which had now expired.

Personal actions lay for the recovery of goods or money, most commonly money. One of the oldest was the Action of Debt, which lay wherever one man owed money to another as a result of some transaction from which he had obtained a material benefit, such as a purchase of goods. Another important action was that of Covenant which lay to enforce any promise if it was made under seal. Other personal actions were Trespass and the Action on the Case from which the whole modern law of tort was to grow.

In the course of time the cumbersome real actions were superseded by mixed actions, which later litigants in turn found less convenient than the personal action of Ejectment, an offshoot of Trespass, a personal action for damages adapted to try title to land by the use of fictions.

Appeals of felony in which the one party appealed, that is, accused, the other as a felon, were a further group of actions outside the scope of the above classification. They were in effect civil actions against criminals, quite distinct from prosecution for felony by the Crown, and enabled a victim of, say, theft to recover his property from the thief under certain conditions, which included slaying the felon in judicial combat.[52] A royal pardon of the crime was no more a defence to the civil "appeal of felony" than the victim's decision not to appeal was a bar to criminal prosecution.

Expansion of the forms of action in tort

Despite their defects the forms of action did contrive to lay the foundations of most of the modern substantive law. From the twelfth century there was a gradual if intermittent expansion of the Register of Writs. This is partly accounted for by statutory remedies like the Writs of Entry and remedies attributed to statute

---

[52] See LVII Selden Society lxxxv; (1980) 1 Journal of Legal History 135.

like the Grand Assize, in each case remedies which concerned land. A number of new writs, some completely novel, others based on accepted forms, but most of them concerned with title to land, must have been devised by the senior Chancery clerks who alone at this period had the power to issue writs. Such a new form would be submitted to the test of approval by the judges in actual litigation and might then become accepted as a writ "of course" or "common form" writ. In principle this process of developing substantive law by trying out new writs might have gone on indefinitely, but the Barons were anxious to limit the creation of any new actions which might affect title to land. So, in the Provisions of Oxford of 1258, they forbade the Chancellor (*i.e.* his clerks) creating new writs "of course" without the approval of the whole Council. Bracton hints that this was accepted as policy by the courts despite the short life of the Barons' Revolt. Although the courts seem to have limited the applications of the Provisions to real and mixed actions (a novel writ of "conspiracy" was allowed in 1281, for example) there appears generally to have been a pause in legal growth until the Statute of Westminster II in 1285. The Action of Trespass was already well enough established before 1258 to be unaffected, but the Action on the Case had to wait for the statute of 1285 before it could emerge.

In 1285 the Statute of Westminster II encouraged the expansion of the law to a limited extent, although some of its effects were not immediately felt. The precise provisions of the statute were first interpreted as dealing with the succession to an existing action rather than the creation of new actions. Thus no new forms of liability were created but known actions were allowed to be brought against fresh parties, such as a successor in title of the original wrongdoer.

The statute also provided, however, that, where a situation arose similar to one for which a writ was already obtainable, a new writ should be formulated to meet the new case. The procedure laid down merely gave statutory recognition and encouragement to the older practice which had been temporarily inhibited. As before, the plaintiff had to persuade the Chancery clerks to concur in granting a new writ. If these officials failed to agree, then the litigant had to petition Parliament to authorise the new remedy, a step which was already available to him, though not apparently much used.

Defects in the statute were mainly the result of ineffective sanctions. The courts were not bound to uphold a writ even if the Chancery clerks were agreed on it nor is it clear whether Parliament could compel the courts to uphold their writs unless they incorporated them into formal legislation. Equally, if the clerks disagreed, the litigant could not compel Parliament to devise a writ to fit his case. Reference to the rolls of Parliament discloses an interesting situation; before 1285 there are few petitions for new writs; between that date and 1300 there is a marked increase in such petitions but scarcely any of them refer directly to the statute. Litigants did rely on the statute, however, as in *Braybrook* v. *Perot* in 1293[53] where a petition to the Council which referred to the statute was endorsed "Let the clerks agree if they can and if not let the petitioner come back to the next Parliament." A more successful example is the case of *Frowyk* v. *Lewknor* in 1310[54] in which the petitioner was told by Parliament to go to Chancery and pick up the writ he had asked for.

Both these cases were indirectly concerned with land, a field in which litigants might feel the need for statutory authority in view of the Barons' hostility to innovations in the land law. There is no recorded instance in which the statute was used to create a purely personal action sounding in damages. Another reason for this may be that the writ of Trespass was still so elastic in 1285 that it could be applied to new situations without the innovation being obvious. Later, as Trespass became more settled and formal, a new method of legal development had to be found. There are signs in the early fourteenth century of completely new writs, perhaps drawn with the statute of 1285 in mind, at first called Trespass although based on indirect wrongdoing. These new forms gradually came to be distinguished from the older direct Trespass, under the title "Trespass on the Case," or "Action on the Case."

We shall now examine in detail the Actions of Trespass and Case, the two great forebears of the common law as that term is now understood.

The writ of trespass

A word of warning must be uttered at the outset. The word "trespass" was given such a wide meaning in medieval times that crimes, slanders, omissions and nuisances were all loosely referred to as "trespass," in the broad sense of "violation of law." The only common element was that they were all cases in which a wrong had to be remedied (torts) rather than a right vindicated. We are here only concerned with trespass in the technical sense, a writ which lay to recover damages for a positive and direct wrongful act. It was the first to provide a remedy for unliquidated damages, and as it finally developed there were three common and important forms. These were Trespass to land (*quare clausum fregit* being the

[53] LVII Selden Society 168.
[54] 1 Rot.Parl. 278.

distinguishing Latin formula), Trespass by carrying off goods (*de bonis asportatis*) and Trespass to the person which recited an insult to the plaintiff and beating and wounding him.[55]

The procedural advantages which the writ of Trespass offered to a plaintiff suggest that its proliferation was hardly an accident. It alleged a breach of the King's peace so that the defendant could be arrested, thus assuring his prompt attendance in court. It offered trial by an impartial jury (instead of by wager of law, a form of proof by character witnesses which was unfavourable to the plaintiff).[56] Again, Trespass was triable in the royal courts, with their skilled judges and advocates, instead of in the less competent local courts.

The development of the writ was gradual, its origins obscure and defying precise analysis. The derivation of the writ of Trespass has been variously ascribed by scholars to the following sources:

The Assize of Novel Disseisin has some elements in common with the writ of Trespass to land and the theory propounded by Professor Woodbine connecting the two[57] is supported by Bracton's statement that disseisin is "trespass plus."[58] He means that it is a trespass to land plus the added element of an intention completely to dispossess the occupant and evict him from the land. If one subtracted the intention to dispossess, a simple Action of Trespass would be left. Unfortunately there would seem to be more features not common to the two actions, in particular the formulae of the writ and pleadings were completely different.

Appeals of larceny and robbery might in theory have formed the basis of Trespass to goods but would hardly explain the origin of Trespass to land or to the person. Larceny and robbery are also forms of "trespass plus"; subtract from them the felonious and dishonest intention and you have the tort of Trespass to goods.

Procedure by bill is said to have been the origin of Trespass, and to have facilitated its development, since an original summons was not needed. There is no evidence, however, that special leniency was shown to procedure by bill, or that the courts allowed novel remedies more readily in this form.

Roman law was active under Henry III. The idea of an action for damages would be familiar to students of the Roman law and it is

---

[55] Other forms were occasionally used, *e.g.* where A cut the moorings of B's ship, so that it drifted away and was lost, he committed a trespass although he did not himself take the ship, or where A deliberately spoiled B's goods, so B could not sell them.

[56] For wager of law see pp. 21, 54.

[57] 33 Yale L.J. 799; 34 Yale L.J. 343.

[58] See Fifoot, *History and Sources of the Common Law*, 50, 57.

clear that in some contexts our records refer to tort as *injuria*, the same name as that of a Roman delict. Thus a civil plea of self-defence in our law used to end with the words *de injuria sua propria* (by his own wrong) and a case where the law of tort is powerless to provide a remedy is still called a case of *damnum sine injuria*. Yet it is very doubtful how far these terminological echoes of Roman law are significant, particularly as Latin was the language of the records.

Local courts from early times dealt with complaints very like the Action of Trespass and the decline of these courts in the thirteenth century would have left a gap and an opportunity for the common law to step in. Borough courts, however, are the only ones known to have influenced the royal courts, and they did not develop actions like Trespass as much as the rural courts. It is more likely that the local courts would follow the example of the royal courts than the other way round.[59]

Breach of the peace was always recited in a writ of Trespass though in many cases it was little more than a legal fiction.[60] It is difficult to see any real disturbance of the peace in a situation where a man crossed another's land by mistake and without being seen by the owner, but an Action of Trespass would lie on these facts. It would seem likely therefore that the phrase "breach of the peace" was used in order to bring Actions of Trespass within the jurisdiction of the royal courts, the protectors of the King's peace, and not in any attempt to describe the nature of the writ.

Whatever may be the true origin of Trespass, whether based on one or more of the above theories or something as yet undiscovered, it is certain that in the period between Magna Carta in 1215 and the Statute of Westminster II in 1285[61] divers experimental writs of Trespass were upheld by the courts. In this way, until the emergence of the Action on the Case in the fourteenth century, Trespass was able to develop unimpeded as virtually the only common law tortious remedy. Forms of Trespass were also eventually to supersede most of the older remedies to recover land or goods, so that it came to cover almost the whole of the English civil law.

---

[59] Recent research shows that county courts operated along the same lines as the central courts and generally acted as minor royal courts, R.C. Palmer, *The County Courts of Mediaeval England* (1982).

[60] *Cf.* Milsom (1958) 74 L.Q.R. 589.

[61] For the effect of the Act of 1285 see *supra*, p. 34.

Basis of liability in Trespass

Liability in trespass was originally very strict. If the defendant voluntarily intruded on land it was immaterial that he had not intended to commit a Trespass. He could and often did plead that he had acted with the authority of the law or in avoiding an assailant, thus confessing but avoiding the claim.[62] It was seldom possible, however, to plead that he was not liable because he had acted without any negligence, for if the act was the product of his will he was liable for it. In the case of Trespass to land this rule has survived to modern times, when it has been held that even the insanity of the trespasser is no defence.[63]

There was a possibility, when liability was so strict, of pleading inevitable accident in Trespass, but this has nothing to do with negligence; it meant simply that the defendant's act was not really due to his own volition, but that the effective causation must be found elsewhere. Thus if a third party pushed the defendant's arm as he was shooting, or if a third party threw the defendant bodily onto the plaintiff's land, the defendant was innocent of any Trespass to the person or land respectively.

The first leading case on the question of liability for fault, whether negligent or intentional, is the *Case of Thorns* in 1466.[64] The defendant was clipping hedges along the boundary of his land and clippings fell on his neighbour's land. The defendant was sued for Trespass to land because he then deliberately entered his neighbour's property to collect the clippings. Much of the discussion concerned the question, first, whether he could have avoided allowing the clippings to fall and, secondly, whether in any case this justified a deliberate entry. Negligence was indirectly involved in the first point but had no bearing on the second. The plaintiff won his case but the record shows that he waived some of the damages he recovered, so it may be that he was mainly interested in vindicating his right in principle.

In 1506 judgment was similarly given against the defendant in the *Case of Tithes*, a case of deliberate Trespass to goods in the honest but mistaken belief that it was justified.[65] No question of negligence arose and there was no problem of causation.

The leading case of *Weaver* v. *Ward*,[66] which occurred in 1616

---

[62] See Potter, *Historical Introduction to English Law* (4th ed.), 376; need to obtain access to your own building to carry out repairs is no excuse for a trespass on adjoining land *Trenberth (John)* v. *National Westminster Bank* (1979) 123 S.J. 388; *cf. Case of Thorns, infra.*

[63] *Morriss* v. *Marsden* [1952] C.L.Y. 3400; *cf. Phillips* v. *Soloway* (1956) 6 D.L.R. 570 (Canada).

[64] Y.B. 6 Edw. 4, M., f. 7, pl. 18; Kiralfy, *Source Book*, 128.

[65] Y.B. 21 Hen. 7, f. 27, pl. 5.

[66] Hob. 134; *Source Book*, 132.

and is still often cited, applied the principle of strict liability laid down in the *Case of Thorns* to cases of Trespass to the person. The defendant, who was undergoing military training, deliberately pulled the trigger of his firearm but aimed badly and injured the plaintiff. He was held liable for this Trespass since the accident was not in any sense inevitable. It has been said that[67] it was necessary in an Action of Trespass to the person to prove some element of fault but it appears that the real problem was one of causation. The act must be intentional on the part of the defendant, whereas the consequences need not be intended. *Leame* v. *Bray*[68] in 1803 reflects this idea, for the defendant was held liable for driving a carriage into the plaintiff when he was driving voluntarily although he did not intend to injure the plaintiff. In the case of *Holmes* v. *Mather*[69] the defendant was similarly held liable for an accident with a runaway horse of which he was voluntarily in charge, except while on the highway.

The law of Trespass to the person was radically changed by the case of *Stanley* v. *Powell*[70] which contrasts nicely with the case of *Weaver* v. *Ward*. In *Stanley* v. *Powell* the defendant deliberately aimed and pulled the trigger of a rifle but the bullet ricocheted off a tree and injured the plaintiff. The court, in giving judgment for the defendant, instead of doing so on the obvious basis of causation, decided to lay down the novel principle that negligence was a necessary element of Trespass to the person.

In later times actions for highway and similar accidents were brought as Actions on the Case for negligence and not as Actions of Trespass to the person. The tendency may partly have been the result of the ruling in *Stanley* v. *Powell* but is also the consequence of the impossibility of disentangling the strict liability of each party where both have been injured as, for example, in a collision. In the case of other negligent trespasses to the person either Case or Trespass might be used but Case was generally used in fact. Case came to be used for personal injury claims where the cause was indirect, *e.g.* where the plaintiff was injured by running into an obstacle left by the defendant on the highway, or where the injury was caused by a servant acting within the course of his employment but without any express directions to do the injury, and the plaintiff sued the master.[71]

---

[67] Fifoot, *ubi supra*, 190, 201.
[68] 3 East 593.
[69] (1875) L.R. 10 Ex. 261.
[70] [1891] 1 Q.B. 86; confirmed by *Fowler* v. *Lanning* [1959] 1 Q.B. 426.
[71] See Fifoot, *ubi supra*, 184–187.

The Action on the Case[72]

Trespass began to throw off a new branch, in the middle of the fourteenth century, known as Trespass on the Case. This was a writ designed to fit particular cases, the pleadings simply setting out the facts and containing an allegation of material damage (except in the special case of slander[73]) which the courts would wish to remedy but could not usually bring within the existing forms of action. As the law began to dominate the exercise of brute force it also extended its sanctions to deal with wrongs of a more subtle kind, such as deceit or conspiracy, which came within the orbit of Case.

Apart from the element of wrongful damage the various types of Actions on the Case had little in common, and it is obviously difficult to generalise about such highly individual writs. The following, however, may be considered typical situations in which Case might be used.

(1) Where there was damage but the writ of Trespass could not be used because force had not been exerted and by no stretch of the imagination could a breach of the peace be alleged. Examples would be negligent or unintentional harm, omissions, and cases where damage was the indirect result of a forcible act.

(2) Where the principle of liability was acknowledged at common law by another writ but the plaintiff could not use that writ, for example only a freeholder could bring an action for Nuisance: a leaseholder became able to bring a similar action only as an Action on the Case.

(3) Where the wrong was criminally punishable but no civil writ to recover damages existed, as in the case of public nuisances of various kinds.

(4) Where the wrong violated local or general custom but no royal writ as yet existed, as where a fire was carelessly minded or dogs allowed to worry cattle.

(5) Where a civil remedy was needed for the recovery of damages for the violation of a statute, for example where the plaintiff's title to property was lost or threatened by the defendant's forgery of title deeds.

(6) Where a common law remedy was required for violation of duties imposed by the Law Merchant, which the language of pleadings shows to have had a greater influence on common law developments than is generally believed. An

---

[72] See generally, Kiralfy, *The Action on the Case* (1951).
[73] *Infra*, p. 48.

example of such liability would be where the defendant had accepted but later dishonoured a bill of exchange payable to the plaintiff. If there was no consideration this would not normally have attracted common law liability.

Procedure in Actions on the Case

The obsolescence of most of the ancient common law actions other than direct Trespass created a vacuum into which Actions on the Case were encouraged to expand. They enjoyed procedural advantages over the old actions and in some cases showed procedural differences from Trespass though these were not always advantageous.

The writ in Case was a mere recital of the facts and did not refer to force of arms or breach of the peace or use any other technical phraseology. The defendant, since he had not violated the King's peace, could not be arrested in Case until legislation of Henry VIII. Also because of the violation of the King's peace, direct Trespass was only triable by jury. This advantage was extended to Case but apparently by a lucky accident as there was no reason in principle why trial should not have been by wager of law.[74] The unsuccessful defendant in Case could be imprisoned, but only until he had paid the plaintiff's damages, whereas in Trespass he had also to pay a fine to obtain his release.

Case as an alternative to older forms of action

The authority of the court for the award of Actions on the Case lay in the inherent nature of the common law, that is, the power and duty of the court to provide remedies for wrongs and honour the King's obligation to secure justice for all. The development of Case in the Middle Ages was vexed by the following dilemma. If there was an existing common law writ which provided a remedy for a wrong then Case could not be used instead, even if the common law writ was less advantageous. On the other hand, if the new writ was very remote from any known writ the courts might hesitate to allow it. Reported arguments in the Middle Ages show that opposing counsel more often asked to have a writ on the Case quashed because there was an existing common law writ, than because it was a completely novel action, which would suggest that writs for Case must be unlike, rather than like, other actions. On the other hand the judges did from time to time use the fact that similar cases had been upheld as a reason for upholding a writ

[74] Fifoot, *ubi supra*, 82.

when it came before them, which would show that the judges, at least, regarded Case as expanding by analogy to existing writs.

A briefly reported decision in 1585 finally resolved the dilemma by stating that Case might be used as an alternative to the older actions. Thenceforward there was no longer any fear of a conflict with existing writs and the reports show counsel arguing from one recognised form of liability that another similar form should be allowed. In *Gerrard* v. *Dickenson* in 1590[75] decisions on slander, deceit and conspiracy were cited to support a case of slander of title. Again, in *Symons* v. *Darknoll* in 1628[76] a case about carriers' liability was argued from cases on bailment and detinue.

The origins of the Action on the Case

Why were such different actions all described as "Actions on the Case"? Again, the origins are disputed by scholars as is the importance of the external influences which made it grow away from the earlier and less flexible common law.

Some scholars consider that Case was an extension of direct Trespass in form though it differed very widely in substance. Other scholars consider that the judges always distinguished between Trespass as the generic name of the nascent law of tort and the specific writs of direct Trespass *vi et armis*.[77] Some scholars, as we have seen, would regard the Statute of Westminster II in 1285 as a sufficient authority for the granting of the writ.

Other influences at work in forming the courts' attitude to this writ included the pressure of the rival Court of Chancery, which became strong at the end of the fifteenth century, and clearly impelled the common lawyers to develop the Actions on the Case for Assumpsit and Trover. Emphasis in the writs on ideas of faith, trust and honour again suggest the influence of equity in the Chancery, but such ideas were not alien to the common law itself. The image of a rigid common law is based on procedural defects rather than on the inadequacy of its substantive law, which was reasonably well advanced for the rude conditions of medieval England. A further example which the common law judges may have followed is that of the mercantile law of Europe. The boroughs had piepowder courts, that is mercantile courts, as well as borough courts of pleas, and one jurisdiction seems to have influenced the other. The borough courts of pleas, especially the City of London Court, in any case appear to have offered new remedies in advance of the common law. There is no evidence of a

---

[75] 4 Rep. 18a; Cro.Eliz. 196.
[76] Palmer Rep. 523.
[77] See Milsom, 1954 C.L.J. 105; (1958) 74 L.Q.R. 561.

derivation from Roman law although there are tempting analogies such as the Roman *Actio in Factum* which was also a personal action of wide scope.

Damage as a basis of liability in case

Liability in Case required two elements which may be described as Wrong plus Damage. Material damage to the plaintiff was always a *sine qua non* for a successful action, except in defamation, where damage was usually presumed.[78]

Indirect "consequential" damage, arising from a direct act or omission of the defendant was only actionable in Case. An example would be where the defendant lit a fire on his own property (the direct act) which then spread to and damaged the plaintiff's property (the indirect consequential damage). Some of these cases caused confusion among the lawyers themselves in the Middle Ages since the distinction from direct Trespass was not always immediately obvious, and was further obscured by a tendency to use the words "by force" in the writ to describe the act which started off the chain of causation, *e.g.* if A strikes B's horse which runs away and injures C, B can sue A in Trespass but C can only sue A in Case.

As time went on, the courts grew to regard the causing of damage as a basis of liability in itself and to assume a wrong unless the defendant could show justification. However, as early as 1410, Hankford, a judge of the Court of Common Pleas, said "There are cases of damage without any wrong."[79] This rule, of *Damnum absque injuria*, has been re-emphasised in modern times, to justify the refusal of remedies for damage suffered as a result of acts by the defendant which the law is not prepared to condemn.[80]

Liability in case for fault

Liability in Case, generally speaking, required proof of personal guilt or fault, though the degree of fault varied with each type of case. The reason for this requirement is that in Case there is no recognised precedent liability at the outset and the plaintiff must therefore persuade the court that there is some ground for requiring the defendant to compensate him for the damage suffered. This means showing the court, for example, that the defendant could have avoided the damage whereas the plaintiff could not, so that it was fairer to make the defendant bear the loss.

Where it should have been obvious to the defendant that his

[78] *Infra*, p. 47.
[79] Y.B. 11 Hen. 4, H., f. 47, pl. 2; *Source Book,* 127.
[80] This doctrine is discussed at the beginning of Chap. 6.

conduct was likely to cause harm the court imposed strict liability, so that if he were in charge of a dangerous thing such as a vicious dog which escaped and caused damage, he would be liable for its acts even if he were not personally to blame for the escape. On the other hand where it was the policy of the law to encourage some act, *e.g.* the prosecution of criminals, it hesitated to impose liability for prosecuting groundlessly unless a very definite personal element such as malice was proved.

In between these two extremes were any other types of liability on which the courts had less definite views and in relation to which they varied their policy from time to time. Thus in the Middle Ages a bailee appears to have been liable for damage to goods in his charge only if he had been negligent.[81] In 1601, however, owing to misunderstandings of the authorities, a very strict liability was laid down, in *Southcote's Case*.[82] It was not until *Coggs* v. *Bernard* in 1703[83] that the more moderate modern position was laid down, restoring very much the same rules as those stated by Bracton in the thirteenth century.

An interesting feature of the old law was the concept of the "common callings" which included innkeepers, common carriers, blacksmiths and possibly surgeons. These men could be prosecuted for refusing to accept customers or clients but their civil liability varied. The liability of an innkeeper for his guest's goods was strict, independent of fault, from the time of Edward III.[84] From the seventeenth century the common carrier's liability was also settled as strict.[85] Most actions against followers of other common callings were brought in *assumpsit*[86] which generally required a more specific allegation of negligence.

Liability for negligence

It was not until the end of the seventeenth century that a general liability for damage caused by the defendant's negligence was recognised. The precise terms of this liability are not completely worked out even today, but in most cases the court will expect there to have been a "duty of care" resting on the defendant, which he has neglected, and, as a result of that neglect, damage to the plaintiff has ensued.

In each case, the court must decide that there is some reason to regard the defendant's negligence as sufficiently blameworthy to

---

[81] See *The Action on the Case,* 158.
[82] Cro.Eliz. 815; Fifoot, 161, 169.
[83] 2 Ld.Raym. 909; Fifoot, 163, 173.
[84] Y.B. 42 Ass., f. 260b, pl. 17; *Source Book,* 202.
[85] *Rich* v. *Kneeland* (1613) Cro.Jac. 330; Hob. 17.
[86] *Infra,* p. 55.

make him rather than the plaintiff pay for the damage. From the time of Edward III, as we have seen, liability for careless minding of a fire was very strict. On the other hand, the rule that there could be *"damnum absque injuria,"* that is, damage caused without any wrong, has allowed defendants to escape where the courts felt there were mitigating circumstances (such as a public benefit, despite damage to one or two individuals). Thus, a schoolmaster opening a new school would not be liable to compensate the master of an existing school for the resulting reduction in his income.[87] It was also a well-recognised rule by the seventeenth century that the defendant would not be liable for damage caused by his act if the plaintiff's own (contributory) negligence had been the effective cause of the harm.[88]

Paradoxically, much of our conception of negligent conduct in the law of tort has come down to us through the law of contract, particularly the early semi-contractual Actions on the Case called *assumpsit*.[89] Some historians insist that negligence was immaterial in the developing law of contract as it is immaterial today, *i.e.* the promisor was bound to do what he promised and it did not matter whether his failure to perform the promise was deliberate, careless or quite guiltless. The word *"assumpsit"* which was pleaded in these Actions on the Case arising out of voluntary agreements rather implied that the promisor took the risk of any accident preventing performance of the obligation which he had "assumed." On the other hand the plaintiffs in such cases always specifically pleaded that the defendant had "carelessly, negligently and imprudently" done the act complained of. Later pleadings in negligence with no reference to assumpsit imitated this form of words. A typical Case for Assumpsit is *Marsham* v. *Goldryng* in 1372,[90] where a cargo-owner whose goods were lost in a wreck sued the skipper of the ship for negligently failing to perform his contract to deliver the goods safely at the port of destination. Much the same language was used in 1609 in *Nottingham & Matteson* v. *Carnaby*,[91] an Admiralty Court case between two shipowners for a collision. Under the Commonwealth the common law judges tried Admiralty cases and became familiar with negligence independent of prior contract.

A negligent omission is as old a basis of liability as a negligent positive act, except that a legal duty to act had to be proved. If a man's dog killed sheep, he was liable for failing to keep it locked in

---

[87] See *supra*, p. 43.
[88] *Burford* v. *Dadwell* (1669) 1 Sid. 433; Potter, *Historical Introduction*, 387.
[89] *Infra*, p. 55.
[90] *Source Book*, 188.
[91] *Ibid.* 374.

or for failing to destroy it after receiving notice of its weakness. In later law few new duties to act were created and even as early as 1600 Coke C.J. is reported to have said that you could never make a man a Trespasser on the Case unless he had done something. This was clearly wrong but is significant of the attitude of lawyers.

If Case were brought simply as an alternative to some older common law writ, as it could be after 1585, there was no need to dwell on any mental elements of fault or negligence unless that element had been required by the older writ.

Besides the rule in *Stanley* v. *Powell* that negligence is a necessary element in direct Trespass to the person, there is an increasing trend in recent years to require proof of negligence in many cases where it was formerly unnecessary to do so. The so-called "tort of negligence" includes special cases of negligent damage not as yet classified. We often speak today of the "duty of care" which must exist before negligence is actionable,[92] but the problem facing a modern judge is not a new one. In every Action on the Case the court in effect recognised a duty of care, *e.g.* of innkeeper to guest, surgeon to patient, without using the phrase. The main extension has in reality been from duties arising out of some antecedent relationship, such as contract or local proximity, to duties towards casual strangers as in highway accidents,[93] or towards sub-purchasers with whom the manufacturer does not come in contact.[94] "Who is my neighbour?" takes on a constantly wider meaning.

Case for fraud and malice

There were several old common law writs which gave a remedy for damage caused by fraud, but only if the fraud occurred in the course of legal proceedings or by their abuse. Thus a plaintiff could sue at common law if several persons had conspired to indict him on a false criminal charge. A writ of Deceit also lay against anyone who had impersonated the plaintiff in litigation or sued the plaintiff basing his action on forged documents, or defeated the plaintiff's action by destroying writs or recovered judgment by default against the plaintiff without having summoned him to appear in court.

There was no writ at common law to recover losses suffered as a result of any deception which was not connected with legal proceedings; for example, there was no remedy for a plaintiff from whom the defendant had obtained money by false pretences.

[92] *e.g. Heaven* v. *Pender* (1883) 11 Q.B.D. 503.
[93] *e.g. Cole* v. *Turner* (1705) 6 Mod. 149.
[94] *Donoghue* v. *Stevenson* [1932] A.C. 562.

Possibly an Action of Debt could have been used in some such cases; certainly by the seventeenth century *Indebitatus Assumpsit* was used to recover money paid to the wrong person. This, however, did not cover such cases as a claim to recover expenses incurred by the plaintiff, as distinct from the money actually received by the defendant. General liability for damage caused by deliberate deceit is first referred to in the early seventeenth century but was not put on a firm basis until the leading case of *Pasley* v. *Freeman* in 1789.[95] The defendant in that case, knowing that a certain J.S. was unreliable, nevertheless told the plaintiff that he could safely sell goods to J.S. on credit. The plaintiff did so and was never paid. The defendant was held liable to compensate the plaintiff in an Action on the Case on the principle that a combination of the two elements, fraud and damage, produced liability.

A common type of dishonesty was the sale of defective goods to innocent purchasers, and legal liability for this had a separate history. Here the merchants' courts and borough courts led the way. The royal courts, by the end of the fourteenth century, upheld liability in an Action on the Case for selling defective goods or livestock only if the seller specifically and deliberately warranted their soundness. This remained the law until the end of the seventeenth century, by which time liability in sale of goods could be enforced in two different ways; (1) by the old contractual action based on an express warranty but without proving any guilty intention, or (2) by an Action on the Case for deceit, proving that the seller knew the defect, but not relying on any express warranty. Under the Sale of Goods Act 1893 all these warranties were placed on a statutory basis and the Act, now of 1979, implies terms in the contract as to good quality. These do not require any proof of knowledge of the defect on the part of a dealer, whose liability to deliver sound goods is absolute. Only in the exceptional cases of private sales will the older forms of deceit be of any importance in the sale of goods.

In the sixteenth century the tort of malicious prosecution was developed as a form of Case, extending the old statutory writ of Conspiracy to cases where the false indictment was procured by a single person. The first reported case is *Fuller* v. *Cook* in 1584[96] although some cases do appear on the court rolls some twenty years earlier. This tort has hardly changed since those times. It requires proof of malice and lack of reasonable cause, so as not to

[95] 3 T.R. 51.
[96] 3 Leon. 100.

discourage reports to the police which may lead to the conviction of genuine criminals.[97]

Case for defamation

Slander. The feudal courts could award compensation as well as apologies for defamation of character, while in the ecclesiastical courts public apologies and payment of costs could be ordered. But by 1500 the feudal courts had decayed and the Church courts were unable to award damages. A statute *de Scandalis Magnatum* of 1275[98] had made it a crime to defame the judges or nobles and a civil action for damages could also be brought on the statute, but the earliest civil action which refers to the statute is reported in 1498.[99]

Not all plaintiffs, however, were judges or nobles, and some new remedy was urgently needed. This was found in the Action on the Case, although the action for special damage was a later development. The earliest form of Case was allowed in the reign of Henry VIII for imputation of serious crime, and here no special damage had to be proved. There is a case of slander on the rolls of the common law courts as early as 1521 and one case is reported in 1535 in the Year Books. Slander was usually oral in those illiterate times although some Actions on the Case for written defamation have been found. In modern times, of course, slander is exclusively oral.

The exact origin of the action is not clear. Some of its pleadings sound like those of the writ of Conspiracy created by Edward I or of the later tort of malicious prosecution. It may be that Case for slander was first used where the defendant accused the plaintiff of crime but no criminal proceedings were actually taken; no writ of Conspiracy or malicious prosecution could be used, as proof of trial and acquittal were conditions precedent to an action for conspiracy, but the plaintiff deserved a remedy since he was still in danger of being indicted, and in any case might suffer business and other losses from the reflection on his reputation. He could not bring an action in the Church courts for they were forbidden by statute to try imputations of felony,[1] and he therefore had to have recourse to the royal courts by Action on the Case.

The cases *de Scandalis Magnatum* were quite different from the Actions on the Case for slander and appear to have had no influence in the development of the law of defamation. The form

---

[97] *Jerome* v. *Knight* (1587) 1 Leon. 107; *Source Book*, 163.
[98] 3 Edw. 1, c. 34.
[99] *Lord Beauchamp* v. *Croft*, Dyer 285a, Keilw. 26.
[1] 1 Edw. 3 (1327), st. 1, c. 11.

of writ and pleadings are quite distinct from those in slander so that sixteenth-century references to cases of *Scandalum Magnatum* as Actions on the Case merely reflect the contemporary practice of referring to all statutory civil cases as "on the Case."

Some early Year Book cases seem at first sight to recognise writs for slander before Case for defamation was developed, but this appearance is deceptive. On analysis they prove to be cases of Trespass for intimidation[2] or Case for contempt "in the face of the court."[3]

Slander of a man's professional reputation ("professional slander") was soon recognised as actionable without proof of damage. Damage was obviously likely where the defendant had claimed that the plaintiff, who was a barrister, knew no law, but the difficulty lay in proving which people would have had dealings with the plaintiff had the slander not been uttered. A modern extension of professional slander is brought about by section 2 of the Defamation Act of 1952, which allows a business or professional person to sue in slander for words which are likely to injure him in his business or profession even if they do not refer to his business or professional activities.

Slander actionable on proof of special damage originated in imputations of immoral, as opposed to criminal, conduct. If material loss resulted from such a slander, *e.g.* where a single woman lost a match with a wealthy suitor because of imputations of immorality, then the existing ecclesiastical remedy was inadequate and only an Action on the Case could be used to recover the damages.[4] At first bad character had to be imputed, but today even allegations of misfortune may be defamatory if they make the plaintiff appear ridiculous.[5]

The courts in the seventeenth century introduced what is called the *"mitior sensus"* rule, by which words were construed in an innocent sense if this was at all possible. The courts' own policy had made this rule necessary, for they encouraged actions for slander as outlets for bad feeling which might otherwise have been vented in feuds and duels. This led to such a spate of litigation that the courts were obliged to attempt to curb the trend and did it so severely as to produce ridiculous results. One could, at a certain period, say with impunity that a man had taken the goods of another, as the taking might have been an honest mistake and not

---

[2] *e.g.* claiming that the plaintiff is the defendant's villein.
[3] *e.g.* insulting a judge on the bench.
[4] *Davis* v. *Gardiner* (1593) 4 Rep. 16b, Pop. 26.
[5] *Youssoupoff* v. *M.G.M.* (1934) 50 T.L.R. 581.

done feloniously.[6] In more recent times words are again given their ordinary sensible meaning.

Libel, that is, written or printed defamation, first became recognised as a separate action in the Court of Star Chamber in the sixteenth century and was punished by fine or imprisonment as well as damages. Most of these libels were violent attacks on the Government, in printed pamphlets or other publications of a seditious nature, so that truth was no defence, but equally oral libel was not of much moment. The Star Chamber fell in 1641 but the common law courts had held in 1607 that Action on the Case would lie for libel[7] and in 1670 they filled the vacuum left by the Star Chamber and provided a civil remedy.[8] Although it was an Action on the Case it did not require proof of special damage, because libel was also a crime. Otherwise it resembled slander in most respects.

The Star Chamber's emphasis on the criminal aspect of libel led to the royal judges almost invariably finding against any defendant whose publication even faintly resembled sedition. The result was Fox's Libel Act of 1792. It is now for the judge in defamation cases to rule whether, as a matter of law, words are capable of being understood as defamatory, but it is for the jury to decide whether, as a matter of fact, they were or could have been so understood.[9]

Justification, *i.e.* proof of the truth of an allegation, became a defence to civil proceedings for the tort of libel in the royal courts but, following the rule of the Star Chamber, truth was no defence to criminal proceedings until the Act allowed it in certain circumstances.

Privilege may sometimes be a defence where there has been a false and defamatory statement made on an occasion which the law considers should be protected. In some cases absolute privilege attaches to such statements on the grounds of public policy, *e.g.* a judge must be absolutely free to discuss the behaviour of the parties to a case before him. In other cases privilege is qualified and may be lost if abused, so that an honest but mistaken imputation will not be actionable whereas a deliberate reckless or malicious falsehood will be, although the circumstances are the same. It is for the judge to rule whether an occasion is privileged and for the jury to decide whether the privilege was abused or not.

---

[6] The high-water mark is probably *Holt* v. *Astrigg* (1607) Cro.Jac. 184 where the plaintiff was charged with murder in effect but not in so many words.

[7] *Edwards* v. *Wooton* (1607) 12 Rep. 35, 4 Leon. 240.

[8] *Lake* v. *King*, 2 Keb. 664.

[9] Specific questions are generally put to the jury but their answers finally determine the matter.

Libel is actionable without any proof of damage, for there is no reliable way of assessing damage to character, which is not a commercial article. It is for the jury to assess what damage in fact has been sustained and their awards are often rather inconsistent.

The distinctions between civil and criminal libel are several and interesting. Unintentional libel is a tort but not a crime since the criminal law requires proof of *mens rea*. Some libels, conversely, are crimes but not torts since no individual is damaged by them, for example blasphemous libel which defames God. A civil action will only lie for defamation of the living but a prosecution may be brought for defamation of the dead where the feelings of the living are outraged, *e.g.* a breach of the peace might result. A civil libel must be published to a third party, for a plaintiff does not suffer damage by being accused of some scandalous act in a letter to himself. A criminal libel, however, may be contained in a letter sent only to the prosecutor, as a breach of the peace may result.

It is an interesting but regrettable fact that much of our present law can only be explained by historical and not logical reasons. Thus libel is limited to an imputation in permanent form such as a book, newspaper article, painting or sculpture. It has been extended to films and all forms of broadcasting and television, including unscripted radio broadcasts.[10] On the other hand other spoken words and gestures constitute slander because of their transient character. The test is an accident of historical development but remains useful to distinguish between grave defamations likely to cause substantial harm because of the magnitude of their dissemination and usually the product of deliberation, and insignificant defamation hastily uttered and soon forgotten by the small circle of its hearers.

History of Contract

The modern law of contract is the product of three main forms of action. The first, the Action of Covenant, was always a true contractual action, and lay against a defendant who had failed to perform some promised act other than the payment of money. It still survives in a much modified form in the special rules which apply to contracts under seal. The second of the old forms was the Action of Debt which lay for the recovery of liquidated (*i.e.* exactly specified) amounts of money due under contracts, whether under seal or informal. The third form was the Action on the Case for *assumpsit* which, from the fourteenth century, allowed the recovery of damages from a defendant who had assumed some special duty in relation to the plaintiff for a consideration.

[10] Defamation Act 1952, s.1.

Covenant

The basis of the Action of Covenant, like that of our modern law of contract, was agreement, as may be seen from the name, derived from the Latin word for agreement (*conventio*). Paradoxically, the word "contract," on the other hand, merely signified that the two parties were bound together, but did not stress agreement. Marriage, for example, was a contract, though it could not be dissolved by consent, and judgment debts were contracts although the judgement debtor might be very unwilling to pay them. When the royal courts adopted the rule that a sealed document was required in this action the word "covenant" lost its general meaning of agreement and became identified with formal contracts under seal. The more neutral word "contract" came by the seventeenth century to acquire its modern meaning.

A distinctive feature of Covenant is that it never required consideration, because it was well established long before the development of the doctrine of consideration. Lord Mansfield regarded the requirement of consideration in informal contracts as the equivalent of a seal in a formal contract, equating them both with evidence of intention to be bound. Consideration later, of course, became a matter of substance.

The second feature peculiar to the later Action of Covenant was that a document under the defendant's seal, a deed or "specialty" as it was called, was required before it could be enforced. As late as 1304 it was not clear that a seal was necessary in the royal courts[11] but by 1321 a plaintiff was non-suited because he produced no "specialty"[12] so that the rule was obviously established by then, and it was confirmed by the full court of King's Bench[13] in 1346. A noteworthy consequence of the rule was that the action lay against the estate of the covenantor after his death, as his participation was proved by his seal.

The advantage of the Action of Covenant was that any kind of agreement could at first be brought within it. Many early recorded instances concern land, *e.g.* leases or warranties of title, probably because the royal courts were mainly interested in title to land, but even in the royal courts miscellaneous types of covenant are found[14] and the Statute of Wales in 1284 expressly stated that the scope of the writ was very wide.

The remedy was usually unliquidated damages for breach of covenant, although specific performance was sometimes ordered

---

[11] See Fifoot, *ubi supra,* 257.
[12] *Source Book* 180.
[13] Y.B. 20 Edw. 3, Vol. II (R.S.), 148 *Source Book* 181.
[14] Fifoot, 255–256.

in medieval times and indeed the law of leasehold, mortgages, and the barring of entails would probably otherwise have been unworkable, as all of these were to some extent enforced by Actions of Covenant.

Debt

The Action of Debt lay to recover specified sums owed by the defendant to the plaintiff. It is important because the Action on the Case for Assumpsit took over some of the rules of Debt after *Slade's Case* in 1600. It is also valuable because its origin may lie in older customary law.

Debt is often described as proprietary in origin, that is to say, it is based on rights of property rather than on obligation. The following arguments have been advanced for this view. In the first place the formula of the writ of Debt resembles that of the writs used to recover land.[15] Secondly, it was originally combined with the writ of Detinue which was concerned with rights of property over chattels (all possessions other than land), although the two writs were separated some time before 1284.[16] Again, in the early days of Debt, there are few references to "agreement," the writ simply claiming "the money which you owe me and wrongfully withhold from me." On the other hand it is argued that the importance of the formulae should not be exaggerated. They do not necessarily denote any abstract principle but merely current practice when the various writs were first devised.[17] Detinue moreover seems to have sprung from Debt and not vice versa, so the nature of Detinue throws little light on that of Debt. Glanvil and Bracton equated the Debt obligation with *Mutuum* and *Emptio venditio* which are personal obligations in Roman law and not with Roman proprietary law.

The scope of the Action of Debt was fairly wide. It lay wherever the law recognised a "cause" for the payment of money, whether arising from a contract, which was the more usual case, or from a statutory or customary right. The word "*debet*" in the writ merely assumes that the defendant "ought" to pay the plaintiff and leaves the reason at large, so that mere moral obligation might easily be converted into an Action of Debt if the court felt inclined to allow it, and the later law of quasi-contract is partly based on this flexibility of the action.

Debt did not generally lie on an executory contract, that is one

[15] See Pollock and Maitland, *History of English Law,* Vol. 2, 203–216.
[16] Glanvil describes them as one action, Bracton shows a division, and they are separated by the time of the Statute of Wales.
[17] Plucknett, *Concise History of the Common Law* (5th ed.), 363; Simpson, *A History of the Common Law of Contract* (1975), pp. 75 *et seq.*

in which the plaintiff had not done his part. Performance by the plaintiff was a condition precedent of performance by the defendant, except in the sale of specific ascertained goods where the mere agreement to sell gave reciprocal actions of Debt and Detinue without any offer of performance. The reason for this anomaly in the law was probably commercial convenience.

At some date long after the Action of Debt had become widely used the actual practice of insisting that the plaintiff prove that he had executed his part of the bargin before he could recover his money from the defendant was generalised into a doctrine known as *quid pro quo* which argued that Debt required an exchange of benefits. There is a cursory reference to this requirement in 1338 but no full discussion until 1458, a date at which the newer Action of Assumpsit had become well known.[18] The *quid pro quo* was generally limited to a material benefit received by the defendant.[19]

Other rules limited the action. The Action of Debt would not lie against a debtor's estate after his death unless the debt were under seal. A debt under seal could only be discharged by a deed of release or by cancellation or destruction of the deed creating the debt. If the debtor paid the debt but neglected to get one of these discharges he could be successfully sued again at common law,[20] but Equity would intervene to prevent injustice and in fact that was one of its earliest fields of activity. Again, another rule was that the debt was regarded as "entire" so that the claim failed unless the full amount claimed was in fact proved to be owing. The cancellation of the whole or part of a debt was ineffective unless under seal, and this is the real reason for the rule in *Pinnel's Case* in 1602[21] that payment of a lesser sum cannot discharge the whole debt. At a much later date this rule was said to be based on the doctrine of consideration but in fact consideration played no part in the Action of Debt. Conversely, a debt was not payable until the whole sum was due, so that if A agreed to serve B for five years for £50 A could not sue until after the five years had elapsed, and if he died one day before the end of the term nothing was owing. Debt would not lie in any case if no price was fixed in advance, *quantum meruit*, a claim for a reasonable price, having been introduced in the seventeenth century after Assumpsit had largely superseded Debt. The greatest defect of the writ of Debt and the one which led to its demise was that the defendant could choose to "wage his law." This procedure consisted of an oath by twelve friends of the defendant that he did not owe the money claimed. In

---

[18] Fifoot, 218.
[19] Y.B 7 Hen. 6, M., f. 1, pl. 3; Potter, 454; Fifoot, 225; Simpson, 153, 193.
[20] Fifoot, 232.
[21] 5 Rep. 117, *Source Book,* 175.

the Middle Ages this may have been satisfactory but in later times, when men took oaths more cheaply, it was highly unpopular with plaintiffs. A means of circumventing this rule was the action of Debt *sur covenant* which enforced a promise under seal to pay money in the same way as an ordinary Action of Covenant, where wager of law was never available.

But for wager of law the development of Assumpsit might never have been necessary and Debt might have remained the principal common law contractual action.

Assumpsit

This form of action sprang from the law of Trespass on the Case and gradually changed from an action in tort to one in contract. It covered three situations, Misfeasance, Malfeasance and Nonfeasance.

Misfeasance was the earliest form to appear and consisted in the defendant doing badly and carelessly something which he had agreed or undertaken (*assumpsit*) to do well. The damage caused might be much greater than the defendant's fee, so that the plaintiff was not compensated by merely not paying it to the defendant, and could probably not sue in Covenant because generally people did not bother to execute a document under seal in the everyday situations in which Assumpsit applied. Forms of special Trespass therefore began to be used to recover consequential damages in the latter part of the fourteenth century. They differed from direct Trespass not only in that the damage was done negligently, but in that the plaintiff had asked the defendant to come in contact with him or his property, so that there was no violation of possession nor any breach of the peace. If the defendant pursued one of certain callings[22] he was liable for damage whether or not he had expressly promised to do the work, provided he had in fact started to do it when the negligent act occurred, and the first recorded cases are generally of this type. After an unsuccessful attempt in 1329, an action in the form of Assumpsit against a surgeon succeeded in principle in 1374,[23] although on a technicality the defendant escaped liability. The defendant surgeon had undertaken to cure the plaintiff's wife of an injury to her hand but made it worse by improper treatment, which the court considered would on principle have made him liable. Similarly in 1372 a blacksmith was held liable for wounding a horse by careless shoeing.[24] It became usual to plead in such

---

[22] See Kiralfy, *The Action on the Case*, 137.
[23] Y.B. 48 Edw. 3, H., f. 6, pl. 11.
[24] Y.B. 46 Edw. 3, T., f. 19, pl. 19.

cases that the defendant had "undertaken" to do his work "well and properly" and then done it "badly and carelessly." Occasional alternatives to the word "*assumpsit*" were "*promisit*," "*agreavit*," "*concordavit*" or "*accordavit*,"[25] all of which show that Assumpsit was from the first considered to be contractual in nature.

Some extension of liability for misfeasance followed, as where a doctor started a cure and abandoned it. Misfeasance in Assumpsit could not provide a general contractual remedy, but it established Assumpsit as an action based on agreement. Paradoxically, misfeasance in modern times has become part of the law of tort, as can be seen in actions for negligence against surgeons or against the railways.

Malfeasance meant doing some positively wrongful act which was not actionable in Trespass because it was stealthy or deceitful and not direct and violent, nor was it an honest but negligent misfeasance. An early example was *Somerton's Case* in 1433 where a lawyer helped someone acquire land which his own client had retained him to buy: as the deceit did not take place in the course of litigation the old common law writ of Deceit did not lie.[26] The courts seized on this idea in order to provide an indirect remedy for a failure to perform a promise which was not under seal. If, for example, A took B's money as the purchase price of a piece of land but conveyed it to C, A could be sued for malfeasance for the positive deceitful conveyance to C although the mere negative failure to convey the land to B would not in itself be actionable at all, except in Debt for the return of the money, and this would involve the hazard of wager of law. Malfeasance, however, was a rather unsystematic solution, for it did not apply if A, for example, decided not to convey the land to anyone, so that there was no positive malfeasance.

Nonfeasance developed later to cover this very situation, where there had been an inactive failure to perform a promise. We have seen that in earlier times all promises were enforceable by the Action of Covenant, but that from some date before 1321 a specialty had to be produced in court before Covenant would lie. Such deeds were seldom in fact used but the courts at first refused to allow Assumpsit to be used to evade the requirements of Covenant. By the fifteenth century some of the judges were weakening on this point, at the least to the extent of admitting *obiter* that if actual collateral damage could be proved, as opposed to the mere disappointment of the plaintiff's expectations, then an

---

[25] "promised, agreed, etc."
[26] Y.B. 11 Hen. 6, T., f. 56, pl. 26.

action might lie. In 1505 the King's Bench finally established general liability for mere nonfeasance after an Assumpsit if damage resulted. Typical forms of damage were payment in advance by the plaintiff or performance of his part of the contract.[27]

If neither party had performed his part of the bargain so that the contract was entirely executory there was still no remedy. The Court of Common Pleas considered that reciprocal actions of Debt and Detinue should be used in many such cases, for instance if A had agreed to sell goods to B but refused to deliver them, but the unpopular wager of law again vitiated these actions. The Court of King's Bench began to allow Actions of Assumpsit in these situations but this caused much dissension until finally all the judges in 1600, assembled in Serjeants' Inn, in the Court of Exchequer Chamber, to settle the point once and for all. This learned assembly produced the rule in *Slade's Case*[28] that Assumpsit might be used to enforce a contract even if it were completely executory. This meant that Assumpsit might be used as an alternative to the Action of Debt, and as an extension of the Action of Covenant to cases where no document under seal had been executed and the defendant had failed to perform his contract. It reversed the course of history and made all promises enforceable without any requirement except consideration.

Consideration[29]

In modern law a simple contract, that is, one not under seal, is only enforceable if mutual valuable consideration is exchanged or reciprocal promises to that effect are made. Such a conception first clearly appeared in the sixteenth century, in Actions of Assumpsit, and attempts have been made to ascribe its origins to various sources in the older law.

As we have seen, in the Action of Debt, except where the case was based on a statutory or customary right (in, that is, cases of "debt sur contract"), there was always a mutual bargain, such as a sale of goods, which came to be known as the "cause" or "*causa debendi*," an expression borrowed from Roman law. By the fifteenth century this feature of the action of Debt on a simple contract had come to be known as "*quid pro quo*," a benefit exchanged for a benefit. In Assumpsit some consideration came to be an essential part of the action, and since it closely resembled the

---

[27] Y.B. 21 Hen. 7, M., f. 41, pl. 66.
[28] 4 Rep. 92b, Moo. 667; Baker [1971] C.L.J. 51, 213; Simpson, 295 *et seq.*
[29] See Kiralfy, *The Action on the Case*, Chap. 16; Barton (1969), L.Q.R. 372; Simpson, 316–488.

idea of "*quid pro quo*" in the older Action of Debt consideration has been thought to be an extension of it by analogy. Thus, if a smith shod a horse he provided a *quid pro quo* for the owner's promise to pay him and could sue for his fee in an Action of Debt just as the owner could sue the smith in Assumpsit if the horse were injured. This view has been attacked on the ground that in many early cases the plaintiff sued successfully in Assumpsit without any reference to his part of the bargain, *e.g.* whether he had promised, for example, to pay the surgeon whom he was now suing for negligence. Thus although pleadings in later times always recite the plaintiff's promise, it is not clear earlier that any such promise was required. It is also pointed out that the *quid pro quo* could only be the receipt of a benefit, not the suffering of a detriment, whilst detriment is a good form of consideration. To say *quid pro quo* was a narrower idea than that of consideration, however, does not preclude its having developed into consideration.

Some aspects of the doctrine of consideration may have developed from the medieval judges' tendency to allow an Action of Assumpsit more readily if the defendant would obviously, in already established law, have a reciprocal action against the plaintiff if he in his turn reneged. Thus, in the example already cited, of the negligent smith, the plaintiff owner would refer to his promise to pay the smith for his services in order to satisfy the court that there would have been a reciprocal remedy.[30] This is not very far from the idea of consideration.

It has also been suggested that consideration in Assumpsit was the damage caused by the breach of an undertaking. This theory would argue that the reason that nonfeasance became actionable in 1505 was that the contract money had been paid over by the plaintiff, so that some "loss caused by the deceit" could be shown.[31] There are weaknesses in this point of view. In spite of the facts of this particular case the damage caused by breach of contract does not necessarily coincide with the consideration, for the plaintiff's consideration must have induced the defendant to make the promise sued on, whereas the plaintiff's damage or loss may have taken place later, as a result of the promise, and could not have been relied on by the defendant at the time the promise was made. An early example of a case where the damage and the consideration were clearly separate and unrelated items is *Dogge's Case* in 1442 where the plaintiff paid the defendant £110 and the defendant in return promised to convey property to the plaintiff.

---

[30] Y.B. 20 Hen. 6, T., f. 34, pl. 4; *Source Book,* 194–195, *per* Newton C.J.C.P.; Simpson, 162.
[31] Ames, *Anglo-American Essays in Legal History,* Vol. III, 276.

She never in fact conveyed the land and the court awarded the plaintiff £20 for his damages.[32]

Again, the view has been advanced that consideration was based on cause, in the Roman or canon law sense, some true and legitimate reason or inducement which was sufficient to make a promise legally binding. As we have seen ideas of "*causa debendi*" were familiar to lawyers through the Action of Debt. The words "cause" and "consideration" often bore similar meanings, so that some references to "cause" are found in Actions of Covenant and Deceit as confirming that a contract was willingly entered into without the use of fraud or force.

Conversely, some fifteenth-century royal charters use the term "consideration" as meaning the reason (cause) of the grant, while the term "consideration" also appears in wills to signify the reason (cause) for a bequest. Similar references appear in the beginning of statutes and in describing the judgments of courts, while the common law plea rolls in the sixteenth century talk of "cause and consideration" *uno flatu*. In Equity references to "consideration" in the broad sense of cause are found by 1504 and the term continued to include such things as parental affection or blood relationship in the Chancery courts long after these ceased to be valuable consideration at common law. The common lawyers only gradually reduced the scope of consideration to its present meaning of valuable consideration, so that for much of our legal history the words "cause" and "consideration" have been almost interchangeable.

The idea of a bargain as a basis of liability may have first appeared from the Law Merchant, which was familiar in the borough courts and elsewhere. The essence of a bargain was obviously barter, the exchange of one valuable thing for another, and this implies consideration.

Quasi-contract

This term is a controversial one, used to describe a group of situations in which the courts could only impose liability by using the analogy of a contract, although there might be no actual promise or agreement. The essential factor was that one party had received money which in justice belonged to another.

The earliest form of this liability was *indebitatus assumpsit*, which lay first on a genuine agreement. If A bought goods from B, B could sue in Assumpsit instead of in Debt for the price, by alleging a fictitious subsequent promise to pay, by which A had "assumed" the obligation, as opposed to merely being indebted.

---

[32] Y.B. 20 Hen. 6, T., f. 34, pl. 4; *Source Book*, 192–196.

Quasi-contractual situations in which *indebitatus assumpsit* came to be used are typified by the case of *Manby* v. *Scott* in 1663[33] in which an innkeeper was held entitled to sue the husband of a guest who had not paid for her board and lodging although the innkeeper and husband had not met.

In the eighteenth century the courts added a new principle of liability, which came to be known as "unjust enrichment." This arose wherever the defendant had been wrongly paid or overpaid, the court feigning a promise by him to repay. This has been extended and applied to cases where there was a failure of consideration after one side of a contract had been performed, or where payment was the result of a mistake of fact. The typical formula was that the money was "had and received" by the defendant "to the plaintiff's use." This remedy for unjust enrichment survives in the modern law of restitution, which is still not exhaustive.

Equity

Equity is a system of rules enforced by the Chancellor as keeper of the King's conscience, designed to alleviate, on moral grounds, technical injustices of the common law. Thus it is a "gloss" (*i.e.* a commentary) on the common law, it exists beside and complements it so that all actions in equity formerly contained the disclaimer "and he hath no remedy at the common law." Originally a rule-of-thumb system, fitting remedies to particular cases, equity was once described as being "as long as the Chancellor's foot," *i.e.* varying with the holder of the office. In modern law, equitable remedies can still be granted or refused as the court in its discretion sees fit, having regard to the requirements of the circumstances. Since the Chancellor was not compelled to give a remedy or, if he did, to define his reasons, his decrees were at first informal and unrecorded, and this hampered the systematisation of equity until the seventeenth century, when the Chancellors began to expound a predictable and consistent system.

The characteristic features of equity are usually considered to include the following:

(1) *Moral considerations* were the overriding preoccupation of equity, as is illustrated by many of the Maxims of Equity such as "He who comes to Equity must do Equity" and "Equity looks at the Intent and not the Form" of transactions.

---

[33] 1 Sid. 109.

(2) *The assistance of the poor and the weak* had originally been the concern of the common law General Eyre, but even there local influence and fear of reprisals hamstrung the poor. In the Middle Ages the powerful Chancellor could guarantee against reprisals and would hear oral complaints from those who could not afford a lawyer. Process in the Chancery was therefore at first cheap and speedy, but by the eighteenth century it had become slow and expensive and statutory local courts, called courts of conscience, played much the same part as the early Chancery in giving relief to poor plaintiffs.

(3) *Relief in cases of fraud* was an overall jurisdiction of the Chancery. Some forms of fraud entitled the victim to bring a common law action such as deceit or conspiracy in the course of litigation, while the Action on the Case for deceit covered most of the other forms of fraud and seems to have developed as early as equity itself. The difficulty of proof however in practice vitiated some of the theoretical remedies. The defendant could not testify and so could not be cross-examined. Thus, a debtor who paid the sum secured by a bond, but failed to recover the bond, could at common law be forced to pay again, as oral testimony was unobtainable and in any case could not upset an obligation under seal. The plea *non est factum* was available as a defence at common law where the defendant had been deceived as to the nature of the transaction, but not every form of fraud was sufficient grounds for such a plea; for example a promise under seal, obtained by a trick, was still binding. In all these circumstances it was left open to the Chancellor to summon and interrogate the creditor as to the true facts of the case and administer justice according to equity.

(4) *New remedies* were constantly being developed by equity in the Middle Ages to put right the mistakes of the common law, *viz*:

(i) Specific performance of a contract as stipulated was just such a remedy, developed by equity to remedy a shortcoming of the common law where, generally, only damages in lieu of performance were available. Specific relief was available in the real actions in the early common law and in ejectment when it took their place, but only if the title to land was involved and it had passed to the plaintiff. It was usual in Replevin, a common law action to recover impounded goods, and at first Detinue.[34] Otherwise, however, specific performance gradually developed in equity, mainly in cases of contracts to sell land where seisin or freehold possession had not yet passed.[35] It was extended by the court until the

[34] Until 1341, Y.B. 14 & 15 Edw. 3 (R.S.), p. 30.
[35] *Source Book*, 191–192; Potter, *ubi supra* (4th ed.), 625–626.

modern position was reached in which it may be sought in any action to enforce a contract except a contract for personal service. Nevertheless it remains in the discretion of the court to refuse specific performance and leave the plaintiff to recover damages at common law if he can.

(ii) The injunction was another Chancery remedy consisting of an order from the court addressed to the defendant ordering him to refrain from doing something which in some way injured the plaintiff. It was used not only to protect a plaintiff's legal rights but also as a vehicle for new rights recognised by the Chancellor in that it would sometimes prohibit the defendant's doing something which he had a common law right to do. The injunction would be enforced by committal of the defendant for contempt of court if he failed to obey. The procedure of committing to prison for contempt was not exclusively a Chancery jurisdiction, but it was more frequently used by equity in enforcing private claims for an injunction.

(5) *Effective accounting machinery* was available in Chancery. There was a common law Action of Account available to discover the exact amount due in an Action of Debt, but the procedure was slow and only available in the case of certain relationships such as those of stewards and bailiffs and their lords. The Chancery Masters and clerks, on the other hand, could and did exercise continuous supervision of accounts without reference to the judge and could orally examine the "accountant." This jurisdiction was very efficiently exercised and explains the assumption by the Chancery of jurisdiction over mortgages and the administration of the estates of infants and deceased persons.

(6) *Oral examination of the parties* was only possible in the Chancery, whose system of examination was based on the canonist inquisition, *i.e.* a direct investigation by the court. The parties were not competent to testify at common law: witnesses could be called but could not be compelled to attend. In Chancery the parties were obliged to answer interrogatories (written questions prepared in advance) and they and their witnesses could be compelled by subpoena to attend court, "on pain of" imprisonment for contempt if they failed to appear.

(7) *The interpretation of statutes* was more liberal in Chancery. Before 1400 common law judges had been less rigid in their interpretation of statutes, but after that date they were afraid of antagonising Parliament by presuming to construe its intention rather than its words. The Chancellor was more powerful, and in any case less concerned with the technicalities of the law, so that

equity would forbid the application of any statute where it would be unconscientious to rely on it, and would interpret all statutes in the light of broader considerations.

(8) *Informal procedure* was more frequently used in equity than at common law. The common law would entertain informal "bills" so long as title to land was not in question, but it was in Chancery that such things as oral petitions were really developed. Typically, Chancery proceedings were framed first in Norman-French and then in English, while pleadings at law were still being couched in Latin.

(9) *Trusts and mortgages* were two fields of law developed exclusively in Chancery. Wardship proceedings also became a Chancery jurisdiction, although in the Middle Ages there were appropriate actions at common law. The Chancery exercised this jurisdiction as representing the King in his role as the overriding protector of the weak and helpless. The other major field of Chancery competence was in the enforcement and interpretation of wills, which they acquired after the breakdown of the Church courts as an effective system during the Commonwealth period. The Chancery was the appropriate forum to acquire this jurisdiction as it had available the necessary machinery for administering accounts.

Categories of equitable jurisdiction

Equitable jurisdiction has been considered as divided into three different categories.

The exclusive jurisdiction consisted of all transactions quite foreign to the common law. For example, the beneficiary under a trust of land had no claim which the common law would recognise, and in the same way the debtor or mortgagor had no shred of title to land if he failed to redeem the mortgage by the due date. The entire law on these subjects was equitable, enforced by direct process against the trustee or mortgagee. The Court of Chancery could summon him by subpoena, interrogate him and order him to carry out the duties entrusted to him or, as the case might be, transfer the mortgaged property to the mortgagor by a suitable conveyance which would be effective at common law. If he refused or failed to carry out the court's orders he could be attached for contempt of court.

The concurrent jurisdiction existed for the petitioner who had a right to damages at common law but desired a more satisfactory remedy, such as the specific delivery of an object of unique interest or the specific performance of a contract to sell land, which, by its nature, is always unique in situation. The Court of Chancery would grant these alternative remedies in its discretion but did not itself award damages, leaving these to be sued for at common law where it considered the plaintiff had no need of equitable remedies. Similarly, its issue of injunctions was often to forbid the commission of some wrong at common law, such as a libel, nuisance or waste, where damages would be inadequate or irrecoverable or where the damage had not yet occurred. In these cases the basis of the plaintiff's claim still rested on the common law. It did slightly modify some common law rules in its concurrent jurisdiction; it would, for example, order specific performance of a contract to sell land where there was only oral evidence, whereas the common law would require written evidence before awarding damages.

The auxiliary jurisdiction consisted of procedural machinery which might be needed as a preliminary to a claim at common law. The Chancery had, for example, its procedure for the taking of accounts, which would be useful to a plaintiff in an Action of Debt at common law. Other procedures necessary for common law claims but developed by the Chancery are orders for discovery of material documents and the administration of written interrogatories.

For a clear understanding of the nature of equitable jurisdiction and principles a closer examination of their application in the fields of trusts and mortgages will be necessary.

Uses and trusts

A trust in modern law is an obligation imposed on the apparent owner (the trustee) of property, who in all other respects is the outright owner, to hold any profits and advantages he derives from the property for the benefit of another person (the beneficiary). Trusts were not the main field of the Court of Chancery in the Middle Ages but became very important later.[36] "Trusts" of money and chattels could to some extent be enforced earlier at common law in Actions of Account and Detinue. But the trust as we know it emerged from the "use" of land, under which the legal owner, A, held it in trust for ("to the use" of) B, B being a secret beneficiary. This could not be enforced in the common law courts because it violated the important principles of publicity of ownership and conveyance required by royal and feudal interests

---

[36] Most cases preserved in the early Chancery records concerned enforcement of common law rights.

to enable them to discover and impose liability on the legal owner of land.

In the fourteenth and fifteenth centuries "uses" were being created but could not be enforced by the law. The only exception was that the beneficiary (*"cestui que use"*) was allowed to finance the trustee ("feoffee to uses") when he defended lawsuits affecting the land at common law without the former becoming liable for the crime of maintenance (financing a lawsuit in which one had no personal interest). The common law and the legislature were aware of the existence of illegal uses and, in a sense, indirectly connived at their existence in certain forms by specifically prohibiting particular types. Many fourteenth-century statutes are concerned with restricting "mortmain" gifts, *e.g.* gifts of land to the Church, by which the ecclesiastical authorities accumulated large estates. The donor would try to circumvent this prohibition by creating a "use" with a lay trustee and the Church as secret beneficiary. This type of use became expressly forbidden when the practice was discovered.

Another common situation in which a use would be created was where an elderly property-owner wished to escape "death duty" on his demise. He would transfer the property to the ownership of a young trustee, retaining a life interest for himself in Equity and giving the capital on trust for his successor. By the reign of Henry VIII the Crown was suffering a serious loss of revenue as a result of the creation of such "uses," and yet the King's Chancellor was their legal protector. To remedy this situation the Statute of Uses in 1535[37] sought to vest the legal estate in the *"cestui que use"* (the beneficiary), thus making these duties payable when he died.

The Statute was temporarily successful but its terms were too narrow and a number of "uses" escaped its net. Conveyancers gradually found ways of evading it, creating "uses" which would still operate exclusively in equity. A typical example was the creation of a long lease in favour of the trustee. This escaped the Statute which referred only to trustees being "seised" of land, which a lessee was not, so that equity could continue to enforce such trusts.

Another evasion of the Statute was by way of a bargain and sale. This was originally used by vendors who had no intention of creating a genuine "use" but wished to pass the estate in their property without going through the cumbersome procedure of livery of seisin. Equity already held that when a vendor A entered into a contract for value to sell land to B (a "bargain and sale") the equitable interest vested in B immediately, before the formal

[37] 27 Hen. 8, c. 10.

conveyance of the legal estate by livery of seisin, so that a temporary "resulting" trust (use) was created, with the vendor as trustee and the purchaser as beneficiary. Under the Statute the legal estate now passed in these circumstances, as A was "seised to the use of" B in the words of the Statute. It was later realised that this process could be taken a step further. Possibly because B was not yet technically "seised" of the land, if the vendor wished he could create a "use" in favour of a third party C by bargaining and selling the land to B "to the use of" C, the first use in favour of B exhausting the operation of the Statute, so that no legal estate could pass to C. B was therefore in the position of a trustee and the Chancery would give C a remedy against B.

Whether or not it was based on the procedure of bargain and sale, a practice known as a "use upon a use" became common within a century of the Statute, certainly based on the theory that the first use exhausted the effect of the Statute. The form "unto and to the use of B in trust for C" became common in settlements of land.

The third and most important exception to the terms of the Statute was the "active trust." The Statute had envisaged what had in fact been the previous practice, that the trustee should be nothing more than an inactive figurehead. If land was transferred by A to B "to the use" that B collect rents, execute repairs and pay the balance of the income annually to C, the trustee B became an active practical manager, who needed to keep the legal estate to carry out the duties imposed on him.

The Statute of Uses remained in force until 1926 although its provisions had long ago ceased to be fully effective as a result of the activity of the Court of Chancery. The trust is one of the principal fields of modern equity, the active trust having provided the prototype for the trust as we know it today.

Mortgages

A mortgage arises where land is made security for a loan of money.

In early times this was generally done by granting a lease of land. In *vifgage*, a form obsolete for centuries, a lease was granted to the creditor until the rents and profits had repaid the principal sum owed by the debtor. In the other form, the *mortgage*, the rents and profits from the land leased accrued to the creditor as interest until the debtor had paid off the principal sum from other sources. The disadvantages of this system were that the creditor had no power to realise his security by sale of the land if the debtor showed no signs of repaying the mortgage, and, moreover, the creditor was liable in medieval times to be ousted from the land by third parties, since he enjoyed only a precarious leasehold tenure.

In time it came to be considered that the better way was to convey the freehold to the creditor with a proviso for redemption (*i.e.* for reconveyance to the debtor) if the loan was repaid on a fixed date, usually six months or a year ahead. This made the creditor (mortgagee) the legal owner of the land, but also meant that if the debtor was unable to repay the money within such a short period he lost his title to the land at common law.

The Court of Chancery's attitude was to protect the debtor on the basis of the maxim "Equity looks to the Intent and not the Form." The formal conveyance to the mortgagee was in intention only a security for the repayment of the debt. Moreover outright usury was illegal in the Middle Ages, which raised a prejudice, particularly in the mind of the Chancellor, who was usually a bishop and familiar with the canon law, against allowing a mortgagee to keep land which might be worth much more than the money he had lent on it, giving him in effect a high rate of interest on his outlay.

In equity, therefore, the debtor (mortgagor) could redeem the land after his common law right to do so had lapsed. The debtor might be deprived (technically called "foreclosed") even of this right to redeem the land if the creditor had offered him ample opportunities to repay the mortgage and he had not done so.

Several other rules of equity protected the mortgagor's rights. Until redemption the debtor was said to have a mere "equity of redemption," but equity treated this for most purposes as the true title and attached to it many rights of ownership, which was particularly sensible since the mortgagor generally continued to live on the land as apparent owner. The creditor's interest, logically, was regarded in equity as monetary rather than a right over the land.

Similarly equity was most suspicious of any provision in the mortgage deed which would discourage the mortgagor from redeeming his property. It refused to countenance terms which prevented redemption for a long period or made it prohibitively expensive, or the provision of any excessive advantage for the creditor, particularly where these were to endure even after the mortgage itself had been redeemed.

Equity effectively discouraged a mortgagee from going into possession under his outward legal title and evicting the debtor. Even if the mortgagor fell in arrears with his payments the court offered the appointment of an independent receiver to collect rents and discharge the arrears as an alternative to the eviction of the mortgagor. The mortgagee's power of sale of the land was also restricted by equity to such an extent that in modern times special statutory powers of sale have had to be conferred on him.

It was also equity which laid down the complicated rules of priorities among competing mortgages. As the first mortgagee obtained the legal title, all second and subsequent mortgages could only operate in equity. By modern statutory provisions priority is conferred by the date of compulsory registration and there can be successive legal mortgages.

In recent years statute law and the changed attitude of equity have revolutionised the law of mortgages and the creditor is well protected. The redemption and foreclosure of mortgages, actions to recover the mortgage debt, and the appointment of receivers are assigned to the Chancery Division, since accounts must be taken, adjustments made and general supervision exercised.

Basis of the principles of equity

Most legal systems, but particularly the Roman and Anglo-Norman, have been familiar with the parallel existence of rival bodies of strict law and equity. The Greeks based their form of equity on a residuary power vested in a high magistrate to relax the operation of a valid general rule where its literal enforcement in a particular case would defeat its objective. The Roman and English systems went further and built up new substantive rules which superseded the old rules of strict law. In English equity the chronology of this process is complex. The Chancellor in his earlier days did not apply new rules of law but merely enforced existing common law rights by a different procedure and on different evidence. It was not until about 1500 that the Chancellor can be said to have offered any positive body of legal rules comparable to the Roman Praetorian Edict, and even here the scope of equity was narrowed by the fragmentary way in which appeals against defects in the common law system had been made to the Chancellor. Equity as a system can be said to date only from the latter part of the seventeenth century when its fundamental ideas were expounded by Lord Nottingham and his successors.

Successive Chancellors drew on diverse sources to form the rules which make up the *corpus* of modern equity.

Many of the essential principles of equity clearly have a religious derivation, though the Chancellors themselves did not emphasise this aspect of their jurisdiction. Thus the rule which we have seen exemplified in the law of mortgages, that equity will relieve against the enforcement of a penalty, is in line with the teaching of the canon law on usurious interest.

Other equitable principles reflect a philosophical or moral

approach, and it is significant that "reason" and "conscience" were at first more common expressions than the word "equity" in proceedings in Chancery. A typical maxim reflecting the high ethical standards of the Court is: "Equality is Equity" which applies where a burden has to be distributed or a benefit divided: "Equity looks on that as done which ought to be done" is also a rule which could only be created by a system based on the highest human principles.

Many equitable maxims arise from the discretionary nature of equitable relief, and the "abnormality" of equity. The Chancery is not compelled to give relief at all, so it may lay down stringent conditions before it will grant a remedy. Delay, for example, may bar a request for an equitable remedy if the court thinks the delay unreasonable, even though it would not be long enough to bar common law remedies. Again, what the court regards as dubious conduct on the part of the plaintiff may disqualify him from claiming equitable relief even if it is not sufficient to affect his legal rights. Equitable relief is given on such terms as the court thinks fit, a position which gives it considerable freedom of manoeuvre.

Some principles of equity are based on the precedence of the common law, so that equity will "follow the law" where no cogent reason exists for a departure from it, though where equitable rules do exist they are "superior" to the common law rules. Where no matter of conscience is involved the common law is left to take its usual course, a principle which extended to making equitable interests in land imitate some of the incidents of legal estates. A statement of the scope of the rules of Equity as compared with those of the common law received a limited confirmation from the King himself in the Earl of Oxford's case in 1615.[38] Appropriately, this was the first case reported in the series *Chancery Reports*, the decision laying down that the Chancery was entitled to exercise jurisdiction over-riding the common law where it had done so in the past.

Equity and the common law

The relationship between equity and the common law has fluctuated from period to period, the essential difference between the two being that the common law works from a basis in optimum general rules, the Chancery from a basis of personal moral standards. The practical effect has sometimes been the same, so that both systems, for example, have throughout recognised the rights of bona fide purchasers of land, though for different reasons.

[38] 1 Ch.Rep. 1.

In some cases the mere threat of a rival equitable jurisdiction led to reforms inside the common law, so that no equitable principle developed. Thus the fact that the Court of Chancery in the fifteenth century began to allow informal purchases of land to be enforced hastened the development of Assumpsit at law. Equitable jurisdiction did not survive in these fields, for it would only intervene where the common law was defective and would retire as soon as it had cured the defect.

In some fields the common law and equity exhibited a peculiar dualism. Thus, equity recognised certain defences to an action to enforce a contract which were not recognised at common law, such as innocent misrepresentation inducing a contract. Where such an equitable defence existed a separate suit had to be brought to rescind the contract to prevent the other contractor from obtaining judgment at common law. Equity recognised interests which the common law rejected, such as the interest of a tenant under a lease which was in writing, but not under seal. In such a case equity would issue an injunction to prevent the tenant's eviction by order of the common law courts.

For historical reasons curious paradoxes can be observed, such as that some common law courts in 1200 could be seen acting as the Chancery was to act in 1400. Anticipations of Equity in the common law system itself are only to be expected before the emergence of a regular court of equity. This relationship is further complicated by the growing rigidity of the common law between 1250 and 1400, and the emergence of some substantive equitable principles between 1350 and 1500. In both cases the tendency was towards more rigid, less adaptable rules so that the gap between the two systems was bound to widen. The contradiction in outlook became more obvious with time, especially after the eighteenth-century definitions of equitable doctrines. By the late nineteenth century some action was imperative, not only because of the inherent inconsistency of two parallel systems but also because procedure in Chancery had become incredibly slow and expensive through lack of competition. The result was the Judicature Act of 1873 which laid down that all equitable defences and remedies were to be available in any Division of the High Court. Where they conflict, the rules of Equity prevail over the rules of the common law. The duality of legal and equitable titles persists, so that property may be owned at law by one person but belong in Equity to other beneficiaries, but purchasers of the property are not concerned with the equities.

Equity, then has assumed three successive characters. In the medieval period its function was to correct abuses in the operation of the common law. From the sixteenth to the nineteenth century it became a parallel system offering rival remedies and conflicting rules in identical situations. Since the Judicature Act came into force in 1875 equity has been divided into two parts; first, the old concurrent jurisdiction is largely incorporated into the common law and is no longer the exclusive field of the Chancery Division; secondly, most of the old exclusive jurisdiction, such as the law of trusts, is still administered exclusively in the Chancery Division, which has retained the special facilities for accounting and hearings in Chambers. The old auxiliary jurisdiction in procedural matters, such as the discovery of documents, is now available in all Divisions, including the Chancery itself.

Not least of equity's ancient features was the pressure which the award of equitable relief exerted on the common law, forcing it to move reluctantly forward. The common lawyers are known to have devised such new forms of action as Trover and Assumpsit in response to competition from the Chancery. Even in modern times equity is quicker to recognise and develop new types of interest in property than is the common law. During the nineteenth century, for example, the restrictive covenant was developed in equity after the Real Property Commissioners had refused to allow such an incumbrance at law. Similarly, in the '50s and '60s the Chancery judges provided an interim security of tenure for deserted wives until apt legislation was passed.[39] Today statutes are the main form of legal change. Equity has not been able to develop as a type of law reform, owing to the primacy of statute and the different kinds of issues, *e.g.* less stress on property rights and more on employment, amenity and social welfare.

---

[39] Matrimonial Homes Act 1967.

CHAPTER 3

SOURCES

PRECEDENT

Case law

When any case, civil or criminal, is tried, points of law and fact are always involved. Thus if one party sues another in the High Court for damages for negligent injury, the judge must find the facts of the case and rule whether in law negligence was present.

The judge's decision has three aspects. In the first place it will decide what is to happen to the plaintiff and defendant, *e.g.* whether the defendant pays a sum of money to the plaintiff. In the second place the judge will give his reasons for his findings of fact, *e.g.* that he believes the plaintiff to be telling the truth. In the third place, he will give his reasons for any legal ruling he has to make as to the legal meaning of negligence. These reasons are useful if an appeal should be taken from his decision to a higher court. They are also precedents for other courts of equal jurisdiction to follow, in the interests of consistency, and for inferior courts to follow as a matter of obligation. "While it is the primary duty of a court of justice to dispense justice to litigants, it is its traditional role to do so by means of an exposition of the relevant law."[1]

Owing to the accidents of legal history, the judges in England have been left to develop and elaborate most of the basic principles of our law. It is the judge's duty to decide every case brought before him and he cannot refuse to do so on the pretext that there is no relevant statutory text applicable to the facts. In building up the law the courts have tried to give effect to practice and transactions which are not clearly harmful and to pray in aid such devices as the conduct of the "reasonable man" or "reasonably foreseeable consequences," basing themselves on how respectable people behave to one another.

Inductive approach. Case law is often said to be the result of "inductive reasoning," in the sense that broad principles of law emerge as a result of the collation and study of a large number of

---

[1] *Jacobs* v. *L.C.C.* [1950] A.C. 361, 369, *per* Lord Simonds L.C.

separate decisions on "unwritten" law or on the interpretation of statutory provisions. In contrast, foreign statute law, especially codified law, is said to be "deductive," since the general rules are laid down in advance and are then applied to individual cases. The words of a Code are not varied by judicial decisions, although their exact meaning may be modified. On the other hand, case law changes more easily since it is based on principles not laid down in any fixed formula. Rules of case law are flexible and do not pretend to cover every aspect of a subject, only the case in hand.

Real dispute necessary. This approach is illustrated by the rule that an English court will only give a legal ruling if there is a dispute. Cases involving points of law are generally fully argued by counsel. Under these conditions it is clear that in fact every possible point will be taken and that the judge will have all the necessary materials for a confident decision. The court will not decide "moot" or "academic" points. The Government may not, for instance, ask for a ruling in advance as to the legality of some step. The court will not try a case if it finds that the parties have really settled the case and only want an abstract statement of the law.[2] The courts will also not try an appeal if they learn that the appellant has undertaken to pay the respondent even if the appeal succeeds.[3] But decisions can be referred by the Attorney General to the Court of Appeal for a ruling, which will not affect the parties.[4]

Provided there is a real dispute there is no objection to suing for a declaration of one's rights, without seeking any other remedy. This possibility is subject to the discretion of the judge, and courts have been less reluctant to allow it in recent years than formerly.[5]

The "moot" objection does not apply to a "test case" for this also involves a genuine dispute between hostile parties, even though other persons in similar circumstances may be interested in the result.

The binding force of precedent

Binding decisions. Decisions of higher courts are binding on lower courts,[6] but such decisions are only authoritative if given after reference by the court to any relevant statutes and any previous decisions on the same point of courts higher than the

---

[2] But an appeal on law was allowed in *Z* v. *A-Z* [1982] 2 W.L.R. 288, C.A. after a settlement.
[3] *Sun Life Co.* v. *Jervis* [1944] A.C. 111; *Sumner* v. *William Henderson & Sons* [1964] 1 Q.B. 450; *I.M.I. Yorkshire Imperial* v. *Olender* [1982] I.C.R. 69 (E.A.T.).
[4] Criminal Justice Act 1972, s.36, see *infra*, p. 157.
[5] e.g. *Pyx Granite Co.* v. *Ministry of Housing and Local Government* [1958] Q.B. 554 at p. 571.
[6] See *infra*, p. 84.

court giving the decision. It is for the judge on each occasion to decide whether the statutes or decisions in question are applicable to the case before him, but if they are not brought to his notice his decision may be ignored by a later court as based on an oversight (*i.e.* a decision *per incuriam*).[7]

It is at present the duty of counsel for the parties to undertake the necessary research to discover all relevant statutes and decisions and bring them to the attention of the court, though judges may also, and this happens in particular in the House of Lords, refer to other authorities known to them but not cited by counsel. Counsel should in such cases be asked by the court for their opinion on such authorities.[8]

The issues between the parties to a lawsuit are formulated in written pleadings, and counsel prepare their cases on this basis. The court cannot go beyond these issues in giving its judgment.

Ratio decidendi

Even where the conditions for a binding decision are present, the judge sometimes goes beyond the points raised in the pleadings, *e.g.* he suggests that he would have decided the case in the same way even if the facts had been somewhat different. This part of his judgment is not strictly binding on a later court, being unrelated to the facts before the judge, and generally not covered by the arguments of the parties' counsel. Thus a narrower principle must often be extracted from the literal wording of a judgment, this being the *ratio decidendi*, the rest being *obiter dicta* (asides).[9]

However, it is rather absurd for a later court to ignore a deliberate statement of law on a given set of facts if made by a judge or court of several judges after full discussion, even if it goes a little outside the facts found to exist in the case before them, and in practice it is not uncommon for counsel in a later case to cite such statements of law as opinions of judges worthy to be considered.[10]

If a general principle is accepted by later courts as convincing, it is often applied to quite different circumstances, provided the principle is equally applicable to them. Thus a decision that a will might be signed by a rubber stamp has been followed in a case turning on the signature of a solicitor's bill of costs. The facts were quite different, yet the concept of a signature was held to apply in

---

[7] See, *e.g. Morelle* v. *Wakeling* [1955] 2 Q.B. 379 (C.A.).
[8] *Re Mason* [1928] Ch. 385, 400.
[9] See Goodhart, *Essays in Jurisprudence and The Common Law*, p. 1; R. Cross, *Precedent in English law*, Chap. 2.
[10] Paton and Sawyer (1947) 63 L.Q.R. 461.

both cases in the same way.[11] A court sometimes gives a negative ruling which goes beyond the facts before it, *e.g.* limiting the application of some doctrine. Since this ruling will not have been based on the facts in dispute, later courts are free to ignore it, and to decide new cases for themselves. Thus in denying the liability of a hospital for the acts of a consultant a court held that the hospital would also escape liability for acts of their permanent staff, but a later court ignored this ruling and made them liable accordingly.[12]

Ruling too wide. A statement of law may thus be said to be an authority for all cases which clearly fall under the same principle as the case decided, but not for any case quite different in nature, even if the words used by the judge would in themselves extend to it. Whether a case lays down a wide or a narrow principle often depends on the reception of the decision by other courts. If it is considered to be correct, it may be applied to an increasing range of analogous cases. If it is felt to be unfortunate and ill-considered, it will gradually be isolated and limited to practically identical circumstances. Only a certain intuition will enable the lawyer to predict which course is likely to be followed, and whether he may hope to win his case although some precedent is against him.[13]

Decisions with two or more reasons. An interesting problem may arise where the court founds its legal ruling on its findings of fact, but states that it would be the same on different facts. Thus counsel may argue that his client should recover damages because she falls within a certain category, and the court may hold that she falls within a different category, but that she cannot recover damages for some reason, irrespective of her category. Since she would have no right of action in any case, is their ruling that she fell within a particular category really a precedent?[14] In a later case it has been held that such a solemn ruling is an authority even though not technically necessary to the decision. The ruling that no one could recover is one reason, and the classification of the plaintiff is another. One cannot accept one reason and reject the other as a matter of personal choice. Otherwise no case could be a precedent if the court gave two or more reasons for it.[15]

"In some cases judges may be criticised for diverging into expositions which could by no means be regarded as relevant to the dispute between the parties; in others other critics may regret

---

[11] *In bonis Jenkins* (1863) 3 Sw. & Tr. 93; *Goodman* v. *J. Eban Ltd.* [1954] 1 Q.B. 550 (C.A.).
[12] *Gold* v. *Essex C.C.* [1942] 2 K.B. 293 (C.A.); *Cassidy* v. *Minister of Health* [1951] 2 K.B. 343 (C.A.).
[13] Paton and Sawer, *supra,* 480.
[14] *Fairman* v. *Perpetual Investment Building Society* [1923] A.C. 74.
[15] *Jacobs* v. *L.C.C.* [1950] A.C. 361, 369.

that an opportunity has been missed for making an oracular pronouncement upon some legal problem which has long vexed the profession. But, however, this may be, there is in my opinion no justification for regarding as *obiter dictum* a reason given by the judge for his decision, because he has given another reason also. If it were a proper test to ask whether the decision would have been the same apart from the proposition alleged to be *obiter*, then a case which *ex facie* decided two things would decide nothing."[16] It is for the judge to make clear whether he is basing his decision on alternative principles or is relying on one principle and suggesting others as possibilities.[17]

Extracting the ratio decidendi. An interesting example of the operation of precedent and the extraction of the *ratio decidendi* occurred in *Bonsor* v. *Musicians' Union*.[18] It had been held that a trade unionist might obtain a declaration from the courts that his expulsion was unlawful if it was proved that the expulsion was not carried out in the manner provided for in the rules of the union. He might also obtain an injunction to prevent their expelling him in an improper way. But it was held by the Court of Appeal some years before that no action for damages for breach of contract would lie against the union for such an expulsion.[19] In *Bonsor's* case counsel for the plaintiff argued that that decision was based on a technical rule of law that a man could not sue a group of people of which he himself was one, and that, this rule having been abrogated since 1925, he might sue the union. The Court of Appeal held that the court in the previous case had not given judgment on the ground alleged, but had considered the contract made by a new member as a contract with all the other members, and not with the union. Hence the 1925 legislation had nothing to do with it. The Master of the Rolls also did not agree that the earlier decision had been an oversight. "I cannot conclude that the question of the essential character of a trade union for the purposes in suit was not properly debated in argument."[20]

The House of Lords reversed this decision and held that a trade unionist can recover damages if he is expelled from the union in violation of the union's own rules of procedure, and the contract between the member and his union was a contract with the trade union as a group and not with all its members individually, as was obvious when one considered that membership was constantly

---

[16] *Jacobs* v. *L.C.C.* [1950] A.C. 361, 369.
[17] *Behrens* v. *Bertram Mills Circus* [1957] 2 Q.B. 1.
[18] [1954] Ch. 479.
[19] *Kelly* v. *National Society of Operative Printers and Assistants* (1915) 31 T.L.R. 632.
[20] *Bonsor's* case, at 496.

changing and that individual members could hardly enforce it against one another. The effect of the cases was, therefore, to confer practically all incidents of incorporation on trade unions, though nominally unincorporated bodies, as they could already own property and bring and defend actions.[21]

Differing opinions. Only the majority opinions are authorities where there are several members of a court and there are dissenting judgments. Sometimes the reasoning of the various judges is inconsistent, even if they agree on the result, so that no principle is laid down which is useful in later cases.[22]

If the various opinions are not repugnant but at the same time are quite different, it now appears that all the reasons given are equally binding, at any rate in the decisions of highest courts.[23]

not merely watons

Distinguishing

If the court considers that a precedent cited before it is not in point it will "distinguish" it. If the facts in two cases differ substantially and the earlier decision is based on the facts in the earlier case, it is obviously not binding on the court trying the later case. Thus, in the trade union case mentioned above, it was pointed out that a trade union had been allowed to bring a libel action against a third party,[24] and it was argued that this showed that the law recognised that it had legal personality. The Court of Appeal "distinguished" this case by pointing out that it concerned relations between a union and outsiders, not relations with its own members.[25]

An example of "distinguishing" in the law of tort is the leading case of *Read* v. *J. Lyons & Co.*[26] There is a great principle imposing liability on anyone who collects dangerous things which then escape from his land on to the land of another person, *e.g.* in the event of the flooding of mines by a defective reservoir.[27] In *Read's* case a shell exploded in a munitions factory and injured an inspector on the premises. There was no evidence as to the cause of the explosion, so that no negligence on the part of the firm operating the factory could be shown. It was sought to rely on the principle of liability for escapes. This attempt was rejected by the

---

[21] [1956] A.C. 104; See now Employment Act 1982 ss.15–17.
[22] *G.W.R.* v. *Owners of S.S. Mostyn* [1928] A.C. 7; *Harper* v. *National Coal Board* [1974] Q.B. 614.
[23] *Jacobs* v. *L.C.C., supra.*
[24] *National Union of General and Municipal Workers* v. *Gillian* [1946] K.B. 81 (C.A.).
[25] *Bonsor's* case, *supra.* at p. 502.
[26] [1947] A.C. 156.
[27] *Rylands* v. *Fletcher* (1868) L.R. 3 H.L. 330.

House of Lords. As Lord Macmillan put it,[28] "The doctrine of *Rylands* v. *Fletcher* derives from the conception of mutual duties of adjoining or neighbouring landowners. It has nothing to do with personal injuries. There must be an escape from one man's close to another man's close."[29] In the present case nothing escaped from the defendant's premises to other premises.

In equity. In equity the distinctions are often very fine. A fairly simple distinction may be illustrated by the case of *Re Rose*. In that case shares in a company were transferred by way of gift by Mr. Rose to Mr. Hook. The company was a private company and the directors were not bound to register transfers to outsiders. In fact they delayed registration of the transfer and the transferor died before it was completed. It was argued that the transfer was ineffective. The judge held as follows: "I was referred to the well-known case of *Milroy* v. *Lord*,[30] and also to the recent case of *Re Fry*.[31] Those cases turn on the fact that the deceased donor had not done all in his power, according to the nature of the property given, to vest the legal interest in the donee. In such circumstances it is, of course, well settled that there is no equity to complete the imperfect gift. If any act remained to be done by the donor to complete the gift at the date of the donor's death the court will not compel his personal representatives to do that act and the gift remains incomplete and fails. In this case the testator had done everything in his power to divest himself of the shares in question to Mr. Hook. He had executed a transfer. He had handed that transfer together with the certificates to Mr. Hook. There was nothing else the testator could do. It is true that Mr. Hook's legal title would not be perfected until the directors passed the transfer for registration, but that was not an act which the testator had to do; it was an act which depended on the discretion of the directors. Therefore, it seems to me that the present case is not *in pari materia* with the two cases to which I have been referred."[32]

Overruling

Higher courts may overrule decisions of lower courts. Technically this is not regarded as a change in the law but as a correction of an erroneous statement. Common law is declaratory, and, in a sense, works retrospectively, since in some cases the law

[28] At 173.
[29] "close" signifies land in private ownership or occupation, originally contrasted with open-field agriculture.
[30] (1862) 4 De G.F. & J. 264.
[31] [1946] Ch. 312.
[32] [1949] Ch. 78.

is not known until after the act is done and the court is called upon to give a legal ruling. The higher court in such cases holds that the lower courts incorrectly expounded the law.[33] Where title to property depends on some decision the courts are slow to overrule old cases. Draftsmen of settlements and wills may have relied on an authoritative ruling of the courts, and it would be as unjust to overrule such cases as to legislate with retrospective operation. On the other hand the higher courts have no compunction in overruling well-established decisions if no titles depend on them, especially where the decisions have been the subject of criticism by writers of articles and textbooks, to say nothing of criticisms in dicta of judges.

Examples. An example will illustrate this practice. It was laid down by a decision of the Court of Appeal in *Chandler* v. *Webster*,[34] that a man who paid in advance to view a procession by hiring a room with windows on the route could not recover his money if the procession was cancelled. The court considered that the contract was in itself valid, although its performance had obviously become meaningless. Before the Second World War a Polish firm, *Fibrosa Spolka Akcyjna*, paid £1,000 in advance to *Fairbairn, Lawson, Combe Barbour Ltd.* on an order for goods to be delivered in Poland. When the war broke out it became impossible to deliver the goods and the Polish firm sued to recover their money. The House of Lords held that they could do so.[35] Viscount Simon L.C. referred to the doubt raised "whether this House would be justified in disturbing a view of the law which has prevailed for nearly forty years, which has been so frequently affirmed, which has been constantly applied in working out the rights of the parties to commercial contracts, and which, more-over, at any rate furnishes a simple rule, against the effect of which the parties to a contract can, if they so desire, expressly provide. These are weighty considerations, but I do not think they ought to prevail in the circumstances of this case over our primary duty of doing our utmost to secure that the law on this important matter is correctly expounded and applied. If the view which has hitherto prevailed in this matter is found to be based on a misapprehension of legal principles, it is of great importance that these principles should be correctly defined, for, if not, there is a danger that the error may spread in other directions, and a portion of our law be erected on a false foundation."[36] The new rule was thus laid down.

[33] *Cf. R.* v. *Ramsden* [1972] Crim.L.R. 547 (C.A.); it is generally too late to re-open other cases not themselves the subject of appeal in time.
[34] [1904] 1 K.B. 493.
[35] [1943] A.C. 32.
[36] *Ibid.* 44.

"The man who pays money in advance on a contract which is frustrated and receives nothing for his payment is entitled to recover it back."[37]

Law Reporting

Citation of authority

The general rule of English law is that any case may be cited in court which is relevant (whether or not binding on the court) if the report of the case is vouched for by a member of the Bar present at the time when the reasoned judgment was delivered. The monopoly which members of the Bar enjoy in this respect is based in part on their appreciation of the relevance and meaning of the judgment, and in part on their duty not to mislead the courts, for violation of which they may be censured and even disbarred. In ancient times each court sat in one room and there were three or four judges on the bench. All counsel practising in that court were in attendance and could make notes of everything that happened. Circuit work was done in vacation so that counsel were not likely to miss decisions of the bench at Westminster Hall. In modern times, judges of the High Court sit in separate courtrooms and a number of courts sit concurrently in each Division. It is therefore quite impossible to know what judgments are being given except by using professional reporters, though some series of reports invite other barristers to send in notes of cases in which they have themselves appeared.

Series of reports. Counsel, in preparing his argument, will usually turn to textbooks or encyclopaedic reference works for lists of possible relevant cases. He will then study the cases themselves as reported in regular series of law reports, year by year. The leading series is known as *The Law Reports* which consist of separate volumes issued each year for each Division of the High Court, including appeals from that Division to the Court of Appeal. Most county court appeals to the Court of Appeal are reported in the Queen's Bench Division volume. *The Law Reports* first appear in monthly issues. Cases reported in this series are submitted to the judges who gave the judgments, for revision before publication. Weekly issues also appear, known as *The Weekly Law Reports*, and these also contain many cases of secondary importance which are not printed in the monthly *Law Reports*. Useful reports appear in the London *Times* in advance of the regular reports and these include some cases not reported

---

[37] *Ibid.* 55, *per* Lord Russell of Killowen.

anywhere else. There are also numerous reports in specialised series or journals, *e.g.* on family law, criminal law, road traffic law and property law.

Most reports have a headnote which summarises the facts and the decision. The names of the parties, or of an accused man, the names of the judge, counsel and solicitors, and the dates of hearing, are given. The facts are either summarised or appear from the judgment. In *The Law Reports* the line of argument of counsel is briefly reported, usually by reference to the cases cited. All cases and statutes referred to in the cases reported are indexed in each issue and volume.

Unreported cases

It is obviously not feasible to report every case which is tried in the High Court, as so many are decisions on fact, so that very few cases tried in the Queen's Bench Division, the busiest trial division, are reported. A fair proportion of Chancery cases are reported, as they turn on law almost as often as fact, though this "law" is often merely the interpretation of the language of stereotyped legal documents. Decisions of the Court of Appeal in civil and criminal cases, Divisional Courts, and the House of Lords are reported more frequently.

There is no official system of recording High Court judgments for use as precedents. Cases on Appeal in the House of Lords are filed in the Supreme Court Library in London and in 1951 the Lord Chancellor directed that transcripts of all judgments delivered in the civil division of the Court of Appeal be filed there.[38] Notes of unreported cases in the Court of Appeal have appeared in *Current Law* since April 1973, but leave of the House of Lords is required before they can be cited there.[39]

Reporters develop a considerable flair in selecting cases worth reporting, but oversights inevitably occur. Sir Carleton Allen lists a number of instances in which erroneous judgments were given because relevant unreported cases were not brought to the attention of the court.[40] Textbooks also often tend to be selective. A certain author or editor will decide to treat a reported case in one context and omit to deal with some of its other aspects. Even well-known cases may be lost sight of, where they decide a number of different points. Counsel who engage in active practice are often extremely busy and lack the time to carry out elaborate

---

[38] [1951] C.L.Y. 2566; *Practice Note* [1978] 1 W.L.R. 600. Copies are also available to solicitors in The Law Society's Library (57 L.S. Gaz. 345); for access procedure see (1973) 117 S.J. 110. Judgments of the criminal division are filed in the Criminal Appeal Office.

[39] *Roberts Petroleum* v. *Kenney (Bernard)* [1983] 2 C.L.Y. 432.

[40] *Law in the Making* (6th ed.), 350 *et seq.*

research into every case. Hence the argument for some official minute of all judgments is very powerful. A concise index would make such records accessible.[41] Under the present system government departments and other public bodies maintain their private files of decisions, including unreported cases,[42] which have a bearing on their operations. Counsel in private practice will seldom have facilities of this kind. If he hears of an unreported High Court case, and time and expense permit, he may order a copy of the judgment from the official shorthand writers. However, unreported cases are occasionally relied on as precedents.[43]

Old precedents

A precedent never loses its authority through the passage of time. Provided it is still relevant in principle, it remains authoritative. Many of our fundamental common law principles, such as personal freedom, freedom of contract and freedom of competition depend on very old decisions.[44]

Most of these old principles are exemplified or interpreted in later decisions and often find their apotheosis in an elaborate modern opinion of the House of Lords. In such cases it is seldom necessary to go back to the original cases.

Property law. Occasions on which very old cases are cited usually arise in the slow-moving stream of the law of property, such as doctrines applying to wills and settlements. These rather metaphysical and abstract doctrines have undergone little basic change despite the enormous changes in the material world in which they operate.

Some years ago citation of fifteenth- and sixteenth-century authority was required in order to decide whether a certain tenancy was a lease for a term of years in the legal sense.[45] The right of a legatee under a will to recover his property from another person, to whom it had been mistakenly given by an executor, was finally established, after much confusion, on the authority of

---

[41] Megarry (1954) 70 L.Q.R. 246.
[42] *Pickford* v. *Mace* [1943] K.B. 623. Revenue authorities can maintain complete files as they bring all revenue actions.
[43] *Re Endacott* [1960] Ch. 232; *Willson* v. *Greene* [1971] 1 W.L.R. 635; *Richard West and Partners (Inverness)* v. *Dick* [1969] 2 Ch. 433; *R.* v. *Easom* [1971] 2 Q.B. 3155 (C.A.).
[44] See *Bourne* v. *Keane* [1919] A.C. 815, 817. *R.* v. *Mountford* [1972] 1 Q.B. 28 (C.A.), considering a 1602 case; *R.* v. *Adams* [1980] Q.B. 575, C.A. on search warrants followed a 1794 decision.
[45] *Land Settlement Association* v. *Carr* [1944] K.B. 657, reversed by statute in Agricultural Holdings Act 1948, s.2(1). See also *Att.-Gen. of the Duchy of Lancaster* v. *Overton (G.E.)(Farms)* [1980] 3 W.L.R. 869, following *Case of Mines* (1567) 75 Eng. Rep. 477.

eighteenth-century cases.[46] The question whether the benefit of a covenant could be attached to land in certain circumstances as a property interest fell to be decided on citation of a seventeenth-century book, which drew its conclusions from a principle supposed to be laid down in a fourteenth-century decision.[47]

Naturally, even in this field, modern legislation is very comprehensive. The legislature, however, has seldom laid down broad general principles in its statutes, preferring to use the standard classic meanings of legal terms. Hence even a very modern statute may pose a very ancient problem for the courts.

Criminal law. Old decisions on criminal law are seldom relevant, in view of the great range of modern statutes which define offences with great precision. Murder remains largely a common law crime, however, and old cases and textbooks are occasionally referred to in that connection.[48] Conspiracy and breach of the peace are also non-statutory.[49]

Law of contract. Conditions in the field of personal obligations have changed so radically that old cases are seldom relevant. On the other hand the true basis of modern doctrines may have to be found by recourse to old cases. The House of Lords pointed out in one case on contract that an error of the Court of Appeal had been due to a confusion between two distinct forms of the old action of *assumpsit.*[50] In order to decide the true nature of the legal relationship between a person posting a letter and the Post Office, decisions of 1701 and 1778 were followed.[51]

Law of tort. The wealth of nineteenth and twentieth century cases accounts for the infrequency with which old cases are referred to in the law of tort though some are still relevant in actions of trespass, in view of the antiquity of that form of action.[52] There has been a modern development in the manufacturer/consumer relationship.[53] Such developments as torts of strict liability for dangerous things, on the other hand, have been developed in imitation of very old torts like cattle trespass.[54]

---

[46] *Ministry of Health* v. *Simpson* [1951] A.C. 25; in *Joyce* v. *Barker Bros.* (*Builders*) [1980] 3 C.L.Y. 349; the effect of inconsistent clauses in a deed was decided by following *Slingsby's Case* (1587) 5 Rep. 186.

[47] *Smith and Snipes Hall Farm Ltd.* v *River Douglas Catchment Board* [1949] 2 K.B. 500.

[48] *R.* v. *Page* [1954] 1 Q.B. 170.

[49] *e.g. Shaw* v. *D.P.P.* [1962] A.C. 220.

[50] The *Fibrosa Case* [1943] A.C. 32.

[51] *Triefus & Co.* v. *Post Office* [1957] 2 Q.B. 352; no action lies in the courts today, Post Office Act 1969, s.9(4)

[52] *N.C.B.* v. *J.E. Evans & Co.* [1951] 2 K.B. 861 at 873, 880 (C.A.).

[53] *Donoghue* v. *Stevenson* [1932] A.C. 562.

[54] *Rylands* v. *Fletcher* (1868) L.R. 3 H.L. 330.

Nuisance remains a very ancient tort, with rules of its own which
are not successfully combined with later notions of fault and
negligence.[55] Statutory torts are now coming into ever greater
prominence, but even they are influenced by traditional considerations.

Procedure. Very old cases are occasionally cited on criminal
procedure, which is still uncodified.[56]

The Hierarchy of the Courts

Many precedents are cited in court which are not strictly binding
on it; a judge will generally follow the ruling of another judge
unless there is some strong reason to do otherwise. On the other
hand some authorities are strictly binding on the court, so that the
judge has no alternative but to follow them unless he can succeed
in distinguishing them in some way. It is in this respect that the
English system differs from many other legal systems in which
previous decisions are cited in argument and followed.

The binding force of a precedent depends on the hierarchy of
courts. Decisions of the highest courts are binding on lower courts.

House of Lords. The decisions of the House of Lords as a court
of law bind all other courts in England.[57] This superiority appears
to be independent of the practical explanation that an appeal
would lie to the House of Lords if its decision was ignored. Thus
appeals from Divisional Courts to the House of Lords in summary
criminal cases have only been allowed since 1960, but decisions of
the House of Lords have always bound Divisional Courts.

Court of Appeal. The decisions of the Court of Appeal are
binding on all High Court judges, on all county court judges, on
Crown Courts, and on Divisional Courts in those cases in which an
appeal lies from a Divisional Court to the Court of Appeal.[58]

The decisions of the criminal division of the Court of Appeal are
probably binding on the Queen's Bench Divisional Court,
although no appeal lies to the former court from the latter. It
would be intolerable if different rules existed in the case of some
offence, depending on whether it was tried summarily or by
indictment. Even where an offence is purely summary, so that the

---

[55] *Southport Corp.* v. *Esso Petroleum Co.* [1956] A.C. 218 (see Oil in Navigable Waters Acts
1955, 1963).
[56] *e.g. Wiltshire* v. *Barrett* [1966] 1 Q.B. 312
[57] An attempt by the Court of Appeal to disregard a House of Lords ruling was rejected by the
House in *Cassell & Co.* v. *Broome* [1972] A.C. 1136. *Cf. Duport Steels* v. *Sirs* [1980] 1
W.L.R. 142.
[58] *e.g. Brownsea Haven Properties* v. *Poole Corporation* [1958] Ch. 574 (C.A.).

Court of Appeal would never have to deal with it, the Divisional Court is probably bound by any general rules of procedure and evidence laid down by the courts of criminal appeal for crimes generally. The difficulty has arisen from the piecemeal nature of English legislation. A Court of Criminal Appeal was set up by statute in 1907[59] to try criminal appeals from conviction on indictment at quarter sessions and assizes. These appeals were quite an innovation. The court was not made part of the Supreme Court although its judges were judges of the Queen's Bench Division of that court. In practice the Lord Chief Justice of England played a prominent part in both the Court of Criminal Appeal and the Queen's Bench Divisional Court and the same judges tended to sit, so that conflicts did not often arise. In 1966 the Court of Criminal Appeal became the criminal division of the Court of Appeal.

Until 1966 conflicts sometimes arose between the civil Court of Appeal and the separate Court of Criminal Appeal. If they disagreed an appeal to the House of Lords was necessary in order to decide the final solution. A conflict once arose in an acute form where a trade protection association maintained a blacklist of traders who violated certain price-maintenance agreements. Their rules enabled them to demand payment of a fine as a condition of removal of a trader from a blacklist. The Court of Criminal Appeal held that such a demand was the crime of blackmail.[60] On the other hand the Court of Appeal held that a contract to pay such fine in consideration of deletion of the trader's name from such a blacklist was a perfectly valid contract.[61] The Court of Criminal Appeal announced publicly that it would continue to uphold convictions for blackmail in such circumstances. Finally a civil appeal was taken to the House of Lords which approved the views of the Court of Appeal and decided that no crime was committed in such circumstances.[62] The combination of both courts eliminated these problems in future.

Trial courts. Decisions of High Court judges are binding on county court judges. This appears to be unaffected by the fact that there is a direct right of appeal from the county courts to the Court of Appeal. Rulings of Crown Courts do not appear to bind magistrates' courts, although they try appeals from such courts. If any important point of law is involved it is better to state a case

---

[59] See *infra*, p. 154.
[60] *R.* v. *Denyer* [1926] 2 K.B. 258.
[61] *Hardie and Lane* v. *Chilton* [1928] 2 K.B. 306.
[62] *Thorne* v. *Motor Trade Association* [1937] A.C. 797. Denyer was later pardoned. The law has been modified by later legislation.

from the magistrates' court to a Divisional Court of the Queen's Bench Division for a definitive ruling.

Courts bound by their own decisions

There is no formal rule of law that a court is bound by its own decisions, any more than there is any formal rule that it is bound by decisions of higher courts. The rule has tended to become more and more general, however, in order to secure legal stability.

House of Lords. The main object of an appeal to the highest instance, the House of Lords, is to secure a final ruling. Hence that court always tended to follow its own decisions and finally ruled that it was bound by its own decisions at the end of the last century.[63] If the result is undesirable the remedy was generally to promote legislation to alter it, and this is quite often done where a decision affects any large section of the public. In July 1966 the House declared that where special grounds existed it would feel free not to follow one of its previous decisions, *e.g.* where based on out-dated circumstances or generally criticised as unfortunate.[64]

Court of Appeal (Civil Division). The Court of Appeal held in 1944 that it is now strictly bound by its own previous decisions.[65] There are some limitations on this doctrine. It is not bound by decisions arrived at without full citation of authorities, or by rulings which are in conflict with those of the House of Lords.[66] If the court is referred to several conflicting previous decisions of its own it reserves the right to select one of them, unless it can distinguish between these decisions in some way.[67]

Court of Appeal (Criminal Division). The Court of Criminal Appeal held that it would normally follow its own decisions in favour of appellants. So few criminal appeals are taken to the House of Lords that the Court of Criminal Appeal was in practice the last court of appeal. If a conviction was quashed the court would quash any later convictions in a similar case. On the other hand the court reserved the power to quash a conviction although

---

[63] *London Street Tramways Co.* v. *L.C.C.* [1898] A.C. 375. As to Privy Council precedents, see *Port Line Ltd.* v. *Ben Line Steamers Ltd.* [1958] 2 Q.B. 146.

[64] (1966) 110 S.J. 584; the Case on Appeal must ask specifically for the House to exercise this power; *Practice Direction,* March 18, 1971; *Yorke (M.V.) Motors* v. *Edwards* [1982] 1 W.L.R. 444; the House reversed itself in *Miliangos* v. *George Frank Textiles Ltd.* [1976] A.C. 443 and *British Rail* v. *Herrington* [1972] A.C. 877.

[65] *Davis* v. *Johnson* [1978] 2 W.L.R. 553, at 558. (H.L.); *Regalian Securities* v. *Ramsden* [1981] 1 W.L.R. 611 H.L.

[66] *Worcester Works Finance* v. *Cooden Engineering Co.* [1972] 1 Q.B. 210.

[67] *W. & J.B. Eastwood* v. *Herrod* [1968] 2 Q.B. 923; (C.A.), affirmed by the House of Lords [1971] A.C. 160.

it had previously affirmed a similar conviction, if it felt an error had been made. In one case the Court of Criminal Appeal held that the plea of disappearance of the spouse could be admitted in bigamy cases only in the case of a prosecution for a second, and not a third or subsequent marriage. The same court decided in a later case that their interpretation of the words "a second marriage" had been too literal and not in accordance with the object of the statute, and that "second" really meant "later." Hence an accused person may plead seven years' absence even if the charge of bigamy concerns a third or subsequent marriage ceremony. The distinction between decisions in favour of the convict and against the convict was thus explained by Lord Goddard C.J.: "This court has to deal with questions involving the liberty of the subject, and if it finds, on reconsideration, that, in the opinion of a full court, assembled for that purpose, the law has been either misapplied or misunderstood in a decision which it has previously given, and that, on the strength of that decision, an accused person has been sentenced and imprisoned, it is the bounden duty of the court to reconsider the earlier decision with a view to seeing whether that person had been properly convicted."[68]

The Court of Appeal retains this power; at any rate five judges can overrule a previous decision of three judges in a criminal case.[69]

Divisional Court. The Divisional Court of the Queen's Bench Division is generally bound by a previous decision, unless such decision was an obvious mistake or inconsistent with the authority of a higher court.[70] On the other hand the court may depart from its previous decisions if to do so would favour the accused.[71]

High Court. High Court judges are not bound by decisions of other High Court judges. In practice they usually follow each other, preferring that the matter be taken to appeal if the rule laid down is doubtful. If two contemporary judgments are contradictory they can be made the subject of simultaneous appeals, and the Court of Appeal can dispose of both appeals as it thinks fit.[72]

Judges are generally reluctant to differ from their brethren in cases turning on common form documents or important statutes, to avoid uncertainty in people's conduct of their affairs. They are

[68] *R.* v. *Taylor* [1950] 2 K.B. 368.
[69] *R.* v. *Gould* [1968] 2 Q.B. 65 (C.A.); *R.* v. *Newsome* [1970] 2 Q.B. 711 (C.A.); *R.* v. *Turnbull* [1976] 3 W.L.R. 445 (C.A.).
[70] *Younghusband* v. *Luftig* [1949] 2 K.B. 354; *Police Authority for Huddersfield* v. *Watson* [1947] K.B. 842.
[71] *R.* v. *Fulham Rent Tribunal* [1951] 1 T.L.R. 423, a precedent on jurisdiction.
[72] *Metropolitan Police District Receiver* v. *Croydon Corporation* [1957] 2 Q.B. 154 (C.A.).

more willing to differ when the court can do justice in a non-recurrent situation, *e.g.* the meaning of a home-made will, the rights and wrongs of an industrial accident.

Judges often have discretions given them by statutes, *e.g.* to relieve a tenant against forfeiture of his lease, or to provide for dependents out of the estate of a deceased person. In fact they tend to develop clear principles for the exercise of such jurisdiction.[73]

Development of the Doctrine of Precedent

The authority of the judges to make law by the reasons given by them for the decision of lawsuits is nowhere laid down in any code or statute. It is possible to explain it constitutionally by saying that courts lay down rules of law by tacit acquiescence of Parliament. Parliament certainly passes statutes from time to time to reverse the rules laid down by the courts in certain cases.[74] It would, however, be an historical anachronism to present the matter in this way. The judges in the first centuries after the Norman Conquest were faced with the practical problem of settling disputes without having any legislation to assist them. They did have ancient customs of various kinds, but these seldom decided specific points of principle. Case law is therefore a product of necessity rather than choice.

It was yet another step to the position in which later judges would be influenced in their decisions by the reasons given in earlier cases. There is an obvious practical advantage in the following of precedents which goes beyond the boundaries of the law. It is a waste of time and energy to decide every point that arises in daily life by tracing it back to first principles, like the propositions of geometry. We all form certain routines in dealing with problems of constant recurrence, reserving our energies for the new or the borderline case. The first question anyone asks when some problem is encountered is "What do we usually do?" or "How has this been dealt with in the past?" We assume, as a Lord Chancellor once put it, that our ancestors were not necessarily more stupid than ourselves.

It is often objected that a law built up in this way makes the present the slave of the past, but this is not quite true. The body of effective law is a structure which is constantly changing. Many bad rules have been rejected and eliminated. What is left is presumed

---

[73] *e.g.* under Law of Property Act 1925, s.146; Inheritance (Provision for Family and Dependants) Act 1975.

[74] *e.g.* Local Government (Misc. Prov.) Act 1953, s.10 reversing *Birch* v. *Wigan Corporation* [1953] 1 Q.B. 136 (C.A.); Trade Disputes Act 1965, reversing *Rookes* v. *Barnard* [1964] A.C. 1129; War Damage Act 1965, reversing *Burmah Oil Case* [1965] A.C.75.

to have stood the test of time. We are ourselves constantly adding
to it. Although our ancestors may have lived in a more primitive
material condition they were definitely our equals or superiors in
fine abstract reasoning. The theological refinements of the Middle
Ages demonstrate this, and legal reasoning has much in common
with theological argument, just as the solemnities of our legal
procedure appear to stem from the same source as our religious
rituals.

The development of precedent was encouraged by the declaratory theory of our common law. The judge is not conceived of as
creating law but as declaring pre-existing law. This pre-existing law
is regarded as customary in origin and authority. It is the essence
of custom that it is what is commonly done, that it is universally
observed. Hence judicial decisions must also be consistent. There
cannot be a custom that we drive on the left and also that we drive
on the right. Equally it cannot at the same time be lawful to do a
thing and also unlawful to do it. If decisions are in conflict both
cannot be right, but it is assumed that one of them is. The
consistency of case law reflects in this way the fundamental
uniformity of custom.

Although some other native legal systems have developed the
practice of following precedents, the English system diverged so
widely in this respect from the contemporary doctrines of Roman
Law in Western Europe that legal writers were struck with the
difference. The late Roman Law of Justinian forbade judges
following the decisions of other judges.[75] Bracton noted in the
thirteenth century that English courts, unlike those of ancient
Rome, followed previous decisions in practice. He himself
collected numerous cases from original court records to illustrate
various points of law and procedure and cited them in his major
treatise.[76]

It was not felt in early times that decisions were absolutely
binding on future judges. This is confirmed by a series of cases
which turned on a Council ruling in *William Butler's* case, which
had been enrolled in error among the statutes. The courts
emphasised that they would have been bound by a statute but were
not necessarily bound by this decision.[77]

The Year Books

Most of our information on English case law during its early
formative period derives from the great series of Year Books

[75] *Codex.* 7.45.13.
[76] Pollock and Maitland's *History of English Law,* Vol. I, 183; Plucknett, 343; Bracton's *Note
Book,* 3 vols., edited by Maitland.
[77] Selden Society's Publications, Vol. LXI, xxix.

which covers the period from 1289 to 1535, with earlier and later fragments. The Year Books mainly report cases on the law of real property and on the highly technical law of pleading and procedure in actions to establish title to land, as this was the most important and lucrative legal practice in the Middle Ages. Criminal cases were rather neglected. There are few allusions to the eventual actual trial of a case or the evidence produced in it and the judgment may be missing. As written pleadings out of court became more common the work of the judges tended to concentrate less on refinements of pleading and more on points of law and procedure. The later Year Books reflect this change and supply much more information of interest to the modern lawyer.

Year Book cases vary considerably in length and completeness. There were numerous alternative MS. reports of cases, some much better than others. Many were prepared for purely personal use and are rather cryptic. Others are very good reporting and compel one's admiration for the skill of the practising Bar in those remote times. It is presumed that these Year Books, or Books of Terms as they were earlier called, are the "books" to which the medieval judges so often referred as repositories of legal rules.

Everyone agrees that the Year Books are a law report of some kind, but hardly anyone agrees what kind they were. Modern critical research suggests that jottings were taken down in longhand in court on scraps of parchment and the expense alone of obtaining writing materials may account for the stark brevity of much Year Book material. The jottings were copied on larger pieces of parchment for safe preservation, but no effort was made, at any rate in the time of the earlier Year Books, to extend abbreviations or fill in the gaps which the original author supplied from his own memory. Lawyers attached considerable value to these reports, as is evidenced by the fact that they were constantly being copied and recopied by hand, often undergoing numerous and ludicrous distortions in the process, the copyists not always having had legal training.

Some collections of cases were arranged according to subject-matter or in some other way but the great majority were arranged chronologically. Pamphlet issues seem to have circulated fairly soon after the end of each of the four annual law terms. There must have been several reporters acting independently in some cases, and most parallel reports differ considerably. In other cases the variants in extant sources are consistent with varying copies of a single original. From time to time blocks of terms or years were copied into a single MS. volume. Eventually printing followed, but the reports were not at first printed chronologically. At last the so-called "Black Letter" series was published in which most available Year Book cases were chronologically reproduced in print.

Curiously enough more MSS. of the earlier Year Books than of later Year Books have survived, possibly because they had greater antiquarian value. The extant MSS. of the later Year Books are so much better, however, that this lack of MSS. is not very important. Modern editors have collected and collated all the numerous MSS. of many early Year Books and the Selden Society has produced definitive fully annotated editions of the Year Books of Edward II.

Most scholars agree that student apprentices prepared the notes which were combined into Year Books, but it is not clear whether they did so for their personal use or were hoping to sell their reports to other lawyers. The reporters themselves are anonymous. They wrote for a small circle and seldom stop to distinguish between judges and counsel, simply referring to them by name, on the assumption that the reader would know instantly which was which. As barristers often became judges this would be very confusing to a modern reader unless he constantly referred to biographical collections like *Foss's Judges* and studied the dates of elevation to the bench.

Precedent in the Year Books. Everyone knew Year Book reports had been and were being made. No doubt counsel and judges had formerly made them and might still make them. Yet there are hardly any clear references to the use of Year Books as authorities in court. The explanation obviously lies in the varying degrees of credibility of the various private MS. versions and the absence of any uniform order of cases or pagination. The order of cases in a term varies in various MSS. and the size of the pages or folios differed. Hence citation by page numbers was out of the question. Year Books could only be used to remind the court of precedents and not as reliable reports of such precedents.

It is certainly not true that judges or counsel never used such MSS. in citing decisions. Although many citations of named cases can be explained as based on personal recollection, this would not explain citation of cases from many years earlier. In 1312[78] Bereford C.J. refers to a case 25 years old. In 1410[79] a case is cited by the name of the plaintiff which was decided as far back as 1366.[80] Although the examination of Year Book cases of any one year may throw little light on citation, an attempt to follow a

---

[78] Y.B. 6 Ed. 2 (XIII Selden Society) 43, 44.
[79] Y.B. 11 Henry 4, Trin., pl. 14.
[80] Y.B. 40 Edward 3, Hil. f. 9, pl. 18.

particular rule of law through the Year Books is much more fruitful. Cases rather vaguely referred to in a later report can be identified with earlier reported cases on the subject, and it is difficult to imagine that some Year Book MS. was not used as the source of the citation. The later Year Books show a wide use of citations of previous cases.

Abridgments

Lawyers used to make their own private digests of case law from Year Book MSS. These shortened versions were known as abridgments. All the cases on a given topic were collected under a heading such as "Pleas of the Crown," "Trespass" or "Debt." Within the heading there was no very scientific principle of arrangement. In many cases there was some attempt at a chronological order but there was no attempt to organise the material into a code or textbook. The Abridgment might be regarded as a Digest of Year Books, except that Year Books were not supplied with standard headnotes, so that each lawyer's abridgment differed from every other. The notes were highly abbreviated and in some cases informative only to the author himself. Conflicting cases follow one another in a most mechanical way without any attempt at distinction or reconciliation.

Some Abridgments were produced by great judges, and these were later published and enjoy high authority as repositories of case law. Broke and Fitzherbert are particularly valuable, and Fitzherbert's Abridgment is in many ways the best key to the Year Books. Some cases were digested from Year Book MS. sources now lost so that the Abridgments are our only authority for those decisions.

Rolle's Abridgment, the work of a great judge of the time of the Civil Wars, was published at the Restoration and is far superior in arrangement to its predecessors. Subjects are more logically arranged, divided and subdivided, so that reference is facilitated. It is far better than a mere digest and has some pretensions to being an encyclopaedia. Reported cases had by then to a large extent superseded Year Book cases. As we have original law reports of most cases reported in Rolle and in later Abridgments and Digests, they are now much less valuable to us, though no doubt useful in their day to the practitioner. The practice of preparing encyclopaedic digests went on through the eighteenth century. In recent times the growing volume of statute law, and the abolition of the system of forms of action led to more scientific textbooks and to digests of cases based on subject-matter *e.g.* criminal law or landlord and tenant.

Precedent in the named reporters

The Year Books were hardly dead when their place was taken by the much more modern series of law reporters, who may be styled the "named reporters" because the reports were published under the reporter's name.[81] These private series passed through two phases. During the first phase, reports which had been prepared by eminent judges for their own use circulated in the profession before they were finally published, often posthumously. These reports were authoritative on account of their authors. As the quality of reporting varied considerably their authorship was some guarantee of accuracy and completeness. In many cases the reporter of a case had been the judge who decided it. This system had disadvantages. Some reports were genuine enough but so terse as to mean little to those who had had no connection with the original case. In other cases the author, knowing they were to be published, took the opportunity to elaborate and decorate the report with all sorts of learned notes and observations, so that it ceased to be a true report and became a juristic exercise. Barristers could not cite recent decisions as these were not widely available, so the judges often had to cite them to counsel, the reverse of the modern practice.

Outstanding among these earlier reporters was Coke C.J. Although his reports are in many ways too elaborate and sophisticated to serve as models, they cover a period of most important decisions, and Coke himself was a judge of unique importance in our legal history. Hence most of our fundamental common law principles may be found fully expounded in his reports. For a clear and concise report of the actual decision many more modest reports are superior.

It was of course, inconvenient to wait for a judge to die in order to be able to refer to his decisions! Hence there was a demand for a more regular series of reports. Gradually, permanent law reporters began to publish contemporary reports, *e.g.* the *Term Reports* in 1789. Each case was given a short title stating its subject-matter. The substance of the pleadings was given, details of the facts and full accounts of the arguments of counsel. In many respects the better reporters of the eighteenth century and early nineteenth century present a much fuller picture of a case than do those modern reports based on transcripts of the judgment. Decisions of the House of Lords were not included in any series, as it was considered to be a breach of their privilege to report their judicial proceedings, although they were the most important of precedents

---

[81] See, in general, *Law Reporting in England* (1485–1585), L.W. Abbott (1973).

and already considered as binding on other courts. This anomaly was corrected after 1700.

The cases reported by the named reporters were decisions of courts "*in banc*." That means that they confined themselves to decisions of the full Courts of King's Bench, Common Pleas and Exchequer sitting at Westminster. The decisions of single judges at the assizes (Nisi Prius decisions) enjoyed little authority. As the courts of Exchequer Chamber decided important cases on appeal, the reporters of those decisions are especially important. In Chancery cases there were reporters in the Rolls Court, Vice-Chancellors' courts and the Lord Chancellor's court. Some named series have been the subject of adverse criticism, and the court today still has some preferences among the older series of reports, depending on the reputation of the reporter for accuracy.

Courts, such as the Admiralty and Ecclesiastical Courts, which followed Roman law traditions, did not regard precedents as binding and consequently did not publish reports until modern times although practitioners studied cases.

As the practice of following precedent depends on adequate and reliable reporting, a semi-official Council of Law Reporting was set up in 1865 and is responsible for the modern series of *Law Reports*. Arguments of counsel are reported, and a full transcript of the judgment is provided.

LEGISLATION

Function

A system which depended solely on judge-made law could only remain adequate while conditions remained fairly static and the judicial elements in the society represented the most powerful or influential groups. With the growth of democratic ideas has come the recognition that the voice of the people is entitled to be heard and that law is not the monopoly of an élite. But it would be quite wrong to imagine that the public have any very strong views on the rules of law or that the extension of the electoral franchise has had very striking consequences. Even Members of Parliament, if they do not happen to be lawyers, confess repugnance to debates on legal matters. Most legislation is concerned with new social problems and not with the niceties of legal rules.

Where legislation has proved most valuable is in cutting the Gordian Knot with which the judges have bound their own hands. Owing to the doctrine of precedent (a "one-way street"), it is impossible for the judges to reverse well-established legal doctrines. These doctrines may have been fair enough at their inception, but many have since proved unadaptable to changed conditions. Parliament can solve the problem by legislation which modifies or reverses the rules previously developed by the courts. This is not a product of democracy since legal fictions and equity performed the same function at earlier periods. But legislation is clearly a more rapid and efficient means of effecting such legal changes.

Social legislation. Judges' activities have been confined to adjusting the rights and liabilities of the parties to a "dispute." If a workman suffered an injury, for example, he had to sue his employer and prove some default or negligence on his employer's part, in order to recover damages. Compensation could also be recovered from an insurer in the unlikely event of the workman having a policy of accident insurance. It was not possible for a court to invent such a policy of insurance, or make the employer liable independently of fault. The creation of a completely new system and the imposition of taxes to defray its cost of operation is necessarily a function of Parliament and not of the courts. The modern systems of Social Security are thus the product of legislation.

There is undoubtedly a tension between social legislation and the traditional attitude of the courts. A judge spends much of his time applying common law notions of right and wrong, generally based on moral considerations. He may be uneasy in applying legislation where the result is repugnant to such notions in the individual case, even though the general policy is commendable. Thus the public interest requires that the development of property be controlled and that minimum building standards be maintained. At the same time the public itself is alarmed when a man is ordered to pull down a house laboriously constructed by his own hands at a time when there is a shortage of housing accommodation. It appears alarming that a man can be compelled to sell part of his land to the state for a particular purpose and yet have no preferential right to buy it back when the purpose is fulfilled. Whilst no one would question that the judges administer the letter of such statutory policies impartially in the individual cases coming before them, an increasing feature of their role in modern society may be to give a hearing to, and sometimes relieve, anomalous cases of hardship which otherwise arouse public disquiet with no other apparent means of solution.

Law revision. Within the ordinary judicial sphere of disputes between private persons Parliament seldom pays an active part. If this "lawyer's law" is to be reformed, it is the lawyers themselves who must take the initiative. A Law Revision Committee was set up between the wars, to which the Lord Chancellor could refer various problems of private law. A Law Reform Committee then took its place, and initiated inquiries into legal matters where reform was desirable. Publicity was given to its facilities and lawyers were invited to send in suggestions for topics to be investigated. The Committee presented reports on topics it selected and this often led to reforming legislation, *e.g.* on contributory negligence. A Royal Commission is also often appointed by the Crown using part-time experts, on ministerial advice, to consider rather wider legal reforms, such as important changes in divorce law or the erection of a new type of court. The Government may then issue a "White Paper" explaining its future policy on the subject. Some, but not all, changes recommended in the reports of the commissions are embodied in bills which are introduced in Parliament.

Committees of experts are also appointed temporarily by heads of departments, *e.g.* by the Lord Chancellor to consider civil procedure, by the Secretary of State for Trade and Industry to consider the reform of copyright law. The Houses of Parliament also appointed Special Committees to investigate possible law reform, *e.g.* the Special Committee of the House of Commons on the Army and Air Force Acts.

There is also a full-time Law Commission of five members to act as a standing body to consider and recommend law reform on a large scale and not merely the excision of minor anomalies, The Law Commission has presented a large number of working papers and reports, suggesting legislative changes in family law, property law and other subjects, and a number of new laws have resulted.

A separate Criminal Law Revision Committee has also presented important reports, *e.g.* on the law of evidence in criminal cases.

Private Members of Parliament sometimes use the opportunity afforded them by parliamentary procedure to introduce Bills, often along the lines recommended by Royal Commissions. Important instances of private initiative are the Matrimonial Causes Act 1937, the Inheritance (Family Provision) Act 1938, the Defamation Act 1952 and the Homicide Act 1957.

Consolidation. From time to time Parliament passes a consolidating statute in which all relevant Acts on a subject, *i.e.* the principal Act and amending Acts are incorporated in a single Act. A special speedy procedure is used to pass such Acts.[82]

---

[82] Consolidation of Enactments (Procedure) Act 1949.

Codification. Legislation is sometimes used to codify a whole field of law which is so well developed, with its possibilities so well explored, that no fundamental changes appear to be likely or useful. Codification must include case law as well as statute law. Many aspects of commercial law are codified by statute, since they have been fully worked out by centuries of experience. Legislation is also valuable where the subject is one in which the parties normally take legal advice in advance, *e.g.* the proper formalities of a will or the effect of an insurance policy. In this case it is more important that the rules shall be clearly ascertained than that they shall be ideal rules in themselves. Most crimes are committed deliberately and with knowledge that they are unlawful and a penal code with definite statutory definitions and prohibitions is often advocated. There is also more danger in imposing criminal liability "by analogy" after the crime, than in the case of civil actions, where the measure of liability can be judged by the amount of damage.

Conversely, legislation, and particularly a complete codification, is inappropriate in cases where the main principles are still in process of evolution and where the legal dispute is likely to arise unexpectedly. The law of tort, for example, is still growing and a complete premature codification might be unwise. Most torts are committed without deliberation and the court is required to adjust the resulting situation as fairly as it can. Here justice is more important than certainty.

Authority of statute

The complete internal legislative sovereignty of Parliament is undoubted, provided it is exercised according to the proper procedure. There may have been some doubt about early medieval enactments but none about modern statutes. Chief Justice Coke argued that even Acts of Parliament need not be recognised if contrary to reason,[83] but this suggested limitation has never been seriously applied. At most it simply means that the courts may interpret a statute so as to avoid absurdity if there is any doubt about its meaning. Parliament can change basic common law principles and has often done so. It can equally enact laws which are considered to be contrary to the laws of God, and has, for example, altered the prohibited degrees of marriage in England, contrary to the traditional canon law of the Church. Neither is it bound by the rules of public international law, nor by the terms of international treaties and conventions, unless and

---

[83] *Bonham's Case* (1610) 8 Rep. 107a; see Gough, *Fundamental Law in English Constitutional History; Pickin* v. *British Rail Board* [1973] 1 Q.B. 219.

until these are incorporated in English statutes, and even then such statutes may be repealed at any time. Technically there is no greater difficulty in repealing a fundamental constitutional provision like the Bill of Rights or the Act of Settlement than any other statute.[84] There are no entrenched provisions not subject to alteration.

The European Communities Act 1972, however gives direct force in the United Kingdom to certain European legislation without further enactment. There is some uncertainty whether this country can withdraw unilaterally from the European Communities.

Subordinate legislation. Much subordinate legislation is now made by Ministries and departments under the authority of statute. In order to save time and trouble a statute may limit itself to laying down general principles, leaving routine details, like procedure or finance, to be worked out by statutory instruments. This practice is now inveterate and enjoys some practical advantages. The delegated legislation can generally be altered from time to time without new legislation in Parliament, by tabling fresh instruments, which are almost invariably accepted by Parliament. Some statutes permit alteration of the terms of the statute itself by subordinate legislation.[85] Parliament has an opportunity of disallowing the rules.

Obsolescence. Statutes never become obsolete with the passage of time though this fact may be obscured by the surrounding circumstances. Magna Carta, for example, was regarded as a compact between King and people rather than a statute. So far as it restricted the royal prerogative it was questionable how far it bound John's successors, so each succeeding monarch was asked to confirm the Charter, usually receiving financial aid from Parliament in return. Other statutes were probably designed to have a temporary operation, such as the so-called Star Chamber Act of 1487, which provided for the trial of rioters at the time of accession of the Tudor dynasty. Even if a statute was not temporary in itself it would cease to have any practical operation as soon as the institution with which it was concerned became obsolete, *e.g.* a statute regulating proceedings on the Writ of Right would be ineffective after that writ had become obsolete. Changes in the value of money destroyed the practical effect of some

---

[84] *Manuel* v. *Att.-Gen.* [1982] 3 W.L.R. 821 (C.A.), 1982 Canada Act altered the Canadian Constitution, which had been laid down in an earlier U.K. statute, The British North America Act 1867.

[85] *e.g.* the Land Registration Act and Rules 1925 and ss.87(3), 84(8) of the Supreme Court Act 1981.

statutes, *e.g.* justices of the peace were paid fixed fees, which later were so small as not to be worth collecting. Some statutes were relieving Acts and ceased to be important when the favoured person had died and no longer needed protection. Hence a great many statutes have become so much dead wood.

In modern times regular Statute Law Repeal Acts, are used to clear away these accumulations so only effective legislation remains in existence. A few statutes are technically still in force but are never in fact enforced, such as some Sabbatarian legislation and ecclesiastical and moral provisions. Any attempt to enforce them would probably lead to their repeal—the abolition of the common informer in 1951 has removed the inducement to any person to bring proceedings to enforce such statutes.

Interpretation. Every word of a statute is binding, whereas in judge-made law only the principles and reasons are binding. This produces a special problem, that of statutory interpretation, which takes quite a different form from the analysis of judge-made law. It is a form which, as we shall see, suffers from a certain rigidity and in some cases from positive unreality.

New legislation

Most legislation today is initiated by the Crown. The initiative may have come from the report of a royal commission or departmental committee, pointing out disadvantages in existing law. In other cases the proposed law may be designed to implement part of the policy of a political party, such as the nationalisation of some industry. The Ministry or department most concerned will draw up a brief of the main changes which they desire to make. Their proposals are then submitted, in the form of instructions, to Parliamentary Counsel, barristers who specialise in this work, to draft the appropriate Bill. Each Bill is assigned to one of these counsel, who will frequently consult the Ministry concerned. The final draft must be approved by the responsible Minister. In important cases the Cabinet may have to be consulted.

The Bills are piloted through Parliament, as and when priorities of time can be found for them, by special committees, on which the legal and parliamentary sides are both represented. The counsel assigned to a Bill attends Parliament and drafts the final text of any amendments which are made during its passage.

Private members have an opportunity to introduce some Bills and the Government may assist them in drafting such Bills.

It is very noteworthy that statutes have never had any special authentication. Originals are preserved in the Houses of Parliament but are not easily accessible. The Queen's Printer's copy is most commonly used[86] but a number of private series of statutes have been printed. Annotated editions are generally consulted by lawyers but in citation in court an unannotated copy of a statute is used, in order to leave the judge to decide its meaning for himself. Many textbooks incorporate statutory texts for convenience of reference.

Statutes are generally cited by their short titles followed by the calendar year of their enactment[87] and the chapter number allocated to each statute in order of enactment.

Both judges and public are deemed to know the contents of all statutes in force. In practice counsel and solicitor refer the court to all relevant statutes. Copies of the statutes are also available in the various courts.[88] Every citizen is deemed to know the law and cannot plead ignorance. In case of doubt he should consult a solicitor for legal advice.

Period of operation of statutes

Statutes generally come into force as soon as they have passed both Houses of Parliament and received the royal assent.[89] The courts thereupon take judicial notice of them. The courts will not take any notice of prospective legislation, since many Bills fail ultimately to be enacted. Nor will they enforce statutory sections passed but not yet put into operation.[90] The existence of pending legislation is occasionally relevant, e.g. in deciding whether a person is acting "reasonably" in refusing to give up possession of a dwelling where a statute conferring security of tenure on him is about to pass.[91]

Many statutes contain special operation sections, fixing a date when they are to come into force, to give the public an opportunity to make any necessary arrangements and to become familiar with their contents.[92] The date of operation may be left to be fixed by Order in Council or Statutory Instrument. Separate sections may be brought into force at separate times or for separate purposes,

---

[86] It is issued monthly and in bound annual volumes. Separate statutes are available at the Government Bookshops. (H.M.S.O.).

[87] Acts of Parliament (Numbering and Citation) Act 1962, from July 19, 1962. Regnal years were formerly used.

[88] In olden times boxes or bags were used to house the statutes in the courts at Westminster; Selden Society's Publications, Vol. LVIII, xvi.

[89] Interpretation Act 1978, s.4(6).

[90] *Osgerby* v. *Rushton* [1968] 2 Q.B. 466 (D.C.); *R.* v. *Miah* [1974] 1 W.L.R. 684; 694 (H.L.). See Bridge, (1972) 88 L.Q.R. 391.

[91] *Clifford Sabey* v. *Long* [1959] 2 Q.B. 290; *cf. Mallett* v. *Bournemouth County Borough* (1973) 227 E.G. 135.

[92] Thus the Law of Property Act 1925 came into force on January 1, 1926.

e.g. the Legal Aid Scheme was applied gradually to different courts, being introduced first in the High Court of Justice[93] and then extended. Some sections may be overtaken by later statutes.

Some statutes expressly provide for retrospective operation. This is sometimes necessary in order to relieve some person of possible liability.[94] It is also common to give effect to changes in revenue statutes as from their introduction into Parliament or any other date at which their provisions become known, to avoid evasions. Retrospective legislation may impose liability for an action which was lawful when done and this is obviously undesirable if it punishes the innocent. Hence the courts will hesitate to imply that a statute was intended to be retrospective if it makes no express provision for retrospective operation even if the purposes of Parliament would seem best served by such a construction.[95] They are more willing to imply retrospective operation in statutes which relieve from liability.[96]

A new statute does not affect pending proceedings started under the old law, so far as substantive law is concerned.[97] But pending proceedings can be affected if the new law has, for instance, increased the jurisdiction of the court,[98] changed the powers of the court in giving judgment, *e.g.* reduced the number of grounds on which the court may order possession of a house to be surrendered[99] or increased its powers to adjust the property rights of parties to a divorce.[1] But this does not apply where the sentence is made more severe after a crime is committed.[2]

The further course of proceedings can also be changed if the procedural law is changed, as there are no vested rights in procedure.[3]

The measure of damages in a civil case is regarded as a matter of substantive law and not procedure.[4]

---

[93] Legal Aid and Advice Act 1949 s.24 Sched. I; S.I. 1950 No. 1357.
[94] McManaway Indemnity Act of 1951; Validation of Elections Act 1955.
[95] *London Fan and Motor Co.* v. *Silverman* [1942] 1 All E.R. 307; *Brown* v. *Conway* [1968] 1 Q.B. 222; *R.* v. *Miah, supra,* n. 90 referring to the international conventions against retrospective crime, but in *Selvarajan* v. *I.L.E.A.* [1980] I.R.L.R. 313, (E.A.T.), evidence of earlier facts was admitted to help prove racial discrimination.
[96] *Barber* v. *Pigden* [1937] 1 K.B. 664, at 678; *cf. Chaterjee* v. *C.* [1976] F.D. 199, "relief" generally.
[97] [1937] 1 K.B. 677; *e.g.* Law Reform Act of 1935.
[98] *Empson* v. *Smith* [1966] 1 Q.B. 426 (removal of former diplomatic immunity).
[99] *Hutchinson* v. *Jauncey* [1950] 1 K.B. 574, 578 (C.A.); *cf. Capon* v. *Rees Motors* [1980] I.R.L.R. 294 (C.A.).
[1] *Williams* v. *Williams* [1971] P. 271; *cf. Chaterjee* v. *C.* [1976] F.D. 199.
[2] *R.* v. *Penrith Justices, ex p. Hay* (1979) 123 S.J. 621 (D.C.).
[3] *e.g. Fairey* v. *Southampton C.C.* [1956] 2 Q.B. 439 (C.A.); *cf. Application des Gaz S.A.* v. *Falks Veritas* [1974] Ch. 381 (C.A.) injunction no longer appropriate.
[4] *Wilson* v. *Dagnall* [1972] 1 Q.B. 509 (C.A.).

Geographical operation

Legislation of the United Kingdom Parliament applies throughout the United Kingdom but not elsewhere unless a contrary intention appears.[5] A statute is in fact often expressly limited to England and Wales, owing to the special character of Scots law.

Some statutes are expressed to extend to crimes done abroad. Thus the crime of treason covers aid given to the Queen's enemies abroad.[6] Murder committed abroad may be the subject of proceedings here.[7] Bigamy is another example.[8] Our Merchant Shipping Acts create offences if committed by British subjects on foreign ships.[9]

The court will occasionally construe a statute as implicitly covering things done abroad, e.g. an order may be made against parents to maintain a child here, even if they are living abroad,[10] and English law governs the capacity of any person domiciled in England to marry abroad,[11] and rights to custody of children abroad of British parents.[12]

Form of statute

Statutes are generally uniform at the present day. They have a short title, for reference purposes, e.g. "The Law of Property Act 1925." They may have a long title, which recites the general purpose of the Act, e.g. "An Act to consolidate the enactments relating to conveyancing and the law of property." In some cases there is a preamble, which sets out the reasons for the legislation and the objects which it is intended to serve.

The actual text is generally arranged in sections, unless the statute is extremely short. Each section deals with one subject. In the longer statutes the text is divided into Parts, but the sections are numbered from the beginning of the statute, so that sections 1 to 50 may form Part I and sections 51 to 100 Part II. These Parts may have headings, e.g. "Financial Provisions," "Mortgages."

Many statutes have special definition sections which explain the meaning of some of the terms used. These definitions are seldom

---

[5] *R.* v. *Martin* [1956] 2 Q.B. 272; *Air India* v. *Wiggins* [1980] 1 W.L.R. 815. (D.C.).

[6] Treason Act of 1352; *Joyce* v. *D.P.P.* [1946] A.C. 347, 368.

[7] Offences against the Person Act 1861, s.9; *cf. R.* v. *El Hakkaoui* [1975] 1 W.L.R. 396 (C.A.).

[8] 1861 Act, s.57; *R.* v. *Earl Russell* [1901] A.C. 446.

[9] *R.* v. *Kelly* [1981] 3 W.L.R. 387 (H.L.).

[10] Matrimonial Causes Act 1973, s.18; Domestic Proceedings (Magistrates' Court) Act 1978 s.24.

[11] *Pugh* v. *Pugh* [1951] P. 482; Age of Marriage Act 1929, now replaced by the Marriage Act 1949.

[12] Matrimonial Causes Act 1973, s.42; *Harben* v. *Harben* [1957] 1 W.L.R. 261.

exhaustive and are generally expressed to yield to contrary intention. Acts usually have repealing sections referring to fuller Schedules of repeals at the end of the statute.

Schedules are also used to list matters of detail, *e.g.* fees and names of localities affected, which are not matters of principle. They sometimes lay down procedures, but this is more often done by separate bodies of regulations, the statute containing a section empowering someone, such as a Minister, to make such regulations.

Sections are often provided with marginal notes, for convenience of reference, stating the brief effect of the section, such as "powers of disposition," "effect of registration."

As already mentioned, many statutes also have special operation sections stating whether they apply to parts only of the United Kingdom, and naming the date when the statute is to come into operation or empowering someone to bring it, or any part of it, into operation by Statutory Instrument or by some other procedure.

Repeals and amendments

A statute may repeal the provisions of any earlier statute. Repeal of the later statute does not then revive the original statute.[13]

The problem is more complicated where a later statute does not expressly alter an earlier statute but is clearly inconsistent with it. The effect is to amend the earlier statute to the extent of the inconsistency. In one case an offence was created by statute and a particular penalty provided. A later statute defined the identical offence and prescribed different penalties. The Divisional Court held that the old penalty could not be imposed, as the earlier statute must be deemed repealed.[14] In another case a statute of 1875 excluded a certain remedy. Another statute in 1879 allowed the remedy. In 1896 the 1875 statute was re-enacted. It was held that the statute of 1879 on the subject was repealed and the remedy had gone.[15]

A general Act does not usually repeal a special Act.[16] Thus the Rent Acts, which began in the First World War, restrict the landlord's right to recover possession of a dwelling from a tenant

---

[13] Interpretation Act 1978 s.15; the repeal of a statute providing a defence to a claim revives the claim, *Sifam Electrical Instrument Co.* v. *Sangamo Weston* [1971] 2 All E.R. 1074.

[14] *Smith* v. *Benabo* [1937] 1 K.B. 518.

[15] *Hall* v. *Arnold* [1950] 2 K.B. 543.

[16] *Cf. Pyx Granite Co.* v. *Ministry of Housing & Local Government* [1960] A.C. 260, development under local Act exempt from general planning law.

in certain cases. But they did not affect older special legislation[17] allowing a bishop to recover possession of a parsonage.[18]

A later statute often amends an earlier, by substituting a different section or by amending the text of some section.[19] A good practice is to reprint the old Act in a Schedule, as amended by the new Act.[20]

In recent years it has become common to repeal old statutes *en masse* by special repealing acts.[21]

Interpretation of statutes

This is a matter of law, to which the doctrine of precedent applies. Some statutes have obvious meanings and require little interpretation, *e.g.* an Act declaring annual Bank Holidays. But most statutes contain sections which are somewhat ambiguous or whose effect is doubtful. Some legislators, like the Roman Emperor Justinian, wanted any such doubts to be referred to the legislature itself for solution. There are traces of this notion in English law, in the old practice of appointing Triers of parliamentary petitions, who decide whether or not the problem was met by existing law. Common law judges often served in this capacity. Some old statutes provided for reference of particular problems to Parliament itself.[22] The jurisdiction of the House of Lords as the final court of appeal is certainly derived from the ultimate authority of Parliament to decide what the law of England is.[23]

It is clear, however, that reference to Parliament could not be a routine matter. Parliaments met less frequently than today and as sessions became more frequent the bulk of parliamentary work also increased. It was therefore left to the courts trying a case to interpret the meaning of any statutory provision relied on by a party. The royal justices played an important part in drafting statutes in the twelfth and thirteenth centuries and took it upon themselves to explain what the statutes meant, or at least were intended to mean. They even went so far as to add to statutes provisions which had been omitted by some clerical oversight.[24]

By the fourteenth century the judges were more and more concerned with routine adjudication of disputes and had ceased to

---

[17] The Pluralities Act 1838.
[18] *Bishop of Gloucester* v. *Cunnington* [1943] K.B. 101 (C.A.).
[19] *e.g.* Children and Young Persons Act 1969, s.49; Criminal Justice Act 1982 s.25.
[20] *e.g.* in the Intestates' Estates Act 1952.
[21] *e.g.* Statute Law (Repeals) Act 1981.
[22] *e.g.* the Statute of 1285, Cap. 24, "*In consimili casu.*" The King was in medieval times also entitled to construe the meaning of charters granted by him and to reconcile conflicting charters.
[23] The House represents "the King in Council in Parliament."
[24] Plucknett, *Concise History of the Common Law,* 331.

hold such high positions in the Council or Parliament. They therefore came to feel diffident about usurping legislative authority or taking liberties with the texts of statutes.

Rules of interpretation were gradually developed by the judges, both to assist the courts themselves and to eliminate any risk of arbitrary interpretation. The text of a statute must be examined objectively. It stands by itself and the intentions of Parliament must be ascertained from the words of the statute. If the words are clear no problem of interpretation arises. If there is any ambiguity, the draftsman himself is considered to be the worst interpreter, since he knows what he meant to enact and cannot approach the text dispassionately. The result is that a judge who helped to draft an Act ought to disqualify himself from interpreting it.[25]

There are two main problems facing the lawyer in advising on the meaning of a statute. In the first place it is for the court to decide whether or not the wording of a section is ambiguous. If it is considered ambiguous, it is then for the court to decide which of the many, often conflicting, rules of interpretation to apply, or whether it is to reject all rules of construction and construe the statute by itself. It might seem that some rules could be relied on, *e.g.* the Interpretation Act 1978 lays down a few definite presumptive rules such as that the male includes the female, and the plural the singular.[26] But even these are expressed to be subject to any contrary indications in the particular statute. This Act lays down, for example, that a "person" includes a "corporation." Yet a statute penalising unqualified "persons" who practised as solicitors was held not to apply to a corporation which did legal work, as only individuals can qualify as solicitors.[27] Most statutes contain useful interpretation sections, defining some important terms used in the statute, though seldom all of them. These sections are usually made subject to contrary intention appearing from the context.

Internal aids

These are the various parts of a statute already referred to. The short title has little relevance to the meaning of an Act, brevity being here more desirable than precision.[28] The long title is a

---

[25] *Per* Lord Halsbury L.C. in *Hilder* v. *Dexter* [1902] A.C. 474.

[26] s.6; *R.* v. *Industrial Disputes Tribunal* [1957] 2 Q.B. 483; *Jackson* v. *Hall* [1980] A.C. 854 (H.L.).

[27] *Law Society* v. *United Service Bureau* [1934] 1 K.B. 343; on the other hand an injunction would lie, or separate proceedings could be taken against employees of the corporation. The Solicitors Act 1957, s.22, solved the problem by expressly applying the provisions to corporate bodies; Solicitors Act, 1974 ss.1, 20 is less clear.

[28] *Vacher* v. *London Society of Compositors* [1913] A.C. 107.

relevant part of the enactment as it is open to discussion in Parliament,[29] and may throw some light on Parliament's intentions in doubtful cases. If the text is ambiguous the title is not referred to, and is in no case conclusive. Thus although the title of an Act referred to the prevention of fraud it was held that an offence under it could be committed recklessly.[30] In another case, on the other hand, where the long title referred to the object of Parliament as extending the powers of trustees, and the Act contained provisions which in one respect were more restrictive of their powers than those in previous legislation, it was held that the limitations could be ignored, in view of the wording of the title.[31]

The preamble may be looked at if there is any ambiguity in the text of a statute but not otherwise.[32] Some preambles are too vague and general to be of assistance in interpretation.[33] The court has often refused to control the meaning of a section in a statute by reference to the preamble. A section prohibiting the use of "places" for betting was held not to apply to betting in the open air although the preamble referred to evils which applied as much to that as to betting offices.[34]

Headings are occasionally useful, but cannot control unambiguous wording. In one statute a section was headed "Appeals" and all but one of its subsections referred to appeals. Nevertheless it was held that the general authority in that subsection to conduct legal proceedings applied to all types of proceedings and not merely to appeals.[35]

Marginal notes are not part of the parliamentary text and are generally inadmissible as aids.[36]

Schedules are part of the text of an Act if incorporated into it by reference in some section. If printed merely for the purposes of information or reference they are not part of the Act and cannot be considered by the court interpreting it. If a statute is intended to implement an international convention which is annexed to the text of an Act, the Convention is no part of the Act itself and cannot override the words of the Act, even if they depart from the terms of the Convention.[37]

---

[29] *Ibid.* 118, 128.
[30] *R.* v. *Bates & Russell* (1952) 36 Cr.App.R. 175; Prevention of Fraud (Investments) Act 1939, now 1958, s.13; *R.* v. *Grunwald* [1963] 1 Q.B. 935.
[31] *Re Scarisbrick* [1944] Ch. 229; Settled Land and Trustee Acts (Court's General Powers) Act 1943.
[32] *Ellerman Lines Ltd.* v. *Murray* [1931] A.C. 126; *Prince Ernest of Hanover* v. *Att.-Gen.* [1957] A.C. 88.
[33] *e.g.* the preamble to the Matrimonial Causes Act 1950.
[34] *Powell* v. *Kempton Park Racecourse Co.* [1899] A.C. 143, 157, 184.
[35] *R.* v. *Surrey Assessment Committee* [1948] 1 K.B. 28, 32.
[36] *Chandler* v. *D.P.P.* [1964] A.C. 763.
[37] *Ellerman Lines* v. *Murray* [1931] A.C. 126, 147; *cf. Burns, Philp & Co.* v. *Nelson & Robertson* [1957] 1 Lloyd's Rep. 267 (Australia).

Explanatory notes are sometimes added to published statutes or rules of court to explain their effect on the existing law, or circulated by Government departments. These are most helpful in practice but do not have any authority, and should not be cited in court to influence the court's decision on the meaning of the enactment.[38]

Minute points of punctuation are not to be read as making major changes in the law.[39]

External aids

Dictionaries are generally referred to in order to arrive at the meanings of words which have no particular legal definition, *e.g.* as to the meaning of the word "use."[40]

Reports of parliamentary debates are not generally admissible as aids to construction as the speeches represent the views of individual members only.[41] The Government, when pressing the passage of legislation, may even discourage its supporters from speaking, so that the speeches may not be typical. Again, it is the Act itself which is law, and not the Government's opinion of it.

Reports of Royal Commissions are admissible as evidence of the former state of the law and of the mischiefs which were to be corrected. The general rule has been that such reports are not admissible as aids to construction. The Bill as drafted does not always accept all the recommendations included in such reports. Parliament also sometimes amends a Bill so as to exclude some provisions which were inserted on the basis of the report.[42]

A wider range of materials may be studied where a statute is designed to implement an international convention.[43]

The ejusdem generis rule

This rule means that general words which follow particular words must be cut down to meanings similar to those of the particular words. Thus in a reference to obligations imposed by "custom, prescription or otherwise," the word "otherwise" is limited to imposition by law, like custom and prescription, and does not extend to obligations arising out of contract.[44]

---

[38] *L.C.C.* v. *Central Land Board* [1958] 1 W.L.R. 1296.
[39] See *Tonge* v. *Wilkinson* [1957] C.L.Y. 3054, confirmed by *Piper* v. *Harvey* [1958] 1 Q.B. 439.
[40] *British Motor Syndicate Ltd.* v. *Taylor & Son* [1900] 1 Ch. 577, 583.
[41] *Hadmor Productions* v. *Hamilton* [1982] 2 W.L.R. 322 (H.L.).
[42] *Assam Railways & Trading Co. Ltd.* v. *C.I.R.* [1935] A.C. 445, 458.
[43] *Stag Line Ltd.* v. *Toscolo, Mango & Co.* [1932] A.C. 328; *Fothergill* v. *Monarch Airlines* [1981] A.C. 251.
[44] *Eton R.D.C.* v. *Thames Conservators* [1950] Ch. 540; *cf. James Buchanan & Co.* v. *Babco Forwarding & Shipping. U.K.* [1977] Q.B. 208 (C.A.).

There are several obvious limitations on the *ejusdem generis* rule. It cannot apply if there are not at least two particular words. Thus a reference to a "quay or other place" does not connote any particular class of words so as to cut down in any way the generality of the term "place."[45] This may be contrasted with the decision as to "places" where betting was carried on.[46] A power to introduce a one-way traffic system for "processions, rejoicings . . . and in any case" was held not to cover the entire summer season at a resort.[47]

Again, no class can be postulated if there are no common links among the possible objects of the class. This usually means that such links are conflicting. The *ejusdem generis* rule was held not to apply for example where the particular words are "dispositions, trusts, and covenants": a disposition is a transfer, a declaration of trust may be a transfer, but a covenant is not; a trust and a covenant both create obligations but a disposition need not. Hence no common class or category could be made out.[48]

Presumptions in interpretation

Where a text is not absolutely clear the courts are often assisted by certain presumptions of interpretation. Some of these presumptions conflict with others and it is difficult to predict in such cases what the outcome may be.

Presumption against fundamental changes of the common law by mere implication

This is necessary to prevent unexpected and undesired changes of principle. Some critics of the courts see in it a judicial jealousy of fundamental change by statute but this criticism is hardly justified today. In one case the National Assistance Board sought to recover from a husband the cost of maintaining his wife under a broad general statutory power to recover such costs in the National Assistance Act 1948. The Divisional Court held that the Board could only sue a husband who was in fact liable to maintain his wife by the general law in spite of the wording of the 1948 Act, *e.g.* it had no such power if his wife had deserted him.[49]

A wife at common law might not testify against her husband. When a statute[50] permitted her to testify, it was held she could not

---

[45] *Roe* v. *Hemmings* [1951] 1 K.B. 676.
[46] *Powell* v. *Kempton Park Racecourse Co., supra,* at 105.
[47] *Brownsea Haven Properties* v. *Poole Corporation* [1958] Ch. 574 (C.A.).
[48] *Hood Barrs* v. *I.R.C.* [1946] 2 All E.R. 768, 773 (C.A.).
[49] *National Assistance Board* v. *Wilkinson* [1952] 2 Q.B. 648; *cf. Planmount* v. *Republic of Zaire* [1981] 1 All E.R. 1110, new statute not exhaustive.
[50] Criminal Evidence Act 1898 s.4.

be compelled to testify if she did not wish to, as the change was
fundamental and should not be extended by implication.[51]

*Presumption against the imposition of criminal liability without
     fault*

The courts are reluctant to construe a statute as imposing
absolute liability unless it expressly so provides, fault being
traditionally an essential element of liability in our criminal law.[52]
Fault must attach to all the elements of the crime.[53] Where a
statute[54] made it an offence to fail to report an accident, it was
held that a man who did not know an accident had occurred was
not liable, as the law does not compel the impossible.[55] Even the
fact that a statute provides for some defence does not exclude
freedom from fault as a general defence. In a leading case a
woman remarried in the honest and reasonable belief that her
husband was dead. The law allowed such a defence in bigamy
cases where no news of the husband had been received for seven
years. The accused had married within the seven years but was still
held not to have committed bigamy as she had no intention to
marry while her husband was alive.[56]

There is a tendency in modern legislation to impose strict
criminal liability in many cases. It is difficult to prove by whose
fault, for example, foreign matter came to be present in food. It is
for the manufacturer to take the risk of being prosecuted unless he
positively ensures that such things do not happen. A perfectly safe
system must be provided for the protection of the public.[57] The
same applies to the law of weights and measures,[58] and to factory
safety regulations.[59] The absolute prohibition of dangerous driving
is devoid of any requirement of fault.[60] Absolute liability is often
imposed in economic and financial legislation.[61] Felling a tree

---

[51] *Leach* v. *R.* [1912] A.C. 305. The rule against calling the wife of the accused was described
by Lord Halsbury L.C. as a rule of law which had lasted for centuries.

[52] *Younghusband* v. *Luftig* [1949] 2 K.B. 354, 370; *Reynolds* v. *G.H. Austin & Sons* [1951] 2
K.B. 135, 143; *Coult* v. *Szuba* [1982] R.T.R. 376 (D.C.).

[53] *R.* v. *Hallam* [1957] 1 Q.B. 569, knowingly possessing explosives; *cf. Sweet* v. *Parsley* [1970]
A.C. 132; *Bradshaw* v. *Ewart-Jones* [1982] 3 W.L.R. 1000 (D.C.), navigation rules not
absolutely binding.

[54] Road Traffic Act 1930, s.22, now Road Traffic Act 1972, s.25(2).

[55] *Harding* v. *Price* [1948] 1 K.B. 695.

[56] *R.* v. *Tolson* (1889) 23 Q.B.D. 168, 181.

[57] *Lindley* v. *G.W. Horner & Co.* [1950] 1 All E.R. 234. Food and Drugs Acts 1938, s.83, 1955,
s.8; *Bennett* v. *Hanks* [1954] Crim.L.R. 545.

[58] *Winter* v. *Hinckley etc. Society* [1959] 1 W.L.R. 182 (D.C.).

[59] *Dunn* v. *Bird's Eye Foods* [1959] 2 Q.B. 265.

[60] *Hill* v. *Baxter* [1958] 1 Q.B. 278 (unconsciousness). The section is now Road Traffic Act
1972, s.2; *cf. R.* v. *Cummerson* [1968] 2 Q.B. 534; *Hawkins* v. *H.* (1974) R.T.R. 436 (D.C.).

[61] *R.* v. *Heron* [1982] 1 W.L.R. 41 (H.L.), counterfeiting coin before uttering any.

protected by a preservation order is an offence even if the party
did not know about the order.[62]

Presumption against confiscating vested rights

A statute may make express provision for the treatment of any
valuable property rights which may be adversely affected by its
provisions. The Adoption Act 1950, for example, postponed the
effect of a novel provision that a gift by will to "children" should
include adopted children, to prevent possible injustice. In *Re
Gilpin*[63] the court interpreted this provision to mean that a gift to
the "children" of the testator's son did not include a child adopted
after the making of the will. The Adoption Acts 1958 and 1976, on
the assumption that the change in the law is now well known, have
eroded this exception.[64]

If no express provision is made, the court will generally limit the
operation of a statute so as to reduce interference with property.
Thus a local authority which is charged with providing a sewerage
system is not exempted from liability in damages if the waters of
third parties are polluted, unless the statute specifically, or by
obvious implication, so provides.[65] A local authority, again, has
power to demolish an unsafe slum building, but it must provide the
necessary support for any adjoining building, not itself in such bad
condition, which might otherwise collapse.[66]

Even if some property rights are intended to be confiscated the
courts will not extend the operation of the confiscation where
there is any real doubt. Thus a gift to a hospital has been treated as
a gift to its objects and therefore not "nationalised."[67] This
enabled extra amenities to be provided privately. Again, where a
freeholder had leased land to a hospital, the freehold reversion on
the lease was held not to have been nationalised although the lease
and the hospital undertaking were.[68]

Presumption against ousting the jurisdiction of the courts

It is always within the power of Parliament to exclude any
matter from the competence of the ordinary courts but the courts

---

[62] *Maidstone Borough Council* v. *Mortimer* [1980] 3 All E.R. 552 (D.C.); Ignorance of law is, of course, no defence to a charge.

[63] [1954] Ch. 1.

[64] Adoption Act 1958, ss.16(2), 17(2); Sched.5; under the Adoption Act 1976, s.39(5) there is now no reservation. For a full discussion of the earlier position see Bevan, *The Law relating to Children* (1973), 369–371.

[65] *Pride of Derby Angling Association* v. *Derby Corporation* [1953] Ch. 149 (C.A.).

[66] *Bond* v. *Nottingham Corporation* [1940] Ch. 429.

[67] *Re Bagshaw* [1954] 1 W.L.R. 238; National Health Service Act 1946, s.6.

[68] *Minister of Health* v. *Stafford Corporation* [1952] Ch. 730. 743 (C.A.).

are naturally slow to imply any such exclusion.[69] They prefer to regard special procedures laid down by statute as additional parallel procedures, rather than excluding recourse to the courts.[70] If the courts are clearly made incompetent in some respects they may still hold that they retain a jurisdiction in others. Thus, where a statute provided that certain types of tenancies were to be referred to arbitration for a settlement of appropriate terms,[71] the courts held that it was for the courts to decide whether or not any tenancy fell within this provision in the first place.[72] Where a statute provided that litigants might be prevented from bringing proceedings[73] it was held that this statute must be confined to civil proceedings because of its history and would not be extended to criminal proceedings, where defendants had other remedies, such as an action for malicious prosecution, if such procedure was abused.[74]

From 1958, any older statute which prevents the use of prerogative orders to review the decision of a tribunal for irregularity is repealed, unless the statute provides a right of access to the High Court in some other way, if only within a short time limit.[75]

If Parliament has provided a special speedy method of determining disputes the courts may hold that their general jurisdiction is meant to be excluded.[76]

The Crown is not bound by statute unless named in it[77]

Statutes must be expressed to bind the Crown,[78] as it is not bound by mere implication. Thus the Crown and its departments were not bound by the Rent Restriction Acts, so that they could lease dwellings in order to produce income and then evict the tenants at the end of the leases where a private landlord could not.[79] In the same way the Crown and its departments can evict

---

[69] *Eastbourne Corporation* v. *Fortes* [1959] 2 Q.B. 92.
[70] *Pyx Granite Co.* v. *Ministry of Housing* [1960] A.C. 260; *Construction Industry Training Board* v. *Att.-Gen.* [1973] Ch. 173 (C.A.).
[71] Agricultural Holdings Act 1948, s.2(1).
[72] *Goldsack* v. *Shore* [1950] 1 K.B. 708, 712 (C.A.).
[73] Now the Supreme Court Act 1981 s.42.
[74] *Re Boaler* [1915] 1 K.B. 21 (C.A.).
[75] Tribunals and Inquiries Act 1971. s.14; an example of the exception was the Acquisition of Land (Authorisation Procedure) Act 1946; compulsory purchase orders absolute after three weeks, 1972, reg. 3; *Smith* v. *East Elloe R.D.C.* [1956] A.C. 736.
[76] *Punton* v. *Ministry of Pensions and National Insurance* [1964] 1 W.L.R. 226.
[77] *Wheaton* v. *Maple* [1893] 3 Ch. 48.
[78] *e.g.* Limitation Act 1980 s.37; Road Traffic Act 1972, s.188; Recreational Charities Act 1958, s.5.
[79] *Territorial Association of London* v. *Nichols* [1949] 1 K.B. 35 (C.A.); the Rent Act 1977, s.13, now expressly exempts the Crown.

farm tenants without satisfying statutory requirements.[80] The Crown is not subject to the Contracts of Employment Act 1972.[81]

Presumption against arbitrary conduct and abuse of power

Wherever a statute confers a power or some form of jurisdiction it is implied that such power or jurisdiction will be exercised fairly and objectively. A number of cases illustrate this rule. Thus a chairman of magistrates may not try appeals for the reduction of the assessment of premises for rating if he is himself appealing against assessment.[82] He would have an obvious interest in establishing the principle of reduction in the other cases, even though he might not sit when his own case was discussed.

Where a statute requires reasonable grounds to exist before some administrative action is taken, the court must be satisfied that there are such grounds.[83] During the war some statutes gave a Minister powers if he was satisfied they were needed, whether or not reasons existed, but such wide powers are not readily presumed in peacetime, and the court will inquire into the reasonableness of the grounds.[84]

An arbitrator is disqualified from acting if there is any doubt as to his impartiality.[85] Even before this specific provision however, the court held that its authority to issue an injunction where it was just and convenient permitted the court to restrain an arbitrator from acting under statutory powers if he was under an obligation to one party which might influence his decision.[86]

The statutory rule that bankruptcy may be avoided if a majority of creditors accept a composition is subject to the condition that the majority act in good faith and do not obtain an unfair advantage over the other creditors.[87]

Canons of construction of statute

Construction as a whole

Where the meaning of a section is not clear all relevant sections of the statute must be examined, to decide its meaning. It may

---

[80] *Ministry of Agriculture* v. *Jenkins* [1963] 2 Q.B. 317; *cf.* Rent (Agriculture) Act 1976, ss.5(1), 36.
[81] *Wood* v. *Leeds Area Health Authority Training* [1974] I.C.R. 535.
[82] *R.* v. *Great Yarmouth Justices* (1882) 8 Q.B.D. 525; now Local Government Act 1948, s.67.
[83] *Nakkuda Ali* v. *M.F. de S. Jayaratne* [1951] A.C. 66.
[84] *Ibid.* at p. 76, distinguishing *Liversidge* v. *Sir John Anderson* [1942] A.C. 206.
[85] Arbitration Act 1950, s.24.
[86] Supreme Court Act 1981, s.37; *Beddow* v. *Beddow* (1878) 9 Ch.D. 89; see Judicature Act 1925, s.45.
[87] *Ex. p. Cowen* (1867) L.R. 2 Ch. 563, 569; Bankruptcy Act 1914, s.16(2).

even be necessary to study a whole group of statutes in order to come to a decision. In practice it is seldom necessary to go so far, except where a number of sections or statutes are interdependent. A later statute does not automatically alter the interpretation of an earlier one, if the later Act is a new provision.[88]

Narrow construction of penal provisions

If a statute imposing criminal responsibility is unambiguous it will be interpreted literally. For example, one statute[89] made it an offence to commit an indecent assault on a male person. The section was headed "unnatural offences" and was probably aimed at assaults by males on males. Nevertheless a woman was convicted of assaulting a boy under this section, because she had done what was forbidden.[90]

If, on the other hand, there is an ambiguity, criminal liability will not be imposed, so as not to interfere unduly with personal liberty. The same is true of tax laws and any laws encroaching on personal freedom.[91]

Literal interpretation

Statutes are construed literally, giving words their usual meaning, if there is no real ambiguity, even if hardship results.[92] The only remedy is an amending statute. "It is not the function of any judge to fill in what he conceives to be gaps in an Act of Parliament."[93]

A law prohibiting "any person" charging certain tenants premiums[94] was held not to be limited to landlords.[95] The offence of applying a false trade description to goods[96] was held to apply to a buyer as well as a seller.[97]

---

[88] *C.P.S.S.* v. *Bryers* [1958] A.C. 485 (H.L.), *per* Viscount Kilmuir L.C.

[89] Offences against the Person Act 1861, s.62.

[90] *R.* v. *Hare* [1934] 1 K.B. 354 (C.C.A.); *cf.* Sexual Offences Act 1956, s.14.

[91] *London & County Investments Ltd.* v. *Att.-Gen.* [1953] 1 W.L.R. 312, 319; *Russell* v. *Scott* [1948] A.C. 422; *D'Avigdor-Goldsmid* v. *I.R.C.* [1953] A.C. 347, 362. *Cf. Barnsley Corporation* v. *Lancashire C.C.* [1957] 1 Q.B. 123.

[92] *e.g. Horace Plunkett Fdn.* v. *Pancras Met. B.C.* [1958] 1 W.L.R. 30 (D.C.); *Traill* v. *Buckingham* [1972] 1 W.L.R. 459 (D.C.).

[93] *Magor and St. Mellons R.D.C.* v. *Newport Corporation* [1952] A.C. 189, where ratepayers lost a benefit they were clearly intended to enjoy, because of technical difficulties of interpretation.

[94] Rent Act 1968, s.85.

[95] *Farrell* v. *Alexander* [1976] 3 W.L.R. 145 (H.L.), assignor of tenancy.

[96] Trade Descriptions Act 1968, s.1.

[97] *Fletcher* v. *Budgen* [1974] 1 W.L.R. 1056. *Cf. R.* v. *Davis* [1975] Q.B. 691, provocation need not be by the victim.

The golden rule

If the wording of a statute is equally susceptible of two interpretations, the court will adopt that interpretation which avoids an absurd result. This follows from what is called the golden rule. Thus one statute[98] made it the crime of bigamy to marry a second husband while married to a first husband. Obviously the second "marriage" was legally ineffective and the word "marriage" was construed to mean "going through a form of marriage with one man while still being married to another."[99] Where a person was charged with setting fire to a building, "any person being therein,"[1] it was held that he himself was not included.[2]

Where a statute authorised an order to a mortgagee to go into possession to be suspended where the mortgagor was likely to make good a default,[3] it was held to apply *a fortiori* where the mortgagor was not in default at all.[4]

Where certain acts were forbidden "in the vicinity" of a "prohibited place,"[5] this was held *a fortiori*, to cover acts done inside such place as well.[6]

An interesting example of the same rule arose out of the law which enables disinherited persons to claim maintenance out of the estate of a deceased person. Such persons were required to apply to the court within six months after the first grant of representation (*e.g.* probate).[7] If a man died apparently intestate so that his family took his estate, and a will was discovered a year later which gave the estate to strangers, it would, strictly speaking, be too late for the family to claim. The grant of representation on intestacy, though it would have to be revoked, was technically the first grant and was made more than six months before the application, yet until the will was discovered the family had no reason to apply to the court for provision, as the law of intestate succession provided adequately for them. The Court of Appeal construed the section as referring to the first grant in respect of such a will as left the family inadequately provided for, so as to make the section sensible.[8] The legislature confirmed this.[9]

[98] Offences against the Person Act 1861, s.57.
[99] *R.* v. *Allen* (1872) L.R. 1 C.C.R. 367, 373.
[1] Malicious Damage Act 1861. s.2; replaced by Criminal Damage Act 1971, s.1.
[2] *R.* v. *Arthur* [1968] 1 Q.B. 810.
[3] Administration of Justice Act 1970, s.36(1).
[4] *Wesern Bank* v. *Schindler* [1976] 3 W.L.R. 341.
[5] Official Secrets Act 1920.
[6] *Adler* v. *George* [1964] 2 Q.B. 7.
[7] Inheritance (Family Provision) Act 1938.
[8] *Re Bidie* [1949] Ch. 121.
[9] Sched. IV to the Intestates' Estates Act 1952; the present text is different, Inheritance Act 1975, s.2(1A).

In another case the combined effect of two statutes seemed to be that a claim which had become statute-barred in the defendant's life would be revived on his death, but the court did not have to decide this curious point.[10]

Sometimes the effect of a literal interpretation of a statute is pointless but the meaning is clear and must be applied. A statute[11] required grants of land for educational purposes to be registered with the Minister of Education. Land was conveyed to an Oxford college, whose transactions are exempt from the Minister's authority. The college argued that the requirement of registration was therefore absurd and could be ignored. The court, however, held that the grant must still be registered, and that the title would otherwise be defective, though there was nothing which the Minister could do if the grant were registered.[12] This anomaly was later removed by legislation.[13]

Descendants of the Elector of Hanover have been held entitled to British nationality, under the unambiguous provisions of a statute of 1705, although they have fought against this country in several world wars and a good case for the application of the golden rule might be thought to have been made out.[14]

The mischief rule

Wherever the meaning of a statutory provision is ambiguous the court may have regard to the defects of the older law and the mischief which the statute was intended to combat.[15]

At one time speculators had been buying dilapidated houses cheaply in order to make a profit by suing the tenants on repairing covenants in their leases. A statute was passed to prevent this.[16] It was held that the statute must be given retrospective effect in order to meet the mischief which led to its enactment.[17]

A married woman who is separated from her husband has been treated as a "single woman" for affiliation purposes.[18] A car jacked up on the road has been held to be "used" (though not "driven") on the highway, since it could in some circumstances

---

[10] *Airey* v. *Airey* [1958] 2 Q.B. 300.
[11] Education Act 1944, s.87.
[12] *Re No. 12 Regent Street, Oxford* [1948] Ch. 735, 746.
[13] Education (Misc. Prov.) Act 1953; *cf. Eton College* v. *Ministry of Agriculture, etc.* [1964] Ch. 274.
[14] *Prince Ernest of Hanover* v. *Att.-Gen* [1957] A.C. 88; see 20 M.L.R. 270.
[15] *Norman* v. *Norman* [1950] 1 All E.R. 1082, 1084; *Pratt* v. *Cook* [1939] 1 K.B. 364, 382 (C.A.); *Pugh* v. *Pugh* [1951] P. 482, 492.
[16] Leasehold Property (Repairs) Act 1938.
[17] *National Real Estate & Finance Co.* v. *Hassan* [1939] 2 K.B. 61, 78.
[18] *Kruhlak* v. *Kruhlak* [1958] 2 Q.B. 32. *Cf. Whitton* v. *Garner* [1965] 1 W.L.R. 313 (D.C.).

become dangerous.[19] To protect young girls, it has been held to be a crime to take a single girl under eighteen away from her parents to have "unlawful" intercourse with men, though voluntary illicit intercourse was not in itself otherwise unlawful at her age.[20] Prostitutes who tapped on windows from inside houses to attract the attention of passers-by have been held guilty of soliciting "in the street" to meet the objects of the statute.[21]

Precedents of interpretation

Decisions of appellate courts on the interpretation of statutes are binding on other courts. Hence a body of case law gradually grows up around important statutory sections, though the statute itself must be construed each time, rather than the decisions.[22]

Decisions on quite different statutes may be referred to as aids to interpretation, if they are concerned with similar objects. A cyclist was charged in one case with being drunk in charge of a carriage. He was convicted because a bicycle had been held to be a carriage for the purpose of a statute which dealt with dangerous driving.[23] The principle of a fair sharing of loss which was applied in 1666 after the Great Fire of London was applied to the interpretation of a statute dealing with the effect on leases of war damage in the Second World War.[24]

Where legislation is consolidated, *i.e.* a number of statutes are combined in a single statute without substantial change, decisions on the old statutes remain binding.[25]

Where statutes and case law are combined in codifying statutes substantial changes are often made and old decisions are not necessarily still binding.[26] The same applies if a later statute is expressed to consolidate older statutes "with amendments."[27]

Language judicially interpreted in one statute is usually given

---

[19] Road Traffic Act 1960. s.201, now Road Traffic Act 1972, ss.40(1), (5); *Elliott* v. *Grey* [1960] Q.B. 367.
[20] *R.* v. *Chapman* [1959] 1 Q.B. 100.
[21] *Smith* v. *Hughes* [1960] 1 W.L.R. 830, under the Street Offences Act 1959.
[22] *Goodrich* v. *Paisner* [1957] A.C. 65.
[23] *Corkery* v. *Carpenter* [1951] 1 K.B. 102, under the Licensing Act 1872 s.12. The Road Traffic Act 1930 was limited to mechanically propelled vehicles; this was altered by the Road Traffic Act 1956, s.1, now Road Traffic Act 1972, ss.17–21. *Taylor* v. *Goodwin* (1879) 4 Q.B.D. 228; under the Highway Act 1835, s.78.
[24] *Re Orbit Trust Ltd.'s Lease* [1943] Ch. 144, 151–152, on Landlord and Tenant (War Damage) Act 1939.
[25] *Smith* v. *Baker & Sons* [1891] A.C. 325, 349, now County Courts Act 1959, s.108; *cf. Nokes* v. *Doncaster Amalgamated Collieries* [1940] A.C. 1014, 1033, now Companies Act 1948, s.28; *Re Turner's Will Trusts* [1937] Ch. 15, 24, 26 (C.A.); *Att.-Gen.* v. *Parson* [1956] A.C. 421, 439; *R.* v. *Heron* [1982] 1 W.L.R. 451 (H.L.).
[26] *Bristol Tramways* v. *Fiat Motors* [1910] 2 K.B. 831, 836 (C.A.).
[27] *Beaman* v. *A.R.T.S. Ltd.* [1949] 1 K.B. 550 (C.A.); *Phillips-Higgins* v. *Harper* [1954] 1 Q.B. 411, 415.

the same meaning when repeated in later statutes on the same subject, *e.g.* the meaning of "wreck" in the Merchant Shipping Act 1894[28] as interpreted in one case[29] was applied in a later case[30] to decide the meaning of the same word in the Merchant Shipping Act 1925.[31] The time-hallowed phrase, "in the course of employment," of the old law of Workmen's Compensation has been interpreted in the same way in the case of third-party risk motor insurance requirements.[32]

A higher court, however, is not precluded from overruling decisions of lower courts even if the statute has been re-enacted in the meantime, at any rate in technical fields, where Parliament may not have taken any interest in the decision. The force of precedent would be unduly extended if a case was treated as ratified by Parliament in such cases.[33]

The higher courts have generally proved reluctant to reverse old precedents of interpretation of statutes where titles to property may depend on them. A case decided in 1870 was left in force on this ground in 1945.[34] Later dicta, however, doubted the importance of this rule.[35]

Public policy

The law will not allow a person to gain by a deliberate homicide, *e.g.* a claim to a widow's pension under a statute by a woman who killed her husband.[36]

CUSTOM

In earlier times local custom was an occasional legal source, but today it is rarely applicable. However trade usage is occasionally recognised in mercantile law.[37] Custom may also be the basis of certain rights over land in the countryside, *e.g.* rights of way to church.[38]

---

[28] s.158
[29] *The Olympic* [1913] P. 92.
[30] *Barras* v. *Aberdeen Steam Trawling & Fishing Co.* [1933] A.C. 402, 411.
[31] s.1
[32] *Vandyke* v. *Fender* [1970] 2 Q.B. 292 (C.A.).
[33] *Braithwaite & Co. Ltd.* v. *Elliot* [1947] K.B. 177; *Royal Crown Derby Porcelain Co.* v. *Russell* [1949] 2 K.B. 417, 425, 427, 429.
[34] *Re Warden and Hotchkiss Ltd.* [1945] Ch. 270 (C.A.).
[35] *Bray* v. *Colenbrander* [1953] A.C. 503.
[36] *R.* v. *Chief National Insurance Commissioner, ex. p. O'Connor* [1981] 2 W.L.R. 412 (D.C.), *cf.* Forfeiture Act 1982, s.5, preserving the rule of case law that a murderer cannot inherit from his victim, *Re Sigsworth* [1935] Ch. 89.
[37] *Teheran Europe Co.* v. *S.T. Belton (Tractors)* [1968] 2 Q.B. 545 (C.A.).
[38] *Brocklebank* v. *Thompson* [1903] 2 Ch. 344.

IMPACT OF MEMBERSHIP OF THE EEC

The membership of the United Kingdom in the European Economic Community from January 1, 1973 introduced a system of supra-national law, in accordance with the provisions of the Treaty of Rome and the Treaty of Accession. Legislation has been passed, aimed at fitting these changes into our traditional system of legal sources and the existing framework of Parliamentary sovereignty.

Community law, future as well as present, is automatically binding in England in many cases without local enactment here. Judicial notice is taken by our courts of such community law.[39] Orders in Council and Regulations may be used to implement Community law in matters of detail.[40] In some cases Community law has no direct effect but requires the United Kingdom Parliament to pass specific enactments.[41]

Decisions of the European Court as to the interpretation of the treaties and their effect on community law are binding in England and proved by certified copies of their judgments.[42] There is also a need to refer doubtful points of law to the European Court. The House of Lords must do so and other courts may.[43]

The impact of these changes is most felt in a wide but limited field, such as the law of restrictive practices and company law.[44] But the whole of existing English law inconsistent with the now incorporated Community law is repealed by implication. English courts have to decide, in the first instance, when this has happened, which may entail their using Continental sources.[45]

References to the European Court in recent years have been solicited in a number of cases of alleged discrimination against women in employment.[46] Free movement of goods has been another common field.[47]

---

[39] European Communities Act, 1972, ss.2(1), 3(2); *Garden Cottage Foods* v. *M.M.B.* [1982] 3 W.L.R. 514; *R.* v. *Goldstein* [1982] 1 W.L.R. 804.

[40] *Ibid.* s.2(2); Sched. 2 imposes some safeguards, *e.g.* no criminal responsibility or new taxation.

[41] *Hugh-Jones* v. *St. John's College Cambridge* [1979] I.C.R. 848 (E.A.T.).

[42] Act of 1972, s.3(3).

[43] Art. 177 of the Treaty of Rome; *H.P. Bulmer* v. *J. Bollinger, SA* [1974] Ch. 401 (C.A.); Ord. 114. The case must then be pleaded appropriately for the European Court, *Hagen* v. *Fratelli Moretti (D & G)* [1980] 3 C.M.L.R. 253 (C.A.).

[44] These are dealt with in the European Communities Act, Part 2, s.9 minimises the *ultra vires* doctrine in company law. In *Application des Gaz* v. *Falks Veritas Ltd.* [1974] Ch. 381, "new torts" under EEC law are referred to at 390.

[45] *Cf. James Buchanan & Co.* v. *Babco Forwarding and Shipping (U.K.) Ltd.* [1977] 3 W.L.R. 907 (H.L.)

[46] *Worringham & Humphreys* v. *Lloyds Bank* [1982] 1 W.L.R. 950 (C.A.), (pensions); *Burton* v. *British Railways Board* [1981] I.R.L.R. 17 (E.A.T.) (retirement); *Macarthys* v. *Smith* [1981] Q.B. 180 (C.A.), (pay).

[47] *R.* v. *Hann and Darby* [1980] 1 C.M.L.R. 246 (H.L.); *R.* v. *Thompson* [1980] Q.B. 229; (C.A.).

CHAPTER 4

AN OUTLINE HISTORY OF THE COURTS

Introduction

The modern Supreme Court of Judicature consists of two elements, the High Court of Justice which is a trial court or "court of first instance," and the Court of Appeal. The High Court is divided into three Divisions, each of which has had a separate history, accounting for its separate survival and for the survival of its distinct procedure and terminology. In the early period after the Norman Conquest there was a single royal court, not very clearly distinguished from other branches of government, since the "separation of powers" was not usual in the Middle Ages. Gradually a group of clerks or royal officials began to specialise in the trial of routine cases and withdrew from the King's general administrative councils, which carried on the day-to-day government of the country, to form a permanent court. Appeals lay from these specialist judges to the Great Council, the ancestor of the House of Lords, a body which met from time to time to pass major laws of a permanent character, there being no distinction at that time between the Lords as a legislative body and the Lords as a court. The House of Commons was not yet part of Parliament, and when it came into existence never acted as a court except in connection with its own privileges. The undivided royal court gradually split into three separate courts which have been reunited in the last century in the Queen's Bench Division. The Court of Chancery developed rather later and on different lines, becoming the Chancery Division in the last century. The Family Division is descended from the old ecclesiastical courts.

The criminal courts always constituted a distinct hierarchy and the Court of Appeal has separate civil and criminal divisions.

The methods of appeal from these courts were different and complicated and it was only as a result of the reforms of the nineteenth century that the Court of Appeal was set up as a common court for appeals from all the Divisions of the High Court. The House of Lords hears appeals from the Court of Appeal and has been little modified by changes in the law, though, by strong convention, it now has little in common with the House of Lords sitting as one of the two Houses of Parliament.

119

The history of our courts is marked by two main trends, a supersession by the royal courts of the jurisdiction of local courts, so that justice has become highly centralised, highly efficient but also highly expensive, and a rather unedifying but often beneficial competition among the various courts, the various common law courts which now form the Queen's Bench Division vying with one another to attract litigants by offering better procedures, and the Chancery Court leading the way with reforms which the common law courts had perforce to imitate or risk losing much of their business. The disadvantage of this competition was the need in many cases to sue in several courts simultaneously and the irritation and expense of one court interfering with litigants in connection with their proceedings in another court. And all of this in the name of the same sovereign!

The centralisation of justice

In the first centuries after the Norman Conquest ordinary litigation was conducted in one of three systems of courts, the manor court for disputes arising on the manor, the communal courts of counties and hundreds for rural disputes of a wider aspect, and the borough courts for disputes among merchants and townsmen arising within the walls of the town. However, the substantive law administered in these courts was basically the same as in the royal courts. Just as English feudalism was more highly centralised than that abroad, so the aspirations of the royal courts to administer justice in as many cases as possible led to a gradual usurpation by them of local jurisdiction. They offered superior procedures, such as trial by jury, while preventing the local courts from doing the same. They allowed a claimant to land to pretend that a lord of a manor had freely "waived" his jurisdiction. Corruption and bias were claimed to be rife in local courts. On the debit side, litigants were compelled to travel longer distances and pay higher legal costs.

The Three Courts of Common Law

The growth of separate divisions of the royal court was a matter of the convenience of royal administration and not a clear programme. Thus the first branch of the royal court to become distinct was the Exchequer Court, consisting of those treasury officials whose work consisted of deciding disputes about royal revenue claims, an occupation which became full-time under King Henry II. These "Barons of the Exchequer," as the judges were called, extended their jurisdiction by means of a pretence that a plaintiff suing before them needed the money (the fruits of the action) to pay a debt to the revenue (the *Quominus* fiction). As time went on they constituted a regular law court with a jurisdiction little different from the others.

The royal court was in theory held in the King's presence, though the monarchs were not trained lawyers and in fact made no attempt to take part or even to attend; it is a convention in modern times that they must not do so, so that the judges are not subjected to any kind of outside pressure. However, the theory meant that the judges had to take part in the numerous royal trips or "progresses" about the country, which was a great hardship for litigants and their lawyers, who had themselves to travel with them and discover exactly where the courts were at any given moment. In order to satisfy their complaints on this subject a number of the judges were left behind, usually at Westminster, to deal with cases only of concern to subjects, which were known as "common pleas," and Magna Carta in 1215 confirmed this practice. This was the origin of the principal civil court of the Middle Ages, the Common Bench or Common Pleas. The court had the advantage of fixity of location, but its proceedings were rather slow and expensive. Senior barristers known as "serjeants" had a monopoly of the right of audience, and the court was somewhat conservative, which is understandable in view of the fact that much of its business was concerned with disputes over the title to large tracts of land, the main source of wealth in those times. Because of its antiquity the court also proceeded in an unsatisfactory way, and the methods of proof prescribed in the actions which were tried by it were inefficient. Still, it remained a busy court until modern times and its judges earned higher fees than their colleagues in other courts. Most of the medieval cases reported in the Year Books, a series which covers the period from the thirteenth to the early sixteenth centuries, are Common Pleas cases.

The splitting off of the Exchequer and Common Pleas left a King's Bench court with reduced jurisdiction. It is not easy to define the character of this jurisdiction minutely, except to say that it dealt with cases not assigned to other courts and therefore in most cases of special interest to the Crown. Thus it tried some civil cases to which the King was a party, some cases involving a breach of the King's peace or contempt of the King's writ, appeals from borough courts chartered by the King, and appeals from the Common Pleas Court, to which it was regarded as senior. It did not generally try criminal cases itself, but it supervised the criminal courts and could quash their judgments. Between royal progresses it too sat at Westminster and therefore had a special interest in

Middlesex cases; by a fiction (known as *Latitat*) it came to compete in ordinary disputes between subjects on the supposition that they arose in that county. Junior counsel appeared in the King's Bench and proceedings were therefore cheaper.

The Assizes and the General Eyre

It had already been the practice in Europe before the Norman Conquest of England to send royal judges out into various regions to try disputes and punish criminals. The Norman Kings followed the same practice here. At first commissioners were sent out from time to time as the occasion required, making inquiries and reporting to the King. From the time of King Henry II, however, the country was divided into circuits, each covering several adjoining counties, and judges were sent out regularly to "take the assizes," *i.e.* to try cases locally. At first the major jurisdiction was criminal, but as a result of statutes enacted in 1166 and 1285, judges were also sent out on assizes to receive local jury verdicts in civil cases. The actual trial was thus conveniently held in the locality where the parties and witnesses lived, though the preliminary legal arrangements and final pronouncement of judgment took place at Westminster. As there were only a handful of judges in the Middle Ages they generally went out on circuit during court vacations. Other lawyers and sometimes laymen were joined in the commission. A single trial judge sat, while three or four sat at Westminster to settle pleadings.

Juries at first spoke to local common knowledge but, as they came to be impartial judges of facts presented to them by other witnesses, barristers had also to go on circuit and conduct cases before the judge and jury. In this way the assizes functioned in much the same way as the central courts, though difficult points of law were often reserved for argument and decision before the full bench of the court at Westminster, where better law libraries were also available. The circuit system has been modified in recent years. Cases can be tried in London and in a number of other towns.

The General Eyre of the twelfth to fourteenth centuries resembled the assizes in the sense that it too was a commission sent out to a group of counties to deal with legal administration but it differed from the assizes in being a general inspection or audit of the administration of justice and other matters. The assize judges visited each county several times a year and kept to defined circuits. The Eyre might visit one, two or more counties when it was felt needed and spend a considerable time there, but only every five years or so, often because of some local crisis or an accumulation of petitions and complaints to the King from that locality. It did not itself try routine cases but investigated how cases had been tried and heard of failures of justice, which it tried to correct. Cases actually awaiting trial by other judges were also dealt with.

One of the main tasks of the Eyre was to collect fines and revenues due to the King, *e.g.* for abuses of official position or neglect of duty. It therefore became extremely unpopular and tended in its later years to be compounded for by the payment in advance to the King of a sum representing an estimate of what the Eyre would probably have collected! Once paid for these offences, the King did not trouble to correct them! By the middle of the fourteenth century the Eyre ceased to be used and left a vacuum which was to some extent to be filled by the jurisdiction of the Court of Chancery which began to develop soon afterwards. In its heyday the Eyre had wide powers of doing justice and with less formality and expense than the regular courts.

The jury

Today the criminal jury is far more commonly used than the civil jury. Indeed the two institutions have quite different origins: the criminal jury represents the old petty jury which was developed by the royal judges on their own initiative after the breakdown of the older forms of trial of criminals by ordeal—as a result of non-co-operation by the clergy after 1215; the civil jury now used derives from the trespass jury used in the late thirteenth century and possibly inspired by the criminal jury, since trespass lay on the frontier of civil and criminal law.

As ordeal was the traditional form of criminal trial, the petty jury was for a long time regarded as a voluntary alternative for the accused man who "put himself on his country" or neighbours. There was a preliminary stage in proceedings, only abolished in England a few years ago and still surviving in many common law countries, known as the grand jury. This was a statutory institution which examined accusations and decided if they justified putting a person on trial. Its functions have been absorbed in England by the modern preliminary inquiry before the examining magistrates.

The jury came to be invariably used in civil cases as a result of the replacement of older civil actions by varieties of action like trespass and case for which it was the appropriate form of trial, but at the present day it is only used in a few types of action, principally for libel or slander.

Appeals

There were no special appeal courts in the early periods of English law. Judgments of the court of Common Pleas could be appealed to the court of King's Bench, which also acted as a court of first instance, and judgments of the King's Bench could be appealed to the House of Lords which was also a legislative body.

A notable advance was made in 1585 by a statute designed to reduce the expense and delay of appealing to the Lords. Decisions of the Queen's Bench could be appealed to a joint sitting of the judges of the Exchequer and Common Pleas courts, thus providing a fuller court but one itself composed of trial judges. However, such a court was bound to incorporate some jealousies and prejudices. In 1830 another statute generalised that of 1585 by making an appeal from any of the three common law courts go to a joint sitting of the judges of the other two. The jurisdiction of the modern Court of Appeal in common law cases is based upon this but with special judges. The ultimate appeal to the House of Lords was preserved but subject to obtaining leave to appeal.

From the late medieval period until the seventeenth century civil cases of exceptional legal importance were informally and unofficially reserved for discussion by all the judges and barristers at Serjeants' Inn in London or in the room at Westminster known as the Exchequer Chamber, and their decision was honoured by all the courts. Criminal cases were also reserved for discussion until 1848 when the practice was regularised by statute and a Court for Crown Cases Reserved set up. This is now superseded by the Court of Appeal (Criminal Division) to which appeals lie as of right or with leave, whereas the older court considered cases only on the initiative of the trial judge.

Extensions of jurisdiction of the common law courts

In former times the three courts already referred to, the Queen's Bench, Common Pleas and Exchequer, had to compete with a number of other jurisdictions. Thus the Council, and, by the late fifteenth century, the Star Chamber, tried many civil and criminal cases. As a result of the defeat of the royalists in the Civil War the jurisdiction of the royal Council to try cases, as well as that of the Star Chamber, which stood in a rather ambiguous relation to the Council over which legal historians are still in disagreement, was abolished by a statute of 1641. The Star Chamber had developed several branches of our civil law, such as libel, and these were taken over by the victorious common lawyers.

The High Court of Admiralty, set up in the fourteenth century, at one time claimed a wide commercial jurisdiction but the common law courts interfered with its proceedings by the issue of writs of prohibition, except in cases arising at sea. As a result our commercial law, including contracts affecting carriage of goods by sea, has become part of the ordinary jurisdiction of the Queen's Bench Division since 1971. This also applies to maritime disputes.

Another court which for a time competed successfully with the common law courts was the Court of Requests, designed to be an informal body which decided minor cases cheaply and equitably. It existed by the end of the fifteenth century and became obsolete during the Civil War. It does not seem to have created any body of law which could be taken over, being guided broadly by Roman law rather than common law and setting no precedents. But the title of Court of Requests was imitated by several cities which by statute set up courts to try poor men's cases, thus inspiring the county court system of 1846.

The Chancery Division

Most systems of law recognise a distinction between strict law and equity. The strict law is applied by the courts in all routine cases, whereas in special circumstances of hardship aid may be given outside the strict rules by some other agency, e.g. the Praetor under the Roman system and the Lord High Chancellor under the English. This high magistrate also has duties connected with the business of government and is not a full-time judge.

The notable feature of English equity is that it remained until 1875 the monopoly of a separate Court of Chancery and even today survives to some extent in the separate Chancery Division of the High Court of Justice. In the Roman and modern European systems the rules of equity supplanted the rules of law and were applied by all judges.

The Chancellor in medieval times was usually a bishop or archbishop who was also the leading counsellor of the King in affairs of state. It is quite natural that the royal power to do justice in extraordinary cases should have become associated with the office of Chancellor. This development began late in the four-teenth century, when the General Eyre was no longer in use, to redress abuses of justice, and the common law courts had begun to lose their original informality and insist on rigid rules of law, evidence and procedure. Petitions would be made with increasing frequency to the Chancellor against failures of justice due to corruption or inefficiency and later to hardships caused by strict application of the law itself, which gave little redress for fraud and did not forgive loss of receipts and other documents. The courts represented feudal ideas, the Chancellor a more Christian and classical tradition.

The Chancellor was responsible for a common law court which dealt with certain death duty cases and other matters, such as the revocation of royal charters. This court survived, to be known as the "Latin side" of the Chancery. Beside it grew up under Richard II and later kings an "English side," so called because informal bills in English were used (originally actually medieval French) unlike the stereotyped formal Latin of the common law jurisdiction. This "English side" was concerned with bills or petitions for relief against the rigours of the common law in some of its workings, and the Chancellor dealt with cases himself, calling on the persons against whom complaint was made, questioning them himself, and having them imprisoned if they refused to appear or to comply with his decree. Bills, defences, and so on had no prescribed common form but simply explained the petitioner's grievance or the defendant's objections to the petition.

The new Court of Chancery which thus arose, the court of "equity," was not an ecclesiastical court, although its judge was an ecclesiastic, nor was it a court of Roman law type, although the Chancellors knew something of Roman and canon law and "equity" itself is clearly influenced by ideas based on those two foreign legal systems. From the beginning lawyers trained in common law at the Inns of Court practised before the Court of Chancery. After the Reformation the Chancellorship was also given to lawyers, not clergy, and this further increased the regularity and formality of the Chancery. Indeed its justice became even slower than that of the common law and its legal records and documents longer and more complicated. Specialisation in equity cases led later to a specialisation of the Bar, especially in Lincoln's Inn, and to the appointment of Chancery judges in modern times exclusively from this Bar.

Rivalry of the Chancery and the common law courts

The common law judges were unable to alter the basic common law rules in order to eliminate special cases of hardship. Hence a parallel jurisdiction existed, the common law courts deciding cases one way and the Chancery, where special hardship was caused, altering the result. The common law required documents to be produced where relied on, and other evidence of a type to which third parties might testify; the parties themselves were incompetent to be witnesses in their own case. The Chancellor, on the other hand, could subpoena the parties to appear and could interrogate them personally, thus obtaining admissions to facts which might otherwise have had to be proved by the production of documents, e.g. that money owing under a bond under seal had in fact been repaid although the debtor neglected to recover his bond and destroy it. If a person was taking proceedings at law where the "equities" were against him, the Chancery would forbid him to continue such proceedings, using a "common injunction," on breach of which he could be imprisoned for contempt of court. The common law courts naturally resented this interference with their activities. The conflict was submitted to King James I, who decided, on the advice of Francis Bacon, the then Attorney-General, that the Chancery was exercising an ancient jurisdiction and was entitled to interfere with the law on regular lines in order to prevent the law being used as a means of doing injustice. The Chancery was suspended during the Commonwealth but survived all attacks on it and its limited superiority over the law courts persisted until 1873 when the Judicature Act turned it into a division of the High Court and reconstructed the jurisdiction of the divisions to eliminate future clashes, e.g. by liberalising the common law itself.

Appeals in equity

Until the latter part of the fifteenth century the Chancellor was regarded as acting in the name of the royal Council of which he was the chief official. Hence, when an appeal was taken it was taken to that body. Chancellors had a wide discretion to grant or refuse remedies so that it would be difficult to mount an appeal on any basis of error on their part. The Chancery was a royal court but based on the prerogative rather than the common law. In 1641 the judicial powers of the Council were abolished, as a result of the unpopularity of the Star Chamber, another aspect of the Council. In 1675 the House of Lords decided that appeals lay from the Chancery to them. This was historically untrue but obviously a replacement for the Council had to be found and the Lords could maintain some uniformity in the whole law in this way. Within the Chancery an appeal lay from the Master of the Rolls, a subordinate judge, to the Chancellor himself. The Chancellor was often one of the few legally qualified members of the House of Lords, so that appeals often took the form of an appeal from him to himself! To cure this a special Court of Appeal in Chancery was set up in 1851, which provided the precedent for the appointment of full-time appellate judges, two Lords Justices of Appeal being appointed for the purpose. The 1873 legislation abolished this court and set up the present Court of Appeal which hears appeals from all three divisions of the High Court. In order to help unify law and equity as far as possible, it is usual for one former Chancery judge to sit as one of the three Lords Justices of Appeal in common law cases and one former Queen's Bench judge similarly in equity appeals.

The Probate, Divorce and Admiralty Jurisdiction

The probate and divorce jurisdiction of the High Court was taken over in 1875 from Probate and Divorce courts set up in 1857 with lay judges. Before that date these matters were dealt with by various courts of the Church of England, usually the bishops' Consistory Courts, though the actual judges were lay experts acting in the names of the bishops. The procedure was related to the canon law and Roman law procedures of the European Continent. Lawyers with different training practised before the Church courts, being members of "Doctors' Commons" and not of the Inns of Court. In earlier days the Church courts had also had a wider jurisdiction or claimed to have it, in many matters of contract and tort, but the common law courts only recognised their matrimonial and testamentary jurisdiction and in other cases issued prohibitions to restrain their trying cases.

This jurisdiction passed to a Probate, Divorce and Admiralty Division in 1875.

In 1971 divorce cases were assigned to a new Family Division, and disputed probate cases to the Chancery Division, as part of a general reorganisation of the Courts.

A special maritime court was set up under King Edward III, the High Court of Admiralty. It competed with the common law courts for many years but was restricted in modern times to matters covered by pure Admiralty law, such as collisions at sea. In 1875 an Admiralty jurisdiction of the High Court was created, as part of the Probate, Divorce and Admiralty Division. In 1971 the Admiralty jurisdiction was transferred to the Queen's Bench Division and forms an Admiralty Court with wider jurisdiction since 1981.

The Magistrates' Courts

Minor offences were at one time tried by courts held by the royal sheriff of a county but he had an interest in securing convictions and the jurisdiction became unpopular. The King then appointed local gentlemen of good character and ample fortune to supervise criminal proceedings and by a statute of 1344 empowered these "justices of the peace" to try offences presented to them by the Grand Juries. They held quarter sessions four times a year and sat with juries, trying all but the most serious crimes, which were reserved for the royal judges taking the assizes. Boroughs were also given their own commission of the peace and their officials were appointed justices of the peace. Offences were then created from time to time by statute which were made triable by justices out of sessions and without juries. This summary court came to be known as "Petty Sessions." Quarter sessions were abolished by the Courts Act 1971. The expression "Petty Sessions" has been replaced in modern legislation by the term "magistrates' courts," which now sit under county commissions.

The County Courts

The original county courts were held by sheriffs for the whole area of a county but these courts, though active in Saxon and Norman times, gradually became obsolete with the decline in the value of money, since they had an upper limit in amount in their civil jurisdiction. The need for inexpensive civil proceedings led to several local statutory small claims courts being set up, and finally to the 1846 County Courts Act which set up a nation-wide system of so-called county courts, though the court districts are not counties.

The New Courts

A major reform was effected by the 1971 Courts Act. It provided that the High Court may try civil cases at prescribed provincial trial centres, and that circuit and sessions cases be tried by a new system of Crown Courts held at various towns. Some of these courts have High Court judges while the lower tier courts have circuit judges and recorders.

The offices of county court judge and circuit judge were also merged.

The idea of the reform was to avoid the traditional geographical division and the system of moving courts, substituting for it a flexible system of court sessions concentrated where they are most accessible to the bulk of the population.

CHAPTER 5

CRIMINAL PROCEDURE

PROCEEDINGS ON INDICTMENT

Process

SUSPECTED criminals are brought before the court by summons, warrant or arrest without warrant. Procedure by summons will be considered in connection with summary offences.

(a) By warrant of arrest

If B, a suspect, is believed to have committed a crime which is indictable or punishable with imprisonment or B's address is not known a police officer may apply to the local magistrates' court before the public session opens and swear an information in writing.[1] The magistrate will issue a warrant, if satisfied that a summons might be ineffective.[2] The warrant names or describes the suspect and states the offence charged, so that the suspect is informed of the nature of the case he has to meet.[3]

No date for appearance in court will be specified in the warrant, as it is not known when an arrest will be effected. For the same reason the warrant can be enforced after any delay, however long. If the suspect is known to be abroad a warrant can be issued but kept in suspense until his return. A warrant can also be applied for at any time after a crime is committed, as no limitation of time is usual in proceedings for indictable offences. The warrant need not be produced by the constable who eventually effects the arrest, as a number of police may be searching for the same suspect, but the constable should inform the man, when he arrests him, that there is a warrant out for his arrest[4] and he should be allowed to see the warrant as soon as possible. A warrant, once issued, can only be withdrawn with leave of the magistrate who issued it.[5]

---

[1] Magistrates' Courts Act 1980 s.1(3), (4).
[2] Magistrates' Courts Rules 1981, r. 96.
[3] *Ibid.* r. 97.
[4] Magistrates' Courts Act 1980, s.125(3); these rules do not apply to civil arrest for non-payment of a fine *De Costa Small* v. *Kirkpatrick* (1978) 68 Cr.App.R. 186 (D.C.).
[5] *Ibid.* s.125(1).

A warrant may be executed anywhere in England and Wales and may be "backed" or indorsed for execution in Scotland and Ireland.[6] A warrant may also be backed "for bail" unless the police object, so that the arrested man can obtain his release from custody but may have to provide substantial sureties for his appearance in court.

Bail may be applied for at his appearance before the magistrates with an appeal to the Crown Court against a refusal.[7]

(b) By arrest without warrant

A different example will illustrate some of the alternative possibilities in procedure on indictment. Let us imagine that a police officer is patrolling his beat late at night and notices C and D climbing over a warehouse wall with some furs. The police, in view of their obligation to protect the public, have wider powers of arrest than the private citizen. They may lawfully arrest anyone whom they reasonably suspect of having committed an "arrestable offence," *i.e.* one for which a sentence of five years' imprisonment might be imposed on a first offender.[8]

Private persons are in an anomalous situation for the purpose of arrests. They may arrest persons whom they suspect of responsibility for an "arrestable offence" which has actually occurred.[9]

The police may also arrest persons they suspect of being about to commit an offence.[10] The legal rules are useful in enabling experienced professional inspectors and investigators to effect arrests in some cases when it is not practical to call a policeman in time, *e.g.* if thefts occur on a train or in a large department store.

It is a rule of law that a private subject may lawfully resist arrest if it is not justified by law.[11] If one private person attempts to arrest another it may be desirable to apply this rule. On the other hand it is not conceived to be desirable to resist a policeman who is effecting an arrest. If the party is innocent he will have opportunities of defending himself in due time. If his view of the law is incorrect when he resists arrest he will be committing the offence of obstructing the police officer whether he is guilty of the offence charged or not.[12]

---

[6] *Ibid.* ss.125, 126.
[7] *Ibid.* s.117; Bail Act 1976 s.6 and Supreme Court Act 1981 s.81(4); as amd. by Criminal Justice Act 1982 s.60.
[8] Criminal Law Act 1967, s.2(1), (4); Criminal Law Act 1977, Sched. 12; *Wills* v. *Bowley* [1982] 3 W.L.R. 10; *cf.* Police and Criminal Evidence Bill, cl. 21, 22.
[9] *Ibid.* s.2(3).
[10] *Ibid.* s.2(5); *R.* v. *Howell* [1982] 1 Q.B. 416 (C.A.).
[11] False arrest is a tort; as to *habeas corpus* procedure see works on constitutional law. As to appeals from orders in such cases see Administration of Justice Act 1960, ss.15(1), (2).
[12] See Glanville Williams [1954] Crim.L.R. 17.

In our second example the police officer effects an arrest, the two men are cautioned that they will be charged with an offence in respect of the furs and are taken to the police station. There is no legal duty to answer questions put by the police or to accompany them to the police station unless arrested.[13] A person, once arrested, is entitled to notify someone of the fact and where he is being held, but this right is not absolute.[14] He must be brought before a magistrate promptly but there is no specific time limit.[15]

Prosecution

The majority of prosecutions are brought by the police acting theoretically as private citizens, on behalf of the Crown. The police are informed of the commission of a crime, take statements from the victim, interview possible witnesses, search for weapons, fingerprints, and other evidence. A police officer may conduct the case at the preliminary inquiry and call the victim as a witness for the prosecution.[16] In serious cases, which cannot be tried summarily, a solicitor will prepare the case and counsel may be instructed to appear.

Government departments, public bodies[17] and large commercial firms, often have legal departments and conduct their own prosecutions, e.g. a bank may prosecute an embezzling cashier, a Ministry may prosecute for a violation of a provision of social legislation. The police will co-operate in the investigation of the crime and the collection of evidence if they believe the proceedings are justified.

Occasionally a private citizen insists on prosecuting in a case where the police feel it is not well grounded and advise against the proceedings.[18] In such cases the private prosecutor will have to convince the magistrates that a warrant or summons should be issued. The police must then effect the arrest or serve the summons if so ordered by the court. The prosecutor will have to establish a prima facie case after the accused is arrested or the magistrates will not commit for trial. If the magistrates are dissatisfied with the evidence they may refuse to commit for trial and release the accused. The private prosecutor, however, has yet another string to his bow. He may apply to a High Court judge for

---

[13] *Rice* v. *Connolly* [1966] 2 Q.B. 414 (D.C.); *Ludlow* v. *Burgess* (1982) 75 Cr.App.R. 227.
[14] Criminal Law Act 1977, s.62; 1983 Bill, cl. 50, 52.
[15] Weekly remands in custody are possible. Magistrates' Courts Act 1980, s.128(6). as amd. Criminal Justice Act 1982, s.59 and Sched. 9; Bill, cl. 37.
[16] The police cannot be compelled to prosecute, e.g. R. v. *Commissioner of Police for the Metropolis* [1973] Q.B. 241, cf. A.F. Wilcox, *The Decision to Prosecute,* 1972.
[17] *R.* v. *Reigate Justices* [1956] 1 W.L.R. 638 (D.C.).
[18] *Lund* v. *Thompson* [1959] 1 Q.B. 283; cf. *Gouriet* v. *U.P.W.* [1977] 1 All E.R. 696.

leave to prefer a bill of indictment.[19] A copy of the depositions will have to be obtained from the magistrates' court for the purpose and the reasons for the prosecutor's insistence on continuing the case will have to be given. Counsel may be heard by the judge, but the trial of the application is *in camera* and the defendant is not consulted.[20] If the judge gives leave, the prosecutor applies to the local magistrates for a warrant. They have no power to refuse this. On the accused being produced by the police before the magistrates, the court must commit him for trial, on mere proof of identity and without considering the merits of the case. The prosecutor's expenses in these cases will usually be paid out of county funds. A private prosecutor runs a risk, however, as he may be required to pay the accused's costs if he is acquitted and the trial court considers that the case should never have been brought. Bills of indictment are also used by the police to save unnecessary time and trouble, *e.g.* to add a new defendant after others have been committed for trial, or where the victim dies, after his assailant has been committed for trial for wounding, so that the charge becomes one of murder.

At the other extreme are prosecutions conducted by the Director of Public Prosecutions whose department was set up for this purpose in 1879. The Director acts as prosecutor in name but is represented by counsel in court. He also has his own legal and administrative staff. He is under the direction of the Attorney-General who issues regulations for the department.[21] Only a fraction of all prosecutions on indictment are "public" in this strict sense. The Director conducts three types of prosecutions. In the first place he is the only authorised prosecutor for certain types of offences against public order or good government, such as sedition, bribery, and corruption, offences under the Official Secrets Act 1911, the Sexual Offences Act 1967, and the rather nebulous offence of public mischief. He can be directed to appear by the court and can take over any prosecution. He is especially concerned with important criminal appeals.[22] The Director may take over a private prosecution and abort it by offering no evidence, *e.g.* to protect an informer.[23]

---

[19] Administration of Justice Act 1933, s.2(2); Indictment (Procedure) Rules 1971, rr. 6–11. Circuit judges cannot give leave (*R.* v. *Thompson* [1975] 1 W.L.R. 1425). High Court judges may direct a bill of indictment to be presented, if present when a crime is committed in court; *R.* v. *Butt* (1957) 41 Cr.App.R. 82.
[20] *R.* v. *Raymond* [1981] Q.B. 910 (C.A.).
[21] Prosecution of Offences Regulations 1978.
[22] Prosecution of Offences Act 1979; s.2.
[23] *Raymond* v. *Att.-Gen.* [1982] 2 W.L.R. 849 (C.A.); *Turner* v. *D.P.P.* (1978) 68 Cr.App.R. 70.

The Preliminary Inquiry

The hearing

A "suspect" once charged becomes "the accused." He must be brought without undue delay before the magistrates as "examining justices" who must decide whether or not to commit him for trial by jury. The magistrates are the lay bench or a stipendiary magistrate.

The preliminary inquiry is held in open court unless the magistrates consider that justice requires them to proceed *in camera*.[24] They may prohibit reports of a particular case, but this power is to be sparingly used.

Where the defence has no objection, a shortened type of procedure by filing written statements is possible.[25]

If the defence wishes to cross-examine the prosecution witnesses an oral hearing is used. To avoid prejudicing the jury at the eventual trial in the trial court if the accused is committed for trial, the details which may be published in the Press or on the media are limited to certain matters, *e.g.* the name and address of the accused, the charge against him and the decision of the inquiry.[26] The accused may ask for this restriction to be lifted, but any co-accused person may ask the court to decide if it is proper to do so.[27]

The prosecutor's task at the preliminary inquiry is to satisfy the examining justices that there is sufficient evidence against the accused to justify putting the accused on trial. The prosecution, for example, will produce the victim of the crime or some other witnesses. Each witness will be examined by counsel for the prosecution and cross-examined by the accused or his counsel.[28] If a material witness refuses to appear voluntarily or fails to appear at the hearing, he may be subpoenaed by a witness summons. If that fails, a warrant may be issued directing that he be arrested and produced in court.[29] The hearing may be adjourned from time to time, if necessary, the accused being remanded in custody or released on bail in the meantime.[30] Such adjournments, however, cause considerable delay, especially in busy magistrates' courts. If a witness is too ill to attend court, as may well be true of the

---

[24] Magistrates' Courts Act 1980. s.4(2); *R.* v. *Horsham Justices* [1982] Q.B. 762 (C.A.) under Contempt of Court Act 1981, s.4(2).

[25] *Ibid.* ss.6(2), 102. Magistrates' Courts Rules 1981 r. 6.

[26] Act of 1980 s.8.

[27] Criminal Justice (Amendment) Act 1981, s.1; *R.* v. *Leeds Justices, ex. p. Sykes* [1983] 1 W.L.R. 132 (D.C.)

[28] Magistrates' Courts Act 1980, s.4(3).

[29] *Ibid.* s.97(1), (3).

[30] *Ibid.* ss.5, 128.

victim, the magistrate may go to the hospital or his home and take his testimony as a written deposition. The accused man is also entitled to be present and to cross-examine the witness.[31]

The evidence of all the prosecution witnesses at the inquiry is reduced to writing and read over to the witnesses in the presence of the accused, and signed by them[32] and by the magistrates.[33] Defence counsel may then submit that there is insufficient evidence to justify his client's committal for trial. The magistrates may agree and discharge the accused. Otherwise they will explain the charge to him and tell him that he may testify and call witnesses, or may reserve his defence for the trial. They must warn him to ignore any promise or threat made to induce him to confess and that anything he may say may be used later at the trial by judge and jury.[34]

If he elects to testify or calls witnesses the case proceeds, after any necessary adjournments to enable him to summon his witnesses.[35] The defence testimony is then taken down and signed. His counsel may address the court again, if the court gives leave, in order to sum up the defence case.[36] The prosecuting counsel may criticise the defence evidence.[37] In practice the defence is usually reserved and no defence testimony is given at the inquiry. This gives more latitude in developing the defence which does not show its hand prematurely.[38] It is in any case impossible to plead guilty to a serious crime at this stage as the inquiry has no jurisdiction to entertain such cases and could not pass any sentence.

If the defence does present its case defence counsel may ask the court to discharge the accused at the close of the hearing. The magistrates need not be satisfied a man is guilty before they commit him; it is not their task to anticipate the ultimate result. But they must commit if any reasonable jury could convict on the evidence given. If the prosecution case, as made out before them, is so weak that the trial judge would probably stop the case and direct an acquittal, then the accused should not be committed for trial. The magistrates may commit for trial for a different indictable offence from that with which he is charged before them, if the evidence establishes a prima facie case of that offence.[39] The

---

[31] *Ibid.* s.105(2).
[32] Magistrates' Courts Rules 1981 r. 7(8).
[33] r.7(3).
[34] *Ibid* r. 7(7).
[35] *Ibid.* r. 7(10).
[36] *Ibid.* r. 7(11).
[37] *Ibid.*
[38] *Ibid.* See Devlin, *The Criminal Prosecution in England,* 91.
[39] Magistrates' Courts Act 1980, s.6(1); 1981 Rules, r. 12.

prosecution evidence may for example prove robbery rather than attempted murder.

If the court discharges the accused, he may still be prosecuted at some later date, *e.g.* should sufficient evidence of his guilt then be forthcoming, as the inquiry is not equivalent to a definitive trial. In practice renewed preliminary inquiries are discouraged[40] and the prosecution prefer to use the bill of indictment procedure, already referred to, instead. This also is regarded as harsh and is not very commonly used.[41]

Committal

Committal consists of securing the appearance of the accused at a competent trial court by placing him in custody and directing his production for trial there, or by obtaining bail for his release and voluntary appearance there. The court will generally commit a person accused of crime for trial by a specific Crown Court; the magistrates take into account the convenience of parties and witnesses.[42] The defendant or prosecutor may apply to vary the directions as to the place of trial.[43] The date of trial will generally be between two and eight weeks ahead, subject to extension.[44]

The magistrates' clerk will see that the depositions taken by him are forwarded to the trial court. If a witness should die, become insane or become too ill to travel his deposition may be used at the trial as evidence, if legally admissible, since the accused had the opportunity to cross-examine the witness before the examining justices.[45] The witnesses themselves are required to attend the subsequent trial and testify by a "witness order" issued by the magistrates' court.[46] The clerk of the magistrates' court must also send to the trial court any documents produced in evidence and various papers relating to bail and other matters.[47]

Bail

Bail is the release of an accused person in return for the provision by him or by a personal surety (*e.g.* a relative or friend) of a bond in a sum of money payable if the accused fails to appear

[40] *R.* v. *Horsham Justices, ex. p. Reeves* (1982) 75 Cr.App.R. 236 (D.C.).
[41] Devlin, *ubi supra*, 96, 97 (but see *R.* v. *Manchester City Magistrates' Court* [1977] 1 W.L.R. 911 (D.C.)).
[42] Magistrates' Courts Act 1980. ss.6(3), 7.
[43] Supreme Court Act 1981, s.76(3).
[44] Supreme Court Act 1981, s.77(1); Crown Court Rules 1971, r. 19; *R.* v. *Edwards* (1975) 62 Cr.App.R. 166; *R.* v. *Urbanowski* [1976] 1 W.L.R. 455.
[45] Magistrates' Courts Rules 1981, rr. 11(2), 33.
[46] Criminal Procedure (Attendance of Witnesses) Act 1965, s.1; Magistrates' Courts Rules 1981, r. 8.
[47] 1981 Rules, r. 11.

at the inquiry or trial. Bail may be granted after arrest, before the preliminary inquiry, and during adjournments of the inquiry. Where the justices decide to commit for trial, the accused or his counsel may apply for bail until trial, *e.g.* providing sufficient sureties.[48]

If a defendant could not be imprisoned on conviction he is entitled to bail unless he has previously failed to surrender after bail.[49] Where the offence is punishable by imprisonment (a "prisonable offence") the court may refuse to grant bail if there are good grounds to believe the offender is likely to fail to surrender to custody or may interfere with witnesses or commit another offence while on bail.[50] Reasons must be given for refusing bail.[51]

If the examining justices refuse to release on bail, they must inform the accused of his right to apply to a High Court judge for bail.[52] Application can also be made to the trial Crown Court, with a further application to the High Court.[53]

Corporations

A corporation obviously cannot be arrested, but it can be summoned and appears by representative. It can be "committed" for trial if the crime is of the type of which a corporation can be guilty but cannot be in custody and no question of bail arises.[54]

Trial Courts

As a result of the radical recommendations of the Beeching Report the system of trial courts for indictable cases was completely reorganised. A number of Crown Courts where trial is by a judge and jury,[55] were set up, situated in places determined by the Lord Chancellor.[56] The Lord Chief Justice and Lord Chancellor regulate the allocation of cases to High Court judges, circuit judges and recorders.[57]

---

[48] Magistrates' Courts Act, s.77(1); the sum fixed must not be excessive; *Ex. p. Thomas* [1956] Crim.L.R. 119.

[49] Bail Act 1976, s.4; Sched. 1 Pt. II.

[50] Magistrates' Courts Act 1980 s.6(3).

[51] Bail Act 1976, s.5(3), (4); pleading "not guilty" is not a good reason, *Tarlochan Gata Aura* v. *R.* [1982] Crim.L.R. 49.

[52] Criminal Justice Act 1967, s.22.

[53] Criminal Justice Act 1982, s.60.

[54] Magistrates' Courts Act 1980 s.46, Sched. 3.

[55] Supreme Court Act 1981, s.73.

[56] Supreme Court Act 1981, ss.8, 45, 78.

[57] Supreme Court Act 1981 s.75; *cf. Practice Direction* [1978] 1 W.L.R. 926. Judges try the First 2 of 4 classes of offence, 77,000 persons were convicted on indictment in 1981.

The circuit judge is a new creation. He is appointed on the advice of the Lord Chancellor from barristers or experienced recorders.[58] The judges of the Central Criminal Court in London became circuit judges.[59] Circuit judges are full-time judges.[60]

Recorders continue to be appointed as part-time judges to try the less serious cases.[61] They are appointed for fixed terms.

Lay magistrates may sit with the judge in trying the least serious cases, but the judge sums up and gives all legal rulings.[62]

The Indictment

An indictment is a formal accusation on which the accused is charged and tried. It must give reasonable particulars of the offence charged, and refer to the statute making it an offence. It is delivered within 28 days to or drawn up by the officer of the Crown Court to which the accused is committed for trial.[63] The indictment is drafted on the basis of the original charges in the warrant as supported and modified by the depositions of the prosecution witnesses at the preliminary inquiry. If the charges are changed from those made before the preliminary inquiry the accused may ask for an adjournment if he needs more time to meet the altered charges.[64] The court also has power to amend the indictment before or at the trial.[65] If there is a serious error or omission the indictment may be quashed, on application by the defence.

Indictments may include a number of counts in numbered paragraphs, for related offences which can conveniently be tried together, each count being a separate indictment in law, *e.g.* a series of burglaries on the same night.[66] The counts must be based on the same incidents or be based on a series of similar offences.[67]

The Attorney-General may stop further proceedings after the indictment is signed by entering a *nolle prosequi*.[68] This is a

---

[58] Courts Act 1971, s.16(3); Administration of Justice Act 1977, s.12.

[59] Courts Act 1981, Sched. 2, Pt. I.

[60] Courts Act 1981, s.17(6); *Sirros* v. *Moore* [1975] Q.B. 118 (C.A.). See *Practice Direction (Circuit Judge: Mode of Address)*, *The Times*, January 1, 1982.

[61] *Ibid.* s.21. Barristers or solicitors are eligible.

[62] Supreme Court Act 1981, s.75(2).

[63] Indictments (Procedure) Rules 1971 r. 45; *R.* v. *Sheerin* (1976) 64 Cr.App.R. 68; *R.* v. *Barrett & Kelly* [1981] Crim. L.R. 835.

[64] Administration of Justice Act 1933, s.2; *R.* v. *Dickson* [1969] 1 W.L.R. 405.

[65] Indictments Act 1915 s.5; *R.* v. *Hall* [1968] 2 Q.B. 787; *R.* v. *Radley* (1973) 58 Cr.App.R. 394.

[66] Indictments Rules 1971, r. 4; *R.* v. *Considine* (1979) 124 S.J. 46.

[67] *Ibid.* r. 9; *R.* v. *Kray* [1970] 1 Q.B. 125 (C.A.); *Ludlow* v. *Metropolitan Police Commissioner* [1971] A.C. 29.; *R.* v. *Barrell* (1979) 69 Cr.App.R. 250.

[68] See [1958] Crim.L.R. 573, 578 *et seq.*

complete bar to a trial, on that indictment, but technically does not bar another later prosecution.

The Jury

All indictable cases are tried with a jury of twelve laymen whose verdict decides all issues of fact.[69] The arrangements for the jury system are made by the Lord Chancellor.[70] Jurors are summoned by an officer appointed by him.[71] He extracts their names from the electoral register drawn up each year by local registration officers in which persons of age to serve are specially noted.[72]

In deciding on the number of jurors the number of cases on the list to be tried is material, and the probable length of each. Allowance must be made for challenges with and without cause. Many of the accused will plead guilty but this cannot be predicted. If the accused pleads guilty on arraignment the jury then have nothing to do with the case. The jury will have to remain in attendance until all the accused have pleaded guilty or been convicted or acquitted after trial.

Jurors must be local government electors between the ages of eighteen and sixty-five. They must have been resident for five years in this country.[73]

Persons convicted of certain offences are disqualified.[74] Members of the judiciary are ineligible.[75] So are lawyers, police and probation officers.[76] Clergy are ineligible,[77] as are persons of unsound mind.[78]

Peers and Members of Parliament are excused attendance, as are practising doctors, dentists and nurses.[79] Exemption continues in some cases for ten years after ceasing to qualify. Ex-Judges and JPs are ineligible.[80]

The officer supplies the clerk of the court with a list or panel of jurors chosen by him on an impartial basis and having due regard to spreading the burden of service evenly. The parties may inspect the panel.[81] Each juror has a name-card, and these name-cards are

[69] Cf. R. v. Guttridge [1973] R.T.R. 135 (C.A.).
[70] Juries Act 1974, s.2.
[71] Ibid. 58. 2(5), 23(2).
[72] Ibid. s.3.
[73] Ibid. s.1.
[74] Ibid. Sched. 1, Pt. II.
[75] Sched 11, Pt.I, Group A.
[76] Ibid. Group B.
[77] Ibid. Group C.
[78] Ibid. Group D.
[79] Ibid. Pt. III.
[80] Ibid. Pt. I, Groups A, B; Pt. II.
[81] Ibid. s.5(2).

picked from a box at random, to ensure fairness.[82] Jurors have an opportunity to request deferment for good cause, *e.g.* illness.[83] Jurors are paid travel and subsistence allowances, where necessary, and can claim for loss of earnings.[84]

Each juror may be challenged as his name is called and he is about to be sworn. The party challenging cannot interrogate the juror to try to discover a reason for a challenge, but may challenge him for some cause known to him, *e.g.* if the juror has expressed an opinion about the case or is personally connected with it. The accused may also challenge not more than three persons without cause.[85] Where a challenge is disputed the judge decides whether to allow it.

The Crown is permitted to "vet" a jury by asking jurors to stand by without giving any cause, *e.g.* to obtain a fair racial balance or exclude a juror likely to be unsuitable in particular cases.[86]

The same jury may be used to try more than one case if the later trial begins within 24 hours of picking the jury.[87] No juror may by law be called on to serve oftener than once in two years.[88]

Persons at or near the court may be impressed to make up a jury if not enough regularly impanelled jurors are left.[89]

Secrecy of jury deliberations is guaranteed by law.[90]

The Trial

A cause list is screened at the opening of a sitting of the Crown Court, listing the order of trial of the cases committed for trial. Trial is generally in open court and places for the public are provided. In some exceptional cases the public may be excluded from the court, *e.g.* where a child or young person is testifying as to indecent offences.

The Press are generally entitled to be present and to report details of all evidence given in criminal proceedings. In charges of blackmail the identity of the victim is generally kept secret. In rape cases the identities of the defendant and complainant are kept anonymous in news media unless the judge otherwise directs.[91]

---

[82] *Ibid.* s.11(1).
[83] *Ibid.* s.9(2). *Practice Direction* [1973] 1 W.L.R. 134.
[84] *Ibid.* s.19; Jurors Allowances Regs. 1980.
[85] Juries Act 1825, s.29; Juries Act 1974, s.12; Criminal Law Act 1977, s.43.
[86] *R. v. Mason* [1980] 3 W.L.R. 617; *R. v. Binns* [1982] Crim.L.R. 522.
[87] Juries Act 1974, s.11(5).
[88] *Ibid.* s.8.
[89] *Ibid.* s.6. They are called "talesmen."
[90] Contempt of Court Act 1981, s.8.
[91] Sexual Offences (Amendment) Act 1976, ss.4, 6.

The court may require a report of a case to be postponed to avoid prejudicing the trial.[92]

Pleas

The accused person is "arraigned," that is to say, brought to the bar of the court, the indictment is read, and he is asked how he pleads, whether guilty or not guilty. The prisoner must plead "guilty" or "not guilty" to each charge.[93] He may be allowed by the judge to plead "guilty" to another charge not in the indictment if the law would allow him to be convicted of it on such indictment.[94] On a plea of guilty the prosecution summarises its case against him and the proceedings are like those after conviction on a plea of guilty.[95] The prosecution will often drop one charge if the accused will plead guilty to another. A plea of guilty may be the reason for a reduced sentence. The judge must not, however, press for the defendant to plead guilty by promising to impose a lighter sentence.[96]

The jury should not hear the pleas taken, since a plea of guilty on one count may prejudice the trial of a plea of not guilty on another.[97] Once a person pleads not guilty he should not change his plea. The jury may, however, convict him on his making an admission of guilt during the trial without further evidence.

If the defendant refuses to plead either way, the first question for the jury is to decide whether he is obstinate or really physically incapable of speech. If he is dumb the jury decides whether he can plead in writing or by using signs. It is often claimed that the defendant is mentally unfit to plead, *i.e.* that he is in no fit mental state to conduct his own defence or to instruct counsel properly. This question may be raised on arraignment or at the close of the prosecution case. If raised at the outset the jury decide whether or not the man is fit to plead; if they decide that he is fit, the trial usually proceeds with a different jury.[98] If he is found unfit to plead he is sent to hospital but may be tried later if he recovers.[99] The question is best left until the prosecution have presented their case, as the defendant may then succeed in having the case

---

[92] Contempt of Court Act 1981, s.4(2); *Practice Direction* [1982] 1 W.L.R. 1475.
[93] *R.* v. *Ellis* (1973) 57 Cr.App.R. 571; trial *in absentia* is seldom permissible; *R.* v. *Howson* (1982) 74 Cr.App.R. 172.
[94] Criminal Law Act 1967 s.6(1); *R.* v. *Dodd, Pack, Wallace, Byrne* (1982) 74 Cr.App.R. 50.
[95] *Practice Direction* [1968] 1 W.L.R. 529. In exceptional cases, evidence may be heard, *R.* v. *Milligan* [1982] Crim.L.R. 317, (D.C.).
[96] *R.* v. *Turner* [1970] 2 Q.B. 321, "plea bargaining"; *R.* v. *Inns* [1975] Crim.L.R. 182; *Practice Direction* July 26, 1976; *R.* v. *Ryan* (1977) 67 Cr.App.R. 177.
[97] *R.* v. *Lashbrooke* (1958) 43 Cr.App.R. 86.
[98] Criminal Procedure (Insanity) Act 1964, s.4.
[99] *Ibid.*

dismissed and be set at liberty.[1] If the defendant is merely obstinately silent, a plea of "not guilty" is entered.[2]

The plea of not guilty in criminal cases is very broad. It covers a flat denial of the facts charged and also a confession of the facts and the addition of new facts to explain away any criminal responsibility. It may also be used to challenge the jurisdiction of the court. A plea of guilty must admit the offence, including any requisite mental element such as a dishonest intention, and not merely the act complained of.[3] The court does not go behind a deliberate plea of guilty in court although it is suspicious of prosecution evidence of previous confessions on a plea of "not guilty."

Most criminal cases are fought on issues of fact. Legal objections by the defence are usually based on irregularities as to evidence or procedure during the trial rather than on disputes as to the meaning of the criminal law. An objection based on substantive law may be made by pleading a demurrer[4] or moving to quash the indictment as disclosing no offence,[5] or by a submission, after the prosecution evidence, that it does not establish any offence, even if true, so that there is no case to go to the jury; or by a motion in arrest of judgment after a verdict against the defendant.

Order of speeches and evidence

As the burden of proof in criminal cases generally rests on the prosecution it is the task of prosecuting counsel to open the proceedings. He refers to the charges in the indictment, outlines the facts which he hopes to establish by the prosecution evidence, explains how these facts constitute the elements of the offence charged and refers to the witnesses whom he is calling to prove these facts.[6]

The prosecution witnesses will generally have appeared before the examining justices and a witness order made directing them to appear at the trial. In other cases the trial court can issue a witness summons, or a warrant if the summons is unlikely to be obeyed.[7]

---

[1] R. v. Webb [1969] 2 Q.B. 278 (C.A.), R. v. Burles [1970] 2 Q.B. 191. Criminal Law Act 1967, s.6(1)(c).

[2] Criminal Law Act 1967, s.6(1)(c).

[3] Ex p. Virgo [1952] 2 Q.B. 1; R. v. McNally [1954] 1 W.L.R. 933.

[4] Criminal Law Act 1967, s.6(1)(a); R. v. Inner London Quarter Sessions [1970] 2 Q.B. 80 (D.C.); R. v. Dytham [1979] Q.B. 722, C.A.

[5] e.g. R. v. New (1957) 41 Cr.App.R. 207; R. v. Hale [1974] Q.B. 819.

[6] This opening speech is not itself evidence, R. v. Lewis [1971] Crim.L.R. 414 (C.A.). See p. 282 post.

[7] Criminal Procedure (Attendance of Witnesses) Act 1965, ss.1, 2, 4; R. v. J.R. Dadlani (1970) 54 Cr.App.R. 305. Evidence is given on oath or affirmation. Oaths Act 1978. The Competence of a witness to testify may be challenged. R. v. Yacoob (1981) 72 Cr.App.R. 313.

Additional witnesses can be summoned if due notice has been given to the accused before the trial. Witnesses receive allowances for expenses.[8] If the opposing party does not object, signed statements may be used, without the witness being called.[9]

Prosecution witnesses should withdraw from court when the case is called until they are called in to testify. They must not leave the court after testifying, without leave of the judge, to prevent their telling later witnesses what to say.

Each witness called by the prosecution is examined "in chief" by prosecuting counsel.[10] After evidence of identity the witness will be asked to recall the events of the day of the offence. The victim of a crime of violence will be called, for instance, and will explain the circumstances of the alleged attack on him. The questions may not be so framed as to suggest the answers expected ("leading questions").

Defence counsel will cross-examine each prosecution witness to shake his testimony, e.g. to cast doubt on his veracity, to seek an admission that he is not able to identify the defendant as his assailant and to put to him the defence version of what happened. "Leading questions" may be asked, as the prosecution witness is supposed to be hostile to the opposing side. The defence are entitled to information by the prosecution about their witnesses.[11] The purpose of defence questions is not always clear at this stage, and the judge may ask counsel what his object is in asking these questions. The defence may have decided to deny the identification of the defendant with the assailant. They may plan to plead self-defence or accident. If an acquittal cannot be secured, the defence may still hope for a conviction of a less serious offence. Their questions will be directed to putting to the prosecution witnesses all possibilities of this kind in the hope of getting admissions that these defences are compatible with the facts as they testify to them. The defence will often seek an admission that the witness's powers of observation were weak, or that it was difficult to observe clearly, or that the witness's memory is vague on the facts to which he is testifying. They may seek an admission that the witness dislikes the defendant or has some motive for lying.

Cross-examination by the defence counsel should also be directed to refuting statements of the witness which have been made in examination in chief which are damaging to the

---

[8] Costs in Criminal Cases (Allowances) Regulations 1975.
[9] Criminal Justice Act 1967, s.9.
[10] Solicitors have the right of audience in some Crown Courts, Supreme Court Act 1981, s.83.
[11] Att.-Gen.'s Guidelines (1982) 74 Cr.App.R. 302.

defendant, since it may be assumed that these statements are accepted by the defence unless they clearly contest them.

The prosecuting counsel may re-examine his witness, if he has made any admissions damaging to the prosecution case or his credibility has been shaken in cross-examination. No new questions can be asked, but questions may be asked in order to elicit answers which will rehabilitate the witness and explain any apparent contradictions in his former testimony.

At the close of the prosecution's case, when prosecuting counsel indicates that he is calling no further witnesses, defence counsel may submit that there is no case to answer, *i.e.* that the evidence against the defendant, even if believed, is insufficient to justify a conviction, whether there is a defence case or not. The judge may accede to this submission and direct the jury to acquit the defendant.[12]

If no submission is made, or the judge rejects it, there is a considerable ramification of possibilities. Let us assume that the defendant is represented by counsel. If he is calling no other witnesses he may, if he wishes, testify after the last prosecution witness, *e.g.* denying identity. Prosecuting counsel then sums up the case for the prosecution. Defence counsel finally addresses the jury and sums up the evidence in the light of the case for the defence.

The defendant may, on the other hand, intend to call defence witnesses, *e.g.* to prove an alibi,[13] to prove that he was attacked by the victim and had to defend himself. In this event prosecuting counsel will sum up his case after the last witness for the prosecution has testified. Defence counsel will then "open" the defence, stating the defence version of the facts, which was already hinted at in his cross-examination of prosecution witnesses. The defendant himself will generally be examined "in chief" as the first witness. He need not give evidence on oath unless he wishes to do so. If he does he may then be cross-examined by prosecuting counsel and re-examined by the defence.[14] The defence counsel makes the closing speech if he wishes.[15] The prosecution should not press for a conviction at any price, but should act objectively to see that justice is done.

---

[12] An appeal is possible if the judge does not accede; *R.* v. *Abbott* [1955] 2 Q.B. 497; the submission is made in the absence of the jury, *R.* v. *Falconer-Atlee* (1973) 58 Cr.App.R. 348.

[13] Advance notice of an alibi must be given. Criminal Justice Act 1967, s.11(1); *R.* v. *Watts* (1980) 71 Cr.App.R. 136.

[14] The right to make an unsworn statement was conferred by the Criminal Evidence Act 1898 but abolished by the Criminal Justice Act 1982, s.72.

[15] Criminal Procedure (Right of Reply) Act 1964, s.1.

Evidence in rebuttal of the defence case may be given, with leave of the court, after the closing speeches.[16]

The judge is entitled to ask the witnesses questions to clear up doubts which might be left in the jury's mind. He may also stop counsel from time to time, to ensure that they confine themselves to relevant points, but counsel for the defence should not be interrupted unduly or disturbed in the presentation of the defence case, nor should the judge show that he disbelieves it.[17] The judge may occasionally himself call a witness if he believes such a person may throw light on the case.[18]

The burden of proof

After all the evidence is in, the judge will sum up and the jury give their verdict. The burden of proof is here most material, since the testimony may be conflicting.

The burden of proof in criminal cases generally rests on the prosecution. It is for them to establish positively that the crime was committed, and that the accused committed it. The jury must acquit if not fully satisfied on both points by the prosecution evidence. The defendant must be given the benefit of any serious doubt.[19]

It is not generally for the defendant to disprove guilt or prove innocence. The burden of proof does not shift after the prosecution have made out a prima facie case.[20] If the accused pleads some defence, e.g. self-defence or provocation, the burden of disproof of this defence rests on the prosecution.[21]

Under various statutes the burden of proof is shifted to the defence, e.g. where the defence pleads insanity, though in some homicide cases the prosecution can plead diminished responsibility instead, or vice versa.[22] Possession of stolen goods on an earlier occasion may be treated as proof of theft unless the new possession is otherwise accounted for.[23] Even in such cases, however, the burden upon the defence is lighter. It is sufficient if the defence can provide evidence which establishes a probability in their favour, without completely disproving guilt.[24]

[16] R. v. Owen [1952] C.L.Y. 760; R. v. Flynn (1957) 42 Cr.App.R. 15.
[17] R. v. Sainthouse [1980] Crim.L.R. 506 (C.A.).
[18] e.g. R. v. McKenna (1956) 40 Cr.App.R. 65. R. v. Wallwork (1958) 42 Cr.App.R. 153.
[19] R. v. Murtagh & Kennedy (1955) 39 Cr.App.R. 72.
[20] R. v. Bradbury [1969] 2 Q.B. 471.
[21] R. v. Abraham [1973] 1 W.L.R. 1270.
[22] R. v. Bastian [1958] 1 W.L.R. 413; R. v. Nott (1958) 43 Cr.App.R. 8; and see Homicide Act 1957, s.2(2); (1957) Crim.L.R. 711, and R. v. Podola (1960) 1 Q.B. 325; Criminal Procedure (Insanity) Act 1964, s.6.
[23] Theft Act 1968, s.27(3); cf. Coinage Offences Act 1936, s.9; Prevention of Crime Act 1953, s.1, R. v. Powell [1963] Crim.L.R. 511. Cf. John v. Humphreys [1955] 1 W.L.R. 325.
[24] R. v. Dunbar [1958] 1 Q.B. 1 (C.C.A.); R. v. Brown (1971) 115 S.J. 708 (C.A.).

The burden of proof shifts to the defence in some cases where the facts can be more easily established by the defence than the prosecution.[25]

The Summing up

Summing up is the most important function of the judge in a jury trial and he takes notes throughout the trial for the purpose. The summing-up may last for several hours in a complicated case and contains several elements.

The judge must explain to the jury the various legal principles which are involved and the way in which the evidence which they have heard is directed to these. If there has been legal argument on any disputed points of law the judge will embody his decision on these in the directions of his summing-up. In this way the verdict of the jury will be general and will conclude the case. Otherwise the jury could only give special verdicts as to specific facts which might or might not enable the judge to complete the case. If the indictment contains several counts, the judge should deal with each of them separately. He should remind the jury that they may convict or acquit separately on each count of the indictment. He should also point out that the jury may convict of offences not referred to in the indictment, *e.g.* in murder cases they may convict of manslaughter or attempted murder, though such alternatives are not joined as counts in murder indictments.[26]

The judge reminds the jury of the duty of the prosecution to prove their case. If warnings about the evidence are to be given he should make them here, *e.g.* point out that B was not cautioned before he confessed, that the testimony of A's infant son is not to be given too much weight.

The judge must refer to the main elements of the cases for the prosecution and defence. He should not influence the jury's decision but may and should point out contradictions or weaknesses in testimony. He need not refer to every point of the defence case, so long as he deals with it fairly.[27]

Where several persons are tried at the same time, the jury must be warned against inconsistent verdicts. They may generally acquit one man and convict the other, but in some cases the guilt of one depends on the guilt of the other. Thus, if X and Y are charged

[25] *e.g. R.* v. *Ewens* [1967] 1 Q.B. 322, that the defendant acquired drugs under a medical prescription; *Tynan* v. *Jones* [1975] R.T.R. 465, possession of a driving licence; *Leathley* v. *Drummond* [1972] R.T.R. 293, possession of an insurance certificate for a car; *R.* v. *Edwards* [1975] Q.B. 27, possession of a liquor licence.
[26] *Bullard* v. *R.* [1957] A.C. 635 (P.C.).
[27] *R.* v. *Olliffe* [1955] Crim.L.R. 570.

with conspiring together to defraud Z, the jury should not, generally, acquit X and convict Y.[28] Again if T is charged with stealing a ring and R with dishonestly handling it, if the jury acquit T of the theft, they cannot convict R. X cannot be convicted of being an accessory to a crime committed by either A or B if both A and B are acquitted, even if one of them must have done it but it cannot be proved which.[29]

The jury may take notes during the trial and ask questions. Any communication between judge and jury should be oral or read out in court.[30]

Withdrawal of Charges

If the prosecution offer no evidence against some person at the trial, the judge can record a verdict of "not guilty."[31] The prosecution may decide at some later stage of a trial not to ask for a conviction, and the jury can then be directed to acquit.

The Attorney General may enter a *nolle prosequi* to stop a trial at any time before conviction. A *nolle prosequi* is only entered where there is no likelihood that adequate evidence will ever be available to secure a conviction.

Verdict

The verdict is given in court by the foreman of the jury in the presence of the accused in response to the judge's question whether the jury have arrived at a verdict. The jury may first retire to consider their verdict, if they wish, and then return to the jury-box. No undue pressure should be exerted by the judge to obtain a quick verdict.[32] If another case is being tried the verdict may be given from the well of the court. The secrecy of the deliberations of the jury is important and what they say should not be published except as ground for upsetting their verdict.[33] The foreman is in theory elected by the jurors but in many cases no election takes place, the first juror sworn being treated as foreman. The foreman also acts as a spokesman for the jury on other matters, *e.g.* to ask the judge to repeat part of his direction or to refer to some item of testimony as to which the jury have no clear recollection.

[28] Criminal Law Act 1977, s.5(8); *R.* v. *Holmes* [1980] 2 All E.R. 458 (C.A.).
[29] *Surujpaul* v. *The Queen* [1958] 1 W.L.R. 1050 (P.C.).
[30] *R.* v. *Ion* (1950) 34 Cr.App.R. 152; *R.* v. *Green* [1949] 1 W.N. 488.
[31] Criminal Justice Act 1967, s.17; *Turner* v. *D.P.P.* (1978) 68 Cr.App.R. 70.
[32] *R.* v. *Rose* [1982] 3 W.L.R. 192, (H.L.).
[33] Contempt of Court Act 1981, s.8.

A majority verdict is possible, *i.e.* a verdict by ten out of eleven or twelve jurors, or nine out of ten.[34] The smaller juries refer to juries depleted during a trial.[35] The jury must deliberate for at least two hours before a majority verdict is accepted.[36] The foreman must state how many agree.[37]

The jury will sometimes convict on a less serious count because they are not quite convinced of the accused's guilt on a more serious count. If the evidence establishes a different offence, not charged in the indictment, it is sometimes necessary for the case to be retried.[38] In many cases, however, the common law or some statute permits a conviction for a different offence from that charged, provided it is expressly or impliedly included in the offence charged.[39]

In practice, convictions are sometimes commoner than acquittals, though these convictions are often for a less serious crime than the crime charged. The jury may add a rider recommending a lenient sentence, but judge and counsel should not suggest such a step to them.[40]

If there is a verdict of not guilty on all counts the accused will be at once acquitted and discharged. He may be rearrested for some other offence arising out of the same incident. But if he could have been convicted of it on the indictment or it could have been incorporated in that indictment the accused can plead "autrefois acquit" as a bar to any further proceedings. Thus an acquittal of murder is a bar to a prosecution for attempted murder.[41] An acquittal in summary proceedings also bars proceedings by indictment for the same offence.

Convictions are bars to fresh proceedings for the same offence but not a repetition of it. Continuing offences are barred up to the date of conviction.[42]

Convictions and acquittals are bars to proceedings in respect of specific offences, not in respect of particular facts. Thus a person can be convicted of robbery after an acquittal of murder during the robbery, and can be convicted of perjury for evidence which secured his acquittal of another charge.[43]

---

[34] Juries Act 1974, s.17; *R.* v. *Paley* (1976) 63 Cr.App.R. 172.
[35] *Ibid.* s.16.; *R.* v. *Richardson* [1979] Crim.L.R. 694 (C.A.).
[36] *Ibid.* s.17(4).
[37] *Ibid.* s.17(3); *R.* v. *Pigg* [1983] 1 W.L.R. 6 (H.L.).
[38] Act of 1851, s.12; *R.* v. *Springfield* (1969) 113 S.J. 670.
[39] Criminal Law Act 1967, s.6(3).
[40] *R.* v. *Black* [1963] 1 W.L.R. 1311.
[41] *R.* v. *Barron* [1914] 2 K.B. 570; Criminal Procedure Act 1851, s.28; *cf. Lloyd* v. *Roberts* (1965) 109 S.J. 850, first charge a nullity.
[42] *Edwards* v. *Bull* (1956) 54 L.G.R. 338; *R.* v. *Thomson Holidays* [1974] Q.B. 592 (C.A.).
[43] *Connelly* v. *D.P.P.* [1964] A.C. 1255; *R.* v. *Maskell* (1970) 54 Cr.App.R. 429; *D.P.P.* v. *Humphrys* [1976] 2 W.L.R. 857.

Sentence

Up to the moment of the conviction the court is concerned with discovering the facts. Thereafter, whether the accused pleaded guilty or was tried and convicted, the judge must decide on the sentence appropriate to the offender, rather than the offence. The jury may recommend mercy in their verdict, but passing sentence is the exclusive responsibility of the judge.

The judge has a record of the previous convictions of the accused available to him during the trial, though this must not be shown to the jury before their verdict. They are read out after verdict by a police officer and the convict is asked if he admits them.[44] The convict is given a copy of the Prison Commissioners' report on his suitability for a prison sentence.[45] The police also prepare reports on the family life and employment record of the accused. If these are disputed by the defence they must be proved by evidence.[46] Provision is made in certain cases for a "social inquiry" by a probation officer or other appointed person.[47] Prosecuting counsel examines the police officer and any probation officer or prison medical officer who testifies, and they may be cross-examined by the defence for admissions favourable to the convict.

The defence may call witnesses in mitigation, *e.g.* to explain provocation, temptation, or the influence of other persons over the accused. Counsel will then address the judge, pressing for a lenient sentence and bringing up anything that can be said in favour of the convict.

The convict may ask for other undetected offences to be taken into consideration. It is convenient to have all the facts as it would be uneconomic and oppressive to prosecute separately for each crime. The judge, by a convention which is traditional but has no precise legal authority, will deal with all these "considered" offences in fixing the sentence. The offences must be of the same kind as the offence actually charged, *e.g.* a series of thefts or burglaries. Technically the conviction is only for the offence charged, but the convict is never in fact prosecuted for the other offences he admitted. The effect is that he may make a fresh start on his release from prison.[48]

---

[44] "Spent" convictions are not read out; *Practice Direction* [1975] 1 W.L.R. 1065, under the Rehabilitation of Offenders Act 1974.

[45] *R.* v. *Wintle* [1959] C.L.Y. 806; *Practice Note* [1959] 2 All E.R. 734 (C.C.A.).

[46] *R.* v. *Campbell* (1911) 6 Cr.App.R. 131; *Practice Direction* [1966] 1 W.L.R. 1185 (C.C.A.); *R.* v. *Dwyer* (1974) 60 Cr.App.R. 39.; *R.* v. *Wilkins*; (1977) 66 Cr.App.R. 49, (C.A.).

[47] Powers of Criminal Courts Act, 1973, s.45.; Criminal Justice Act 1982, s.62.

[48] *R.* v. *Webb* (1935) 37 Cr.App.R. 82; [1959] Crim.L.R. 18, 197; *R.* v. *Davies* [1981] Crim.L.R. 192.

A court cannot take into consideration offences which are outside its jurisdiction, *e.g.* a court trying an indictment should not take purely summary offences into consideration.[49] Certain sentences, *e.g.* probation, can only be imposed with the consent of the convicted person.[50]

The convict must be present when sentence is pronounced.[51] There must be a distinct sentence on each count of the indictment on which he is convicted. It is usual to make the sentences run concurrently. Sometimes the court directs that the sentences should be consecutive, with the result that the statutory maximum sentence for any one of the offences may be exceeded.[52]

The court may vary or rescind a sentence or other order, after a trial on indictment within 28 days,[53] and it may also defer passing sentence for six months, to consider how the defendant behaves.[54]

Punishment

The fact that a sentence is aimed to suit the character of the convict himself makes it impossible to lay down any lines of policy in sentencing which refer solely to the circumstances of the offence. A judge will take these into account as well, *e.g.* whether the convict betrayed a trust, whether the injuries done were serious, whether he was guilty of brutality. His past record and likelihood of reform are relevant. A hardened criminal will be treated more severely than a duped accomplice. However, if two offenders are equally guilty the fact that one has a worse previous record may not in itself justify differentiation of sentences. The welfare of others may be taken into account, *e.g.* where both parents could be sent to prison, but their children would suffer.

Mandatory sentences are unusual but in murder cases life imprisonment must be imposed.[55]

If a crime is created by statute and no sentence is prescribed, the maximum sentence is two years' imprisonment.[56]

---

[49] *R.* v. *Simons & Simons* [1953] 1 W.L.R. 1014.
[50] See p. 152.
[51] *R.* v. *Lloyd* [1958] C.L.Y. 784.
[52] *Practice Direction* [1959] 1 W.L.R. 491 (C.C.A.); *R.*v. *Blake* [1962] 2 Q.B. 377 (C.C.A.); *R.* v. *Faulkner* (1972) 56 Cr.App.R. 594.
[53] *Customs and Excise Commissioners* v. *Menocal* (1979) 123 S.J. 372 (H.L.).
[54] Supreme Court Act 1981, s.47; Powers of Criminal Courts Act 1973, s.1; Criminal Law Act 1977, Sched. 12; *R.* v. *Jacobs* (1975) 62 Cr.App.R. 116; *R.* v. *Smith* (1976) 64 Cr.App.R. 116; *cf. R.* v. *Annesley* [1976] 1 W.L.R. 106 (C.A.).
[55] Murder (Abolition of Death Penalty) Act 1965; the court may recommend a minimum period to be served *ibid.* s.1(2). *R.* v. *Aitken* [1966] 1 W.L.R. 1076.
[56] Powers of Criminal Courts Act 1973, s.18. This is seldom required.

Common law misdemeanours have no definite sentence and may be punished by a fine or imprisonment. Imprisonment for these should not normally be for more than two years.[57]

Most offences are statutory and the statute prescribes a maximum punishment but sentences in practice are usually below the maximum.

About one-third of all sentences after trials on indictment are to terms of imprisonment of various kinds. typical sentences range from six months to two years. Overcrowding of prisons has led to a trend to avoid or reduce prison sentences, as has industrial action by prison officers.[58] A "life" sentence is considerably shorter in fact as it is reviewed from time to time.[59] Persons under 21 cannot be imprisoned but may be sentenced to youth custody for a corresponding period.[60] Persons over 21 should not normally be sentenced to imprisonment for a first offence.[61] Provision is made for a prisoner to earn remission of a third of the term during service of sentence, by hard work and good behaviour.[62] The court must not, however, consider this possibility in advance and increase the sentence. The Home Secretary may remit part of a sentence for special causes.[63]

Sentences to not over two years may be suspended unless the offender commits another offence punishable with imprisonment.[64] The period of suspension specified in the order may be from one to two years.[65] On committing another serious offence the sentence or part of it may be revived.[66] Part of a sentence may also be suspended.[67]

If a man accused of a serious offence were convicted, say, of some type of assault, but acquitted of more serious charges, he might be punished by a fine. Fines are fairly common in procedure by indictment.[68] There is no maximum but they must not be

---

[57] See *Verrier* v. *D.P.P.* [1967] 2 A.C. 195 (H.L.).
[58] *R. v. Upton* (1980) 124 S.J. 359; *cf.* Imprisonment (Temporary Provisions) Act 1980 on alternative places of detention. Criminal Justice Act 1982, s.32 foresees early release of all but the most serious offenders from time to time.
[59] Twelve years is typical. Life sentences should only rarely be imposed in cases other than murder, *R. v. Picker* [1970] 2 Q.B. (6) (C.A.); *R. v. Caroline Johnson* (1982) 4 Cr.App.R. 143.
[60] Criminal Justice Act 1982 ss.1(1), 6, 7.
[61] Act of 1973 ss.20, 20A (1982), Criminal Justice Act 1982, s.62.
[62] Prison Act 1952, s.25(1); Prison Rules 1964–81.
[63] *R. v. Maguire* (1956) 40 Cr.App.R. 92.
[64] Powers of Criminal Courts Act 1973, s.22.
[65] *Ibid.* s.22(1).
[66] *Ibid* s.23; Criminal Justice Act 1982, s.31.
[67] Criminal Law Act 1977, s.47 (quarter to three-quarter Criminal Justice Act 1982, s.30).
[68] Criminal Justice Act 1977, s.32; 8,500 cases out of 77,000 cases of convictions on indictment in 1981.

excessive in the light of the offender's means.[69] They are also suitable where corporations are convicted as these cannot be imprisoned. Fines constitute a civil debt to the Crown and are also recoverable from the estate of a deceased convict.[70] A large fine may be substituted for a sentence of imprisonment on grounds of the prisoner's ill health.[71] A fine may be imposed as well as imprisonment.[72] A pre-fixed term of not more than 2 years' imprisonment and proportionate to the amount of the fine may be directed as an alternative if the fine is not paid, but only imposed if the convict can afford to pay.[73]

Probation is coming to be used in a fair proportion of sentences on indictment.[74] Probation subjects the convicted person to certain restrictions, *e.g.* he may be required to report to a probation officer, do or refrain from doing various things, or to avoid the company of certain persons. This sentence is available to the court on a conviction for any offence other than murder[75] but it is not commonly used in serious cases. It is useful where the convict has no previous convictions and is not a professional criminal, but is also sometimes used in other cases. The actual operation of the system is left to the magistrates' courts, who appoint probation committees to supervise the work of the probation officers.[76] The offender must consent to the order being made and to co-operate with the probation officer. If its terms are violated he may be summoned before the local magistrates' court and recommitted for sentence by the Crown Court; if he commits another offence he will be dealt with by the later court on both offences.[77] The judge has a number of alternative powers in such cases.[78] If the terms of the probation are kept, no "conviction" is considered to have occurred for the purpose of any later proceedings in which previous convictions are material, *e.g.* to increase the possible sentence, but an appeal against conviction is possible.[79]

---

[69] *R.* v. *Churchill* [1967] 1 Q.B. 190; *R.* v. *Tester* [1969] Crim.L.R. 214; *R.* v. *Khan* [1982] 1 W.L.R. 1405 (E.A.T.).

[70] *Treasury* v. *Harris* [1957] 2 Q.B. 516; *Dawes* v. *I.R.C.* [1965] 1 W.L.R. 323.

[71] *R.* v. *Miller & Hanoman* [1958] C.L.Y. 787.

[72] Powers of Criminal Courts Act 1973, s.30.

[73] *Ibid.* s.31(2), (3), (3A) (1982); persons under 21 are liable to a corresponding period of detention, Criminal Justice Act 1982, s.9.

[74] 5,000 cases in the Crown Courts in 1981.

[75] Powers of Criminal Courts Act 1973, s.2; (4A) (1982), the currency of the order is 6 months to three years.

[76] Powers of Criminal Courts Act 1973. Sched. 3 (amd. 1982).

[77] Powers of Criminal Courts Act 1973, s.8(7); *R.* v. *Slatter* [1975] 1 W.L.R. 1084.

[78] *Ibid.* s.6(2), (3).

[79] *Ibid.* s.13(1); Criminal Appeal Act 1968, s.50 (amd. 1982).

An absolute or conditional discharge may be given, *e.g.* conditional on the accused not committing any other offence for a specified period not exceeding three years.[80] A discharge of this kind is not technically a conviction except for the purpose of an appeal, but is a bar to any other prosecution for the offence.[81]

Persistent offenders may be given extended terms of imprisonment.[82] The instant offence must be punishable with at least two years. The effect is that the sentence may exceed the normal maximum period.[83] The offender must have a history of several previous convictions or aggregate lengths of imprisonment.[84]

By "community service orders" a convicted person of 16 or over may, with his consent, be ordered to do useful unpaid work in lieu of punishment for from 40 to 240 hours.[85]

Articles used to commit a crime, *e.g.* house breaking equipment and get-away cars, may be forfeited,[86] but this does not extend to land, *e.g.* a house in which a crime was committed or in which the proceeds of crimes are kept.[87]

Prisoners may be released on licence after they have served a third of their sentence or 12 months, whichever expires first. The Home Secretary is advised by a Parole Board.[88] Persons sentenced to life imprisonment are subject to special restrictions in this connection.[89] The licence may be revoked if necessary to protect the public or if the person on parole commits another crime. Young short-term prisoners may be subjected to supervision after release.[90]

Convictions are treated as "spent" and not generally material after specified subsequent periods of good behaviour by the offender.[91]

---

[80] *Ibid.* s.2.
[81] *Ibid.* ss.7, 13(1), n. 79.
[82] Powers of Criminal Courts Act 1973, s.28(1).
[83] *Ibid.* s.28(2).
[84] *Ibid.* s.28(3).
[85] *Ibid.* s.14 Criminal Justice Act 1982, s.68 and Sched. 12. Crown courts made 6,000 such orders in 1981.
[86] *R.* v. *Ackers* [1977] R.T.R. 66 (C.A.); *cf. Solomon* v. *Metropolitan Police Commissioner* [1982] Crim.L.R. 606, car bought with proceeds of theft is "stolen" within Theft Act 1968, s.24(2); *cf. R.* v. *Cuthbertson* [1981] A.C. 470 (H.L.), proceeds of sale of drugs not forfeitable.
[87] *R.* v. *Khan* [1982] 1 W.L.R. 1405.
[88] Criminal Justice Act 1967 ss.59, 60, 62.
[89] *Ibid.* s.61.
[90] *Ibid.* ss.62, 63.
[91] Rehabilitation of Offenders Act 1974, s.4; *Practice Direction* [1975] 1 W.L.R. 1065; *Property Guards* v. *Taylor & Kershaw* [1982] 1 R.L.R. 175 (E.A.T.).

Appeals

A person convicted on indictment may under certain conditions appeal to the criminal division of the Court of Appeal (formerly the Court of Criminal Appeal).[92] The court consists when trying appeals against conviction of at least three judges, who may be Lords Justices of Appeal or judges of the High Court required to sit at the request of the Lord Chief Justice.[93]

An appeal on a point of law may be taken without leave. This includes misdirection of the jury as to the law, and wrongful admission or exclusion of evidence which might have influenced the jury. Appeals on points of law are not very common.[94] The court may substitute a verdict of guilty of a different offence if the view of the jury clearly was that he was guilty of that offence.[95]

There is a right to appeal to the Court of Appeal against a finding of unfitness to plead[96] and against a finding of not guilty by reason of insanity.[97]

Leave is required before an appeal can be taken from conviction on the facts or from sentence. A defendant who intends to appeal against conviction or sentence may ask the trial court for a certificate of leave to appeal, and this course has certain advantages, but few such certificates are obtained.[98] The more usual procedure is to apply to a single appellate judge for leave to appeal against conviction.[99] If he refuses leave the application may be heard by three judges.[1]

Leave to appeal is applied for in a fraction of the cases,[2] not unnaturally being relatively most common after conviction for murder. Grounds of appeal must be stated. Most of them simply repeat the convict's original defence or claim that the accused was wrongly persuaded to plead guilty. To discourage futile appeals sentence may be prolonged where leave is refused.[3]

The appeal court may set aside a conviction if it seems to them unsafe or unsatisfactory or there has been a material irregularity at the trial.[4]

---

[92] Criminal Appeals Act 1968, s.1; Supreme Court Act 1981, ss.3(1), 3(2), the Lord Chief Justice is its President.
[93] Supreme Court Act 1981, ss.53(2), 55; the trial judge is excluded, s.56(2).
[94] There are no statistics however.
[95] Criminal Appeal Act 1968, s.3.
[96] Criminal Appeal Act 1968, s.15.
[97] *Ibid.* s.12.
[98] *Ibid.* s.1(2), 11 (1A) (1982).
[99] *Ibid.* s.31(2)(*a*); Criminal Appeal Rules, r. 11.
[1] *Ibid.* s.31(3); r. 12, Form 15.
[2] In 1981, 5,822 applications, 1400 heard, out of 77,000 convictions.
[3] *Practice Direction* [1980] 1 W.L.R. 270.
[4] Act of 1968, s.2; Criminal Law Act 1977, s.44.

No new defence can be raised which was not raised in the court below. Fresh evidence cannot be adduced by the appellant unless relevant and credible and not procurable earlier, *e.g.* a new witness is found whose existence was not previously known, or a witness not compellable to testify now volunteers to do so.[5] No evidence of facts occurring since the trial is admissible for the defence.[6] The respondents, on the other hand, can support the conviction by such evidence, *e.g.* an admission of guilt in a letter sent to a third party by the convict in prison.[7]

The court has a general power to dismiss an appeal even if it finds that a technical irregularity has been committed, if no miscarriage of justice has occurred, *e.g.* if some inadmissible evidence was received, but the evidence against the accused was very strong without it, or if the summing-up was somewhat defective but the accused's guilt fully established. This is known as "The Proviso."[8] Appeals with no real merit can also be disposed of summarily without a hearing.[9]

The hearing of an appeal is generally open to the public.[10] Each side is usually represented by counsel, though the appellant is also entitled to attend.[11] If the appeal is on a point of pure law there will be legal argument only. If the ground is the wrongful admission or exclusion of evidence, the court will be supplied with a note of the evidence in question. If the ground is that the verdict was against the weight of the evidence the whole of the shorthand note of the testimony will have to be transcribed. The cost of this is seldom justified, in view of the court's reluctance to upset verdicts on facts. The judge's summing-up will generally be transcribed, and his own notes made during the case will be available.[12]

The court has no general power to order a new trial so as to obtain the verdict of another jury, unless the first trial was a nullity, or fresh evidence is admitted.[13] This means that if, for example, some improper evidence was admitted or the summing-up was misleading, the convict must have his conviction quashed

---

[5] Criminal Appeal Act 1968, s.23; *R. v. Ditch* (1969) 53 Cr.App.R. 627 (C.A.); *R. v. Lomas* [1969] 1 W.L.R. 306; *R. v. Lattimore* (1975) 62 Cr.App.R. 53.
[6] *R. v. Thomas* [1959] 1 W.L.R. 1086.
[7] *R. v. Robinson* [1917] 2 K.B. 108.
[8] Criminal Appeal Act 1968, s.2(1) proviso. *Stirland* v. *D.P.P.* [1944] A.C. 315; *R. v. Samuel* (1956) 40 Cr.App.R. 85; *R. v. Hallam* [1957] 1 Q.B. 569; *R. v. Thomas* [1957] 1 W.L.R. 1091; *R. v. Folley* [1978] Crim.L.R. 556 (C.A.).
[9] *Ibid.* s.20.
[10] *Ibid.* s.23(4), r. 9(2); *R. v. Stafford* [1972] 1 W.L.R. 1649 (C.A.).
[11] *Ibid.* s.22.
[12] Criminal Appeal Act 1968, s.32, Criminal Appeal Rules, rr. 18–20; *R. v. Le Caer* (1972) 56 Cr.App.R. 727; *R. v. Kluczynski* [1973] 1 W.L.R. 1230; *R. v. Campbell* (1981) 7 C.L. 352a.
[13] *R. v. Gee* [1936] 2 K.B. 442; see Tucker Report (1954) Cmd. 9150; Criminal Appeal Act 1968, ss.7, 23.

and will escape punishment, even if his guilt might still be established by a second trial. The "proviso"[14] may be used to prevent such a result, but it would not be applied where there was real doubt as to the convict's guilt. It is argued, against granting the court power to order a new trial, that the man should not be put in jeopardy twice for the same offence. This reflects the same notion as the plea of "autrefois convict." The argument, however, has little merit. The new trial would be part of the same proceedings and not a new proceeding. There is ample precedent for retrial of criminals, *e.g.* where a jury disagree on a verdict, or are discharged before verdict because inadmissible evidence has been given, and where the Crown Courts hear appeals from convictions by magistrates' courts. It is argued that the second jury would know about the accused's previous convictions, which are read out before sentence in the first trial, but this is unlikely after a time. The retrial would not be held at the same sessions, in case the new jury had attended the first trial.[15] One of the few advantages of the present system is the meticulous care required of the prosecution, as they know a serious irregularity will lead to an appeal and a guilty man may escape.

In appeals based on fresh evidence the appeal court has a discretion and may order a new trial when quashing a conviction, instead of directing an acquittal.[16] The case is re-tried by the original court unless the appeal court directs trial by another court.[17] If the convict is again found guilty the sentence may not be more severe than that originally imposed.[18]

A convict may apply for leave to appeal against sentence unless it is fixed by law, whether or not he is appealing against conviction and even if he pleaded guilty.[19] Such applications are much commoner than applications for leave to appeal against conviction.[20] The court will not interfere with the sentence unless the trial judge has approached the problem on the wrong lines or the sentence is very excessive. The appeal court cannot increase the sentence as a whole, although it may increase a sentence on one charge, *e.g.* where it quashes others.[21]

The granting of leave to appeal shows that the application may have some merit, and about half the convictions appealed against are ultimately reversed. Judgment of acquittal is then entered.[22]

---

[14] *Supra*, n.8.
[15] This is very unlikely under the latest jury system.
[16] Criminal Appeal Act 1968, s.7; *R.* v. *Saunders* (1973) 58 Cr.App.R. 248.
[17] Criminal Appeal Act 1968, s.8(1), as amended by Courts Act 1971.
[18] *Ibid.* s.8(4), Sched. 2(2).
[19] *Ibid.* s.9.
[20] In 1981 4,800 applications were against sentence only, 1,000 against conviction.
[21] Act of 1968, s.11(3).
[22] Act of 1968, s.2(3).

Sentences are often reduced by the court. The small effect of appeals proves the stability of criminal procedure.[23]

A single judgment is delivered in this court, representing the opinion of at least two of the three judges. If there is a dissenting opinion it is not read unless the presiding judge considers it convenient to do so.[24] Judgments are seldom reserved in practice.

It is possible to take a further appeal to the House of Lords from the decision of the appeal court.[25] This appeal is possible from a reversal of a conviction as well as from its affirmation, though no appeal from an acquittal at the trial is allowed. Only a few criminal cases are appealed to the Lords each year[26] but they prove to be of great importance in deciding the principles of law, procedure and evidence to be applied by all courts. The procedure is in two stages. First the appeal court must be asked to certify that a point of law of general public importance is involved, the appellant stating the point of law which he wishes to be certified.[27] The second stage is an application to the appeal court for leave to appeal to the House of Lords, but an application can be made to the House if the appeal court refuses.[28] A convicted person may apply to the Home Secretary for a pardon if no possibility of appeal remains.[29] The Home Secretary may refer the matter to the Court of Appeal.[30]

A reference may be made, where a person has been acquitted, by the Attorney-General to the Court of Appeal, and also a further reference to the House of Lords. The decision does not re-open the acquittal.[31]

Preliminary Reference under EEC Treaty

Where a judge of a Crown Court or the Court of (Criminal) Appeal finds that he cannot arrive at his judgment without resolving some difficulty of interpretation of the treaties governing

---

[23] In 1981 only one-tenth of convictions appealed against were quashed and one-fifth of sentences quashed or varied.

[24] Supreme Court Act 1981, s.59; no dissenting judgments appear in recent law reports.

[25] Criminal Appeal Act 1968, s.33. At least three Lords of Appeal must take part, s.35.

[26] 15 Cases in 1981. See p. 249 for the composition of the House of Lords.

[27] Criminal Appeal Act 1968, ss.33(2), Criminal Appeal Rules, r. 23(1), Form 17 *Practice Direction* (H.L.) (1979) 123 S.J. 324; *R. v. Taaffe* (1983) 4 C.L. 343.

[28] Act of 1968, s.34(1); *R. v. Cooper* (1975) 61 Cr.App.R. 215.

[29] Criminal Law Act 1967, s.9.

[30] Criminal Appeal Act 1968, s.17; *Stafford* v. *D.P.P.* [1974] A.C. 878.

[31] Criminal Justice Act 1972, s.36; *Re Att.-Gen. References* [1974] Q.B. 744, [1975] Q.B. 773, esp. at p. 778 *per* Lord Widgery, L.C.J., to prevent wrong legal rulings becoming accepted *cf.* [1981] 1 W.L.R. 148 (C.A.), policeman signed deponent's name to statement; [1981] 1 W.L.R. 705 (C.A.) one of two acts by accused caused death but it was uncertain which.

the European Economic Community, he may refer the point to the European Court for decision before deciding the case.[32]

SUMMARY PROCEEDINGS

General Procedure

Summary proceedings, *i.e.* trials of offences by a magistrate or magistrates, as contrasted with trials with a jury, are of great importance in the day-to-day administration of the legal system. Several million cases are tried annually. Most of these cases concern minor criminal offences but there is also a civil jurisdiction, mainly concerned with family matters. The explanation for this jurisdiction lies in the history of the justices of the peace or (lay) magistrates, as they are now described, on whom a constant succession of statutes has imposed judicial and semi-judicial duties.

Summary jurisdiction is entirely the product of statute. General matters of procedure and the constitution of courts are now regulated by a few consolidating Acts, but much magisterial law must be sought in individual Acts conferring jurisdiction on magistrates to try particular offences.

The jurisdiction of justices to try non-indictable crimes developed gradually and unsystematically. It was recognised that many minor offences did not justify a full-dress trial, though various safeguards exist under which trial by jury may be claimed in some cases. Many indictable offences may also conveniently be tried summarily, by arrangements to which reference will be made later, and in practice the great majority of indictable cases are so tried, which speaks well for the standing of magistrates' courts.

The term "summary procedure" is best illustrated by considering, in contrast, how the justices act as examining justices inquiring into an indictable offence. There, if the accused is committed for trial he may have to wait for some time in custody or on bail. He will then be tried by a judge with a jury at some length and the possible sentence may be severe. If, on the other hand, the offence may be dealt with "summarily" the same justices may hear the evidence and finally dispose of the case without delay or without more than a short adjournment, and will impose a

---

[32] Treaty of Rome, Art. 177; *Henn & Darby* v. *D.P.P.* [1980] 2 W.L.R. 597 (H.L.); *R.* v. *Plymouth Justices, ex p. Rogers* [1982] 3 W.L.R. 1 (D.C.). The procedure in England is laid down by Crown Court and Criminal Appeal (References to the European Court) Rules 1972. Only a highest court of appeal is obliged to make such a reference, and a judge cannot in any case be forced to find that a difficulty of interpretation exists.

lighter sentence. The actual hearing is not cut short in any way, though most summary offences by their nature can be fully heard in a much shorter time than the more complicated cases.

There is a six-month time limit for prosecutions.[33]

A summary case

Road traffic offences make up three-quarters of summary offences. In most of them summary trial is invariable.

Highway cases general commence with police action. If the police report justifies criminal prosecution, a summons will have to be served by a policeman on the defendant, in this case within the short period of fourteen days, or a notice of prosecution served within that time unless he was warned at the time of the offence.[34]

The police officer lays an information in closed court before the local bench of magistrates for the magistrates' courts district in which the offence occurred, assuming there is no professional magistrate.[35] The information is usually oral and states in simple language the offence which the defendant is alleged to have committed.[36] If the magistrate so decides, the summons will be issued, on the lines of the information.[37] Proceedings cannot then be dropped without leave of the bench.[38]

The summons must identify the date and place of the offence and the statutory provision under which it is brought. It must also inform the defendant as to the place, date and time at which he must appear.[39]

A summons may be served on the defendant by a policeman, or left at his house in such circumstances that he is sure to receive it. There is also a procedure by post but this is only effective on proof of receipt by the defendant unless it was registered or sent by recorded delivery.[40]

It is not generally known in advance whether the defendant intends to appear or defend the charge. Some clerks to magistrates write to defendants asking them whether they propose to appear. If personal appearance is essential the defendant should be warned, to avoid adjournments. He may appear personally or by

---

[33] Magistrates' Courts Act 1980, s.127.
[34] Road Traffic Act 1972, ss.180, 179(2).
[35] Magistrates' Courts Act, 1980, s.1(1). A justices' clerk may act, Justices of the Peace Act 1979, s.28; Magistrates' Courts Act 1980, s.127; R. v. *Manchester Stipendiary Magistrate* [1982] 3 W.L.R. 331 (H.L.).
[36] Magistrates' Courts Rules 1981, r. 4.
[37] *Ibid.* 98; R. v. *Brentford Justices,* [1975] Q.B. 455 (D.C.); R. v. *Fairford Justices* [1976] Q.B. 600; R. v. *West London Justices* [1979] 2 All E.R. 221 (D.C.).
[38] R. v. *Redbridge Justices, ex. p. Sainty* [1981] R.T.R. 13 (D.C.).
[39] r. 98(2) details of the charge may be given, Criminal Law Act 1977, s.48.
[40] Magistrates' Courts Act 1980, s.145.

solicitor or counsel.[41] An absent or unrepresented defendant cannot generally be sentenced to imprisonment.[42] The attendance of the police officer will be necessary in any case. The defendant is not excused from appearance in court because the summons has formal defects, *e.g.* misspelling of his name or giving the wrong date for the offence, though he may apply for an adjournment while the summons is amended.[43]

Where the court does not pass a sentence of imprisonment the case may proceed in the absence of the defendant, *e.g.* many motoring offences are committed some distance away from the motorist's home and the cost of fares and loss of working time would be more expensive than any probable fine. The defendant may be required, however, to send his driving licence to the court, since the court is under an obligation to indorse it in many cases and may do so in others.[44]

The defendant may plead guilty by letter, if he is sent a statement of the facts to be presented by the prosecution. He may also send, in writing, a statement of any mitigating circumstances. These statements may be read in court if he does not attend the hearing.[45] If any previous convictions are to be referred to after conviction, written advance notice of this must be sent to the defendant.[46] If the court, in the event, decides to sentence the defendant to imprisonment or to disqualify him from driving it must adjourn the case, so that he may appear and oppose this.[47]

A form of on-the-spot fine is also possible. In certain minor cases the defendant has the option of paying a fixed penalty instead of attending court.[48] This procedure is being introduced area by area.

In purely summary cases the court must grant bail if the defendant is in custody, unless he has previously dishonoured bail or, in the case of prisonable offences, certain conditions are present.[49]

---

[41] *Ibid.* s.122.

[42] Criminal Justice Act 1967, s.26; Powers of Criminal Courts Act 1973, s.21.

[43] Magistrates' Courts Act 1980, s.123(2); *R.* v. *Newcastle-upon-Tyne Justices* [1976] 1 W.L.R. 517 (D.C.).

[44] Road Traffic Act 1972, s.101(4), Magistrates' Courts Rules, 1981, r. 32.

[45] Magistrates' Courts Act 1980, s.12; *R.* v. *Oldham Justices* [1959] 1 W.L.R. 58. This applies only to purely summary offences with limited punishments, s.1(2)(iii). The appropriate forms are given in the 1968 Forms Rules, rr. 29, 30; the accused cannot claim jury trial in such cases, *ex p. Shields* (1969) 113 S.J. 124.

[46] *Ibid.* s.104; previous convictions and pending charges must be kept from the court until after conviction; *R.* v. *Liverpool City Justices* [1983] 1 W.L.R. 119 (D.C.).

[47] *Ibid.* s.11; the court must disqualify the driver in certain cases; Road Traffic Act 1972, s.93.

[48] Road Traffic Regulation Act 1967, s.80; Fixed Penalty Regulations 1974–75.

[49] Bail Act 1976, s.4, Sched. 1.

The hearing

The courts open about 10 a.m. and the daily cause list is screened in the corridor. The hearing is generally public.[50] The defendant may ask for an adjournment if he needs more time to find witnesses and prepare his case.[51]

The magistrates' clerk first reads the charge and asks how the defendant pleads. If he pleads not guilty the police solicitor or counsel then examines the informant and other witnesses as to the facts of the case. The defendant is entitled to cross-examine the informant. The defendant may then testify on his own behalf and give his version of the case.[52] He may also submit that there is no case to answer.[53] Written statements may be used, if the other side does not object, to save producing witnesses.[54]

In the case of some summary offences the burden of proof of innocence is thrown by the relevant statute on to the defendant, e.g. if foreign matter is found in food, or bread is shortweight.[55]

Lay justices

Many offences are tried by lay magistrates. At least two lay justices of the peace must sit for the trial of such cases. The maximum number is regulated by rules[56] but the normal maximum is five, with two justices on each side of the chairman. This facilitates easy consultation on the bench before deciding whether or not to convict. The justices may also retire to discuss their decision.

The justices on local benches of magistrates are generally laymen who receive an allowance for expenses and loss of earnings.[57] The justices of each petty sessional division are appointed by the Lord Chancellor on the recommendation of local advisory committees.[58] Each county in England and Wales has a single commission of the peace, to which magistrates are appointed.[59] The counties are sub-divided into petty sessional

---

[50] R. v. Denbigh Justices [1974] Q.B. 759; there are exceptions for cases of state secrets.
[51] Magistrates' Courts Act 1980, s.10.
[52] Magistrates' Courts Rules 1981, r. 13; Simms v. Moore [1970] 2 Q.B. 327.
[53] Disher v. Disher [1965] P. 31; Practice Direction [1962] C.L.Y. 1876.
[54] Criminal Justice Act 1967, s.9, Magistrates' Courts Rules 1981, r. 70.
[55] Chingford Borough Council v. Gwalter (1959) 124 J.P. 21, under the Food and Drugs Act 1955; Read v. West Wales Bakeries (1962) 60 L.G.R. 515 (D.C.) under the Bread Order 1953.
[56] Justices of the Peace Act 1979, s.18.
[57] Justices of the Peace Act 1979, s.12.
[58] Ibid. s.6; Administration of Justice Act 1982, s.65.
[59] Justices of the Peace Act 1979, ss.1, 4; London has five.

divisions and areas.[60] About one-third of the justices of the peace are members of local authorities.[61]

As courts generally sit during business hours it is difficulty for employed persons and owners of one-man businesses to sit as justices. The tendency is for the older men and women to sit, and to sit part-time only. After attaining the age of seventy, however, a justice can no longer sit on the bench.[62] He may also be directed not to sit if he is incapable or neglects his duties.[63] The same applies if he is found to have committed irregularities or acted unjudicially, but he will be given an opportunity by the Lord Chancellor to meet such charges.[64] In recent times attempts have been made to lower the average age of magistrates and to broaden the social and economic make-up of the bench. Justices and their clerks are entitled to an indemnity out of local funds in cases where they have acted reasonably and in good faith but damages or costs have been recovered against them in any proceedings in connection with their official duties.[65]

Magistrates elect a chairman for the division each year by secret ballot, to take general charge of all the courts.[66] If magistrates have to hold courts in two or three court rooms the other benches may be presided over by the deputy chairmen.[67]

The clerk

If any legal point or procedural problem arises, the bench is assisted by the clerk to the magistrates. The clerk performs many routine duties. He sees that all summonses are in proper time and in proper form. He swears the witnesses. He generally takes a longhand note of the substance of all testimony.[68] He must be a barrister or solicitor of at least five years' standing[69] and is generally a solicitor. The clerk is appointed by the magistrates' courts committee for the county, on which the various petty sessional divisions are represented, and not by the local bench, and the Home Secretary must confirm the appointment.[70] The justices of the local division ought to be consulted, but this does

---

[60] *Ibid.* s.4.

[61] Justices of the Peace Act 1979, s.64, disqualifies them from sitting where the local authority is itself interested in the case.

[62] Justices of the Peace Act 1979, s.8(1); judges may act until aged 75 if also JPs.

[63] *Ibid.* s.8(4).

[64] *Ibid.* s.6(1). Justices have been removed for refusing to enforce a statute and asked to resign for meeting an applicant for a liquor licence privately. See also *Iwi* v. *Montesole* [1955] Crim.L.R. 313; *The Times*, March 8–15, 1955; (1955) 71 L.Q.R. 335.

[65] *Ibid.* s.53. The local magistrates' courts committee decides the questions with an appeal to a person appointed for the purpose by the Lord Chancellor.

[66] *Ibid.* s.17.

[67] *Ibid.* s.17.

[68] He has received further powers, Justices of the Peace Act 1979, s.28.

[69] *Ibid.* s.26.

[70] *Ibid.* s.25; s.20 regulates the Magistrates' Courts Committee.

not appear to be essential if the appointment is in fact confirmed.[71] Some clerkships are part-time but in very busy courts the position is a full-time appointment.[72]

The clerk should not take an active part in making decisions; his role is to advise the bench whether they have jurisdiction, whether any point of law or procedure arises, and as to the rule of law governing the matter.[73] The bench may send for the clerk if they require his advice in the retiring room, but should not retire or return with him.[74]

The decision

If the magistrates dismiss the case the defendant will be discharged. The bench may dismiss some charges and convict on others, usually less serious. They may not convict of a lesser offence but may allow a different charge to be made. If the magistrates decide to convict the defendant they will briefly announce that the case is proved and ask what is known about him. The police will then report on previous convictions (including those no longer indorsed on his present driving licence). The defendant may be heard in mitigation of sentence, *e.g.* if his past record is good.

The appropriate sentence is then considered. The clerk may advise the court as to maximum sentences and cite typical sentences by other benches. Imprisonment is limited to six months, and fines to £200.[75] A common sentence is to a small standard fine and payment of the prosecution's costs. The fine is paid to the magistrates' clerk. Time may be allowed on the defendant's establishing grounds for temporary inability to pay.[76] Defaulters are not imprisoned unless they have the means to pay the fine and it cannot otherwise be enforced.[77]

Lay character

There is some criticism of entrusting the responsibilities of magistrates to men and women without legal training, even though assisted by a clerk. Many magistrates, however, are lawyers or have studied law, and regular provision is now made for courses of instruction for lay magistrates.[78] Magistrates' courts committees organise lectures by professional lawyers which new magistrates

---

[71] Justices of the Peace Act 1979, s.25(3).
[72] *Cf. ibid.* s.27(5).
[73] *Ibid.* s.28(3); *Practice Direction* [1981] 1 W.L.R. 1163.
[74] *R. v. Southampton Justices* [1974] Crim.L.R. 108; *cf. R. v. Aberdare Justices* [1973] Crim.L.R. 45; *R. v. Worley Justices ex p. Nash* (1982) 8 C.L. 170 (D.C.).
[75] Magistrates' Courts Act 1980, ss.31, 34(3).
[76] *Ibid.* s.75.
[77] *Ibid.* s.82.
[78] *Ibid.* s.63(5). As to professional magistrates, see pp. 165, 166.

attend on appointment. A National Advisory Council on the Training of Magistrates has also been set up.[79] The senior magistrates have generally learned by experience enough of the principles involved in their work. Their real task is to be judicious judges, not technical experts.

Alternative Procedures

Some offences may only be tried by jury on indictment and may be severely punished.[80] Others are purely summary in character and more leniently treated.[81] There are a number of offences, however, which can be tried "either way," depending on the circumstances of the case and the previous record of the accused.[82] Some of these were created "hybrids" by a statute providing for alternative forms of trial; others are in principle indictable but there is statutory provision for summary trial.

The right to claim jury trial for some purely summary offences has been abolished.[83]

The magistrates who first hear a case must, where it can be tried "either way," provisionally select either to enquire into it as examining justices[84] or try it summarily themselves. They will hear the views of prosecution and defence on this.[85] Their decision to proceed to a preliminary examination is final, but if they decide to try the case themselves the consent of the accused is required. He must be warned that they may opt for jury trial where the law so allows and that he may, after summary conviction, be committed for sentence to the Crown Court if a more severe sentence is indicated by his previous record then made available to the court,[86] than the court has power to impose.

In a number of cases only summary trial is possible if the amount involved does not exceed £200; the maximum sentence will then be three months' imprisonment or a £500 fine.[87]

Where an offence triable "either way" is tried summarily the maximum fine is £1,000,[88] but this limit may be raised by the Secretary of State.[89]

---

[79] [1964] C.L.Y. 2306.
[80] See *ante*, p. 130.
[81] See *ante*, p. 158.
[82] Magistrates' Courts Act 1980, s.17, Sched. 1.
[83] Criminal Law Act 1977, ss.15, 30, 31, Sched. 1.
[84] *Ante*, p. 134.
[85] Magistrates' Courts Act 1980, s.19.
[86] *Ibid.* s.20.
[87] *Ibid.* ss.22, 33; *R.* v. *Leicester Justices, ex p. Lord* [1980] Crim.L.R. 581 (D.C.).
[88] Magistrates' Courts Act 1980, s.32.
[89] *Ibid.* s.143.

Stipendiaries

In areas where stipendiary magistrates have jurisdiction they may try offences on a full-time professional basis. The Crown may appoint such magistrates in any commission of the peace area outside Inner London. Such magistrates must be barristers or solicitors of not less than seven years' standing.[90] They must generally retire on attaining the age of 70.[91] There is an upper limit of 40 stipendiaries.[92] Provision is made for the fixing of their salaries.[93] Existing appointments under current legislation were protected.[94]

Crown Court procedure after committal for sentence

The accused is asked if he admits the convictions and if he was warned at the trial that he might be committed for sentence.[95] Defence counsel may cross-examine the police officer as to any facts favourable to the accused, such as a good service record and good references by employers. He may produce and examine witnesses for the defence to testify to his being the dupe of men of worse character, his being pressed by his wife for money for the family and things of that kind. Defence counsel then addresses the court in mitigation. The court may sentence the defendant to any punishment which could have been imposed after trial by jury on indictment.[96] The maximum punishment which the magistrates could have inflicted would have been six months.[97] This procedure may seem rather harsh but it is superior to the older practice of inquiring into previous convictions in court before deciding to try a case summarily, which must have prejudiced the chances of the defence. If however the Crown Court imposes a sentence of more than six months in such a case the convicted person may appeal to the Criminal Division of the Court of Appeal against sentence in the same way as if he had been convicted after trial by jury on indictment.[98]

The defendant can also apply for an order of certiorari to the Divisional Court of the Queen's Bench Division if the magistrates commit him for sentence without real grounds.[99]

---

[90] Justices of the Peace Act 1979, s.13(1).
[91] *Ibid.* s.14.
[92] *Ibid.* s.13(4).
[93] *Ibid.* s.15(3).
[94] *Ibid.* s.71.
[95] *R.* v. *Faithful* [1950] W.N. 550; *R.* v. *Vallett* [1951] W.N. 4.
[96] Magistrates' Courts Act 1980, s.38; Powers of Criminal Courts Act 1973, s.42.
[97] See n. 75.
[98] Criminal Appeal Act 1968, s.10.
[99] *R.* v. *Warren* [1954] 1 W.L.R. 531.

The defendant may in any case appeal against his conviction by the magistrates even if they have committed him to the Crown Court for sentence. He may be released on bail in the meantime but must surrender to his bail or a bench warrant will issue for his arrest.[1] He has the advantage that, on such an appeal, the court cannot impose a heavier sentence than the original magistrates' court could have imposed.[2] On the other hand the Crown Court may see his previous convictions on the record, since they are referred to on his committal for sentence by the magistrates.[3]

Appeals

Appeals are heard in the Crown Court by a High Court judge, a circuit judge or recorder, and several lay justices,[4] and may be against conviction or sentence. We may take a case which originated in London. Special arrangements apply in the Greater London area.[5] This has an inner and four outer areas for the purposes of summary jurisdiction, the outer area being served by lay courts.[6] The Inner London area has two types of courts, lay and professional,[7] serving nine petty sessional divisions.[8] There are certain limitations on the powers of the lay justices[9] and there is a committee of magistrates which directs the division of work between lay justices and the professional magistrates.[10]

The professional magistrates are known as Metropolitan Stipendiary Magistrates and are appointed on the advice of the Lord Chancellor from barristers or solicitors of not less than seven years' standing.[11]

Assume that a man is charged before a magistrate with a violent assault. He is sentenced to imprisonment. He gives notice of appeal[12] and in the meantime is released on bail.[13] The appeal is heard by a Crown Court, which may give a final judgment.[14]

If the facts are not disputed but the appeal is against sentence, the court acts in the same way as a trial judge after conviction and before sentence.[15] The court may be unfavourably impressed by a

---

[1] Bail Act 1976, ss.1, 7.
[2] Supreme Court Act 1981, s.4.
[3] *R.* v. *O'Brien* [1956] 1 Q.B. 452n. See *Practice Note* [1956] C.L.Y. 5415.
[4] Supreme Court Act 1981, s.74.
[5] London Government Act 1963, s.2 and Sched. 1.
[6] Outer London Petty Sessions Order 1964, No. 1529.
[7] Justices of the Peace Act 1979, s.33(1).
[8] S.I. 1964 No. 854.
[9] Justices of the Peace Act 1979, s.33(2).
[10] *Ibid.* s.35(1)(c).
[11] *Ibid.* s.31; there are 60 in Inner London.
[12] Magistrates' Courts Act 1980, s.108; Rules 1981, r. 74. Crown Court Rules 1971, r. 7.
[13] Magistrates' Courts Act 1980, s.113; Supreme Court Act 1981, s.81.
[14] Supreme Court Act 1981, ss.45(2), 48.
[15] See p. 149.

record of previous convictions for crimes of violence. The appeal will therefore be dismissed and the defendant remanded in custody to serve his sentence.

An appeal to the Crown Court against a conviction on the facts is a complete rehearing and the evidence taken before the magistrates is not relied on. The prosecutor-respondent opens the case just as if it were being tried for the first time. The court must not be prejudiced by being shown any record of the appellant's previous convictions.[16] A shorthand note is taken. The court has power to impose a heavier sentence than that imposed by the magistrates, in this case, provided it is below the maximum possible sentence which could be imposed by magistrates.[17]

Statement of a Case

Instead of appealing on the facts either party to a summary case may ask magistrates, or a Crown Court trying an appeal from magistrates, to state a case on a point of law for the opinion of a Queen's Bench Divisional Court of the High Court of at least two judges.[18] The case is not confined to points of law actually argued before the magistrate.[19] The parties should agree on a common draft statement of facts and on the legal problem in dispute.[20] The "case" should be concise and not enter into evidence unless the objection is that there was no evidence to justify the decision,[21] insufficiency of evidence being a matter of law.[22] Irregularity of procedure is also a legal error on which a case may be stated.[23] A sentence may also be legally irregular, e.g. beyond the jurisdiction of the court.[24]

The bench must state a case or an order of mandamus may be obtained to require them to do so.[25] The right of appeal is lost where a case is stated.[26]

When the case is tried in the Divisional Court the burden is on the appellant to show that the magistrates were wrong in law.

---

[16] R. v. Grimsby Borough Q.S. [1956] 1 Q.B. 36.

[17] Supreme Court Act 1981, s.48(4).

[18] Magistrates' Courts Act 1980 s.111; Supreme Court Act 1981, ss.28, 66, Magistrates' Courts Rules, 1981, r. 76, 179 cases were stated in 1981.

[19] Whitehead v. Haines [1965] 1 Q.B. 200.

[20] Spicer v. Warbey [1953] 1 All E.R. 284; see [1955] 1 W.L.R. 101; [1955] Crim.L.R. 491; Maskhar v. Smith (1963) 107 S.J. 375.

[21] Magistrates' Courts Rules 1981, r. 81. Magistrates' Courts (Forms) Rules 1968, Form 148. Practice Direction, December 16, 1971.

[22] Bracegirdle v. Oxley [1947] K.B. 349.

[23] Magistrates' Courts Act 1980, s.111, Rigby v. Woodward [1957] 1 W.L.R. 250.

[24] R. v. Green [1959] 2 Q.B. 127; R.S.C., Ord. 59, r. 33; Practice Note [1958] 1 W.L.R. 1016.

[25] Magistrates' Courts Act 1980, s.111(6).

[26] Act of 1980, s.111(4).

If the Divisional Court considers that the defendant has not committed an offence, as a matter of law, they will adjudge an acquittal. If they consider that the facts stated constitute, in law, the offence charged, they will adjudge a conviction.[27] If the facts stated constitute a different offence from that charged, the Divisional Court has power to amend the conviction and substitute a conviction for that other offence, but the court will not generally do this, as the defendant might have been able to produce evidence to acquit himself of the other charge.[28]

Under some statutes creating offences it is provided that the decision of the magistrates is final, and no appeal or statement of a case is possible in such cases.[29]

There is a further appeal from the Divisional Court's decision on a case stated, to the House of Lords.[30] The procedure follows that used in appeals from the criminal division of the Court of Appeal in indictable cases.[31]

In relation to the two million annual adult convictions appeals are relatively uncommon.[32] Statements of cases are even rarer.[33]

Judicial Review

As magistrates' courts are inferior jurisdictions[34] their decisions may be reviewed by the High Court as part of its supervisory powers.[35] The High Court may use the order of certiorari, for example, in order to quash a decision made irregularly or without jurisdiction. The inferior court may in an appropriate case be required to reconsider the case in the light of directions by the High Court.[36]

There is some overlap between judicial review and other remedies. Judicial review is hedged about with restrictions; it must be applied for within three months of the decision complained of and requires leave of a High Court judge after a hearing in open

---

[27] Magistrates' Courts Act 1980, s.112.
[28] *Shackell* v. *West* (1859) 2 E. & E. 326.
[29] *e.g. Hall* v. *Arnold* [1950] 2 K.B. 543.
[30] Administration of Justice Act 1960, s.1; 7 such appeals were tried in 1981.
[31] *Supra*, p. 157.
[32] In 1981, 6,200 appeals against conviction were brought to the Crown Court. One-fourth succeeded. 11,000 appeals were brought against sentence one-half succeeded in some respects.
[33] 179 cases were stated in 1981 from Magistrates' Courts and 18 from Crown Courts on appeal from Magistrates.
[34] See textbooks on constitutional and administrative law on the relations of the various courts.
[35] This jurisdiction is exercised by the Queen's Bench Division. *Cf. Bousfield* v. *North Yorkshire County Council* (1982) 44 P. & C.R. 203; *R.* v. *Wolverhampton Crown Court ex. p. Crofts* [1983] 1 W.L.R. 204.
[36] Supreme Court Act 1981, s.31(5).

court.[37] It has been held that a statement of a case by magistrates is better than judicial review if the facts of a case are complicated.[38] On the other hand other remedies should not be sought merely to defeat the restrictions placed on applications for judicial review.[39]

Punishment

No discussion of individual cases can give a general picture of trends in punishment. Magistrates are guided as to proper sentences by instruction and by their clerk and acquire experience in the course of their work. The wide range of punishments does sometimes lead to inconsistencies.

There is a statutory prohibition of sentencing first offenders to prison except for special cause, to be stated by the magistrates.[40]

Magistrates may adjourn sentence to determine the most suitable punishment, or for medical examination.[41] Detentions for four days or less may be ordered[42] or imprisonment for eight days or more.[43]

Summary cases

The statute creating an offence may limit the punishment to a fine generally or for a first offence. In some cases either a fine or imprisonment, but not both, may be imposed. Statutes often fix maximum sentences but much lighter sentences are usual. Six months is generally the maximum term of imprisonment that can be imposed by magistrates even for a number of offences charged together.[44]

In fact imprisonment is imposed in very few purely summary cases, usually where the defendant has a previous bad record and needs a strong deterrent. Many offenders, especially first offenders, get an absolute discharge after conviction.[45] It is irregular to dismiss a charge if it is proven, the absolute discharge being the appropriate form of leniency.[46]

---

[37] *Ibid.* s.31(3). R.S.C. Ord. 53.
[38] *R.* v. *Felixstowe Justices, ex. p. Baldwin* (1981) 72 Cr.App.R. 131.
[39] *O'Reilly* v. *Mackman* [1982] 3 W.L.R. 1096 (H.L.), review of a decision of a Prison Board of Visitors; *Practice Direction* [1982] 3 All E.R. 800; *cf. Davy* v. *Spelthorne Borough Council* (1983) 10 C.L. 414b, civil law liability.
[40] Powers of Criminal Courts Act 1973, s.20.
[41] Magistrates' Courts Act 1980, ss.10(3), 30.
[42] Act of 1980, ss.10(4), 128(6).
[43] *Ibid.* s.132.
[44] *Ibid.* s.33.
[45] Nearly 17,000 cases in 1981.
[46] *Evans* v. *Jones* [1953] 1 W.L.R. 1056.

In practice the fine is the usual sentence in magistrates' courts.[47]
It is generally possible to exact a fine even if the original statute
creating the offence provided for imprisonment only.[48] Fines tend
to be rather standardised in routine summary cases, but the court
is entitled to consider the offender's means.[49] A standard scale has
been introduced to facilitate taking inflation into account. Statutes
can refer to levels on this scale rather than specific amounts; and
existing fines or maximum fines are converted into these levels.[50]

A fixed proportionate term of imprisonment can be imposed for
failure to pay a fine but only if the offender has the means to pay.[51]
A defendant who refuses to be bound over or breaks the terms of
his recognisance can also be imprisoned.[52]

Indictable cases tried summarily

Where a magistrates' court tries an indictable offence summarily
the position is slightly different. Absolute discharges are about as
frequent as in summary cases.[53] Probation is more commonly
used, as the greater gravity of the offence justifies such
treatment.[54] If the terms of probation are not kept, the proba-
tioner may be resentenced or again put on probation. An offender
may be fined or imprisoned.[55] Community Service orders are
being increasingly used.[56]

Youth custody and detention

Where a term of imprisonment would be imposed on a youth
between 15 and 21 or a girl between 17 and 21 years of age, it is
replaced by a sentence of youth custody.[57] Youths between the

---

[47] Fines were imposed in 98 per cent. of motoring and 91 per cent. of other offences in 1981.
Earnings can be attached if the fine is not paid: Criminal Justice Act 1967, s.46; Attachment
of Earnings Act 1971, s.1(3) (6).
[48] Magistrates' Courts Act 1980, s.34(3).
[49] Act of 1980, s.35;
[50] Criminal Justice Act 1982, ss.37; 46, the Home Secretary may vary the standard scale
Magistrates' Courts Act 1980, s.143 (as amended Criminal Justice Act 1982, s.48).
[51] Magistrates' Courts Act 1980, s.82; Sched. 4; *R. v. Southampton Justices, ex. p. Davies*
[1981] 1 W.L.R. 374 (D.C.). Payment by instalments may be arranged, under Act of 1980
ss.85, 85A (1982).
[52] *Ibid.* s.115(3).
[53] About 3,000 out of 412,000 convictions in 1981.
[54] In about 6 per cent. of cases in 1981.
[55] Powers of Criminal Courts Act 1973, s.6(3). In 1981 5 per cent. were imprisoned and 50 per
cent. fined.
[56] Magistrates' Courts Act 1980, s.37. Criminal Justice Act 1961, s.1, Sched. VI; Children and
Young Persons Act 1969, s.7(1); 2800 in 1981.
[57] Criminal Justice Act 1982, s.6. This applies to summary or indictable cases. Older offenders
may be committed for reference to a Crown Court, if a heavier sentence is required,
Magistrates' Courts Act 1980, s.38.

ages of 14 and 21 may be sentenced to be detained in a Detention Centre for not more than four months.[58]

Binding over

Binding over is a curious institution. A defendant convicted of a summary offence such as assault or insulting behaviour may be bound over to keep the peace and be of good behaviour. Imprisonment may be ordered if the terms are broken.[59]

The power to bind over is used in some cases where no charge is brought, e.g. the person bound over appears as a witness but is clearly involved in a long-standing feud. If a defendant objects to being bound over, he can appeal to the Crown Court.[60] A binding over is not regarded as an acquittal and cannot be the basis of an action of malicious prosecution.[61]

Domestic Proceedings

Local magistrates' courts have jurisdiction to grant "matrimonial orders" on various grounds, such as cruelty, desertion and wilful neglect to maintain a spouse or child.[62]

As some of these grounds may also be relevant in divorce proceedings in the Family Division of the High Court, the magistrates will not try a case which could be more conveniently dealt with in the High Court.[63] Orders may be made by magistrates in the domestic court for custody of, and access to, children.[64]

At the hearing the case will be tried separately from other summary cases,[65] and certain days or parts of days must be set aside for such cases. A stipendiary or metropolitan magistrate may sit, or three lay justices of the peace, with at least one man and one woman.[66] There is a special domestic court for Inner London, consisting of a metropolitan stipendiary and one or two lay justices, e.g. from special domestic court panels.[67] The domestic

---

[58] *Ibid.* ss.4, 5. See below, p. 173 Juvenile Proceedings, for details on offenders aged 15 and 16.

[59] Act of 1980, s.115; no violence need be apprehended; *Bamping* v. *Barnes* [1958] Crim.L.R. 186 (street photographer stopping passers-by).

[60] Magistrates' Courts Act 1980, s.108(1), (3); *Shaw* v. *Hamilton* [1982] 1 W.L.R. 1308, (D.C.).

[61] *Everett* v. *Ribbands* [1952] 2 Q.B. 198, 201.

[62] Magistrates' Courts Act 1980, s.65.

[63] Domestic Proceedings and Magistrates' Courts Act 1978, s.27.

[64] *Ibid.* s.8.

[65] Act of 1980, s.69.

[66] *Ibid.* s.66; Domestic Proceedings & Magistrates' Courts Act, 1978, ss.1, 2, 3; 67(2); Domestic Courts (Constitution) Rules, 1979.

[67] *Ibid.* s.66(2); Domestic Courts Constitution (Inner London) Rules 1979.

courts are not open to the general public.[68] The press are present but they are restricted to publishing the substance of the dispute and the decision.[69] It is one of the tasks of the court to reconcile the parties, if possible,[70] and probation officers are used for the purpose.[71]

The defendant may be summoned personally or by post and is usually given two opportunities to appear. If he still fails to appear the court, if satisfied he has had notice, may proceed to decide the case without him. If he does appear the court explains the complaint to him, in the presence of the wife.[72] The wife then testifies and may be cross-examined. Solicitors or counsel may represent the parties and the order of speeches and the rules of examination and cross-examination are like those in summary criminal cases.[73] The court must assist the parties if they are conducting their own cases.[74] The defendant may plead that his wife is unwilling to have him back, deny mistreatment or drunkenness or claim that she is responsible for the breakdown of the marriage, e.g. by quarrelling, neglecting the home or children or herself misbehaving.

The court may make orders for the parties to cease to cohabit and for custody and care of children.[75] A common order is for payment of support by the husband. The court will consider the husband's means and expenses and award an appropriate sum to the wife, with additional amounts for the children maintained by her.[76] Payments can be made directly to the child.[77]

The husband may be re-summoned if he falls in arrear. The clerk of the court is the collecting officer but some other person may be made the recipient by the order.[78] A husband may claim that he cannot afford to pay, but the order takes priority over all other expenses, e.g. the cost of maintaining some other woman. For default in payment he may be sent to prison.[79] The husband may also apply to have the amount of the order reduced if his earnings are reduced or the wife's position improves. The wife may apply to have it increased if another child is born or her

---

[68] *Ibid.* s.69(2).
[69] *Ibid.* s.71.
[70] Act of 1978, s.26(1).
[71] *Ibid.* s.26(2).
[72] Act of 1980, ss.52, 55.
[73] *Ibid.* s.122, there is usually no submission of "no case to answer," *Clifford* v. *C.* (1963) 107 S.J. 515.
[74] Act of 1980, s.73.
[75] Act of 1980, ss.8, 16; Magistrates' Courts (Matrimonial Proceedings) Rules 1980, Form 13.
[76] Act of 1978, ss.1, 3.
[77] *Practice Direction* March 10, 1980.
[78] Act of 1978, s.32(2).
[79] Act of 1980, s.76(1), Sched. 4.

income is reduced.[80] Divorce does not automatically mean a discharge of the order unless the High Court's findings are inconsistent with those of the magistrates.[81] However, the order will cease to have effect if the person maintained re-marries.[82]

A husband's earnings may be attached, by an order to his employer, if he has wilfully refused or culpably neglected to satisfy a maintenance order.[83] The husband must give the court details of his wages and employment.[84]

A wife can be ordered to support a husband if he is unable to support himself and to support children of the marriage.[85]

The clerk of the court must take a longhand note of domestic cases, which means that some hearings are rather protracted. There is an appeal to the Family Division of the High Court.[86] The justices are required to provide reasons for their decisions.[87]

There is a further appeal to the Court of Appeal by leave of either the Court of Appeal or the Divisional Court.[88] A case may be stated for the Family Division.[89]

The domestic court deals with applications concerning custody and maintenance of children[90] and consents to the marriage of minors under eighteen.[91]

The domestic court has also taken over guardianship and adoption cases.[92]

Juvenile Proceedings

A special semi-criminal juvenile procedure applies to young persons aged under seventeen, and children aged under fourteen at the time of appearing in court, for summary offences, or many indictable offences.[93]

A juvenile case may commence by a police officer discovering a group of boys under seventeen committing some petty theft. He

---

[80] Act of 1978, s.20.
[81] *Wood* v. *Wood* [1957] P. 254; *Sternberg* v. *Sternberg* [1963] 1 W.L.R. 1036.
[82] Act of 1978, ss.4(2), 35.
[83] Attachment of Earnings Act 1971, ss.1(3), 3(5); Attachment of Earnings Rules 1971.
[84] *Ibid.* s.14.
[85] (The present law refers to spouses, not wives.)
[86] Act of 1978, s.29; Supreme Court Act 1981, s.61, Sched. 1; *D.* v. *M.* [1982] 3 W.L.R. 891, new evidence admissible.
[87] Other evidence may be used if the clerk's notes are not available (R.S.C. (1971), Ord. 112, r. 6(6)). Act of 1980, s.74; Magistrates' Courts Rules, r. 36; Act of 1980, s.111; Ord. 56, rr. 4A, 5.
[88] Supreme Court Act 1981, ss.15(2), 18(1).
[89] Act of 1980, s.111; Ord. 56, rr. 4A, 5.
[90] Act of 1978, s.3(2), 8; Supreme Court Act 1981, s.61, Sched. 1.
[91] Marriage Act 1949, s.3(5); s.79(2); Family Law Reform Act 1969, s.2(2).
[92] See p. 177.
[93] *R.* v. *Tottenham Juvenile Court* [1982] 2 W.L.R. 945; 130,000 were prosecuted in 1981, two-thirds for indictable offences.

will take them to the police station where they are kept separate from any adult offenders.[94] The parents are told to attend the local juvenile court at the hearing unless the court does not wish it or regards requiring their attendance as unreasonable.[95] Notice is then given to a probation officer attached to that court. The local authority are also notified, as the responsible children's authority.[96]

Juvenile courts consist of specially experienced justices.[97] Justices may not act after having reached the age of sixty-five.[98] Provincial juvenile magistrates are appointed by the Lord Chancellor and then elected by the justices of the petty sessional division to a special juvenile panel, which acts for three years at a time.[99] The London panels and chairmen are nominated by the Lord Chancellor.[1]

Juvenile courts must in any case always be held in different court rooms or at different times from ordinary magistrates' courts.[2] Juvenile cases are often tried on special days. The object is to avoid association with adult offenders and preserve a different atmosphere.

Juvenile courts are not open to the public.[3] Accommodation is in any case fully taken up, because a number of probation officers will be present, to report on cases awaiting sentence. Representatives of local authorities also attend. The Press is represented but it may not publish the name of any person under seventeen or reveal his identity, unless the court expressly so orders.[4]

The young persons charged are called in when their case is reached and the police complainants are called. The parents are also admitted to the court for the hearing of their child's case and may be heard, and in some cases have a right to be heard. The court will act as examining justices and commit a young person for trial by jury where the charge is homicide or an offence for which a long prison sentence is likely.[5]

---

[94] Children and Young Persons Act 1933, s.31; provision is made for release, bail or further detention: Children and Young Persons Act 1969, s.29; and Sched. 5, para. 24, amending Criminal Justice Act 1948, s.27.

[95] Children and Young Persons Act 1963, s.25; Magistrates' Courts (Children and Young Persons) Rules 1970, r. 5.

[96] Children and Young Persons Act 1969, s.9.

[97] Juvenile Court Rules 1954, r. 12.

[98] Juvenile Court Rules 1954, r. 1(2).

[99] Children and Young Persons Act 1963, Sched. 2, Pt. I.

[1] Administration of Justice Act 1964, s.12, amending Children and Young Persons Act 1963, Sched. 2, Part 2, para. 15. (There are nine juvenile courts in Inner London, Act of 1964, s.14; Juvenile Courts (London) Order 1975).

[2] Children and Young Persons Act 1933, s.47.

[3] *Ibid.*

[4] *Ibid.* s.39; Children and Young Persons Act 1969, s.10.

[5] Children and Young Persons Act 1969, s.6; Criminal Law Act 1977, s.25.

Assuming that the juvenile court is to try a boy apprehended by the police, he will be called to the justices' table. The offence charged will be explained to him in simple language.[6] The police officer complainant will outline the circumstances of the offence and refer to any statements made by the boy, and the boy will be asked if these are correct. An admission is then commonly made. If the offence is not admitted the child or his parent may cross-examine the police officer,[7] and defence witnesses may be called. Occasionally solicitors or counsel represent the accused, and address the court in the same way as on the trial of adults.[8]

No child under the age of fourteen is criminally responsible.[9]

The findings of the court are announced after consultation among the magistrates. The decision may be by a majority. It does not technically constitute a conviction.

The court receives reports on the circumstances of the child or young person before deciding what order to make.[10]

The boy then appears with his parents to hear the order. They are entitled to know the substance of the reports and the probation officer will be present in case they wish to dispute his conclusions.[11]

First offenders are often conditionally discharged and warned that they may be sentenced if they commit another offence during some period of not more than a year. Fines are the most common punishment for children and young persons for purely summary offences but less common for thefts or housebreaking.[12]

Parents must pay these fines unless this would be unreasonable in the circumstances.[13]

Youths of 15 and 16 may be sentenced to Terms of Youth Custody of over 4 but under 12 months where non-custodial sentences would be ineffectual, provided the magistrates give reasons for their decision.[14] The object is to provide a training programme, and the sentence is served in special centres if possible.[15]

Youths under 21 may be required to attend Attendance Centres

---

[6] Magistrates' Courts (Children and Young Persons) Rules 1970, r. 6.
[7] *Ibid.* r. 8: the court assists the young person if he has no other assistance.
[8] *Ibid.*r. 5(1).
[9] Children and Young Persons Act 1963, s.16; Act of 1969, s.70, "child."
[10] Magistrates' Courts (Children and Young Persons) Rules 1970, r. 10.
[11] r. 10(2).
[12] Magistrates' Courts Act 1980, s.24.
[13] Children and Young Persons Act 1933, s.55 (amd. 1982).
[14] Criminal Justice Act 1982, ss.6, 7; 6 months is maximum for one offence, but 12 months may be imposed by the Crown Court if committed there for sentence *ibid.* s.37.
[15] *Ibid.* s.11. The general rules about remittance of sentence apply, Criminal Justice Act 1967, s.60 (1982).

by various courts for periods of 12 to 36 hours but without interfering with school or work.[16]

Care Proceedings

Care proceedings are used where young people are in need of care or control, *e.g.* are neglected or play truant. They may also be used where an offence is committed. A policeman or the local authority may start proceedings.[17] A summons or warrant can be issued to ensure attendance.[18] Proceedings may also be initiated by parents unable to control their children.[19]

The young person may be taken to a safe place for his own protection,[20] or detained by the police.[21] Parents or guardians must be notified of this.[22]

The general procedure is the same as that already described for juvenile court proceedings against offenders.[23]

The court may make a care order or supervision order or require the parents to take proper care or exercise proper control.[24] Care orders are carried out by the local authority.[25] They may place the young person in their institution, a "community home" in serious cases (including prison-like accommodation where necessary)[26] or he may be boarded out or placed in a voluntary institution, or allowed to live with relatives or friends.[27] Supervision orders resemble adult probation orders. The person supervised may be required by the court or the supervisor to comply with certain conditions, *e.g.* as to residence, going out, activities, education.[28]

Care orders expire at the age of eighteen or nineteen.[29]

---

[16] Criminal Justice Act 1982, ss.16–19.

[17] Children and Young Persons Act 1969, s.1(1).

[18] *Ibid.* s.2(4).

[19] Children and Young Persons Act 1963, s.3; Children and Young Persons Act 1969, Sched. 5, para. 47; Magistrates' Courts (Children and Young Persons Act) Rules 1970, r. 22 and Sched. 2, Form 4.

[20] Children and Young Persons Act 1933, s.40; Children and Young Persons Act 1969, s.28.

[21] Children and Young Persons Act 1969, ss.1(2), 28(4), 29(1).

[22] Children and Young Persons Act 1933, s.34; 1970 Rules, r. 14(3) and Sched. 2, Form. 5.

[23] 1970 Rules, rr. 16–20, *supra* p. 173.

[24] Children and Young Persons Act 1969, s.7; Criminal Justice Act 1982, s.28. In 1981, 17,000 supervision orders and 4,000 care orders were made.

[25] Domestic Proceedings and Magistrates' Courts Act 1978, s.10; 1970 Rules Form 3J. "Local authority" is defined in s.70(1); the local authority is not personally liable in damages for harm done by the child, *Leeds City Council* v. *W. Yorks Metropolitan Police* [1982] 2 W.L.R. 186 (H.L.).

[26] Act of 1969; ss.35–48; Criminal Justice Act 1982, ss.23, 24, 25.

[27] Children Act 1948, s.13(1), as amended by Children and Young Persons Act 1969, s.49. "Child" is anyone under 18 for this purpose, Children and Young Persons Act 1969, s.70(1).

[28] Children and Young Persons Act 1969, s.12 as amended 1977–1982. Instructions operate for up to 90 days (s.12(3)).

[29] Children and Young Persons Act 1969, s.20(1).

Supervision orders expire after three years at the latest, or at age eighteen.[30]

Parents are summoned to appear in care proceedings and may be required to contribute to the maintenance of the subject of a care order.[31]

Appeals from juvenile courts

There is an appeal by the child or young person as if the findings and orders of the juvenile court were convictions and sentences. Parents may also appeal, *e.g.* if ordered to bind themselves to exercise proper care, or to contribute towards the child's maintenance at a community home.[32] Parents may appeal against care orders, on a young child's behalf.[33]

Appeals are tried by a Crown Court.[34] The judge is assisted by two magistrates from the juvenile court panel.[35]

Foster-children

Juvenile courts supervise the living conditions of foster-children.[36] Appeals from their orders go to the Crown Court.[37]

Adoption and guardianship

Applications were made to the juvenile court, but are now assigned to the domestic court.[38] The court appoints a special temporary guardian to investigate the proposed adoption and report to the court. There is an appeal to a judge of the Family Division of the High Court.[39] Guardianship cases are also dealt with.[40]

Inquests

The coroner's inquest is a very ancient institution and partakes of the nature of an administrative as much as of a judicial inquiry.

[30] *Ibid.* s.17.
[31] Children and Young Persons Act 1933, ss.86–88; Children and Young Persons Act 1969, s.62; 1970 Rules, rr. 24, 25, Forms 53, 54.
[32] Children's Act 1933, s.102.
[33] *B.* v. *Gloucestershire County Council* [1980] 2 All E.R. 746 (D.C.).
[34] Act of 1969, ss.2, 3; Magistrates' Courts Act 1980, s.108; *R.* v. *Snaresbrook Crown Court, ex. p.* S [1982] Crim.L.R. 682 (D.C.).
[35] Crown Court Rules, r.3(4).
[36] Children Act 1958, ss.5, 7, 10.
[37] *Ibid.* s.11; Foster Children Act 1980, s.14.
[38] Magistrates' Courts Act 1980, s.65; Adoption Act 1958, s.9(5); Adoption (Juvenile Court) Rules 1959–1973; Administration of Justice Act 1970, s.1; Children Act 1975, ss.21(3), 58, 100(2)(*d*). Adoption Act 1976 not yet in force.
[39] Adoption Act 1958, s.10; Children Act 1975, ss.20, 101(3). Supreme Court Act 1981, s.61, Sched. 1.
[40] Guardianship Acts 1971–73, Magistrates' Courts (Guardianship) Rules 1974. (amd. 1981).

This is seen in the active function of the coroner in conducting the inquiry and in the different objectives of inquests and trials. The purpose of the inquest is to identify the deceased and determine the medical cause of death, and to seek to prevent such deaths in future.

There is a statutory duty to hold an inquest wherever there are reasonable grounds to believe that a death has been violent or unnatural, as distinct from death due to old age or natural illness.[41] Deaths in traffic and railway accidents or from overdoses of drugs would be examples.

Information as to all unusual deaths is sent to the coroner for the district where the body is found. The first intimation may come from the police who find a body, or from a doctor who is unable to certify that a death was natural, or from a registrar of deaths where the cause is not stated as natural.[42] The coroner may view the body[43] and direct a post-mortem.[44] It is often possible to dispense with an inquest as a result of this examination.[45]

In some cases the coroner is under a duty to hold an inquest although the cause of death is illness, e.g. in the case of some industrial diseases.

The coroner is appointed for a coroner's district. A coroner must be a barrister, solicitor or doctor.[46] In London there are four coroners, each of whom is a barrister who is also a qualified medical practitioner. This is valuable since much of the coroner's work is concerned with technical medical details and he must examine the medical witnesses. A coroner may be removed from office by the Lord Chancellor.[47]

The coroner is supplied with various police and medical reports before the inquest. He has his own staff of police who can interview witnesses and fill in details, which expedites the conduct of the inquest itself. If more time is needed to establish the causes of death the inquest will confine itself to evidence of identification and the direct medical causes of death. The inquest can be resumed later and the burial can proceed in the meantime.

In many cases the coroner must sit with a jury, e.g. under various statutes dealing with traffic deaths, factory accidents and

---

[41] Coroners Act 1887, s.3; H.O. Circular 68/1955; see the Brodrick Report on Coroners, Cmnd 4810 (1971); cf. R. v. W. Yorkshire Coroner [1982] 2 W.L.R. 1071 (C.A.), body returned to England from abroad.
[42] Registration of Births, Marriages and Deaths Rules, 1968; Re Hull (1882) 9 Q.B.D. 689.
[43] Coroners (Amendment) Act 1926, s.14; this is not obligatory, Coroners Act 1980.
[44] Coroners Rules 1953, No. 205, rr. 2–3 and Sched. I; Coroners Act 1954.
[45] Coroners (Amendment) Act 1926, s.21(2).
[46] Coroners (Amendment) Act 1926, s.1.
[47] Act of 1887, s.8; Act of 1926, ss.30, 31.

deaths in police custody or by police action.[48] This jury is taken
from the usual lists, as in Court proceedings.[49] The coroner may
summon any material witness, and witnesses may be fined if they
refuse to appeal or to testify.[50]

The coroner conducts the entire inquest, questioning each
witness and making notes.[51] He is absolutely privileged in respect
of anything he says.[52] There are three main types of witness. First
the widow or near relative describes having identified the body and
explains something of the deceased's antecedents. If the death was
a fall from a window, for example, the witness may be asked
whether the deceased suffered from fainting spells. If the accident
occurred at work the skill and experience of the deceased at his job
are material facts. Then the medical or professional experts are
heard. The deceased's doctor will testify as to any treatment for
illness he had received and the doctors who performed the
post-mortem will report their findings. Where the death was
possibly due to mechanical defects there will be a report by an
expert, *e.g.* a railway inspector. The third set of witnesses are
asked as to any circumstances which might explain the cause of
death in the remoter sense, *e.g.* whether the deceased jumped
from the window or fell, why he fell, if any part of the building
gave way, if he could have fallen accidentally, and so on. Plans and
drawings are used, *e.g.* a plan of a house or machine or a street
intersection.

During the third stage reflections may be made on some third
party, *e.g.* an employer who ordered a man to climb on to a roof.
Such persons are entitled to appear and may retain a solicitor or
counsel to cross-examine each witness as may relatives, insurance
companies and the police[53] after the coroner has examined him.[54]
Any person whose conduct the coroner thinks may be called in
question at the inquest and who has not been summoned as a
witness should be given due notice of the date, hour and place of
the inquest.[55]

In straightforward non-jury cases the coroner may use leading
questions, as he already has reports of the witnesses' statements
in writing before him. He may also accept heresay evidence,

---

[48] Act of 1926, s.13; Administration of Justice Act 1982, s.62; *R.* v. *H.M. Coroner, ex. p. Peach* [1980] Q.B. 211 (C.A.).
[49] Coroners' Juries Act 1983.
[50] Act of 1887, ss.4, 19, 21; Act of 1926, ss.21, 22, 30, Sched. II.
[51] He may use a tape recorder; *R.* v. *London Coroner, ex. p. Thompson* [1982] C.L.Y. 458.
[52] *Thomas* v. *Churton* (1862) 2 B. & S. 475.
[53] Coroners Rules 1953–80 r. 16.
[54] *Ibid.* r. 17.
[55] *Ibid.* r. 19.

e.g. suicide notes and statements by the deceased when in hospital as to the cause of the accident.[56]

The coroner than proceeds to state his findings, *e.g.* identity, date and place of death, medical and general causes of death.

In practice, the strict rules of evidence are observed in coroner's courts wherever civil or criminal proceedings are expected to follow. This makes it possible for the statements made at the inquest to be put in evidence at the trial if the witness dies in the meantime or goes abroad.

Where a jury is used, any person obviously implicated will have his legal representatives cross-examine witnesses more vigorously. There is nothing corresponding to the opening of a case by counsel, however, and counsel has no right to address the jury so as to influence their verdict.[57] At the close of the evidence the coroner sums up the case and directs the jury as to any legal principles involved.[58] The verdict is that of the jury.

The Press attend inquests and the proceedings are open to the public.[59] Accommodation, however, is rather limited in practice.

Coroners' inquests were able to make findings of guilt of homicide, charging the person so found, and committing him for trial.[60] Now, once the coroner is informed of the commencement of criminal proceedings arising out of a death, he must adjourn the inquest until those proceedings are completed, unless the Director of Public Prosecutions otherwise decides.[61] After the criminal proceedings are terminated the coroner may resume the inquest if he believes such a step is justified.[62] The inquest cannot, however, make any finding which is inconsistent with the outcome of the criminal proceedings.[63]

The coroner's inquest is not a civil court and no question of civil liability can be decided.[64] The verdict should not exonerate any person from fault, as this might prejudice civil claimants, *e.g.* an exoneration of an engine driver might prejudice the trial of a civil action for damages against the railways brought by relatives of the deceased. The coroner may make a report to the appropriate authority, designed to prevent a recurrence of an accident, *e.g.* that a pond or railway line should be fenced, or that a traffic

---

[56] *Ibid.* r. 26, Form. 18.
[57] *Ibid.* r. 31.
[58] *Ibid.* s. 32.
[59] *Ibid.* r. 14; *McCarey* v. *Associated Newspapers* [1965] 2 Q.B. 86.
[60] The leading statute was the Coroners Act 1887, s.4.
[61] Criminal Law Act 1977, Sched. 10, amending Coroners (Amendment) Act 1926, s.20.
[62] *Ibid.* s.20(13).
[63] *Ibid.* s.20(7)(*a*).
[64] Coroners Rules 1953, r. 33.

"black spot" should be corrected by widening, removing obstructions or adding pedestrian crossings.[65]

The Divisional Court may review an inquest verdict, on the application of the Attorney-General.[66] It may also order a fresh inquest or, by certiorari, quash an inquisition if the coroner's findings appear not to be justified by the facts, *e.g.* findings of suicide where an accident is an equally plausible finding.[67] A new inquest can also always be held if new facts come to light.[68]

There are many statutory inquiries which are not inquests, *e.g.* into railway accidents, shipwrecks and mine disasters. These also aim at finding the reasons for the disaster and preventing its recurrence.

Suicide verdicts go back to the times when suicide was followed by forfeiture of property. Suicide was a crime until recently and there is still a presumption against it.[69] Some testimony at inquests may be very harmful to persons who are under no legal liability, *e.g.* where a man died after being dismissed from work or after his fiancée broke the engagement. Whether such a death was an accident or a suicide may seem legally irrelevant. On the other hand it is very material for the protection of the public to decide whether a machine was dangerous, a railway platform unsafe, or a gas or electric appliance defective. Murders can also be camouflaged as suicide. Such questions can, therefore, hardly be eliminated.

Coroners also hold inquests on treasure trove (*i.e.* buried precious metals or coins) and other Crown prerogatives.[70]

[65] R. 34 (1980); *R. v. Surrey Coroner ex. p. Campbell* [1982] 2 W.L.R. 626 (D.C.), lack of medical care.
[66] Act of 1887, s.6; *R. v. Howe* [1954] Crim.L.R. 715; *R. v. London Coroner, ex. p. Thompson* [1982] C.L.Y. 458.
[67] *R. v. Cardiff City Coroner, ex p. Thomas* [1970] 1 W.L.R. 1475.
[68] Act of 1926, s.19.
[69] Suicide Act 1961; *R. v. Cardiff Coroner, ex p. Thomas* [1970] 1 W.L.R. 1475. The offence of abetting suicide remains (1961 Act, s.2) and is a homicide case for the purpose of the new s.20 of the 1926 Act, added in 1977.
[70] See *Hill on Treasure Trove*; *Att.-Gen. of the Duchy of Lancaster* v. *Overton (G.E.)* [1982] 2 W.L.R. 397 (C.A.).

CHAPTER 6

CIVIL PROCEEDINGS IN THE HIGH COURT (QUEEN'S BENCH DIVISION)

PROCEDURE BEFORE TRIAL

IN order to obtain a remedy for a civil wrong a plaintiff must show that the rules of substantive law in the circumstances imposed a liability on the defendant in favour of the plaintiff. Normally he will consult his solicitor before taking legal action and if the legal position is obscure the solicitor may obtain counsel's opinion. If the defendant is not liable in law, the plaintiff will be advised not to bring the action.[1] Considerations of law are also important in anticipating what defence the defendant may be able to make and framing the action in such a way as to avoid or meet such defence.

The plaintiff and his legal advisers must also consider what evidence will be necessary in order to prove his case. The court can only decide cases on the evidence put before them. If the necessary evidence is lacking there is little point in bringing the action, *e.g.* if the law requires a written memorandum of contract and no such memorandum exists, as in actions on guarantees.[2]

The plaintiff must also consider various procedural prerequisites, *e.g.* whether he must or should join other parties as plaintiffs, whether he should sue one or more persons as defendants, whether the English courts have jurisdiction.

Parties

The rules as to joinder of parties vary considerably from case to case. If two passengers in a vehicle are hurt in a collision on the highway they may jointly sue either driver, as the cause of action

---

[1] Not every injury is susceptible of redress by civil action. *Chapman* v. *Essex C.C.* (1956) L.G.R. 28 (statutory duty to provide a type of school); *Winchester* v. *Fleming* [1958] 1 Q.B. 259 (harbouring a husband); *Re Korda* [1958] C.L.Y. 2740 (reburial of ashes); *Hargreaves* v. *Brotherton* [1959] 1 Q.B. 45 (damage caused by perjury); *Chapman* v. *Honig* [1963] 2 Q.B. 502 (damage caused by contempt of court); *Hudson* v. *Hodson* [1966] Ch. 207 (undertaking given to the court broken); *R.C.A. Corp.* v. *Pollard* [1982] 3 W.L.R. 1007 (C.A.) (pirated records); *McKay* v. *Essex Area Health Authority* [1982] Q.B. 1166 (C.A.) (defective child no right not to be born).

[2] Law Reform (Enforcement of Contracts) Act 1954. See Note on Evidence, *infra*, p. 282.

will be the same in each case. On the other hand separate actions are desirable where the evidence will be different, *e.g.* if the defendant libels two different people in the same book, but makes different imputations against each.[3]

If the plaintiff is a passenger and is injured in a collision between two vehicles, he should join both drivers as defendants, since either one may be liable, and the evidence will be the same in both cases.[4]

Representative actions are used for various purposes, *e.g.* to save the expense of joining a large number of plaintiffs. Some shareholders, for example, may sue in the name and with the authority of the others. The fact that the action is brought in a representative capacity must appear on the writ. Such actions will not be allowed where the parties' interests are adverse to each other, *e.g.* if an action of directors benefits one class of shareholders and damages another. In such cases each class of claimant should be separately represented so that their interests can be protected and their point of view presented to the court.[5]

It sometimes happens that a plaintiff begins an action in the wrong capacity, *e.g.* as widow when she should have sued as executrix, or vice versa. The defendant can then apply to have the writ set aside. The plaintiff may be allowed to amend the writ, and proceed in the other capacity. If the period of limitation has run, she can still proceed as executrix, but there is no corresponding provision in favour of an administratrix on intestacy.[6]

Test cases

Test cases are sometimes brought. These are cases where a dispute exists as to the law and a number of different parties will be affected by a decision either way. A single lawsuit between one plaintiff and one defendant may be commenced, to save the expense of multiple action. The decision will be binding on all other persons in the same legal position, though they are not directly concerned with the lawsuit. Associations or trade unions, for instance, may help to fight an important case arising out of an industrial accident, or in order to have the correct principle determined, even if the amount involved in the case is small. The Revenue authorities may wish a judicial decision on some important point of liability to tax. In a leading case the British

---

[3] *Marchant* v. *Ford* [1936] 3 All E.R. 104 (C.A.).
[4] *Bullock* v. *L.G.O.C.* [1907] 1 K.B. 264 (C.A.).
[5] R.S.C., Ord. 15, r. 12; *Smith* v. *Cardiff Corporation* [1954] 1 Q.B. 210.
[6] R.S.C., Ord. 20, r. 5; Cmnd. 6923 [1977] p. 68.

Transport Commission agreed to pay the plaintiff's costs in the Court of Appeal as well as in the House of Lords, in order to get a final ruling as to the proper measure of damages payable by them to the victims of railway accidents.[7]

Jurisdiction

Jurisdiction is based on the defendant's presence in England or Wales. The writ runs throughout the country, and the High Court in London and the provinces can deal with all civil cases. There is no upper limit of amount to this jurisdiction. Small claims should be brought in the county court.[8] Any Division of the High Court can, in theory, try any type of case. Of course there is a well-defined system assigning cases to various Divisions. If an action for damages for personal injuries arising out of an accident were begun in the Chancery Division, it might be transferred to the Queen's Bench Division. In the same way, an action in the Queen's Bench to redeem a mortgage or dissolve a company might be transferred to the Chancery.[9] If a plaintiff does bring an action in the "wrong" Division he may have to pay the costs thrown away by the transfer.

The plaintiff may issue his writ out of the writ office of the Supreme Court or out of the district registry of the High Court situated in the local county court respectively. If the plaintiff proceeds locally and the defendant lives locally he must accept service there.[10] If he does not reside locally, however, he may do this in London.[11] After pleadings have been concluded the ultimate place of trial is decided by the master of the High Court or local district registrar on the hearing of the summons for directions.[12]

If a defendant whose home is in England or Wales is temporarily abroad, he can be sued here. The same is true where a contract is made or a tort is committed here by a person who is abroad, *e.g.* an employee in England is wrongly dismissed by a foreign company, or a libel is published in a foreign newspaper circulating in England.[13] In such cases, application must be made to the High Court for leave to serve the writ or notice of the writ out of the

---

[7] *Gourley* v. *B.T.C.* [1956] A.C. 185.
[8] See *infra*, p. 235.
[9] Supreme Court Act 1981, ss.61, 65, Sched. 1.
[10] R.S.C., Ord. 12, r. 2(3).
[11] R.S.C., Ord. 12, r. 2(4); *Davies* v. *British Geon Co.* [1957] 1 Q.B. 1.
[12] R.S.C., Ord. 25, r. 1.
[13] *The St. Elefterio* [1960] 1 Q.B. 187. *Official Solicitor* v. *Stype Investments (Jersey)* [1983] 1 W.L.R. 214. Within the U.K. and E.E.C. there are analogous rules to be applied when the Civil Jurisdiction and Judgments Act 1982, Sched. 1 is in force.

jurisdiction.[14] The judge must be satisfied that there is an arguable case that a wrong of the kind covered by this procedure has been done in England, without prejudging the ultimate result. The court has a discretion to grant or refuse leave and it will refuse leave if such a case is not made out.[15]

The plaintiff should not commence any action in the High Court where he knows he is unlikely to recover more than a specified amount, now £600. If he does, he will not generally be allowed to recover any costs against the defendant.[16]

Furthermore, if the plaintiff recovers less than a specified amount, now £3,000, he will as a rule only be allowed costs on the county court scale,[17] unless a reasonable man would have thought it possible that he might recover that amount.[18] The case will be treated as if it had been commenced by plaint in a county court and the appropriate amounts allowed in the county court scales of costs will be allowed for each item of costs in the High Court.[19] As the plaintiff will still be liable to pay his solicitor's costs on the High Court scale, he will lose a considerable sum for having commenced the action in the High Court.

There are special exceptions to these rules, e.g. a small counterclaim may be set up in a High Court action, as the plaintiff, not the defendant, chose to sue in that court.

Limitation of Actions

The law requires legal proceedings to be commenced within certain periods after the facts which have given rise to them because of the inconvenience of stale claims and the difficulty of disproving them. The debtor need not, of course, take advantage of such a limitation and many big firms will not do so. It is in the option of the defendant to plead the limitation statutes and the plaintiff need not specifically plead that his claim has been brought within the time allowed by law.[20] The plaintiff's legal advisers, however, should take care that a writ is issued within the prescribed time, as most defendants will plead such a defence if they know of it. The period usually begins when the facts which are the basis of the claim occur, and ends when the writ is issued.

---

[14] R.S.C., Ord. 11. Application is made to a master, accompanied by an affidavit showing that the case is appropriate. If the master refuses leave, there is an appeal to a judge in chambers, and from him to the Court of Appeal.
[15] *George Monro Ltd.* v. *The American Cyanamid Corporation* [1944] K.B. 432 (C.A.).
[16] County Courts Act 1959, s.47(1)(*b*); County Court Jurisdiction Order 1981.
[17] *Ibid.*
[18] *Hopkins* v. *Rees & Kirby* [1959] 1 W.L.R. 740.
[19] *Infra*, p. 269.
[20] *Ronex Properties* v. *John Laing Construction* [1982] 3 W.L.R. 875 (C.A.).

Breach of contract

There is a six-year period in which to sue for a breach of a simple contract and a twelve-year period in the case of contracts under seal,[21] unless the breach has been concealed by fraud.[22]

Time begins to run in favour of the defendant from the date of the breach of contract, as no wrong is done and consequently no right of action arises until that date. Where, however, a loan is repayable on demand, time starts to run in favour of the borrower at once, except in the case of bank accounts and similar deposits where such an interpretation would be inconsistent with the banker's duty to his customer and the obvious intention of both parties.

A part-payment of a debt or a clear acknowledgment of liability by a debtor forfeits all time run in favour of the debtor to date and the period starts to run again from the beginning.[23]

Tort

The usual period of limitation is six years.[24] There are several important statutory exceptions; thus an action by dependants of a deceased person for the loss of financial support caused by the death of their husband or father as a result of the negligence of a third party is subject to a special time-limit of three years after the death.[25]

Another important exception exists in the case of claims for damages in respect of personal injuries, such as bodily disablement, which form a considerable part of the business of the Queen's Bench Division in modern times. These must be brought within three years of the right of action accruing.[26] The provision includes claims sounding in trespass, nuisance, negligence, breach of contract, tort at common law and the so-called statutory torts, such as cases of injuries caused by failure to fence machinery or other violations of statutory duties. The court may waive the limit where reasonable to do so.[27]

Where a tort is wrongful *per se,* as in the case of libel or false arrest, time will start to run in favour of the defendant as soon as the wrong is done, *e.g.* from the moment of publication of a libel

---

[21] Limitation Act 1980, ss.5, 8.
[22] *Ibid.* s.32; *Applegate* v. *Moss* [1971] 1 Q.B. 406 (C.A.); *King* v. *Victor Parsons & Co.* [1972] 1 W.L.R. 801.
[23] Act of 1980, s.29 *Re Overmark Smith Warden* [1982] 1 W.L.R. 1195.
[24] Limitation Act 1980, s.2.
[25] Fatal Accidents Act 1976; Limitation Act 1980, s.12.
[26] Act of 1980, s.11(4). *Letang* v. *Cooper* [1965] 1 Q.B. 232; *Lang* v. *Hepworth* [1968] 1 W.L.R. 1299.
[27] Limitation Act 1980, s.33; *Thompson* v. *Brown* [1981] W.L.R. 744 (H.L.).

or the arrest. Fresh actions cannot be brought should fresh damage occur after judgment has been given.[28] If a tort is of such a nature that no action will lie until damage is suffered, time will not run until such damage occurs and successive actions may be brought if damage recurs.[29]

If a tort is based on fraud, *e.g.* deceit, or concealed by fraud, time will not run until the fraud is, or should have been, discovered.[30] Time will, however, run in favour of an innocent purchaser.[31]

If a tort is a "continuing one," *e.g.* a nuisance, or an unsafe system of work at a factory, time will not run in favour of the defendant as long as the tort continues, no matter when the damage was suffered.[32]

Where two or more persons are entitled by law to contribution from one another towards the payment of damages for a wrong for which both are liable, there is a two-year limitation period from the date of a judgment or admission of liability against either.[33]

Time will not run so long as the plaintiff is insane or under age. If, however, he is sane at the moment of the cause of action accruing, time will not be suspended should he subsequently become insane.[34]

The Writ

Issue of the writ

Proceedings in civil actions in the Queen's Bench Division are usually begun by the issue of a writ. This writ must be prepared in accordance with the form prescribed by the rules. In practice standard printed forms of writs are commonly used.

On the front of the writ the name of the appropriate Division of the High Court must be entered, if not already printed, and the names of the plaintiff and defendant. This, together with the serial number to be allocated by the court on the issue of the writ, becomes the title of the action.

The writ requires the defendant to satisfy the claim referred to

---

[28] *Archer* v. *Catton* [1954] 1 W.L.R. 775.

[29] *Darley Main Colliery Co.* v. *Mitchell* (1886) 11 App.Cas. 127; the plaintiff need not have been able to discover the damage *Pirelli General Cable Works* v. *Oscar Faber and Partners* [1983] 2 W.L.R. 6 (H.L.).

[30] Act of 1980, s.32; *Kitchen* v. *R.A.F.A.* [1958] 1 W.L.R. 563; *Clark* v. *Woor* [1965] 1 W.L.R. 650. There is no time limit in the case of theft of goods.

[31] Act of 1980, s.32(3); *Eddis* v. *Chichester* [1969] 2 Ch. 345 (C.A.).

[32] *Clarkson* v. *Modern Foundries* [1957] 1 W.L.R. 1210.

[33] Limitation Act 1980, s.10.

[34] Act of 1980, s.28, unless the wrong caused the insanity to supervene, *Kirby* v. *Leather* [1965] 2 Q.B. 367.

on the back or acknowledge service[35] and state whether or not he contests the claim.[36]

The writ concludes with the name and address of the solicitor issuing it on behalf of the plaintiff, whose address must also be given.

In order to issue the writ, two copies must be prepared by the plaintiff or his solicitor and these are taken to the Central Office of the Supreme Court or to the District Registry. A court official will see that they are in conformity with the form laid down by the Rules of the Court.

If they are in order, a serial number is allocated to the writ, which contains the year of issue and the initial letter of the plaintiff's surname and is dated. One copy is retained for the court records, and the original is handed back to the plaintiff or his solicitor.

In some cases, *e.g.* a pure point of law, an originating summons may be used.[37]

The indorsements

(a) A concise indorsement. This is merely a general description of the character of the plaintiff's claim, *e.g.* "for personal injuries arising from the defendant's negligence in driving a motorcar," or "for assault and battery."[38] No details of the claim are required, except in cases of libel where the publications complained of must be identified.[39] It also states the exact amount claimed or any other remedy sought. Where the "concise" indorsement is used, the plaintiff will in due course have to deliver to the defendant a statement of claim giving full particulars of his claim.[40]

(b) An indorsed statement of claim. This may now be used in all actions, not only claims to fixed sums.[41]

Service of the writ

A writ is a writ of summons and its main object is to secure the attendance of the defendant. If the defendant is an individual the writ may be served upon him personally, or by post or through his letter box.[42] If the defendant is a limited company the writ is

---

[35] See p. 190. A form for acknowledgment of service is attached to the writ.
[36] Ord. 6, r. 1 (1979), Form no. 1.
[37] Ord. 5, r. 4(2).
[38] Ord. 6, r. 2.
[39] Ord. 82, r. 2; *cf.* Ord. 83, r. 3, particulars in moneylenders' actions.
[40] See *infra*, p. 195.
[41] Ords. 6, r. 2; 18, r. 6.
[42] Ord. 10, rr. 1, 2, (1980).

served by leaving a plain copy at the company's registered office, or by sending it there through the post.[43]

Personal service is effected by handing the defendant a sealed copy of the writ, and showing him the original if he desires to see it. If the defendant has no known address an application may be made for an order for substituted service.[44] The application is made to the Practice Master by filing an affidavit.

When service of the writ has been effected, an affidavit of personal service must be made by the person who has effected such service or stating that the summons if sent by post, has not been returned undelivered, or that a summons left at the door will have reached the defendant within seven days.[45]

There is one case in which service of a writ is not required, and that is where the defendant's solicitor undertakes to accept service on behalf of his client, and subsequently acknowledges it for him.[46] In such a case, it is usual for the plaintiff's solicitor to send the original writ to the defendant's solicitor, who then indorses upon it his acceptance of service. It is not then necessary to complete the indorsement of service on the writ.

Life of the writ

We have seen, in connection with the limitation of actions, that the plaintiff must commence his action within a given period of time or find his claim against the defendant statute-barred. "Commence his action" means "issue his writ." The rules provide that the writ only remains in force for twelve months and this is stated on the writ. If the plaintiff has any difficulty in serving the writ he may, at any time before the twelve months are over, apply for renewal of the writ, by way of affidavit placed before the Practice Master.[47] The extension given will be for up to twelve months.

Although the court has an additional general power to enlarge any time-limit imposed by the rules,[48] it appears to be the practice not generally to do so in the case of a writ after the twelve months have expired. Where the application is made in such circumstances that, apart from any enlargement of time, the right of action would be statute-barred, the court will certainly refuse to grant a

---

[43] Companies Act 1948, s.437; *Thomas Bishop* v. *Holmville* [1972] 1 Q.B. 464; Ord. 65, r. 3; *cf.* Ord. 81, r. 3.
[44] Ord. 65, r. 4; *e.g.* by advertisement in the press.
[45] Ord. 10, r. 1(2). This is necessary if judgment by default is likely.
[46] Ord. 10, r. 1(4).
[47] Ord. 6, r. 8(2).
[48] Ord. 3, r. 5.

renewal, as otherwise the plaintiff could stop time running against him without any serious effort to serve the writ.[49]

The limit placed upon the life of the writ is for the purposes of service only. If the plaintiff serves the defendant with the writ out of time and the defendant, not appreciating this point, acknowledges service, the action will proceed in the usual way.

Acknowledgment of service

The defendant must either personally or by his solicitor complete the form provided for acknowledgment of service attached to the writ, giving the title of the action as it appears on the writ, the full names of the defendants and his address for service, which will be his residence if he appears in person or the business address of his solicitor if one has been instructed. The Form must be taken to the Central Office or District Registry or sent there by post.[50] All further pleadings or summonses in the proceedings can be served by post by sending them to the address for service. The Central Office then sends a copy to the plaintiff or his solicitor.[51]

Acknowledgment of service does not waive any irregularity in the writ[52] for if the defendant disputes the jurisdiction of the court, he may apply to the court to set aside the writ or service.[53]

Judgment in Default of Acknowledgment of Service (Ord. 13)

Entering judgment

We have seen that a defendant is commanded by the writ to reply to it within 14 days of service upon him. If he fails to do this, or to satisfy the claim, the plaintiff is entitled in most cases to proceed to enter judgment against him by default. Most actions in practice end in this way.

Forms of judgment in default are drawn up, which merely contain the title of the action, a recital that the defendant has not acknowledged service of the writ, and a declaration that judgment is given against him. Service must be proved by the plaintiff by affidavit.

What the plaintiff does next depends upon whether he has obtained a final or an interlocutory judgment by default.

---

[49] Ord. 6, r. 8; *Battersby* v. *Anglo-American Oil Co. Ltd.* [1945] K.B. 23; *E.* v. *C.* [1959] 1 W.L.R. 692; *Heaven* v. *Road Rail Wagons* [1965] 2 Q.B. 355.
[50] Ord. 12, r. 1(3).
[51] Ord. 12, r. 4.
[52] Ord. 12, r. 7.
[53] Ord. 12, r. 8.

Final judgment

A final judgment is obtained where the plaintiff has claimed a liquidated sum (*e.g.* repayment of a loan or the price of goods sold), or the recovery of land. Here no further step is required.

Interlocutory judgment

An interlocutory judgment is obtained where the plaintiff has claimed pecuniary damages at large (*e.g.* for physical injuries), or he claims goods or their value in the alternative. The judgment settles the issue as to liability but the damages have still to be assessed. These are assessed at a hearing before a master, district registrar or special referee.[54] The plaintiff may be previously required to deliver particulars of his claim before the hearing, which is then conducted in very much the same manner as a full trial before the judge, with both parties represented by solicitor or counsel (if so desired) and calling such witnesses as they wish on the point at issue, who may be subjected to cross-examination. When the damages have been assessed, the plaintiff enters final judgment for the amount awarded to him. There is an appeal to the Court of Appeal on the assessment of damages.[55]

Effect of judgment in default

A final judgment in default can be enforced by all the means of execution that would be at the plaintiff's disposal if the action had proceeded to a full-scale trial before a judge. The only difference is that a judgment entered by the direction of the judge can only be upset by the Court of Appeal, whereas a judgment in default can be set aside by a master of the court.

Setting aside judgment in default

The application to the master to set aside the judgment in default is by way of summons served on the plaintiff. If the judgment has been obtained irregularly (*e.g.* by fraud, if process was not in fact served or by error, where process was mistakenly served on the wrong person), then the judgment is set aside as of right. Where, however, the writ has been properly served, the defendant will have to satisfy the court by affidavit, first that he had a good reason for not replying in time, such as illness, and, secondly, that he has a bona fide defence as to the whole or part of the claim. In this case, the judgment may be set aside in the court's

---

[54] Ord. 37.
[55] Ord. 58, r. 2.

discretion and upon such terms as to costs or otherwise as it thinks just.[56]

Judgment in Default of Defence and Summary Judgment

We must now consider what happens where a defendant acknowledges service and gives notice of his intention to defend the action.

If the writ is not indorsed, the plaintiff must deliver his full statement of claim within 14 days.[57] If, on the other hand, the writ is indorsed with a statement of claim he may:

(i) Wait for 14 days from the acknowledgment of service for the defendant to deliver his defence, and, if he does not do this, enter judgment against him in default of defence in very much the same way as he would have done in default of acknowledgment, or

(ii) Proceed immediately for summary judgment. Some claims, *e.g.* for fraud or libel, are excepted. The plaintiff will only make his application for summary judgment where he believes the defendant has no real defence to the action. The application is made by way of summons before the master and is supported by an affidavit sworn by the plaintiff verifying the cause of action and the amount claimed and stating that in his belief there is no defence to the action. The summons and affidavit are then served on the defendant. On the hearing of the summons the defendant will be given ten days in which to show he has a prima facie defence, and may file an affidavit declaring his grounds for this on oath. The master hearing the summons is not concerned to try the action between the parties and to probe into the truth of the defence or whether it is one that would entitle the defendant to succeed at the trial, but the master must be satisfied that, on the facts as disclosed, there is an arguable issue between the parties to be tried by the court. If he is in any doubt, he may adjourn the summons in order to give the plaintiff an opportunity of replying to the defendant's affidavit by filing an affidavit in reply.

When the master is satisfied that he has heard all that has to be said for both parties he may either—

(a) Order that the plaintiff be at liberty to enter judgment against the defendant on the grounds that the latter has no prima facie defence to the action (subject to an appeal to a judge in chambers).

---

[56] Ord. 13, r. 9, 10.
[57] For the details of a statement of claim see *infra*, p. 195.

(b) Give the defendant leave to defend, conditional upon his payment of the whole or part of the claim into court, or giving security for it.

(c) Give the defendant unconditional leave to defend.[58]

On granting leave to defend, the master will frequently give directions on the future conduct of the action, e.g. that a defence be filed within eight days, that there be discovery by affidavits whereby each party discloses to the other the documents in his possession relating to the matters at issue, and that the action be set down for trial within 21 days after discovery and inspection of documents.[59]

Delivery of the Defence

We have now come to the stage in all the various kinds of proceedings where the defendant, if he has survived the preliminaries, must deliver his defence. This must be done within 14 days after he acknowledges service or receives the statement of claim, and, if he does not, he runs the risk of judgment in default being entered against him or, in certain cases, of the plaintiff going straight into court before the judge on a motion for judgment.[60]

If the defendant is in difficulties with his defence, e.g. where a great deal of correspondence or of accounts must be sifted before he can formulate it, he may ask the plaintiff for extensions of time, which are usually given as a matter of courtesy, and in the last resort where the plaintiff has tired of his delay, the defendant may apply to the master. Reasonable extensions will usually be given, as the courts are reluctant to bar a man from a just trial for non-compliance with strict formality.

Pleadings

Nature and purpose of pleadings

The issue of the writ and the acknowledgment are registered with the court. Further pleadings are exchanged between the solicitors for the two parties and not lodged with the court until the

---

[58] *Yorke (M.V.) Motors* v. *Edwards* [1982] 1 W.L.R. 444 (H.L.); *Agualite* v. *Jaymer International Freight Consultants* [1980] 1 Lloyds Rep. 36 (C.A.). Appeal from the master lies to a judge who will rehear the matter, *European Asian Bank AG* v. *The Punjab & Sind Bank* [1983] 3 C.L. 366 (C.A.).

[59] Ord. 14, r. 6; Ord. 25. Nearly 97 per cent. of all Queen's Bench actions in 1981 ended in judgment by default or summary judgment (76,000 and 5,000).

[60] Ord. 18 and Ord. 19. For details of the defence see *infra*, p. 196.

case is set down for trial. Pleadings are a series of documents which have replaced actual appearances in court to decide various preliminary matters. The plaintiff's main pleading is known as the statement of claim. The statement of claim is an expanded version of the claim in the writ and is dispensed with if the writ was indorsed with it. The defendant delivers a defence or answer to the claim within 14 days of receiving the statement of claim[61]; this will put the defendant's side of the case and refute the statements in the statement of claim. If it incorporates new facts the plaintiff may have to deliver a reply within 14 days thereafter, stating how far he refutes these facts. If there is no further pleading within 14 days of the last pleading delivered, the parties are said to reach an issue for trial and the pleadings are closed.

An alternative procedure by exchange of affidavits is also possible.[62] It will be assumed in the following account that this procedure is not followed.

Pleadings must refer concisely and clearly to matters of fact, and not evidence. They need not identify the points of law, but can do so.[63] Imagine that X has assaulted Y, and that Y issues a writ against him. Y must not allege that X "legally wronged him" or "committed a tort." He must plead facts which his advisers consider to constitute the tort of assault in law, *e.g.* that X struck or wounded Y. X, in his turn, will not plead that he "is not legally liable" or "committed no tort." He will plead facts which his advisers consider establish a recognised legal defence to assault, *e.g.* that Y attacked him first and he only struck Y in self-defence.

Pleadings serve a double purpose. One object is to eliminate uncontested material and isolate the issues of fact before trial, *e.g.* whether X will deny striking Y, or claim he was justified in doing so. Unfortunately, the modern rules are very lax. Plaintiffs may claim on a number of alternative grounds, for safety's sake, when they really depend on one of them. Defendants are allowed to plead several alternative and even inconsistent defences, *e.g.* to deny that a contract was made or, if made, that it was broken.[64] The general costs of the proceedings are not substantially increased by this laxity, but it does defeat a main purpose of pleadings.

The other object of pleadings is to assist the court. Only evidence which is relevant to the facts pleaded can be adduced in

---

[61] Ord. 18, r. 2.
[62] R.S.C. Ord. 18, r. 21.
[63] Ord. 18, rr. 7, 11. *Re Vandervell's Trusts (No. 2)* [1974] Ch. 269.
[64] *e.g. Barclays Bank* v. *Thomas* [1979] 2 Lloyd's Rep. 505.

court. Issues of fact not referred to in the pleadings cannot be dealt with at the trial.[65]

A party must not normally try to anticipate his opponent's case. A plaintiff, for example, need not deny that the defendant in an assault case was acting in self-defence, but should simply allege that the defendant assaulted him, and let the defendant raise the question of self-defence. Quite often an opposing party may be ignorant of a possible defence or decide, on various grounds, not to rely on it. If, however, the plaintiff knows the defendant intends to plead limitation of time as a defence, for example, it is advisable for him to plead the facts taking the plaintiff's claim out of the statutes of limitation, to save wasting time.[66]

The statement of claim

Care must be taken in drafting the statement of claim. It is divided into numbered paragraphs and should be sufficiently clear and detailed to dispense with requests for further particulars. In actions for personal injuries there are certain standard types of particulars of negligence and of the extent of the injuries which are appended to the statement of claim. It must also state whether special damage has been suffered, if that is essential to the cause of action. Particulars of special damage are always given in actions for personal injuries, e.g. medical expenses, and loss of wages before trial. Claims for interest must be made in detail and the rate of interest claimed.

The statement of claim must not depart from the cause of action shown in the writ which preceded it. It must not set up a new head of claim. On the other hand, it may cure the inadequacy of the writ by supplying sufficient particulars of the nature of the claim and the circumstances on which it is based.[67]

There must be no ambiguity in the claim. Thus, if a loan of £500 was to have been repaid on January 1, 1977, the plaintiff must state clearly that he has never received that sum or any part of it on that or any other date, or state what part he has received.

The statement of claim abandons any part of the claim in the writ to which it does not refer.[68] If the writ refers to several claims and the statement of claim to some or one of these only, the other claims will be treated as waived for the purpose of the present

---

[65] *Davis* v. *Hall* [1954] 1 W.L.R. 855; *Esso Petroleum Co.* v. *Southport Corporation* [1956] A.C. 218; Master Jacob [1960] *Current Legal Problems* 171.
[66] *Busch* v. *Stevens* [1963] 1 Q.B. 1; see Ord. 18, r. 8, generally as to pleading statutory defences.
[67] *Waterhouse* v. *Reid* [1938] 1 K.B: 743 (C.A.); *Grounsell* v. *Cuthell* [1952] 2 Q.B. 673; *Hill* v. *Luton Corporation* [1951] 2 K.B. 387.
[68] *Tazewell* v. *South of England Homes* (1967) 111 S.J. 91a.

action. If a plaintiff sues in two capacities and the statement only refers to one, the claim cannot be continued in the other capacity.[69] If a writ asks for two remedies and the statement of claim only for one, the other remedy is waived, unless the court gives leave to amend.[70]

If a writ is generally expressed, e.g. refers to wrongful interference with support to land, the statement may specify several facts consistent with the writ which support two different heads of a claim, e.g. the positive wrong of unlawfully tunnelling under land and the wrongful omission to provide support for the land.[71]

The plaintiff may later amend his statement of claim with leave of the master. If this presents new facts the defendant is given an opportunity to plead further defences.[72] Thus if the plaintiff originally relied on an oral contract and then amended his pleadings so as to rely on a written contract, the defendant must be given time to plead a defence to such contract.[73] It is too late for the plaintiff to raise a new head of claim by amendment if the limitation period on it has run.[74]

If a plaintiff fails to follow up his writ by delivering a statement of claim, or fails to prosecute his action thereafter, the defendant may apply to a master to strike out the action for want of prosecution, but the master may refuse if the limitation period has not expired.[75]

The defence

This is delivered 14 days after the statement of claim is received by the defendant, or after leave is given to defend.[76] A defendant is permitted, as we have seen, to plead alternative defences, e.g. that he never ordered goods and also that he paid for them.

All statutory defences must be pleaded or they will be treated as waived, e.g. the absence of a written memorandum, lapse of time, or a claim to contribution.[77]

The defendant's denial of the facts in the claim is known as a "traverse," e.g. if the statement of claim alleges an assault the

---

[69] *Harries* v. *Ashford* [1950] 1 All E.R. 427 (C.A.).
[70] *Harries* v. *Ashford, supra*, at 429; *Morley London Developments* v. *Rightside Properties* (1973) 117 S.J. 876.
[71] *Graff Bros. Estate* v. *Rimrose Brook Sewerage Board* [1953] 2 Q.B. 318 (C.A.).
[72] Ord. 20, rr. 2, 5, 8.
[73] *Loufti Pasha* v. *C. Czarnikow* [1952] W.N. 481.
[74] *Hall* v. *Meyrick* [1957] 2 Q.B. 455 (C.A.).
[75] *Birkett* v. *James* [1978] A.C. 297; *Bremer Vulkan Schiffbau und Maschinenfabrik* v. *S. India Shipping Corp.* [1981] 2 W.L.R. 141 (H.L.).
[76] Ord. 18, r. 2.
[77] *Adler* v. *Dickson* [1955] 1 Q.B. 158, *Bowes* v. *Sedgefield D.C.* (1980) 125 S.J. 80 (C.A.).

defendant traverses by denying that he ever threatened or touched the plaintiff. The traverse must be clear and unambiguous. The object of a traverse is to require the opponent to prove his case, and it is immaterial whether it takes the form of a denial or a refusal to admit.[78]

If the defendant admits the facts alleged by the plaintiff he may plead "in confession and avoidance" new facts which put the matter in a different light. This may refer to the original incident, e.g. "I struck you, but in self defence," or it may refer to a later incident, e.g. "I borrowed the money but I paid it back." The defendant is deemed to admit all the facts in the statement of claim unless he traverses them.

A defendant may be permitted to amend his defence, e.g. if his grounds of defence could not have been discovered by him when he delivered his original defence.[79] An example is where an executor is sued on a bond of his testator and only discovers it to be a forgery late in the proceedings. Procedure in such cases is by summons before a master. Late amendment may be penalised by requiring the defendant to pay the costs which have been wasted as a result. If the plaintiff shifts his line of attack at the trial the defendant is also entitled to amend his defence to meet it.[80]

Legal objections

Legal objections may be taken in two ways. If the plaintiff's case even if true, discloses no legal wrong the defendant may apply to strike out the action, e.g. where the plaintiff claims a declaration that a proposed treaty is unconstitutional.[81] The same procedure is followed if the plaintiff's pleading show that some necessary elements of liability are missing,[82] or, in a negligence action, that no prima facie case of negligence has been made out.[83] But if the plaintiff's claim has a sound legal basis on the face of it, the defendant must put in a defence if he wishes to prove that in fact he has a reasonable answer to it.[84]

---

[78] *Warner* v. *Sampson* [1959] 1 Q.B. 297.
[79] *Cadam* v. *Beaverbrook Newspapers* [1959] 1 Q.B. 413 (C.A.). *Associated Leisure* v. *Associated Newspapers* [1970] 2 Q.B. 450.
[80] See *Davie* v. *New Merton Board Mills* [1956] 1 W.L.R. 233n. (liability for quality of tool first raised at trial of negligence action); *G.L. Baker* v. *Medway Building & Supplies* [1958] 1 W.L.R. 1216 (C.A.) (claim to trace property altered to claim of personal liability).
[81] R.S.C., Ord. 18, r. 19. *Blackburn* v. *Att.-Gen.* [1971] 1 W.L.R. 1037 (C.A.); *cf. Asher* v. *Secretary of State for the Environment* [1974] Ch. 208.
[82] *e.g.* an action for breach of covenant where pleadings do not recite any covenant (*Whall* v. *Bulman* [1953] 2 Q.B. 198 (C.A.)); a claim based on a statute which gives no civil remedy (*R.C.A. Corp.* v. *Pollard* [1982] 3 W.L.R. (C.A.)).
[83] *Price* v. *Gregory* [1959] 1 All E.R. 133 (C.A.).
[84] Ord. 18, r. 19; *Aero Zipp Fasteners* v. *Y.K.K. Fasteners* [1973] C.M.L.R. 819.

The defendant may alternatively plead a legal objection to be dealt with at the trial.[85]

A defence may similarly be struck out if not justified in law.[86]

It would be a waste of time and money to try a case, however, if there is a legal objection which, if upheld, would end the case even if the facts stated by the plaintiff were true. Hence a useful procedure is provided for deciding preliminary points of law.[87]

This procedure is not to be used where evidence may have to be heard anyway. Thus, in libel, apparently innocent words may be shown to have been defamatory in the circumstances, while many defences exist even if the words are clearly defamatory. Hence a preliminary objection to the defamatory character of words is not generally appropriate.[88]

In most cases there is also some dispute about the facts of a case, and legal points are saved for the trial, when the law is applied to the case made out by the evidence.

Particulars

Each party is entitled to sufficient details of his opponent's claim or defence. If these are not supplied in the first instance he may request further and better particulars. Should his opponent refuse or claim that he has already given adequate particulars, the master can be asked to make an order, with an appeal from such order to the judge.[89]

Third party notices

It sometimes happens that some third person may be liable to indemnify the immediate defendant in whole or in part. He is therefore, really equally interested or more interested, and should not be expected to satisfy the defendant if the latter pays the claim where it could have been resisted. The third party must be given an opportunity of helping to defend the action and often pays the defendant's costs, as part of his obligation to indemnify the defendant. Examples are cases where a retailer is sued by a customer for defects in goods which are due to their faulty manufacture and joins the manufacturer as co-defendant, or

---

[85] R.S.C., Ord. 18, r. 11.

[86] *e.g. British Leyland Motor Corp* v. *T.T. Silencers* [1980] 2 C.M.L.R. 332; *cf. Butcher* v. *Dowlen* (1980) 124 S.J. 883 (C.A.).

[87] Ord. 33, r. 3; *Eastman Co.* v. *G.L.C.* [1982] 1 W.L.R. 2; (internal company dispute); *Babanaft International Co. S.A.* v. *Avanti Petroleum Inc.* [1982] 1 W.L.R. 871 (claim in any case barred by lapse of time).

[88] *Morris* v. *Sanders Universal Products* [1954] 1 W.L.R. 67.

[89] Ord. 18, r. 12; *DDSA Pharmaceuticals* v. *Times Newspapers* [1973] Q.B. 21 (C.A.); *Samuels* v. *Linzi Dresses* [1981] Q.B. 115 (C.A.).

where a defendant claims that someone else is jointly liable with him, or that he is only vicariously liable for the default of another person as in the case of the employer of a servant who is himself directly to blame.[90] Application is to the Practice Master by affidavit, explaining the circumstances. If granted, a notice is issued and served as a summons.

Set-off and counterclaim

If the plaintiff claims a precise sum, such as £5,000, the price of goods delivered to the defendant, the latter may set off any lesser sum which the plaintiff owes him on a different basis, such as £2,000 for money lent. If the defendant claims he has already paid £2,000 on account for the same goods, he claims this as a deduction rather than a set-off.

A defendant may also plead a defence and counterclaim. A counterclaim is in fact a separate cross-action by the defendant against the plaintiff. For instance, if a carrier sues the defendant for freight charges for the carriage of his goods, the defendant may counterclaim for damage to the goods caused by the plaintiff carrier's negligence. A counterclaim can also be used in collision cases, where each party blames the other.

A counterclaim, unlike set-off, can claim a larger sum than the amount of the plaintiff's claim, as it may be fortuitous which party sues first. If the plaintiff abandons his claim, the counterclaim can still proceed as an independent action. Judgment is ultimately given both on the claim and on the counterclaim. If any party is successful judgment will be entered for the final balance due to one party by the other.

Reply

Whenever the defendant counterclaims in his answer, the plaintiff must enter a defence by his reply and defence to counterclaim or be taken to admit the counterclaim. Where there is no counterclaim the plaintiff need not reply if he merely wishes to dispute the defence and reassert his claim in spite of it. A reply will be needed, however, if the plaintiff wishes to introduce new facts to explain away any facts put forward in the defence. A reply may sometimes be necessary because the statement of claim must not anticipate the line of defence which the defendant will take. If a plaintiff sues for a debt, the defendant may defend, by a plea of confession and avoidance, that the debt has been released. The plaintiff may then reply that the defendant obtained the release by

---

[90] R.S.C., Ord. 16; *Myers* v. *N.J. Sherick* [1974] 1 W.L.R. 31.

fraud. Wherever the defendant shields himself behind some statutory defence, such as lapse of time or want of written evidence, the plaintiff's reply may allege facts which take the case out of the statute, such as concealment of the cause of action by fraud (which prevents time running in favour of the defendant, or part performance of the oral contract (which dispenses with the need for writing). The reply must not depart from the statement of claim.[91]

Discovery

Each party to an action must supply the opponent with a list of all documents in his possession which are material to the dispute, within 14 days of close of pleadings. Otherwise the court may dismiss the claim or strike out the defence.[92]

The summons for directions

A summons for directions will have to be taken out at the close of pleadings, unless directions have already been given by the master in proceedings for summary judgment or for trial without pleadings or it is a personal injury case. The plaintiff must take out the summons within one month and it is returnable in 14 days. A copy is served on the defendant.[93]

The master, at the hearing of the summons, reads the pleadings and finds out from the parties how many witnesses are to be called. He will then direct how the action is to be tried (*e.g.* by judge alone or by judge and jury), and where the trial shall take place—in London or a trial centre elsewhere (depending on convenient dates and where the majority of witnesses live).[94] The estimated length of trial and difficulty of the case will be stated, and the kind of trial list specified.[95] The master will also give

---

[91] Ord. 18, r. 10; *Herbert* v. *Vaughan* [1972] 1 W.L.R. 428.

[92] Ord. 24, rr. 1–3. Early discovery may be ordered in some cases, r. 7.

Privilege against production of documents may be claimed for communications between lawyers and clients (*Waugh* v. *B.R.B.* [1979] 3 W.L.R. 530 (H.L.)) and for State secrets and Cabinet minutes and the like. Not all Crown documents are privileged and there is no simple test (*Air Canada* v. *Secretary of State for Trade* [1983] 3 All E.R. 336; *Burmah Oil Co.* v. *Governor and Company of the Bank of England* [1979] 3 W.L.R. 722 (H.L.)). Professions like doctors, priests and journalists have no automatic privilege (*B.S.C.* v. *Granada Television Ltd.* [1980] 2 W.L.R. 774).

Since the making of an order for discovery is in the discretion of the court, it will weigh up the public interests involved on each side, *e.g.* it will generally refuse to order disclosure of school or social workers reports on children (*D.* v. *N.S.P.C.C.* [1978] A.C. 171; *Gaskin* v. *Liverpool City Corporation* [1980] 1 W.L.R. 1549) but not always (*Campbell* v. *Tameside Metropolitan Borough Council* [1983] 3 W.L.R. 74 (C.A.), (record of violence of child assaulting teacher).

[93] Ord. 25, r. 1; (1980) 8 C.L. 215.

[94] Ord. 33.

[95] Ord. 34; [1958] 1 W.L.R. 1291; [1972] 1 W.L.R. 5.

directions concerning matters of evidence, for the purpose of shortening the trial and lessening costs. The master should press for savings in costs by allowing agreed secondary evidence, *e.g.* by ordering documents to be admitted as proof of facts stated therein or allowing evidence by affidavit, to dispense with producing witnesses at the trial. He must also press the parties to admit any facts which they do not intend to dispute at the trial and penalise any party in costs if he is obstinate in this respect. He may also consider whether the parties may call expert evidence.[96]

In personal injury cases, the parties must automatically make discovery of documents and exchange written reports by their experts.[97] Police accident reports are also receivable in evidence. The action must be set down for trial within six months.[98]

Appeal lies to a judge in chambers in London or some provincial centres from decisions of the master.[99]

Interim payment

An application may be made by a plaintiff for an interim payment where the only dispute is as to the amount of damages or the court is satisfied the plaintiff is likely to succeed and obtain substantial damages. The payment ordered will be less than those, and is repayable if the plaintiff recovers less in the event. No order is made in personal injury cases if the defendant is not insured and unable to pay. Directions may be given on the application as if it were a summons for directions.[1]

Interrogatories

Interrogatories are numbered questions on issues of fact delivered by one party to the other, which must be answered on oath. They are used for the purpose of discovering the exact nature of the opponent's case where he has not made it clear in his pleadings, and of the facts upon which he relies in support of it. The interrogatories may not, however, be directed to discovering what evidence the other party proposes to call in order to prove these facts. They are perhaps most commonly used in libel actions where a defendant has pleaded justification and wants to obtain

---

[96] Ord. 25, r. 3(*a*) (*b*).

[97] *Kirkup* v. *British Rail Engineering* [1983] 1 W.L.R. 190. Discovery may even be ordered before issuing a writ.

[98] Supreme Court Act 1981, s.33(2) Ord. 25, r. 8 (1980); *cf.* Ord. 38, r. 37(2).

[99] Ord. 58, r. 1; *Practice Direction* (Q.B.D.), December 10, 1971; *Whiteoaks Clifton Property Services* v. *Jackson* [1975] 1 W.L.R. 658.

[1] Supreme Court Act 1981, s.32; R.S.C. Ord. 22, Ord. 29, rr. 9–15; *Fryer* v. *London Transport Executive* (1982) 12 C.L. 357. The trial judge is not informed of such orders.

admissions from the plaintiff that statements in the alleged libel are in fact true.[2]

Setting down for trial

The onus is on the plaintiff to do this within the time ordered by the master on the hearing of the summons for directions.[3] His solicitor prepares two copies of the pleadings and these are filed in London actions in the Supreme Court with the order for directions. District registries are used in trial centres in the provinces. One copy is used by the judge at the trial, and the other serves as the record of the case.[4] The plaintiff lodges a certificate of readiness for trial outside London, which must estimate the length of the trial.

Provision is made for the allocation of cases to appropriate lists and for the advance publication of these, so that cases can be ready for trial when reached on the lists. Alternatively, a fixed date may be applied for.[5] The plaintiff must inform the defendant of his setting the action down for trial, and the eventual date of trial.[6]

Publicity of Documents

All documents and proceedings filed in the Central Office of the Supreme Court are open to inspection by the public on payment of fees. This enables newspapers, for example, to confirm whether or not any litigation is pending.[7]

Jury Actions

A party can only claim jury trial in actions for libel, slander, false imprisonment, fraud, and malicious prosecution.[8] In all other cases the award of a jury is in the discretion of the court and it is infrequently awarded even where the case is analogous to those listed above.[9] The application must be made on the summons for directions.[10] Plaintiffs, particularly those who have suffered

---

[2] Ord. 26, r. 1. *Cf. Ramsey* v. *Ramsey* [1956] 1 W.L.R. 542.
[3] Ord. 34, r. 2. See *Practice Directions* [1972] 1 W.L.R. 4.
[4] Ord. 34, r. 3; it includes legal aid documents.
[5] Ord. 34, rr. 4–7; *Practice Directions* [1972] 1 W.L.R. 4.
[6] Ord. 34, r. 8.
[7] Ord. 63, r. 4; *cf.* [1959] 2 C.L. 232(2); 10 C.L. 330. The remedy for refusal is mandamus: *Ex p. Associated Newspapers* [1959] 1 W.L.R. 993 (C.A.). But an undertaking not to publish such material may be made a condition of an order for discovery *Home Office* v. *Harman* [1982] 2 W.L.R. 338 (H.L.).
[8] Supreme Court Act 1981, s.69. *Rothermere* v. *Times Newspapers* [1973] 1 W.L.R. 448 (C.A.); *Stafford Winfield Cook* v. *Winfield* [1980] 1 W.L.R. 458.
[9] *Holford* v. *Bloom* [1963] C.L.Y. 1681 (C.A.) (enticement of a wife).
[10] Ord. 33, rr. 2, 4, 5 see pp. 204, 211, 212, as to the course of trial by jury.

serious injury, often prefer juries, since they feel that considerations of humanity might with them outweigh strict legality. Juries are less able than judges, however, to keep awards of damages consistent and it is now the practice that jury trial shall not be granted in personal injury cases except in very special circumstances.[11] Special juries of business men used to be awarded in commercial cases.[12] An issue of fact, where there is no right to a jury, may be referred to a circuit judge for report.[13]

Preparation for Trial

After an action has been set down for trial the solicitor for each party will send all his papers to counsel, including those obtained on discovery, and statements taken from his client and witnesses for the purpose of obtaining counsel's advice on evidence.[14] Counsel will consider the case and advise what evidence is needed to prove the facts relied on by the client. Each solicitor must obtain copies of documents and plans, prepare preliminary proofs of testimony of witnesses, issue *subpoenas* against those who are reluctant to attend court, and draw the brief for counsel. He must note fixed dates for trial or watch the trial calendars and see that all his witnesses are present.

Termination of an Action without Trial

A defendant sometimes satisfies a claim without delivering a defence or by withdrawing his defence, and the plaintiff then enters judgment for his costs.

The plaintiff may discontinue his action after he receives the defence if he believes he may lose the case. If he wishes to discontinue later, he must obtain leave of the court and this is generally made conditional on an undertaking not to revive the action.[15]

The parties may agree to settle their differences before trial and even during the trial. It is a matter of public policy to discourage litigation, and the court is always happy to see parties reach an amicable agreement. The court should, however, be informed promptly of the progress of settlements.[16] A day's notice should be

---

[11] *Ward* v. *James* [1966] 1 Q.B. 273. It was held that the "discretion" to award a jury is not absolute. *Cf. Hodges* v. *Harland & Wolff* [1965] 1 W.L.R. 523 (C.A.).

[12] These were abolished by the Courts Act 1971, s.40.

[13] Ord. 36, as amended Supreme Court Act 1981, s.68. The right of appeal on fact is limited, Ord. 58, r. 5.

[14] See Note on Evidence at the end of this book.

[15] Ord. 21; *Castanho* v. *Brown and Root* (*U.K.*) [1980] 3 W.L.R. 111 (H.L.).

[16] Ord. 34, r. 8(2).

given, wherever possible, so that the lists of cases for trial can be rearranged.[17]

The terms of settlement may be kept private, unless the parties agree that counsel make a statement in open court approved by the judge, *e.g.* withdrawing a defamatory statement.[18]

CIVIL TRIAL

Characteristics of a civil trial

Civil procedure reflects a balance between the parties. It differs considerably from criminal procedure, which incorporates special safeguards for the accused. We have seen that a judge in a criminal case may discharge an offender with a nominal sentence or a conviction be quashed on a technical irregularity. Civil proceedings are in quite a different tradition. The plaintiff who claims payment of a debt or damages has a right to his remedy, which cannot be overridden by a lenient judge or pardoned by the Home Secretary. The damages awarded by the court must face the test of comparison with objective measurements of damage. The remedy must fit the wrong, whereas the criminal sentence is passed to fit the criminal. Again, whereas most crimes are the work of anti-social elements, plaintiffs and defendants may be equally obstinate and equally respectable. A civil trial must aim at a precise result which is objectively justifiable. Hence civil law is far more complicated and technical than criminal law. As decisions must be based on strict law there is far more importance attached to legal argument than in criminal cases and the rules of substantive law are more detailed and refined.

The judge preserves an even greater neutrality than in criminal proceedings. His judicial oath prescribes that he must "do right to all manner of people after the laws and usages of this realm,[19] without fear or favour, affection or ill will."[20] The judge must also avoid unduly interrupting counsel or witnesses.[21]

In recent years, jury trials have become less common, so that the judge is now usually a judge of fact as well as law.[22] This has simplified trials. Thus a judge may shorten a hearing by indicating that further evidence need not be given on a point on which he

---

[17] *Practice Note* (1959) 103 S.J. 373.
[18] See *Liebrich* v. *Cassell & Co. Ltd.* [1956] 1 W.L.R. 249.
[19] A phrase meaning "according to law."
[20] Promissory Oaths Act 1868; Supreme Court Act 1981, s.10(4). Magna Carta 1215 contains a famous provision "That right and justice must not be sold, denied or delayed."
[21] *Jones* v. *N.C.B.* [1957] 2 Q.B. 55 (C.A.).
[22] As to trials by judge and jury, see pp. 211, 212, *infra.*

already feels satisfied. He may indicate points on which he wishes clarification. Questions of admissibility and relevance of evidence are dealt with as they arise. No summing-up will be necessary. At the conclusion of the evidence legal argument will generally be heard and the judge will proceed to give judgment on both fact and law and assess damages. Occasionally a "view" of buildings or other real evidence outside the court may be necessary but the parties must generally be able to attend.[23]

The judge is absolutely privileged in respect of anything he does in his judicial capacity. This extends to remarks which are not part of his judgment, such as observations reflecting on any party to a case.[24] The same rule applies to counsel on both sides. This privilege is essential to the proper conduct of the trial. The parties and other witnesses are not civilly liable[25] but will be liable for the crime of perjury if they knowingly give false testimony. It is not an offence or a legal wrong to bring a groundless civil action or make a groundless defence, but the party responsible will have to pay all costs occasioned thereby.

Counsel have the exclusive right of audience as legal representatives before the judge in the High Court. A litigant occasionally appears in person to conduct his case, but seldom does himself justice in view of the specialised experience required of a professional advocate. He may receive some unofficial assistance from a lawyer.[26]

The Queen's Bench Division of the High Court

We have seen that small claims are brought in county courts, unless unlikely to be contested, or where an important point of principle is involved. Other claims, and these excepted claims, are brought in the Royal Courts of Justice in London or in provincial trial centres.[27]

The High Court may sit wherever it is directed; 23 provincial cities are authorised trial centres.[28]

The law administered in the Queen's Bench Division is largely common law, generally involving claims for debt or damages, and most barristers practise in this field. The Lord Chief Justice presides.[29]

[23] e.g. Buckingham v. Daily News [1956] 2 Q.B. 534; Salburg v. Woodland [1970] 1 Q.B. 324; Tito v. Waddell [1975] 1 W.L.R. 1303.
[24] Anderson v. Gorrie [1895] 1 Q.B. 68; Law v. Llewellyn, [1906] 1 Q.B. 487; Sirros v. Moore [1975] Q.B. 118 (C.A.).
[25] Evans v. London Hospital Medical College [1981] 1 W.L.R. 184.
[26] McKenzie v. McKenzie [1971] P. 33. The availability of free legal aid for persons unable to pay a lawyer will normally dispense with this: see p. 272.
[27] In 1981 the Queen's Bench Division tried 2,000 cases and entered judgment in 93,000 cases.
[28] Supreme Court Act 1981, s.71.
[29] Supreme Court Act 1981, s.5(1).

The judge

A High Court judge is appointed by the Crown on the advice of the Lord Chancellor from among barristers of at least ten years' standing. Men then receive a knighthood. High Court judges are appointed for life and can only be removed by addresses of both Houses of Parliament, or, possibly, by the Crown for misconduct in office, unless earlier unable to continue through illness.[30] There are statutory limits on the number of High Court judges who may be appointed, owing to the expense.[31] The salaries of judges are charged on the Consolidated Fund and are not subject to annual vote. The amounts of the salaries are fixed by law.[32] Judges retire at the age of seventy-five.[33]

Temporary (Deputy) High Court judges may be appointed and the Lord Chancellor may ask a circuit judge or Recorder to sit with the powers of a High Court judge.[34]

The Lord Chief Justice is appointed by the Crown on the recommendation of the Prime Minister.

A High Court judge is assigned to one Division of the court but may sit as an additional judge in another. He sits alone when trying civil cases at first instance, but is one member of a court of two or three judges when sitting in the Divisional Court and generally one of three judges in the Civil Division of the Court of Appeal.

A puisne judge of the High Court may be assigned to the Commercial Court which forms part of the Queen's Bench Division.

Date of trial

Application may be made for the date of trial to be fixed in advance.[35]

In other cases in the High Court a list of pending actions is issued weekly and a "warned list" issued daily gives 24 hours' notice of a possible hearing; the case will then appear in a daily cause list. As soon as a case comes into the warned list, solicitors and counsel must keep the Clerk of the Lists informed of the probable length of trial, so that the daily lists are kept effective, and do not collapse, leaving the judge without any cases to try.[36]

---

[30] *Ibid.* s.11(3), (8).
[31] The maximum number of High Court judges is now 80; Supreme Court Act 1981, s.4(1)(*e*).
[32] *Ibid.* s.12, with power to increase.
[33] *Ibid.* s.11(2); Judicial Pensions Act 1981.
[34] *Ibid.* s.9; Administration of Justice Act 1982, s.58.
[35] Ord. 34, r. 4; *Practice Direction* (1981) 10 C.L. 186.
[36] Ord. 34, r. 8; *Practice Direction* [1959] 1 W.L.R. 258.

The hearing

Trial is in open court and the public is admitted so far as room permits. The press is also entitled to attend. In exceptional cases a trial *in camera* (*i.e.* in closed court) is held, *e.g.* where details of secret processes are in question.[37] The judge's associate, an officer of the court, makes notes of orders of the court and administers the oath or affirmation to witnesses and jurors.

If neither side appears, the case is struck out of the list and must be set down afresh within a reasonable time. If only one side appears he will get judgment by default, but his opponent may apply within a week to have the judgment set aside, on paying the costs resulting from his non-appearance.[38]

The burden of proof

(a) How heavy is the burden of proof? In civil cases the successful party must prove his case by a preponderance of evidence; it need not be proved beyond a reasonable doubt.

(b) On whom does the burden lie? A person alleging any fact must generally prove it—the opponent need not disprove it—unless the law presumes some fact until rebutted.[39] Where the defendant denies facts alleged by the plaintiff the latter must make out his case. If the defendant admits the facts alleged but introduces new facts, *e.g.* a release from liability, the defendant must prove these. A case is opened by counsel for the party on whom the burden of proof lies. An exception is the case of a plea by a defendant that the claim against him is barred by lapse of time, where the plaintiff must prove that the statute of limitations does not apply, *e.g.* that the obligation has been acknowledged within the limitation period.

Order of speeches

Plaintiff's counsel usually "opens" the case by explaining the general background of the case and the points of law which are relevant.[40] He then traces the events which have happened, in chronological order, referring to facts which he expects to prove by evidence, or which are admitted.

---

[37] *e.g. Vandervell Products* v. *McLeod* [1957] R.P.C. 60. The Patent Appeal Tribunal may elect to sit *in camera*: Rules of 1950 (as amended in 1971), r. 7A.

[38] R.S.C., Ord. 35, rr. 1, 2; time may be extended for good cause; *Schafer* v. *Blyth* [1920] 3 K.B. 140.

[39] *Grunther* v. *Federated Employers Insurance Association* [1976] Lloyds Rep. 259 (C.A.).; *Howard* v. *Bemrose* [1973] R.T.R. 32; *cf. Elizabeth* v. *Motor Insurers Bureau* [1981] R.T.R. 405 (C.A.).

[40] Ord. 35, r. 7.

The plaintiff's witnesses are then called in, one by one, and examined by his counsel, "in chief," commencing with the plaintiff himself. A witness not yet called to testify may not remain in court while previous witnesses are being examined. Each witness testifies from the witness-box. A witness does not narrate an entire occurrence but replies to questions by counsel for the party producing him. These are directed to establish the facts pleaded by that party and must relate to those facts. No "leading" questions (*i.e.* questions suggesting the expected answer) may be asked, except on formal matters, such as names and addresses. The witness may be asked where he was on a particular date, who was there, and what happened. He is asked if the defendant was present and whether the defendant did anything. He is not asked for conclusions or opinions or about the legal effect of any act. The judge, or opposing counsel may object to questions put by counsel on irrelevant matters.

Expert witnesses are often produced, *e.g.* in tort actions doctors who testify to the truth of their medical reports on the nature of the plaintiff's injuries. They should not be asked for legal opinions.

The defendant's counsel cross-examines each of the plaintiff's witnesses after the witness has testified "in chief," to endeavour to shake the witness's story or weaken his credibility. Counsel must be prepared to reframe questions and change his approach according to the turn taken by the answer. He attempts to catch the witness in contradictions or elicit admissions. He must also put his client's version of all incidents and facts to the witness even if the latter obviously disagrees with it since if he omits to cross-examine on any point, the witness's statement is assumed to be accepted. He may and does ask "leading" questions, as the witness is assumed to be hostile to his case and unlikely to follow his lead. He may ask questions which are irrelevant to the issue but only where they tend to show that the witness is unworthy of belief. By thus shaking the credit of the witness he is establishing a fact relevant in itself since it may suggest his relevant answers are also untrue. A witness may not go beyond the answer required or give added details which are not asked, or address questions to counsel, as it is for the counsel for the party calling him to add these details in the course of re-examination. Counsel is absolutely privileged in what he says to witnesses, provided the question is in any way relevant, *e.g.* he may suggest to him that his testimony is untrue or that he has a bad reputation. If a witness denies any imputation this denial is conclusive, except in the case of a conviction for crime, which can be proved in spite of it. Witnesses need not answer incriminating questions.

Each witness may be re-examined by counsel for his own side. This is unnecessary if his testimony was unshaken during cross-examination. It is necessary, however, if he has made apparently contradictory statements, so that he may have an opportunity to reconcile them. He may also be asked further questions designed to clear up any imputation of dishonesty or untruthfulness made by counsel for the other side. Witnesses must remain in court until discharged by the judge as it is sometimes necessary to recall them for further questioning, and they might "prime" later witnesses as to what to say.

The judge may ask a witness to clarify some point in his testimony, such as a slip of the tongue in referring to the plaintiff when he meant the defendant. He may also ask the witness questions to clear up a point left obscure by the course of cross-examination. These matters can generally be dealt with by opposing counsel in re-examination however, and the judge must be studious to avoid undue interruption of counsel or any temptation to take over their conduct of the case.[41]

Submissions

At the close of the plaintiff's case in a jury action the defendant's counsel may submit that the plaintiff has not made out a case, even before the defence case is put. Lack of minimum proof is a matter of law, and the judge may therefore give judgment for the defendant if he accepts the submission.[42] The judge may also withdraw a case from the jury in such circumstances, without any submission by counsel.[43] Otherwise he might be faced with a jury verdict which could not legally be justified.[44]

If the judge rejects the submission the defence may then put on their case and try to refute the case made out by the plaintiff.[45]

Where, as is now usual, the judge sits alone, counsel runs a risk in making such a submission, as, if it fails, the plaintiff will win his case at once, as it would be difficult for the judge to keep an open mind thereafter.[46]

[41] [1952] C.L.Y. 1041, 1043. Final Report of the Evershed Committee on Supreme Court Practice, p. 104.
[42] See *Cavanagh* v. *Ulster Weaving Co.* [1960] A.C. 145.
[43] *Cf. Grinsted* v. *Hadrill* [1953] 1 W.L.R. 696 (C.A.).
[44] *Young* v. *Rank* [1950] 2 K.B. 510, 514–515.
[45] *Ibid.*
[46] *Alexander* v. *Rayson* [1936] 1 K.B. 169, 178; *Portland Management* v. *Harte* [1976] 2 W.L.R. 174.

The case for the defence

The defence may content themselves with the points made in cross-examination of the plaintiff's witnesses, and counsel may state that he will offer no evidence.[47] Plaintiff's counsel then addresses the judge or jury, and sums up his case, trying to obtain acceptance of his version of the facts. Defendant's counsel then addresses the court and criticises the plaintiff's case, in this way having the last word.

On the other hand the defence often call their own witnesses to the same act or transaction and rival expert witnesses. In this case counsel for the defendant addresses the court and "opens" the defence at the close of the plaintiff's case. Each defence witness is examined "in chief" in the way as were the plaintiff's witnesses, and will be cross-examined by plaintiff's counsel.

Whether a witness appears for plaintiff or defendant is often arbitrary. The best witnesses are often indifferent to both parties and either side may subpoena them to appear at the trial. A party calling a witness cannot cross-examine him or attack his testimony, however damaging to him, unless the witness is clearly antagonistic to that party.

Plaintiff's counsel usually attempts to refute the defence case in advance, in the light of the defendant's pleadings. He will call evidence of this kind as part of his own case. He cannot call new evidence after the defence case, in rebuttal of the statements of defence witnesses unless the judge agrees beforehand.[48]

Counsel for the defendant addresses the court on behalf of his client at the close of the defence case. Plaintiff's counsel has the right to the last word and may address the court on all the evidence.

Notes of testimony

The judge takes notes of all important details throughout the case. He uses them to prepare his judgment and his summing-up to a jury in jury cases, and they are available to the Court of Appeal. A shorthand note is also taken by a shorthand writer of all testimony. This is not generally transcribed except in case of an appeal on the ground that the judge's findings or the jury's verdict are against the weight of the evidence, which is not very common. The judge may ask for a transcript of evidence during the trial in special cases, *e.g.* where the witness speaks broken English, to confirm any points which the judge did not get down.[49] Parties

---

[47] Ord. 35, r. 7(3).
[48] *Beevis* v. *Dawson* [1957] 1 Q.B. 195.
[49] *Theocharides* v. *Joannou* [1953] 2 All E.R. 52.

may also order transcripts of evidence from the shorthand writers at their own expense, as the case proceeds.

Legal argument

If there is some dispute as to the law applicable to a case, either because the legal principle is unsettled or obscure or because it is not clear which legal principles apply to the circumstances of the case, the judge will give rulings after legal argument. The judge is supplied with a list of the legal authorities to which counsel intend to refer. Legal argument is usually heard in the absence of the jury after all the evidence is completed so that all the facts are known, and the witnesses are not detained. If the judge is sitting without a jury he will give judgment on the facts and law after this legal argument. If he is sitting with a jury he will hear legal argument and embody his rulings in his directions to the jury before they consider their verdict.

Sometimes the judge must give rulings at an earlier stage, *e.g.* on a submission of no case, already referred to. The judge may also have to give legal rulings on the relevance of some line of examination or cross-examination, to decide whether some evidence which is offered is admissible as proof of the facts pleaded, or whether some line of argument is consistent with the pleadings on which the case is being tried. Such matters are also dealt with in the absence of the jury.

Summing up in jury cases

A judge must sum up in all jury cases and will refer to his own notes for this purpose. He summarises the main points of the case, indicating the conflicting versions of the facts presented by the two sides and any factors which support or militate against the acceptance of each. He must not interpret the facts so as to usurp the jury's right to be the judges of fact but he may comment on the weakness of the case made by one party or the other, and give his impression of the credibility of witnesses.

The second element in summing up lies in his rulings on relevant legal principles which may precede or accompany his account of the facts, *e.g.* what constitutes a binding contract in law; whether words are capable of bearing a defamatory meaning; what the standard of care is in particular circumstances; whether and what exceptional circumstances will excuse a wrong, *e.g.* whether a letter containing an alleged libel was written on a privileged occasion so that the defendant must succeed unless the jury find he abused his privilege. The judge must also advise the jury on any legal principles affecting the weight of evidence, *e.g.* the danger of relying on the uncorroborated testimony of a young child or the motive which the author of documentary evidence may have had to state untruths.

The judge should generally direct the jury that they may find for one party or the other, or partly for one and partly for the other in cases of counterclaims or multiple claims. He may put specific questions to the jury, *e.g.* in a libel action he may ask whether the words published were understood to be defamatory, or whether the defendant was malicious, and base his judgment on their answers.

The judge must, in the third place, sum up on the question of damages, referring to the legal principles governing their assessment, and the evidence and arguments as to damages, *e.g.* the extent of the physical incapacity caused by an accident and any circumstances aggravating or mitigating the damages.

The verdict in jury cases

Juries usually give a general verdict, *e.g.* they find the defendant liable and assess the damages or they find him not liable. Counsel for the successful party asks for judgment after the verdict. A special verdict, on the other hand, finds specific facts and leaves it to the judge to apply the law to those facts. In such cases there may be legal argument as to the effect of the verdicts.

A majority verdict is possible, so long as ten of eleven or twelve jurors agree on it, or nine of ten jurors, if the jury have had adequate time to deliberate.[50]

Judgment

In jury cases the judge gives his judgment after the verdict. In non-jury cases he embodies his findings of fact in the judgment[51] and himself assesses the damages to be recovered.[52] By tradition, reasons are usually given for a decision on law in the higher courts, especially if there has been any legal argument. Reasons are also generally given for findings of fact by the judge, but this is not strictly necessary.[53]

A judge is bound to come to a decision, whereas a jury may be unable to reach a verdict and have to be discharged. A judge is not excused from deciding a case because the facts are complicated or the law is obscure. If the facts for and against the plaintiff are

---

[50] Juries Act 1974, s.17.
[51] *Cf. Craven* v. *Craven* [1957] C.L.Y. 1126, petitions dismissed without facts found.
[52] Usually in sterling but it can be in a foreign currency; *Miliangos* v. *George Frank Textiles* [1976] A.C. 443 (H.L.).
[53] *Automatic Woodturning Co.* v. *Stringer* [1957] A.C. 544.

evenly balanced, the judge will decide against the party on whom the burden of proof lay, usually the plaintiff. If both parties are partly to blame for an accident or collision the judge may apportion the damages.[54] If one party is claiming and the other is counter claiming, and one or the other is clearly solely liable the judge must decide for one or the other.[55] If the two parties bring separate actions against each other and each one wins, the only remedy is to appeal to the Court of Appeal for a final decision of the case.[56] The judge must also decide all counterclaims and may give judgment for one party on the claim and the other on the counterclaim.

A judge may indicate for which side he gives judgment, but reserve his reasons; but it is much more usual to deliver extempore judgment immediately.

Counsel for the successful party then asks for costs and there may be legal argument on this. Counsel for the unsuccessful party may ask for a stay of execution pending an appeal. This may be refused or made conditional on payment of the damages and costs into court.

The terms of the judgment are noted by the associate on the bundle of pleadings. He then draws up a certificate embodying these terms. The solicitor for the successful party calls for the certificate and draws up a formal judgment to the same effect, which is entered at the Central Office of the Supreme Court. Judgments may be recalled before they are filed.[57]

If the costs are agreed or assessed by the judge the initial judgment will be complete. If the costs are ordered to be taxed by the taxing officer, the amount assessed by him will be certified and added to the judgment later.[58]

Execution may issue for damages and costs after taxation. If it is desired to issue execution of judgment before taxation a separate execution for costs will have to issue after the certificate of the taxing officer is received.[59]

The judgment will finally conclude the matter between the parties, unless successfully appealed, even if the judgment is given after the writ has issued in a related action. Findings are not binding on third parties, however, *e.g.* a passenger may sue a

---

[54] Law Reform (Contributory Negligence) Act 1945.
[55] *Bray & Bray* v. *Palmer* [1953] 1 W.L.R. 1455; *cf. Nesterczuk* v. *Mortimore* (1965) 39 A.L.J.R. 288.
[56] *Baker* v. *Market Harborough Industrial Co-operative Society* [1953] 1 W.L.R. 1472.
[57] *Re Harrison* [1955] Ch. 260; in *Stewart* v. *Daily Telegraph* [1958] C.L.Y. 1848 it was held that a judgment could not be varied at this point if the matter could have been raised earlier.
[58] *Re a Debtor* [1954] 1 W.L.R. 1190 (C.A.). As to costs see pp. 264 *et seq.*
[59] Ord. 46. *Bell* v. *Holmes* [1956] 1 W.L.R. 1359.

driver of a car for negligence even if a court has exonerated the driver in an action by another driver.[60]

DAMAGES

Assessment of damages

Damages are the loss suffered by the plaintiff as a result of the defendant's wrongful conduct. In some cases the damages are liquidated by the parties. Thus, in an action for failure to repay a loan, to pay for goods sold on credit, or to pay rent, the damages will be liquidated in advance and will be specified in the statement of claim. The defendant may, however, be able to show that the figures are wrong or that he has a set-off.

In other actions the court assesses the damages at the trial, *e.g.* for personal injuries.

Damages are generally assessed as a lump sum, including estimated future damages, although periodic damages might in theory be awarded. Future inflation is not taken into account as the sum awarded may be invested so as to offset inflation.[61]

Personal injury cases

In actions for personal injuries it is difficult to arrive at a definite figure. The plaintiff will recover general damages for loss of earning capacity, so far as can be foreseen[62] and for bodily deterioration, pain, and other matters which cannot be estimated exactly. He may wish to recover special damages as well, *e.g.* cost of special treatment, and loss of wages while in hospital after the accident. Such items must be pleaded and proved by him. At the trial the extent of the plaintiff's injuries will be referred to in evidence. The defendant's counsel may call evidence to refute the amount of damage claimed, and may cross-examine the plaintiff or his witnesses in order to elicit admissions that less damage has been suffered, *e.g.* that the plaintiff has obtained a new employment which is equally remunerative, in spite of the accident. Lump sums are awarded but may be reviewed if the plaintiff's condition

---

[60] *Randolph* v. *Tuck* [1962] 1 Q.B. 175; *cf. Bell* v. *Holmes, supra; Wood* v. *Luscombe* [1966] 1 Q.B. 169.

[61] *Mallett* v. *McMonagle* [1970] A.C. 166; *Cookson* v. *Knowles* [1978] 2 W.L.R. 978 (H.L.).

[62] *Fairley* v. *John Thompson* [1973] 2 Lloyd's Rep. 40 (C.A.); *Croke (A minor)* v. *Wiseman* [1981] 1 W.L.R. 71 (C.A.). The issue of damages can be deferred under Ord. 33, r. 3; *Hawkins* v. *New Mendip Engineering* [1966] 1 W.L.R. 1341 (C.A.); *Coenen* v. *Payne* [1974] 1 W.L.R. 984.

changes.[63] Damages for bereavement and loss of support can be claimed in case of a fatality.[64]

Damages in libel

In libel cases damages are particularly difficult to estimate, *e.g.* it is impossible to know how many people read a libellous article and how it influenced their attitude to the plaintiff. As a trial by jury is often claimed the judge is in some difficulty in directing the jury, as he should not specify any particular sum, the assessment being their concern, and it is not possible to apply any particular test which will give a predictable result.

Nominal damages

If the plaintiff wishes to vindicate his rights but no actual damage has occurred, nominal damages may be awarded. This is not possible where proof of actual damage is a necessary element of the cause of action.[65]

Punitive or exemplary damages

Punitive damages may no longer be awarded except where officials make or continue clearly unjustified arrests[66] or where the defendant was hoping to gain a particular profit from committing the wrong, *e.g.* from libels in his newspaper or book.[67] Such damages, if desired, must be claimed in the pleadings.[68]

Role of judge and jury

The jury assess damages in those cases in which a jury is still used, the judge directing them as to the legal principles which apply. If a judge is sitting without a jury he will assess the damages himself. He may also refer the question to a master.[69] Where it is clear that the plaintiff has suffered some damage but the liability of the defendant is disputed, the judge may give judgment for the defendant on a question of law but assess the damages in case an appeal is taken to a higher court, thus saving the expense of a new

---

[63] Supreme Court Act 1981, s.32 (1982).
[64] Fatal Accidents Act 1976, as substituted by Administration of Justice Act 1982, s.1.
[65] *The Mediana* [1900] A.C. 113; *Sedleigh-Denfield* v. *O'Callaghan* [1940] A.C. 880.
[66] *Reynolds* v. *Commissioner of Police of the Metropolis* [1982] Crim.L.R. 600 (C.A.), *cf.* *Derbyshire* v. *Lancashire County Council* (1983) 133 New L.J. 65.
[67] *Rookes* v. *Barnard* [1964] A.C. 1129; *Cassell & Co.* v. *Broome* [1972] A.C. 1136 (H.L.). *Beloff* v. *Pressdram* [1973] 1 All E.R. 241; such damages are not claimable on death, Administration of Justice Act 1982, s.4(2).
[68] Ord. 18, r. 8(3).
[69] R.S.C. Ord. 37.

trial. If there is some difficulty as to the proper method of assessment of damages, the judge may assess them on alternative principles, and give judgment according to one of these. This will again obviate a new trial if a higher court reverses the judge on this question.

Measure of damages in contract

The general rule in sale of goods is that a seller who fails to perform a contract to supply goods is only liable for the difference between the contract price and the market price, if the latter is higher, or a drop in the re-sale price before the buyer can obtain alternative supplies. A buyer is liable for the difference between the contract and market prices if he refuses to accept delivery and the market price is lower.[70] In hire the amount promised is recoverable, unless the demand exceeds the supply.[71]

Damages have been awarded for disappointment, such as a failure to provide tourist accommodation of the type offered.[72]

Lost profits and other consequential damages may be recoverable, if they were foreseeable by both parties, but must be specifically claimed at the outset.[73]

Damages in employment contracts are fairly liberal. Loss of increased earning power may be recovered.[74] A star may be liable for losses if a film or play has to be abandoned when he walks out.[75] Damages may take into account the employee's personal distress.[76]

Time of assessment of damages

When a tort is actionable in itself, the damages awarded are assessed so as to provide complete compensation for existing and prospective damage and no further action can be brought if further damage subsequently occurs as a result of the original tort.[77] If a trespass or nuisance is continuing, e.g. where the defendant places an obstruction on the plaintiff's land or causes continuous noise or vibration, repeated actions can be brought so long as the wrongful

---

[70] Sale of Goods Act 1979, ss.50, 51; *W.L. Thompson* v. *Robinson* [1955] Ch. 177; *cf. Lazenby Garages* v. *Wright* [1976] 1 W.L.R. 459 (C.A.), loss of a customer though price on a sale higher.

[71] *Interoffice Telephones* v. *Robert Freeman & Co.* [1958] 1 Q.B. 190.

[72] *Jarvis* v. *Swan's Tours* [1973] 1 Q.B. 233. This is becoming common.

[73] *Perestrello e Comp. Ltd.* v. *United Paint Co.* [1969] 1 W.L.R. 570 (C.A.); *AMF* v. *Magnet Bowling* [1968] 1 W.L.R. 1028; *Mitchell (George)* v. *Finney Lock Seeds* [1982] 3 W.L.R. 1036 (C.A.).

[74] *Dunk* v. *George Waller & Son* [1970] 2 Q.B. 163.

[75] *Anglia Television* v. *Reed* [1972] 1 Q.B. 60.

[76] *Cox* v. *Philips Industries Ltd.* [1976] Q.B. 638.

[77] *Rowntree* v. *Allen* (1936) 41 Com.Cas. 90.

condition continues.[78] If damage is essential to the cause of action successive actions can be brought each time any damage occurs.[79] In contract damages are generally assessed as of the time of breach of contract. Inflation up to the date of trial may be taken into account.[80]

Wrongs to property

Generally the actual material loss suffered by the plaintiff can be recovered, *e.g.* the reduction of the value of a building due to the defendant's wrong[81] or the value of the plaintiff's chattels detained or disposed of by the defendant.[82] In some cases the relevant value is that at the time of loss, in others at the date of judgment, the difference depending on whether the plaintiff asserts his title to the goods.[83]

Interest

Damages in the nature of interest are recoverable in respect of the period after the due date for repayment of a debt. The court has a discretion to award interest for the whole or any part of the period from the date when the cause of action arose to the date of judgment.[84]

The court will award interest on damages in tort actions for personal injuries.[85] The period runs from the date of service of the writ up to the date of trial, at half-rate.[86]

Mitigation of damages

This term is used in two distinct senses. (a) Proof that the plaintiff has not suffered some item of damage in respect of which he claims, *e.g.* that defective goods have been used to some advantage and not proved a total loss. If X wrongfully injures B's leg and Y later wrongfully further injures it and it has to be

---

[78] There may be a good case for an injunction; see p. 222.
[79] *Darley Main Colliery* v. *Mitchell* (1886) 11 App.Cas. 127, successive subsidences.
[80] *Philips* v. *Ward* [1956] 1 W.L.R. 471, negligent survey. *Wroth* v. *Tyler* [1974] Ch. 30; *Horsler* v. *Zorro* [1975] Ch. 302.
[81] *Moss* v. *Christchurch R.D.C.* [1925] 2 K.B. 750, negligent fire.
[82] *Building and Civil Engineering Holidays Scheme Management* v. *Post Office* [1966] 1 Q.B. 247 (C.A.); *Brandeis Goldschmidt* v. *Western Transport* [1981] 3 W.L.R. 181 (C.A.).
[83] See *Sachs* v. *Miklos* [1948] 2 K.B. 23; *Strand Electric & Engineering Co.* v. *Brisford Entertainments* [1952] 2 Q.B. 246.
[84] *Riches* v.*Westminster Bank* [1947] A.C. 390; Supreme Court Act 1981, s.35A(1); *Practice Note*, February 24, 1983. Judgment debts carry interest; the Lord Chancellor may fix the rate, Administration of Justice Act 1970, s.44.
[85] *Ibid.* 35A(2) apart for special reasons.
[86] *Cookson* v. *Knowles* [1978] 2 W.L.R. 978; there is no interest on damages for pain and suffering.

amputated, that does not reduce the damages recoverable from X.[87] Insurance benefits are not deducted from claims to damages as the defendant was no party to the plaintiff's contract with his insurer. A pension received by the plaintiff as a result of his injury is not taken into account if he contracted for it as part of his contract of service.[88] A public pension is not taken into account if damages are deductible from it.[89] Unemployment benefit and supplementary benefit are set off against damages, but not social security payments, retirement pensions, redundancy payments or national health care.[90] In recent years, with the high incidence of taxation, it has been held that a plaintiff can only recover for loss of net earning capacity, *i.e.* his pay after deduction of tax, although the various allowances personal to individuals make this complicated to assess.[91] (b) Proof that the plaintiff need not have suffered some item of damage, *e.g.* where the plaintiff refused to undergo a necessary operation to cure personal injuries,[92] or to accept a suitable substitute for the article contracted for.[93]

EXECUTION OF JUDGMENT OF THE HIGH COURT

The court does not of its own motion enforce its judgments but leaves it to the successful plaintiff, known thenceforward as the judgment creditor, to take the initiative afresh, by suing out some form of execution. He must apply to the court and produce a copy of the judgment. The forms of execution differ according to the type of property which the judgment debtor owns. Direct execution is in the charge of the under-sheriff, an administrative and not a judicial officer. High Court money judgments may be enforced through the county court.[94]

Movable goods, securities, negotiable papers and leasehold interests in land are liable to seizure by writ of *fi. fa.*[95] As soon as the judgment debtor is warned of the issue of the writ he will

---

[87] *Baker* v. *Willoughby* [1970] A.C. 407.

[88] *Judd* v. *Hammersmith Hospital* [1960] 1 W.L.R. 328; *Parry* v. *Cleaver* [1970] A.C. 1 (H.L.D.); *cf. Cunningham* v. *Harrison* [1973] Q.B. 942 (C.A.).

[89] *Elstob* v. *Robinson* [1964] 1 W.L.R. 726. See also Fatal Accidents Act 1976.

[90] *Foxley* v. *Olton* [1965] 2 Q.B. 306; *Hewson* v. *Downs* [1970] 1 Q.B. 73; *Daish* v. *Wauton* [1972] 2 Q.B. 262; *Basnett* v. *J. & A. Jackson* [1976] 1 C.R. 63; *Nabi* v. *British Leyland (U.K.)* [1980] 1 W.L.R. 529.

[91] *Gourley* v. *B.T.C.* [1956] A.C. 185; *W. Sussex C.C.* v. *Rought* [1957] A.C. 403; *cf. Herring* v. *B.T.C.* [1958] T.R. 401; *Parsons* v. *B.N.M. Laboratories* [1964] 1 Q.B. 95 (C.A.).

[92] *Luker* v. *Chapman* [1970] 114, S.J. 788; *Morgan* v. *T. Wallis* [1974] 1 Lloyd's Rep. 165; *cf. Spartan Steel Alloys* v. *Martin & Co.* [1973] Q.B. 27 (C.A.).

[93] *Sotiros Shipping Inc.* v. *Solholt* [1981] Com.L.R. 201.

[94] County Courts Act 1959, s.139.

[95] *Fieri Facias, i.e.* cause to be levied: Ord. 47.

generally raise the sum needed, by borrowing from friends or by selling property, unless he is insolvent. Hence there is seldom any necessity for actual seizure and sale of the debtor's goods.[96] The issue of the writ forces the debtor to realise his assets himself for it is otherwise difficult for the creditor to ascertain what assets the debtor has and where they are. The sheriff's officer leaves a man in possession between the time of seizure of the goods and sale.[97]

Clothing, bedding and tools are privileged from execution up to prescribed values.[98]

(2) Where a plaintiff is successful in an action for the recovery of land he will obtain a writ of possession, and actual possession will be delivered to him.[99]

(3) Land and securities, e.g. shares, can be made liable to be taken in execution for money judgments by the court imposing a charge on them to secure payment of the judgment debt.[1] This court order may be registered as a land charge, in order to prevent the judgment debtor selling or mortgaging land.[2]

(4) A committal order may be used to enforce an order to do some act other than to pay money, e.g. to discontinue a nuisance on land. There may be imprisonment in default of compliance.

(5) Interests in land, legacies under wills or interests under trusts and settlements, may be intercepted by applying for the appointment of a receiver.[3]

(6) Debts owing to a judgment debtor can be attached by garnishee proceedings. The judgment debtor can be examined as to his financial position and the payment diverted to the judgment creditor. Money in current deposit or other prescribed accounts at banks can be attached, but not wages or at present National Savings. The sub-debtor must not repay the debt until it is decided whether the creditor is entitled to garnishee it.[4]

(7) Pressure is often put on a judgment debtor by issuing a judgment summons in the county court. As a result the debtor may arrange to pay the debt by instalments, or he may be declared insolvent. It is better to take insolvency proceedings than have numerous creditors sue out separate writs of execution.

---

[96] 55,000 writs of *fi. fa* were issued by the High Court in 1981 on 93,000 judgments of all kinds.
[97] As to "walking possession," see *Watson* v. *Murray* [1955] 2 Q.B. 1.
[98] The Protection from Execution Order 1980 fixes £100 for clothes and bedding and £150 for tools.
[99] R.S.C., Ord. 45, r. 3; *Practice Direction* [1955] 1 W.L.R. 1314.
[1] Charging Orders Act 1979; *National Westminster Bank* v. *Stockman* [1981] 1 W.L.R. 67; *Roberts Petroleum* v. *Kenney (Bernard)* [1982] 1 W.L.R. 301 (C.A.).
[2] Land Charges Act 1972, s.6.
[3] Supreme Court Act 1981, s.37(4).
[4] *Ibid.* ss.40(4), 139(2). Ord. 49.

(8) A writ of delivery is used to obtain possession of specific goods.[5]

(9) A writ of sequestration may be used against personalty, *e.g.* to enforce payment of money into court or to a litigant, or to recover unpaid costs.[6]

(10) The judgment debtor's earnings may be attached to satisfy the debt.[7] The debtor is entitled to certain deductions first.[8] He may be required to give details of his employment and earnings.[9]

(11) Some judgments are self-enforcing, *e.g.* declarations.[10]

INSOLVENCY

This is a statutory procedure to call in all the assets of an insolvent debtor and divide them fairly among his creditors.[11] Some debts are paid in priority to others. The debtor may ultimately obtain a discharge and begin life anew. Where a company is insolvent it may be put into liquidation by its creditors.[12]

SECURING EFFECTIVENESS OF EXECUTION

Until recently English law only assured the effectiveness of a court judgment in a few fields. Thus a pending action against land could be registered so as to bind third parties,[13] assets disposed of so as to defeat claims on divorce could be recovered[14] as could assets disposed of so as to defeat claims by dependants on death.[15]

A general remedy, similar to that used in Europe, has now been provided in suitable cases. An interlocutory injunction may be obtained to prevent a defendant moving or transferring assets to frustrate the effects of a future judgment in an action brought against him. This practice originated in cases with defendants domiciled abroad who might remove assets from this country, and

---

[5] Ord. 45, r. 4; s.29, r. 2A; *Howard E. Perry & Co.* v. *British Railways Board* [1980] 2 All E.R. 579.
[6] Ord. 45, r. 5; *Phonographic Performance* v. *Amusement Caterers (Peckham)* [1964] Ch. 195; *Bucknell* v. *Bucknell* [1969] 1 W.L.R. 1204; *Webster* v. *Southwark London Borough Council* [1983] 2 W.L.R. 217, local authority defied declaratory judgment on electoral law.
[7] Attachment of Earnings Act 1971; *Practice Direction*, September 2, 1981.
[8] *Ibid.* Sched. 3.
[9] *Ibid.* s.14.
[10] *e.g. Leco Instruments (U.K.)* v. *Land Pyrometers* [1981] F.S.R. 325.
[11] Bankruptcy Act 1914, Insolvency Act 1976.
[12] Companies Act 1948, s.218.
[13] Now Land Charges Act 1972, s.15.
[14] Matrimonial Causes Act 1973, s.37(2).
[15] Inheritance Act 1975, s.10.

in maritime and mercantile cases.[16] But it is now applicable to any type of action and to cases of domestic defendants, although in such cases it will not necessarily be granted as a matter of course.[17] The practice has been confirmed by legislation.[18]

The defendant's bank account may also be "frozen" and previous dealings traced.[19] However the injunction is a discretionary remedy and will not be used so as to prejudice third parties acting in good faith.

---

[16] The leading case is *Mareva Compania Naviera S.A.* v. *International Bulk Carriers S.A.* [1975] 2 Lloyd's Rep. 509, also noted in [1980] 1 All E.R. 213 (C.A.). There have been numerous later cases with foreign defendants.

[17] *A.J. Bekhor & Co.* v. *Bilton* [1981] 2 W.L.R. 601.

[18] Supreme Court Act 1981, s.37(3).

[19] *A. & B.* v. *C. D. etc.* [1980] 2 Lloyd's Rep. 200; *A.* v. *C.* [1981] 1 Q.B. 956.

CHAPTER 7

OTHER CIVIL PROCEEDINGS

PROCEEDINGS IN THE CHANCERY DIVISION

THE Chancery Division has far fewer judges than the Queen's Bench Division, but the judges do not sit in appellate courts and generally sit in London and eight other cities.[1] Chancery judges try cases without juries.

Part of their jurisdiction is of an advisory or administrative character and exercised in Chambers, but hostile actions, *e.g.* for an injunction or specific performance, and actions involving decisions on points of law, including the interpretation of documents, are heard in open court.[2]

The organisation and conduct of the business of the division is entrusted to a Vice-Chancellor nominated by the Lord Chancellor.[3]

Motions for an injunction

A striking instance of the use of motions is the application for an injunction. An injunction is a court order requiring or prohibiting the doing of some act. Most injunctions are prohibitory, *e.g.* forbidding the publication of a libellous pamphlet, the distribution of books which infringe the plaintiff's copyright, the erection of a fence across the plaintiff's right of way or of a building which will obstruct the plaintiff's ancient lights. A mandatory injunction may also be ordered, *e.g.* to demolish a wall.[4]

The court has a discretion to grant or refuse an injunction.[5] It need not be granted where damages would be an adequate remedy. It is considered better in most cases, however, to prevent threatened damage being suffered, by issuing an injunction, than

---

[1] Ord. 7 (as amended), *Practice Direction*, [1982] 1 W.L.R. 1189. The District Registrars there have the powers of Chancery Masters: Ord. 32, r. 26 (as amended).

[2] There is now a special Patents Court, Supreme Court Act 1981, ss.6, 62. In 1981 Chancery judges tried 300 witness 380 non-witness actions There were large numbers of insolvency cases and companies proceedings.

[3] *Ibid.* s.5(1)(*a*); the Lord Chancellor is President but does not generally sit.

[4] *Esso Petroleum Co.* v. *Kingswood Motors* [1974] Q.B. 142 (re-conveyance of land); *Wakeham* v. *Wood* (1981) 8 C.L. 325 (demolition).

[5] Supreme Court Act 1981, s.37.

to wait until serious damage occurs, especially as the defendant may not be wealthy enough to make amends for it.[6] Even if some damage has occurred, an injunction is useful to prevent further damage, *e.g.* continued sale of a book which contains libellous passages. An injunction is also useful to prevent a wealthy man from buying immunity from the law, as by defiantly undermining the plaintiff's house and offering to pay for the damage.

An injunction is also very appropriate for repeated wrongs. If a neighbour constantly trespasses on your land as a short cut, it is pointless to sue him for each trespass; indeed you might get only nominal damages and have to pay the costs. On the other hand an injunction will render the neighbour liable to be committed to prison for contempt of court if he trespasses again. If the land-owner fails to take some kind of action he may find that the neighbour has acquired a legal right to cross his land through his acquiescence.

Occasional use is made of injunctions to restrain the repetition of minor offences, for which repeated small fines prove no deterrent.[7] In such cases the civil rules as to the extent of the burden of proof apply.[8]

Injunctions can be used in industrial cases, *e.g.* to restrain the wrongful expulsion of a trade unionist from his union, as damages may be an inadequate remedy.[9]

A valuable employee, *e.g.* a film star, can be restrained by injunction from working for any other employer. This is very important because the law will not force any person to perform personal service. An employee is usually unable to pay a large enough sum in damages to compensate the company for the loss they would otherwise suffer: *e.g.* if a star walks out in the middle of a film, all the film already taken is lost, as well as the salaries paid to other performers and technicians.[10]

An injunction will not be granted unless it is a meritorious case, the applicant has acted properly, and the application is made promptly. Notice of the motion is given to the person whom it is desired to enjoin or restrain.[11]

---

[6] Ord. 29; *Hooper* v. *Rogers* [1975] Ch. 43 (C.A.); *Evans Marshall & Co.* v. *Bertola S.A.* [1973] 1 W.L.R. 349 (C.A.).

[7] *Att.-Gen.* v. *Harris* [1961] 1 Q.B. 74; *Att.-Gen.* v. *Wellingborough U.D.C.* (1974) 72 L.G.R. 507 (C.A.); *Burnley B.C.* v. *England* (1978) 76 L.G.R. 393.

[8] *Post Office* v. *Estuary Radio*, pirate radio station [1968] 2 Q.B. 740.

[9] See p. 76, *supra*. *Cf.* Restrictive Practices Act 1968, s.7; *Re Flushing Cistern Makers' Agreement* [1973] 3 All E.R. 819 (trade restrictions).

[10] *Lumley* v. *Wagner* (1852) De G.M. & G. 604; *Warner Brothers* v. *Nelson* [1937] 1 K.B. 209; *Marco Productions* v. *Pagola* [1945] K.B. 111; *Hivac Ltd.* v. *Park Royal Scientific Instruments Ltd.* [1946] Ch. 169.

[11] *Godfrey Phillips* v. *Investment Trust Corp.* [1953] Ch. 449; *Armstrong* v. *Sheppard & Short* [1959] 2 Q.B. 384.

An interim or interlocutory injunction may be sought after an action is begun. The motion must be supported by affidavits, stating the ground on which an injunction is claimed.[12] The opposing party is then entitled to an adjournment in order to file an answering affidavit.[13] If the matter is urgent the court may grant a temporary or interim injunction even without hearing the other side.[14]

The interim injunction may be granted by consent or granted subject to an undertaking in damages by the plaintiff should he lose the case. The court may refuse an interim injunction without prejudice to the eventual result of the action and will do so if the grant of the injunction would pre-judge a matter which will later have to be decided.[15] The trial court will grant or refuse a final injunction, on the strength of oral testimony or affidavits. The trial of the motion may, by agreement of both parties, be treated as the trial of the action, to save further costs.

Undertakings to desist from some steps are sometimes accepted by the court from the defendant instead of submission to an injunction. Injunctions may be for some period, subject to renewal, or they may be suspended, e.g. while the defendant executes building or demolition work in order to terminate the damage complained of by the plaintiff.[16]

Damages may be awarded in substitution for an injunction.[17] This is a limited remedy. It means that the case is of a kind in which an injunction would normally be appropriate, but that an injunction ought not to be issued in the particular circumstances. In some cases the loss to the defendant, were an injunction granted, would be out of all proportion to the loss suffered by the plaintiff.[18]

Action for specific performance

A suit for specific performance is one of the most important hostile actions in the Chancery Division. A common example is the action by a purchaser to insist on performance of a contract of sale of land, not contenting himself with damages. A writ is

[12] *Silber* v. *Lewin* (1889) 33 S.J. 757.
[13] R.S.C., Ord. 29, r. 1(7).
[14] R.S.C., Ord. 29, r. 1(2); this is not appropriate in the case of mandatory injunctions; *Shepherd Homes* v. *Sandham* [1971] Ch. 340.
[15] *Sim* v. *H.J. Heinz & Co.* [1959] 1 W.L.R. 313 (C.A.); *American Cyanamid Co.* v. *Ethicon* [1975] A.C. 396.
[16] *e.g. Charrington* v. *Simons & Co.* [1970] 1 W.L.R. 725; Three-year suspension.
[17] Supreme Court Act 1981, s.50; *Baxter* v. *Four Oaks Properties* [1965] Ch. 816.
[18] *Redland Bricks Ltd.* v. *Morris* [1970] A.C. 652; *Wrotham Park Estate Co.* v. *Parkside Homes* [1974] 1 W.L.R. 798; *Kennaway* v. *Thompson* [1980] 3 W.L.R. 361.

served, as in a Queen's Bench proceeding, pleadings are exchanged, and interlocutory applications are dealt with by a
Chancery master, an adjournment before the judge taking the
place of an appeal in interlocutory matters. The judge may decide
such matters in chambers but will adjourn them into court if a legal
principle or an important rule of practice is involved. There is
provision for summary judgment where the defendant has no
arguable defence to the claim.[19]

Fixed dates for the trial of witness actions may be applied for.[20]
Non-witness actions are set down on the lists and tried when
reached. Cases may be set down for trial in London, and eight
provincial cities.[21] Many cases of contracts for the sale of land turn
purely on correspondence or on the effect of the contract or
conveyance, or on printed conditions of sale; here documents are
examined by the court and no oral testimony may be needed.
Other evidence is often given by affidavits, which are filed in the
court while copies are exchanged among the parties. Deponents
can be ordered to appear to be cross-examined on their affidavits
before the master or judge on application by the opposing side.[22]
Oral evidence may be desirable to clarify the circumstances of a
contract.[23]

The order of speeches by counsel is similar to that in other civil
cases. There is no jury and the judgment will therefore deal with
facts and law and with the right to a decree.

Chancery judgments

Counsel for the two parties endorse the terms of the judgment
on their briefs. The registrar draws up the order after studying the
endorsements, pleadings and affidavits. In difficult cases counsel
for the parties may agree on the terms of the order. If counsel do
not agree on these terms the matter must be referred to the
judge.[24]

Judgment by default is a much more cautious proceeding in the
Chancery Division than in the Queen's Bench. If the defendant
fails to enter an appearance the plaintiff files his statement of claim
in court, as he cannot deliver it.[25] He then makes a motion for

---

[19] R.S.C. Ord. 86; *Practice Direction,* February 20, 1974 .
[20] *Practice Direction,* November 25, 1974. The listing of cases is governed by the *Practice Direction* [1983] 1 All E.R. 1145.
[21] *Practice Direction,* [1982] 1 W.L.R. 1189, but may be adjourned elsewhere, *St Edmundsbury & Ipswich Diocesan Board of Finance* v. *Clark* [1973] Ch. 323.
[22] R.S.C., Ord. 38, r. 2(3), *Practice Direction* [1969] 1 W.L.R. 983.
[23] *N.C.B.* v. *Hornby* [1950] Ch. 10, 15; *cf. Bird* v. *Treasury Solicitor* [1951] Ch. 298, 301.
[24] *Cf. Practice Note* [1884] W.N. 91; *Ex p. Skerratt* (1884) 28 S.J. 376; *General Share Co.* v. *Wetley Brick and Pottery Co.* (1882) 220 Ch.D. 130; *Practice Direction* (1960) 12 C.L. 270a.
[25] Ord. 13, r. 6.

judgment, notice of this motion being filed in the court.[26] If the defendant entered an appearance but has failed to deliver a defence, the plaintiff must move for judgment and serve notice of this motion on the defendant.[27]

Where a judgment directs further steps to be taken, *e.g.* the preparation of an inventory, taking of accounts or a sale of land, a "summons to proceed" is taken out and the parties' solicitors appear before the master, who gives directions as to the necessary action to be taken.[28] If the solicitors do not accept the master's directions they may appear by summons before the judge in chambers. If a point of principle is involved the matter will be tried in open court and argued by counsel.[29] If some step results in an account or report which is disputed by either party, the matter can also be brought before the judge.[30]

Procedure by originating summons[31]

This procedure is appropriate where there is no substantial dispute of fact or the sole or principal issue is a point of law, including the construction of a statute, deed, will or contract.[32]

One form is used to ask the Chancery judge to perform some administrative action, *e.g.* to appoint trustees when there is no other way of doing so,[33] or to authorise some transaction which is not authorised by the general law.[34] This jurisdiction is usually exercised in the judge's chambers or at a district registry, but will be tried in open court if the court prefers.[35] Another form is a construction summons taken out by some person claiming to be interested under a deed or will and applying to have the meaning of the instrument interpreted by the judge in open court. Under an analogous procedure the court may be asked to rule on the identity of beneficiaries or creditors or the extent of their rights, or on problems which arise in the course of administration.[36] The court may, for example, order that the estate be distributed on the footing that some missing claimant is dead.[37] It may direct

---

[26] Ord. 8, r. 2.
[27] Ord. 19, r. 7; *Butterworth* v. *Smallwood* [1924] W.N. 82.
[28] Ord. 44, rr. 2, 4.
[29] Ord. 44, r. 20.
[30] Ord. 44, r. 24; Harman Report (1960), p. 25.
[31] 8,224 writs and originating summonses were issued in 1981. There are no separate figures.
[32] Ord. 5, r. 4; Ord. 7, r. 2. *Practice Direction,* November 5, 1974.
[33] Trustee Act 1925, s.41; Ord. 5, r. 3.
[34] *Cf.* Settled Land Act 1925, s.64; Ord. 5, r. 3.
[35] *e.g.* under the Variation of Trusts Act 1958, s.1; *Re Chapman* (*No.* 2) [1959] 1 W.L.R. 372.
[36] Ord. 85, r. 2.
[37] *Neville* v. *Benjamin* [1902] 1 Ch. 723; *Re Newson-Smith's Settlement* [1962] 1 W.L.R. 1478; *Re Westminster Bank's Declaration of Trust* [1963] 1 W.L.R. 820.

inquiries where the usual advertisements for claims prescribed by law[38] have been unsuccessful.[39] Application may also be made by summons for an order for the administration of a deceased person's estate, *e.g.* where creditors have not been satisfied.[40] A general order will then direct the taking of accounts and the making of inquiries, so as to determine all debts and ascertain the value of the assets of the estate.[41] The order may reserve liberty to apply for another order on further consideration.

There are two forms of originating summons[42] and special forms for acknowledgment of service.[43]

Procedure on originating summons differs from that in an action. There are no pleadings. The document to be construed will be filed,[44] and a specific point will be raised in the summons, supported by an affidavit explaining the facts.[45] A copy is served on the opponent.[46] Discovery of relevant documents may be ordered by a Master on application.[47] On the summons for directions the defendant will be given time to file an affidavit in opposition or deponents may be required to attend for cross-examination, and an appointment is made for the hearing.[48] A case will illustrate the objects of the system. A testator had been interested in certain coal mines which were nationalised. In a codicil to his will he left his mines to one person; in another codicil he left the rest of his personal estate to another person. The state was bound to pay compensation to the testator for his mines. The executors of the estate applied to the court for a ruling as to which of the two legatees was entitled to this compensation money.[49]

The judge will try such a summons in court, and hear argument by counsel, as all points of construction are points of law and should not be decided in chambers. Chambers decisions are not reported whereas decisions on a summons adjourned into court often are.

Masters in Chancery may not decide questions of law or construction or make certain orders, though they may otherwise

[38] Trustee Act 1925, s.27.
[39] *Re Lord Letherbrow* [1935] W.N. 34.
[40] Ord. 85, r. 1.
[41] Ord. 85, r. 5.
[42] Ord. 7, r. 2 Forms 8 and 10.
[43] Ord. 10, r. 5 Form 15.
[44] [1949] W.N. 441.
[45] Ords. 7, r. 3; 28, r. 3(3); *Re Caines The Times,* November 8, 1977.
[46] Ord. 28, r. 3(1).
[47] Ord. 24, r. 3.
[48] Ord. 28, r. 4(4); *Isaac v. Isaac* [1972] 1 W.L.R. 921 (C.A.).
[49] *Re Galway's Will Trusts* [1950] Ch. 1. The court may also have to decide at what date a condition must be satisfied, on what basis capital and income are computed, and whether some proposed transaction is consistent with the terms of a trust.

act as judges subject to a right of appeal to the judge, unless any party insists on trial by the judge or some rule forbids it.[50]

There are limitations on the court's powers to rule on such summonses. Thus, like any other court, it will not give a hypothetical ruling. It will readily advise trustees or executors whether they have power to do some act in the future, but it will not advise, for example, as to the legal effects of such acts before they are done.[51] Future problems will not generally be anticipated, e.g. what will have to be done when some person dies. In particular the court does not like to rule as to the rights of persons under age or not yet born or identified, though there is provision for separate representation of such persons.[52]

Repeated recourse to the judge in chambers may be necessary after the original hearing of an originating summons, as where inquiries or accounts are ordered, and recourse will always be necessary where future points are left outstanding. Hence the various orders made by the court will generally include "liberty to apply" until all matters are finally disposed of. Even a final order may be reopened in suitable circumstances.[53]

Where the court has power to allow steps to be taken which are not authorised by the general law it has a wide discretion. Expediency, rather than strict law, is often decisive[54] provided the judge has jurisdiction under the appropriate statute.[55]

A summons is not generally appropriate for hostile litigation, e.g. charges involving fraud or disputes of fact. In such cases an action should be commenced by writ.[56]

On the other hand the originating summons is the procedure prescribed for applications to secure provision for dependants left unprovided for by a will, the executor of the will being made defendant to the summons.[57] Evidence is generally by affidavit, but the court may direct a deponent to be cross-examined. The proceedings, if successful, result in an order for payment of maintenance out of the estate. They are often hostile actions, and writ procedure might be more suitable. The same objection

---

[50] Ord. 32, r. 14(2); *Practice Directions* [1975] 1 W.L.R. 131; [1977] 1 W.L.R. 1019, December 30, 1982. This appeal may amount to a rehearing, Ord. 58, r. 1, *Practice Direction* July 29, 1982.

[51] *Re Barnato* [1949] Ch. 258.

[52] *Re Staples* [1916] 1 Ch. 322.

[53] *Re Tate's Will Trusts* [1959] Ch. 615; applicant lost right of appeal by relying on a promise which was not kept.

[54] *Cf. Re Leman's Trusts* (1883) 22 Ch.D. 633; *Re Henderson* [1940] Ch. 764.

[55] *Re Chapman's Settlement Trusts* [1954] A.C. 429; see n. 34.

[56] *Re Parkinson & Co.* [1965] 1 W.L.R. 372. *Re Old Wood Common Compensation Fund* [1967] 1 W.L.R. 958, *Re Deadman* [1971] 1 W.L.R. 426.

[57] Ord. 99, under Inheritance (Family Provision) Act 1975; *Practice Note*, March 26, 1976; *Practice Direction* [1978] 1 W.L.R. 585; *Re Christie* [1979] 2 W.L.R. 1051.

applies to the extension of the summons procedure to use against squatters and trespassers on land.[58]

Limitation of actions in equity

Limitation of actions is statutory and equity has never allowed statutes to be used as a cloak of fraud. The Limitation Act 1980 assimilates common law and equitable principles.

A general period of 12 years' adverse possession will bar any claim by one beneficiary to recover personal estate from another. The common example is where the wrong legatee has received a legacy or land has been transferred to someone other than the devisee under a will.[59] The same rule applies if an estate is distributed on the assumption that some provision in a will or settlement is valid, whereas it is in fact ineffective and another claimant is in law entitled to the property.[60]

Where the action is brought against fiduciary defendants, such as trustees, executors or administrators, a further subdivision of possible cases must be made. If the trustee, for instance, is sued for his negligence in paying the wrong legatee or transferring land to the wrong person, he can plead six years lapse of time. On the other hand he may not escape liability in spite of any lapse of time if he was guilty of fraud or still retains the trust property or has used it for his own benefit.[61] The same rule applies to persons acquiring trust property from a fraudulent trustee otherwise than in good faith and for value.[62] No time runs in favour of a trustee who has fraudulently concealed a negligent loss of assets, until the facts are discovered.[63] In one case a woman died intestate in 1923. Her husband occupied her land until 1944, although her son was legally entitled to it. It was held that the son could still recover the land, together with a fair occupation rent for the whole period since 1923.[64]

In claims for discretionary remedies like injunctions or specific performance, and in claims against trustees where they cannot plead the Limitation Act 1980,[65] the Chancery Division will refuse a remedy if the plaintiff has been guilty of laches (unreasonable

---

[58] Ord. 113; [1970] 1 W.L.R. 1250.
[59] Limitation Act 1980, s.22. Interests under a trust for sale of land are claims against land, though themselves personalty.
[60] Re Diplock [1948] Ch. 465, 508–512.
[61] Limitation Act 1980, s.21.
[62] G.L. Baker v. Medway Building & Supplies [1958] 1 W.L.R. 1216.
[63] Act of 1980, s.32; Beaman v. A.R.T.S. [1949] 1 K.B. 550, 559 (C.A.).
[64] Re Howlett [1949] Ch. 767.
[65] Godfrey Phillips v. Investment Trust Corp. [1953] Ch. 449.

delay) or acquiescence, *i.e.* appearing to waive or condone the defendants' torts or breach of contract.[66]

PROBATE AND ADMINISTRATION

Non-contentious business

The intervention of the court is usually required in order to transfer the property of a deceased person to his successors.[67] All people die testate or intestate. A man dies testate if he has made a will in proper form, *i.e.* duly signed and attested, provided also he was of sound mind in the sense that he could properly assess all his normal obligations.

If the testator has made a will and appointed an executor, the executor, unless he wishes to renounce his office, may apply for a grant of probate, *i.e.* a judicial authentication of the effectiveness of the will. The executor must apply at the Principal Registry of the Family Division at Somerset House in London, or at a district probate registry.[68] If the estate is large enough to attract liability to taxation it will have to be valued and tax will have to be paid before any grant is made. The original will must be filed at the registry with an affidavit by the executor undertaking to administer the estate properly.[69]

Most wills are undisputed. Any person who disputes the validity of a will or relies on a later will or codicil, however, may lodge a *caveat* at the registry and trial takes place in the Chancery Division.[70] In order to anticipate disputes about mere formal objections, a will usually contains an "attestation clause" which recites compliance with the provisions of the Wills Act 1837 as to formal execution. This forces the party contesting the will to prove positively that it was not properly executed; *e.g.* that the witnesses signed before the testator. Many of these formal defects are difficult to prove if the will appears validly executed on the face of it. If there is no attestation clause or there are unattested alterations on the will, the validity of the will must be verified by affidavits of attesting witnesses or other witnesses.[71]

---

[66] Limitation Act 1980, s.36(2); *Bullock* v. *Lloyds Bank* [1955] Ch. 317.

[67] Supreme Court Act 1981, ss.25, 105, there are exceptions: Administration of Estates & Small Payments Act 1965 and Order [1975] C.L.Y. 1396.

[68] Supreme Court Act 1981, ss.104, 105. Probate must generally be applied for within three years of the death, but there is no limitation period if reasons can be shown for delay. *Re Flynn* [1982] 1 W.L.R. 310. Postal applications are possible, *Practice Note* (F.D.), April 15, 1975.

[69] Form 121. See Probate Rule 53; any person in possession of a will may be required to produce it, Supreme Court Act 1981, ss.122, 123.

[70] Supreme Court Act 1981, ss.107, 108, Sched. I(1)(*h*).

[71] Non-contentious Probate Rules, r. 10.

The registry will grant probate if the will is not rejected. A probate order is issued, which is used as proof of the passing of the title to the testator's property to the executor. A copy of the will is also issued, the original being kept on file.[72]

If there is a will but no executor is appointed or the executor named in it refuses to act, a grant of "administration with the will annexed" will be made. The applicant will have to find security for due administration.[73]

If a man dies wholly intestate, *i.e.* leaving no effective will, an administrator "on intestacy" will have to be appointed.[74] Administrators may be required to provide guarantees in some cases.[75]

If a will or intestacy, fails to make reasonable provision for the testator's or testatrix spouse or ex-spouse or dependants and they are in need, application may be made for maintenance by proceedings in the Chancery Division, or Family Division.[76]

It sometimes happens that a later will or codicil is found after a grant of probate, or a valid will after a grant on intestacy. Application must then be made to revoke the grant and have an appropriate new grant made.[77]

Contentious business

Few probate or administration cases are litigated.[78] Trial is in the Chancery Division.[79] A writ is used, indorsed with a statement of the nature of the plaintiff's and defendant's interest in the deceased's estate.[80] The executor or administrator is made a party. The grant is lodged in Court and an affidavit is made as to any other testamentary documents known to exist.[81] Grounds for opposition to the will, *e.g.* lack of due execution of the will or the insanity of the testator must be specifically pleaded.[82]

---

[72] Supreme Court Act 1981, ss.124, 125.
[73] *Ibid.* ss.119, 120; there is an order of priorities, *e.g.* a person entitled under a residuary gift is entitled to a grant before a person receiving a specific legacy; Non-contentious Probate Rules 1954, r. 19.
[74] *Ibid.* ss.105, 113. Priority rights to a grant follow the law of intestate succession. A surviving wife will usually be the obvious choice: Non-contentious Probate Rules, r. 21.
[75] Non-contentious Probate Rules, r. 38 as amended by r. 8 of 1971 Supreme Court Act 1981, s.120.
[76] Inheritance (Family Provision) Act 1975, see n. 57, *supra.*
[77] Supreme Court Act 1981, s.121.
[78] 118 probate suits were fought whereas the Family Division Registry made 265,000 grants in respect of wills and intestacy in 1981.
[79] Supreme Court Act 1981 Sched. I(1)(*h*).
[80] New Ord. 76 (1971), r. 2; it is issued only in London.
[81] rr. 4, 5.
[82] r. 9.

COMMERCIAL COURT

Rules of court assign some commercial cases to this branch of the Queen's Bench Division.[83]

ADMIRALTY COURT

This is a branch of the Queen's Bench Division dealing with salvage, collisions at sea, freight and other marine disputes.[84]

COURT OF PROTECTION

This is a special department of the High Court which undertakes the management of the property of persons mentally incapable of such administration.[85] The master exercises its powers under the supervision of the Lord Chancellor and nominated judges of the Chancery Division. The court is financed out of charges made on the estates administered.

RESTRICTIVE PRACTICES COURT

This court, with a judge and expert assessors, investigates whether restrictive trading agreements offend the public interest. The Court may sit in the Law Courts in London, or elsewhere.[86]

MATRIMONIAL PROCEEDINGS

All matrimonial causes[87] now commence in a divorce county court designated as such by the Lord Chancellor, or in the Principal Family Division Registry in London, which is equated with those courts.[88] If the cause remains undefended by the other spouse the county court also tries it, if designated as a trial court.[89] A number

---

[83] Supreme Court Act 1981, ss.6(1), 62(3).

[84] Supreme Court Act 1981, ss.20, 24, 62(2).

[85] Mental Health Act 1983, s.93; Court of Protection Rules 1982; 26,763 estates were being administered in 1981. And see *M.* v. *Lester* [1966] 1 W.L.R. 134; *Re W.* [1971] 1 Ch. 123.

[86] Restrictive Practices Court Act 1976, s.6. The procedure is governed by rules of 1957 and 1973.

[87] As defined by the Supreme Court Act 1981, s.26; 266,000 matrimonial cases were started in 1981.

[88] Matrimonial Causes Act 1967, ss.1(3), 4; r. 12.

[89] *Ibid.* s.1(1). 141,068 decrees were granted by county courts in 1981.

of county courts have been so designated.[90] The Lord Chancellor also designates various county court judges to sit in such cases.[91]

If no intention to defend is notified and no answer to the petition is filed, the case is regarded as undefended, even if the parties are in dispute about financial matters[92] or about the future of the children of the marriage.[93]

If the case is defended it is transferred to the Family Division of the High Court.[94] The county court may also transfer undefended cases to the High Court if it deems it desirable,[95] *e.g.* if the case is difficult or important.[96] Divorce cases in the High Court may be tried at the Royal Courts of Justice in London or in certain divorce towns where there are trial courts of the High Court.[97]

Petition and pleadings

Although no specific matrimonial wrong need now be put in issue, the petitioner must satisfy the court that the marriage has broken down and the evidence will be similar to that used in the past, matrimonial offences being proof of breakdown.[98]

The petition must describe the family circumstances and state facts relevant to prove the alleged breakdown of the marriage.[99] It is served on the respondent personally or posted to him with a form for acknowledgment of receipt.[1]

The respondent may give notice of intention to defend.[2] He must then file an answer,[3] denying the facts alleged in the petition or setting out further facts supporting his opposition to the petition.[4] Where the only ground for divorce is five years separation, the respondent may also object that grave hardship would be caused to him if a divorce were decreed.[5]

In undefended cases there is a special procedure and new forms of petition are provided.[6]

---

[90] Divorce County Courts Order 1978.
[91] Act of 1967, s.5, Courts Act 1971, s.20, now "circuit judges."
[92] Matrimonial Causes Rules 1977, rr. 49, 50.
[93] Act of 1967, s.2.
[94] Act of 1967, s.1(3). Supreme Court Act 1981, s.61, Sched. 1, the President is head of the Division.
[95] Act of 1967, s.2.
[96] rr. 32, 80.
[97] *Ibid.* r. 43. 10,386 decrees were granted in 1981 in the High Court and its District Registries.
[98] Matrimonial Causes Act 1973, s.1.
[99] r. 9, App. 2.
[1] r. 14.
[2] r. 15.
[3] r. 18, *Sims* v. *Sims* (1979) 10 Fam.Law. 16 (C.A.); *Day* v. *Day* [1979] 2 W.L.R. 681 (C.A.).
[4] r. 21.
[5] Act of 1973, s.5.
[6] *Practice Direction,* March 7, 1977.

The stress in divorce litigation is now on financial provision, custody of children and similar matters; but the relative behaviour of the two spouses is still relevant, and will have to be considered.[7]

Particulars may be requested in divorce proceedings.[8] Discovery of documents may be ordered, and interrogatories may be administered.[9]

An attempt must also be made at reconciliation.[10] Court welfare officers will act to assist in this.[11]

Trial arrangements

The registrar may give directions, on written request by a party, as to the place and form of trial. The party's request, where he suggests the place, will generally be acceded to, but in defended cases the opposing party will be consulted and general convenience will be decisive.[12]

Causes are set down for trial at the Principal Family Division Registry or at a divorce town registry.[13] A fixed date may be obtained in county court cases[14] and may be applied for in High Court cases.[15]

Divorce cases are tried after a delay of at least ten days.[16]

Trial

Trial is by a hearing in defended cases.[17] The order of speeches will be decided by counsel. Affidavits will be filed but oral testimony may be required. Procedure at the trial will be similar to that in the past, and like the practice in civil trials in the Queen's Bench Division. When the case is undefended there is no formal hearing.[18]

Ancillary relief

Wide powers are conferred on the court to deal with the financial position of the parties and their children and each family situation is unique.[19] The petitioner or respondent must therefore

[7] *Infra.* Ancillary relief.
[8] r. 26.
[9] rr. 28, 29.
[10] Act of 1973, s.6.
[11] *Practice Note* [1971] C.L.Y. 3690.
[12] rr. 33, 34, 34(7).
[13] rr. 2, 44, 46.
[14] r. 33(2).
[15] Matrimonial Causes Rules 1977, r.33(4) (as amended 1978).
[16] r. 47.
[17] r. 43(1). The Registrar may act in some cases, rr. 33, 48.
[18] Matrimonial Causes (Amendment No. 2) Rules 1976.
[19] Matrimonial Causes Act 1973, Pt. II; *Sharpe* v. *Sharpe* (1981) 11 Fam.Law. 121 (C.A.).

apply for rulings in their petition and answer respectively.[20] The court may, however, permit a later application instead.[21] Financial matters may be decided in chambers by the registrar.[22] Proposals on such matters must be made by the parties.

A prayer for custody, if desired, must be included in the petition and answer.[23] Custody may be dealt with by the judge at any time in the proceedings.[24]

The decrees

The first decree is a decree *nisi*. A decree absolute must be applied for within twelve months of the decree *nisi* or reasons for the delay must be given.[25] A period must elapse between the two decrees.[26] Orders for financial provision may be made even after the decree absolute.[27] The Queen's Proctor may also show cause against the decree being made absolute, if the material facts were not before the court.[28] No decree may be made absolute until the court makes an order declaring that it is satisfied that proper arrangements have been made for the children of the marriage.[29]

Appeals

Appeals are provided from the registrar to the judge.[30] Appeal lies from a decree *nisi* to the Court of Appeal, from the county court[31] and the High Court.[32] Four special lists are provided in the Court of Appeal.[33]

Where the judge has been guilty of some irregularity which has prejudiced the trial, application may be made to the Court of Appeal for a new trial.[34]

PROCEEDINGS IN COUNTY COURTS

The county court is a statutory creation of the nineteenth century, being designed to provide less costly remedies for small claims and

---

[20] *Ibid.* s.26(2)(*a*), r. 68(1).
[21] *Ibid.* s.26(2)(*b*), r. 68(2).
[22] rr. 77, 78. Pre-trial review was tried but dropped, [1980] 2 C.L.Y. 186; [1981] 6 C.L.Y. 701.
[23] Act, App. 2, para. 5, r. 21.
[24] Act of 1973, s.42, r. 92.
[25] *Ibid.* s.9(2), r. 65.
[26] *Ibid.* s.1(5); *Practice Direction* (F.D.). June 15, 1977.
[27] *Ibid.* s.23.
[28] r. 61 *Savage* v. *Savage* [1982] 3 W.L.R. 418.
[29] Act, s.41.
[30] r. 124; *Practice Direction* (F.D.) February 26, 1979.
[31] Supreme Court Act 1981, s.15.
[32] Supreme Court Act, 1981, s.18(1).
[33] Ord. 59, r.3(2), (4).
[34] r. 54(8), *McKenzie* v. *McKenzie* [1971] P. 33.

a forum more easily accessible to litigants. Judgment is entered in about a million cases a year but few of these are contested cases. Small claims are transferable by the High Court to the county court, but the High Court may take over some cases from it.[35] The County Court may transfer a case to the High Court if it involves an important question of law or fact.[36]

Commencement of proceedings

The creditor or his solicitor must ascertain in which county court district his debtor resides or trades. He must then fill in a form of plaint known as a request which states the names and addresses of the parties, particulars of the claim and the sum claimed.[37] The registrar's clerk fixes the date of a pre-trial review of the case. He then issues the summons, which reproduces the information given on the request. This summons can be served by a party or a bailiff of the court.[38] The bailiff need not serve the summons on the defendant personally but can leave it in his letter-box or with some other person at his home to hand to the defendant. Postal service is permissible if proof of receipt is forthcoming.[39]

We have seen that the court takes a more active part in proceedings than in the case of the High Court, by serving process instead of leaving it to private process servers.[40] The summons is accompanied by special reply forms which provide for the defendant to state his defence or to admit liability.[41]

Jurisdiction

The county court may try claims for tort or breach of contract not exceeding £5,000.[42] If an important question of law or fact is likely to arise, the defendant, on giving security for costs, may ask for the case to be transferred to the High Court.[43] The monetary maxima may be raised.[44]

Some types of action cannot be brought in the county court at all, except by agreement, namely, libel or slander. It may try malicious prosecution, false imprisonment or cases where a party

[35] County Courts Act 1959, ss.75A, 75B, in Supreme Court Act 1981, Sched. 3. In 1981 18,000 contested cases were tried in county courts.
[36] County Courts Act 1959, s.75(c) (1981).
[37] Ibid. s.1; County Court Rules (1981) Ords. 3, 6.
[38] County Court Rules 1981, Ord. 7.
[39] Ord. 7, r. 10 and 2.
[40] See n. 38.
[41] Ord. 9, r. 2.
[42] County Courts Act 1959, s.39; cf. s.192; Administration of Justice Act 1969, s.6; County Courts Jurisdiction Order 1981.
[43] Act of 1959, s.75c (1981).
[44] Ibid. s.192 (1982).

is charged with fraud.[45] In all such cases a jury of eight would have to be used, taken from the same jury books as the High Court jury.[46]

The parties may agree to the trial by a county court of any type of common law action, even if generally excluded from the jurisdiction of such courts or for an amount above the maximum.[47]

The county court now has a substantial equity jurisdiction, up to £30,000.[48]

Certiorari will lie to set aside a judgment if the county court judge exceeds his jurisdiction.[49]

Default and fixed date procedure

A "default procedure" is used in the case of liquidated claims such as the price of goods sold.[50] The summons is served on the defendant or left at his address. The defendant must put in a defence within 14 days or the plaintiff will recover judgment. The defence is filed at the court office, a copy being sent by the registrar to the plaintiff.[51]

In the fixed date procedure or where a defence is filed. The registrar holds a pre-trial review of the case and deals with interlocutory matters raised by the parties such as discovery of documents. He may give judgment by default if the defendant does not attend and has not delivered a defence. The registrar fixes a day for the trial if the case is defended.[52]

County Court judge

The county court judgeship is part of the functions of the circuit judges, who will also sit in Crown Courts. High Court judges and Recorders may sit in county courts if they consent to do so.[53]

Registrar

The registrar is a solicitor, appointed by the Lord Chancellor.[54] He disposes of most undefended cases and claims up to £500

---

[45] County Courts Act 1959, s.39; *Lea* v. *Moore* [1955] 1 W.L.R. 38; *Harmsworth* v. *London Transport Executive* (1979) 123 S.J. 825 (C.A.).
[46] *Ibid.* ss. 94, 96. In fact such cases are rarely tried in county courts. Twenty jury trials occurred in 1981. A majority verdict of seven is acceptable under the Courts Act 1971, s.39(2).
[47] Act of 1959, s.42; *R.* v. *Judge Willes* [1954] 1 W.L.R. 136.
[48] *Ibid.* s.52(1); Administration of Justice Act 1969, s.5; County Court Jurisdiction Order 1981.
[49] *R.* v. *Worthington-Evans* [1959] 2 Q.B. 145.
[50] Ord. 3, r. 2.
[51] Ord. 9, rr. 2, 6.
[52] Ord. 17; under Ord. 9, r. 14 summary judgment may be obtained if £500 or more is claimed.
[53] County Courts Act 1959, s.20.
[54] *Ibid.* s.18, 22 he retires at 72, s.23.

(unless an objection is made).[55] The parties may agree to trial of any case by the registrar.[56] There may be a full-time registrar, or a part-time registrar with a private practice, depending on the pressure of the work.

The hearing by the judge[57]

When the day fixed for the hearing arrives several things may happen. If the plaintiff fails to appear the case will be removed from the list, but the action is not dismissed, and the plaintiff may apply to reinstate it, on explaining his reasons for absence; he will be liable for the costs due to his failure to appear. If the defendant does not appear, the plaintiff explains his case orally or by affidavit,[58] and will generally obtain judgment.[59] If both parties appear, the order of speeches is the same as in High Court trials. It is not uncommon for either party or both to appear in person to conduct the case, though solicitors or counsel often represent the parties.[60]

The judge may give judgment for the defendant or, in a proper case, non-suit the plaintiff but leave him free to sue again.[61] He may give judgment for the plaintiff for a lump sum or for payment by instalments.[62] In any case the judgment debtor may apply for a stay of execution and an order for payment by instalments or ask for more time.[63] Specific performance may be ordered, and in some cases an injunction issued.[64]

Appeals from registrar

The judge hears appeals from interlocutory decisions of the registrar's court.[65] He also hears appeals from decisions of cases. The grounds of appeal must be stated. The judge may give judgment as he thinks fit or order a retrial.[66] In some cases the facts cannot be reopened.[67]

---

[55] County Courts Acts 1959, s.102(3)(c); and County Court Rules Ord. 21, r. 5.
[56] Ord. 21. In 1981 registrars tried 125,000 cases.
[57] Judges tried 33,000 cases in 1981; 838,000 cases went by default.
[58] Ord. 20, rr. 4, 6.
[59] Ord. 21, rr. 1, 3.
[60] County Courts Act 1959, ss.89, 89(a); Administration of Justice Acts, 1969, s.7; 1977, s.16; In some cases legal executives may appear. County Courts (Right of Audience) Direction 1978.
[61] Ord. 21, r. 2; *Clack* v. *Arthur's Engineering* [1959] 2 Q.B. 211.
[62] County Courts Act 1959, s.99; interest may be awarded s.97a (1982).
[63] *Ibid.* s.123.
[64] County Courts Act 1959, s.74(1); *Hatt & Co.* (*Bath*) v. *Pearce* [1978] 1 W.L.R. 885.
[65] Ord. 13, r. 1(10).
[66] Ord. 37, rr. 5, 6.
[67] *Cf. Perry* v. *Stopher* [1959] 1 W.L.R. 415 (C.A.); *Meyer* v. *Leanse* [1958] 2 Q.B. 371.

Satisfaction of judgment

Money in satisfaction of judgment is paid into court. The court office keeps a record of payments and notifies the creditor.

If the debtor fails to satisfy a judgment he may be orally examined as to his means.[68] Goods, *e.g.* a motor-car, can be taken by warrant of execution if the debtor fails to pay.[69] The county court bailiff takes "walking possession" but does not actually take the goods for about a week. During this time the debtor generally raises the money, *e.g.* by borrowing from friends or mortgaging the car.

If the debtor has not sufficient goods a judgment summons may be issued, and served personally or by post.[70] Such summonses may be tried in county courts on judgments of the High Court as well.[71] If the debtor fails to appear for examination as to his means the summons is adjourned and he is again summoned to show cause for his default. An administration order may also be used, to divide the debtor's assets among his creditors as in insolvency proceedings.[72] Money in deposit accounts may be attached (garnished).[73]

A judgment debtor's earnings may also be directly attached at their source. The employer must make periodic deductions from his earnings.[74]

Special statutory jurisdiction

Various statutes confer specified jurisdictions on the county courts, as, for example, in the field of landlord and tenant.[75] Landlords who are proceeding to sue for possession of land of a net annual value of £1,000 or less may proceed in the county court.[76]

Many county courts outside the London area have insolvency jurisdiction.[77] Appeal lies from them to a Chancery Divisional Court of two judges.[78]

---

[68] Ord. 25, r. 3; Form 149. The forms of admission of liability require the debtor to state his means.
[69] Ord. 26 (1981). One million warrants were issued in 1981.
[70] Ord. 28, Form 172; 6,500 were issued in 1981.
[71] Ord. 25, r. 11.
[72] County Courts Act 1959, s.148; Administration Order Rules 1971.
[73] County Courts Act 1959, s.143. Ord. 30. *Gandolfo* v. *Gandolfo* [1980] Q.B. 359 (C.A.).
[74] Attachment of Earnings Act, 1971, ss.1(2), 6, Sched. 3, Pt. I; County Court Rules; Ord. 27, 32,000 orders were made in 1981.
[75] *e.g.* the Leasehold Reform Act 1967, Race Relations Act 1968; Sex Discrimination Act 1975; Ord. 49.
[76] County Courts Act 1959, s.48; Administration of Justice Act 1973, s.6(1), Sched. 2, Pt. I. 19,000 orders for possession were made in 1981.
[77] 4,000 petitions for receiving orders were filed in 1981.
[78] See *Practice Direction* (Ch.D.) July 24, 1978.

County courts make many adoption orders[79] and have guardianship jurisdiction.[80] Appeal lies to the Family Division.[81]

---

[79] Adoption Act 1976, ss.62–67; Adoption (County Court) Rules 1959–73. 7,842 orders were made in 1981.
[80] Under the Guardianship of Minors Act 1971–73; County Court Rules Ord. 47, r. 6. 978 orders were made in 1981.
[81] Supreme Court Act 1981, s.61, Sched. I.

CHAPTER 8

CIVIL APPEALS

APPEALS TO THE CIVIL DIVISION OF THE COURT OF APPEAL

When appeal lies

Unless parties to civil proceedings in the High Court or county court agree to exclude the right to appeal or a statute excludes an appeal[1] an appeal will lie to the civil division of the Court of Appeal.[2] Appeals lie on a question of law or fact from the High Court in London or elsewhere. Leave is required where an appeal is taken from a decision of the Divisional Court in a civil proceeding.[3]

An appeal will lie from the county court on a question of law or fact but only with leave in cases prescribed by the Lord Chancellor.[4]

Appeals will lie, with leave of the Court of Appeal, from High Court decisions on appeal from administrative appeal tribunals.[5]

Procedure

Procedure is by notice of motion within six weeks of the entry of the judgment. The case is entered on the lists and is tried when reached unless a date is fixed. The party appealing against a decision is known as the appellant, and the party defending the decision as the respondent. Interlocutory matters are decided by a Registrar of Civil Appeals.[6]

---

[1] R.S.C., Ord. 25, r. 5; County Courts Act 1959, s.111; *Re Racal Communications* [1981] A.C. 374.
[2] Supreme Court Act 1981, ss.15, 18; 1,488 appeals were commenced in 1980.
[3] *Ibid.* ss.16, 54, *e.g.* cases of habeas corpus, mandamus, certiorari in civil matters, bankruptcy appeals from the Chancery Divisional Court and appeals from the Family Divisional Court trying an appeal from magistrates. On statutory appeals, see *Huyton U.D.C.* v. *Hunter* [1955] 1 W.L.R. 603.
[4] County Courts Act 1959, s.108, (1981).
[5] Tribunals and Inquiries Act 1971, s.13(2), (4).
[6] Supreme Court Act 1981, s.58. There is an appeal to a judge of the Court, *Stillevoldt (Van) (C.M.) BV* v. *El Carriers Inc.* [1983] 1 W.L.R. 207.

Constitution of Court of Appeal

The civil jurisdiction of the Court of Appeal was established by the Judicature Acts 1873–75 and is now governed by the Supreme Court Act 1981. A quorum consists of any three members of the 21 permanent judges of the court, *i.e.* the Master of the Rolls, its President, and 20 Lords Justices of Appeal. They are appointed by the Crown on the advice of the Prime Minister and must have been High Court judges or be of 15 years' standing at the Bar.[7] Members retire at the age of seventy-five.[8] The Lord Chief Justice and the President of the Family Division sometimes sit in the court. A High Court judge may be asked to sit. It usually consists of three of the permanent members, occasionally of five or seven. Two form a quorum in some cases, and one Lord Justice can hear applications for leave to appeal, where that is required.[9] The Law Lords may sit and one court consisted of three Lords of Appeal in Ordinary.[10]

Grounds of appeal

The notice of appeal must be given within four weeks of judgment and precisely specify the grounds of appeal and it is not generally possible to rely on any other grounds at the hearing.[11] The respondent by a respondent's notice may ask for the decision of the lower court to be varied or affirmed on different grounds.[12] The object is to reduce the time spent at the oral hearing. Counsel are encouraged to supply a summary of their arguments in advance.[13]

Hearing of appeals

The court sits in public in the Law Courts in London, except in very special cases. Dates for hearings of individual cases are not fixed, as the time taken by the trial of the appeal is unpredictable. The appeal gets into a list of forthcoming appeals and then into a warned list. There are 16 separate lists, *e.g.* Chancery Appeals, Queen's Bench Appeals.[14]

The court is supplied with the notices of appeal and the transcribed judgment of the High Court judge against which the

---

[7] Supreme Court Act 1981, s.10(3). In theory the Lord Chancellor may sit in the court but does not sit in practice.
[8] *Ibid.* s.11(1).
[9] *Ibid.* ss.54(4)(7); Court of Appeal (Civil Division) Order 1982.
[10] *Ibid.* s.9(1). *The Times,* December 1, 1977.
[11] Ord. 59, r. 3(2); there is a model form of notice in r. 3(5).
[12] Ord. 59, r. 6.
[13] *Practice Note* [1982] 3 All E.R. 376.
[14] *Practice Statement* (1983) 4 C.L. 232a.

appeal is brought and copies of the pleadings and exhibits.[15] If the appeal is on the facts it may be necessary for the appellant to order a transcript of the testimony given at the trial.[16] To save expense the judge's notes may be used instead, if he intimates that his notes are an adequate statement of the facts.[17] Though the court has power to summon and hear witnesses it does not generally do so. Members of the court study the judgment and the authorities cited by counsel at the trial before the appeal is heard.

The trial of an appeal is often described as a rehearing. This means that the court hears fresh argument on law, the appellant beginning the argument, and may substitute its own judgment for that of the trial court. On the other hand, it is not a full rehearing as the court does not hear the testimony taken again.

The appellant cannot rely on any point of law which was not raised by him in the trial court, unless the Court of Appeal gives him leave, since he ought to have prepared his case properly in the court below.[18] He might be given leave if the point arises on the same evidence, so that the respondent is not prejudiced.[19] An appellant from a county court judgment cannot raise a point of law not raised in the county court,[20] except in certain cases in favour of tenants.[21] The appellant cannot rely on a new head of claim, *e.g.* if he sued in the court below for a breach of statutory duty, he cannot in the Court of Appeal claim that he has a remedy for negligence at common law.[22] On the other hand, the respondent can support a decision on any point, whether or not previously raised.[23]

Decision of the court

The decision of the court is given by a majority or unanimous ruling. Only a fraction of the judgments of the court are reserved. Extempore judgments, after consultation on the bench or during adjournments, are usual. Dissenting judgments are relatively uncommon. This may appear surprising in view of the many

---

[15] Ord. 59, r. 9(1). The Registrar may direct filing of documents to save court time r. 9(3).

[16] *Stevens* v. *Stevens* [1954] 1 W.L.R. 900; R.S.C., Ord. 68. The testimony may be taken down in shorthand or mechanically recorded.

[17] Ord. 59, r. 12.

[18] *Boyer* v. *Warbey* [1953] 1 Q.B. 234.

[19] *The Tasmania* (1890) 15 App.Cas. 225, *per* Lord Herschell; *Moriarty* v. *Evans Medical Supplies* [1958] 1 W.L.R. 66 (H.L.).

[20] *Smith* v. *Baker & Sons* [1891] A.C. 325.

[21] *Boyer* v. *Warbey, supra.*

[22] *Woods* v. *Rhodes* [1953] 1 W.L.R. 1072. The respondent might have been able to defeat this claim had it been raised at the trial.

[23] *Thomas* v. *Marconi's Wireless Telegraph Co.* [1965] 1 W.L.R. 850. But he must give the appellant and Court notice of this in advance. Ord. 59, r. 6 (1979).

dissenting judgments reported, but it is in the difficult borderline cases which are worth reporting that dissent is naturally more usual. The judgment is not read out, unless of public interest; but copies are supplied to the parties and reporters.

Appeals on fact

As the Court of Appeal does not see the witnesses, and the burden of upsetting the findings is on the appellant, it is slow to reverse a decision on facts. Where the decision is that of a judge sitting without a jury this reluctance is not quite so strong as in appeals against verdicts, but the court places great faith in the skill and experience of the trial judge, who is daily having to decide on the credibility of witnesses and other factual matters which less often come before the higher court. Thus they will not reverse a finding where a witness's evidence clearly supports the finding and the judge clearly believed that witness,[24] but they will reverse a ruling inconsistent with the evidence.[25]

The Court of Appeal is free to draw different legal inferences from the facts proven.[26] Where a trial judge said that he believed that the husband had complained of the wife's cooking and therefore was guilty of cruelty in the legal sense, the court could reverse him and hold that it did not constitute cruelty, without doubting that the husband had in fact complained in that way.[27] The trial judge may also have drawn a wrong logical inference from a number of facts so that it is possible to substitute a correct inference without disputing the facts themselves.[28] The court will not always take such a step, however, even if it would itself have come to a different decision.[29]

The appellant cannot rely on any matter of fact not contested at the trial, even if he put it in issue in his pleadings.

Damages

The court may alter a High Court judge's assessment of damages if he has followed a wrong legal principle in making the assessment, e.g. has omitted material elements of damage or applied a test used in a different context, as this is a matter of law.[30] On the facts underlying the award of damages it may alter

---

[24] *Powell* v. *Streatham Manor Nursing Home* [1935] A.C. 243.
[25] *Kirk* v. *Colwyn* [1958] C.L.Y. 1416; *cf. Breen* v. *Amalgamated Engineering Union* [1971] 2 Q.B. 175.
[26] R.S.C., Ord. 59, r. 10(3).
[27] *Simpson* v. *Simpson* [1951] P. 320 (Div.Ct.).
[28] *Watt* v. *Thomas* [1947] A.C. 484.
[29] See *Silver* v. *Silver* [1958] 1 W.L.R. 259.
[30] *Earl* v. *Earl* [1959] C.L.Y. 957.

the amount only if it is clearly much too high or much too low.[31] "The scale must go down heavily against the figure attacked if the appellate court is to interfere, whether on the ground of excess or insufficiency."[32] The court is reluctant to alter a jury's assessment of damages even if out of harmony with typical awards by judges sitting alone.[33] But courts are consequently reluctant to award trial by jury in cases where damages are difficult to estimate without long experience.[34]

County court appeals

There is no appeal, without leave of the county court judge or the Court of Appeal, in some cases.[35] The Lord Chancellor prescribes these cases.[36] A note of the findings of law and fact may be requested of the judge. If the judge's notes are sketchy, he may approve a note by counsel giving an account of what happened.[37] No verbatim record of proceedings is kept in the county court.

Applications for a new trial

This is a more appropriate procedure than an appeal in many cases. It is used when the issues in a case have not been fully and properly tried, or where further evidence will have to be adduced, or where the decision of the court is inconsistent with the evidence but the evidence is inconclusive.[38] If the application succeeds, the retrial will constitute the third hearing of the case, unless the parties consent to the Court of Appeal disposing of the matter when considering the application for a new trial.[39]

Retrials originated when jury trial was general in civil cases. The Court of Appeal might be able to decide that a jury verdict was against the weight of the evidence but it had no right to give a final decision on the facts. Where, as is now usual, a judge acts as judge of fact as well as law, this problem does not arise. The idea of a retrial has been extended to decisions of the judges,[40] but in some

---

[31] *Flint* v. *Lovell* [1935] 1 K.B. 354 (C.A.); *Clarke* v. *Wright & Sons* [1957] 1 W.L.R. 1191 (C.A.).
[32] *Davies* v. *Powell Duffryn Associated Collieries Ltd.* [1942] A.C. 601, 603, 604; *cf. Nolan* v. *C. & C. Marshall* [1954] 2 Q.B. 42; *Wilson* v. *Pilley* [1957] C.L.Y. 960.
[33] *Scott* v. *Musial* [1959] 2 Q.B. 429.
[34] *Supra*, p. 202.
[35] County Courts Act 1959, s.108, as substituted by Supreme Court Act 1981, s.149, Sched. 3.
[36] Supreme Court Act 1981, Sched. 3; at present the minimum claim must exceed one-half the limit of county court jurisdiction; County Court Appeals Order, 1981.
[37] s.112; *Practice Note* [1959] 1 W.L.R. 684; *Arnold* v. *Main Morley* [1970] C.L.Y. 399.
[38] *Powell* v. *Streatham Manor Nursing Home* [1935] A.C. 243; *Tombling* v. *Universal Bulb Co.* [1951] 2 T.L.R. 289. Ord. 59, r. 11.
[39] Supreme Court Act 1981, s.17(1).
[40] Evershed Report, pp. 209, 211.

cases the High Court itself may be asked for a retrial.[41] A new trial may be ordered as the result of an appeal as well as on an application for a new trial.

There are a number of possible grounds for a retrial.

(1) Serious misdirection of the jury by the judge as to the law, if they might have found for the other party had they been directed properly, *e.g.* an error as to the burden of proof in a summing-up,[42] or a ruling which prevented a defendant proving his defence.

(2) Improper admission or rejection of evidence, if a substantial wrong has been done and the matter is left doubtful until retried on proper evidence. If there was enough evidence, apart from the evidence excluded, the decision will be left in force and not retried.[43]

(3) That there was no real evidence to go to the jury, but the judge directed the jury to give a verdict, *e.g.* where words alleged to be libellous were incapable of being defamatory in any circumstances.[44] There may be a converse case, in which the judge held there was no evidence to go to the jury when in fact there was, *e.g.* where he held that an invitation to a wife to elope was not evidence of enticement of the wife from her husband.[45]

(4) That the verdict or finding was against the weight of the evidence. The Court of Appeal is slow to disagree with the judge or the jury who were able to study the demeanour of the witnesses in the box, but it will order a new trial if the jury have clearly put an unreasonable interpretation on the case, as may appear from a study of the documents. If the evidence all points the other way, the Court of Appeal may substitute a judgment for the other party.[46] If the case is inconclusive, especially where the parties are entitled to insist that a jury try the facts, a new trial will be ordered.[47]

(5) If fresh evidence has been discovered since the trial a new trial may be ordered.[48] In one case a witness who could prove the

---

[41] Supreme Court Act 1981, s.17(2).

[42] *Jenoure* v. *Delmerge* [1891] A.C. 73.

[43] Ord. 59, r. 11(2); a new trial has been ordered where witnesses later admitted they had perjured themselves; *Piotrowska* v. *Piotrowski* [1958] 1 W.L.R. 797.

[44] *Tolley* v. *J.S. Fry & Sons Ltd.* [1931] A.C. 333. The ruling of the Court of Appeal was reversed by the House of Lords on their interpretation of the innuendo.

[45] *Place* v. *Searle* [1932] 2 K.B. 515 (C.A.).

[46] *Mechanical & General Inventions Co. Ltd.* v. *Austin* [1935] A.C. 346, 349.

[47] *Metropolitan R.R.* v. *Wright* (1886) 11 App.Cas. 152, 155; *Powell* v. *Streatham Manor Nursing Home* [1935] A.C. 243, 250.

[48] Or an interlocutory proceeding, in the case of an interlocutory appeal: *Nizam of Hyderabad* v. *Jung* [1957] Ch. 185, 226.

plaintiff's contention was in hospital at the time of the first trial.[49] In another case the defendants failed to produce certain documents under the original order for discovery and these documents were later produced.[50]

An application will not be granted if the evidence could have been produced by the applicant with a little more diligence or imagination before. In one case a widow claimed provision out of her husband's estate. At the time of his death his estate was worthless. It later appreciated in value but at the trial the widow had not put this fact in evidence. The court dismissed her claim for want of any assets which could be made available to her. It was held that it was too late for her to produce evidence of the new value of the assets at the appeal court.[51] In another case a plaintiff sued a highway authority for damage caused by a defective drain. At the trial of the action it was not established whether the defendants had in fact constructed the drain. A local resident read about the result of the case in a newspaper and came forward with proof that it had in fact been constructed by the defendants. It was held that it was too late. The plaintiff must have known he would have to prove this fact and ought to have obtained the evidence before he brought his action.[52] One of the supposed reasons for the restriction on fresh evidence is the temptation to manufacture some form of evidence after it has been decided at the trial just what evidence would be needed. But this does not appear to be the real basis of the rule. In one case a landlord could not prove a dwelling was outside the Rent Restriction Acts and in fact clearly admitted that the Acts applied. He could have discovered the truth by more investigations. Later he obtained a copy of an official record which proved that the Acts did not apply to the dwelling. He was not granted a retrial, although the fresh evidence was above suspicion.[53]

It is not enough that the fresh evidence may prove that a witness whose testimony was believed was in fact not entitled to credence,[54] for instance, if a witness who is believed is later convicted of an offence which tends to show that he might have

[49] *Bills* v. *Roe* [1968] 1 W.L.R. 925.
[50] *Davey* v. *Harrow B.C.* [1958] 1 Q.B. 60.
[51] *Leeder* v. *Ellis* [1953] A.C. 52 (P.C.).
[52] *Nash* v. *Rochford R.C.* [1917] 1 K.B. 384 (C.A.); *cf. Crook* v. *Derbyshire* [1961] 1 W.L.R. 1360 (C.A.).
[53] *E.H. Lewis & Son Ltd.* v. *Morelli* [1948] 2 All E.R. 1021 (C.A.).
[54] *Braddock* v. *Tillotsons Newspapers Ltd.* [1950] 1 K.B. 47 (C.A.); *Tombling* v. *Universal Bulb Co.* [1951] 2 T.L.R. 289 (C.C.A.); *R.* v. *Robinson* [1971] 2 K.B. 108.

been lying, it is still impossible to obtain a new trial as it is not proven that he did lie.[55]

These strict rules are not even relaxed in matrimonial cases except possibly where the custody of children is involved.[56] On the other hand fresh evidence is more easily admitted in construction summons cases, as the executor may apply to the court from time to time for help and the court is trying to interpret the will and not decide a dispute.[57]

Fresh evidence may be admitted on the measure of damages as well as on legal liability, *e.g.* where the extent of injuries is not at first appreciated.[58]

(6) Where the party had been surprised, *e.g.* he had been misled by his opponent as to the time of the trial or a material witness had been kept out of the way by his opponent at the time of the trial.

(7) Where the jury were biased or in contact with interested parties or for some reason failed to act responsibly. In one case a member of a local authority served on the jury at the trial of an action brought against that authority. A new trial was ordered, although there was no evidence that he influenced the other jurors.[59]

(8) Where the jury have awarded a grossly excessive or grossly inadequate amount of damages to the successful party. There must be strong grounds for any interference with the province of the jury in this respect.[60] A new trial will be awarded if the jury have followed the wrong principle, *e.g.* ignored clear directions by the judge as to mitigation of damages,[61] or if the award bears no reasonable relation to the facts as to damage which appear in evidence.[62]

New trials in county court cases

A new trial[63] was ordered by the Court of Appeal where a county court judge wrongly admitted or rejected evidence.[64]

---

[55] *Ali* v. *Elmore* [1953] 1 W.L.R. 1300. The plaintiff lost an action for malicious prosecution against four policemen. Two of them were later convicted of corruption. It was held that this had no direct bearing on his case.

[56] *Corbett* v. *Corbett* [1953] 2 All E.R. 69.

[57] *Re Herwin* [1953] Ch. 701.

[58] *Mulholland* v. *Mitchell* [1971] A.C. 166.

[59] *Atkins* v. *Fulham B.C.* (1915) 31 T.L.R. 564.

[60] *Mechanical & General Inventions Co. Ltd.* v. *Austin* [1935] A.C. 346, 377; *Rubber Improvement* v. *Daily Telegraph* [1964] A.C. 234.

[61] *Chapman* v. *Ellesmere* [1932] 2 K.B. 431.

[62] *Tolley* v. *J.S. Fry & Sons Ltd.* [1930] 1 K.B. 467 (C.A.), reversed on another point; [1931] A.C. 333; *cf. Greenlands Ltd.* v. *Wilmshurst* [1913] 3 K.B. 507, 532; *Taff Vale Co.* v. *Jenkins* [1913] A.C. 1, 7.

[63] County Courts Act 1959, s.113.

[64] Admissibility of evidence is a matter of law and not fact.

Where the county court judge gave judgment although the pleadings disclosed no cause of action, a new trial was ordered by the same county court judge.[65] Facts cannot be re-opened.[66]

Setting aside a judgment for fraud

After the time for appeal has expired it is still possible to apply to have a judgment set aside for fraud, *e.g.* where it could be proved that witnesses had been bribed to give perjured evidence.[67] The plaintiff must give full particulars of the fraud in the pleadings in his new action. He must also clearly establish his case by legally admissible evidence, just as if he were suing any other action based on allegations of fraud. It is not sufficient for him to raise a doubt as to the truth of the findings of the court.[68]

APPEALS TO THE HOUSE OF LORDS

Judges of the House of Lords

The House of Lords, as a judicial body, was once the entire House and this remains true in a technical sense, the Appeals Committee and the Committee of Privileges being committees of the House. But in fact it differs in two respects. In the first place there is a strong convention that peers who are not or have not been judges shall not take part in judicial sessions of the House.[69] In the second place provision was made by the Appellate Jurisdiction Act 1876 for the appointment of life peers as Lords of Appeal in Ordinary, to act in a judicial capacity.[70]

The *ex officio* members of the court are the Lord Chancellor and ex-Lord Chancellors. The Lord Chancellor is a Cabinet Minister appointed by the Prime Minister of the day, so that he goes out of office with his Government. The Lord Chancellor receives a peerage on appointment, so that he in any case remains a peer who has held high judicial office and is qualified to sit. In addition to this he receives half his former salary and in practice does often

---

[65] *Whall* v. *Bulman* [1953] 2 Q.B. 198. The appellant received no costs as he should have raised the point in the county court.

[66] See p. 235.

[67] *Hip Foong Hong* v. *H. Neotia & Co.* [1918] A.C. 888; see Gordon (1961) 77 L.Q.R. 369.

[68] *Jonesco* v. *Beard* [1930] A.C. 298.

[69] As to the vestiges of the participation of lay peers, see *Re Lord Kinross* [1905] A.C. 468 at p. 476; R.E. Megarry (1949) 65 L.Q.R. 22, citing *Hansard* (3rd series), Vol. 278, col. 68; *The Times,* April 10, 1883.

[70] This example has been followed for non-judicial peerages: Life Peerages Act 1958.

assist in trying appeals. It is less usual for other peers who have been judges to take an active part.[71]

The office of Lord Chancellor is paradoxical in that he enjoys legislative, executive and judicial powers, being a legislator in the House of Lords, a judge when the House acts as a court, and having executive functions as a Cabinet Minister, including the power to nominate judges.

There are at present nine "Law Lords," in addition to *ex-officio* judges.[72] Appointments of Lords of Appeal in Ordinary are made on the advice of the Prime Minister, in consultation with the Lord Chancellor.[73] A Law Lord must be a barrister of at least 15 years' standing or have been a judge or Lord Justice for at least ten years.[74]

These peers are in no sense inferior to lay peers and the law specifically provides that they shall receive the writ of summons of Barons and can sit and vote in the House when it acts as the Upper Chamber of the legislature.[75] But the separation of function appears in many ways. Thus the judicial body may sit when Parliament is not in session.[76] The position of the Law Lords as life peers in the legislature is unusual. In theory they may take an active part in all its work but there is a convention that they should not take part in party-political discussions and they sit on the cross-benches. They take part in debates concerned with the administration of justice.[77] The judges who have received hereditary peerages may enjoy slightly wider freedom.

In former times, when the House was less strong judicially, it was the practice on some occasions to summon the judges of the common law courts to the House, to advise on difficult points of law. Thus in 1843 the House took the advice of the judges on an important question of criminal law after the accused had been acquitted, so that the case was purely academic.[78] This practice has

---

[71] Reference should be made to textbooks on constitutional law for a discussion of the composition and functions of the Judicial Committee of the Privy Council, which is mainly a Commonwealth, rather than an English, court. The Committee of Privileges of the House of Lords also enjoys judicial powers, but these are best considered in connection with its legislative functions.

[72] Appellate Jurisdiction Act 1947; Administration of Justice Act 1968, s.1(1).

[73] One or two of the Law Lords are generally judges from Scotland or Northern Ireland to help hear civil appeals from their appellate courts. Law Lords enjoy security of appointment for life and are only removable where Supreme Court judges are removable. Lords of Appeal retire at 75, under the Judicial Pensions Act 1959, s.2. Salaries are regulated under the Administration of Justice Act 1973, s.9.

[74] Appellate Jurisdiction Act 1876, s.6.

[75] Appellate Jurisdiction Act 1876, s.6; Appellate Jurisdiction Act 1887, s.21.

[76] 1876 Act, s.8. It was formerly the custom for the House to sit as a chamber of the legislature after the judicial hearings had ended for the day.

[77] *e.g.* on the issues of the flogging of criminals and of capital punishment.

[78] 10 Cl. & F. 200.

been renewed in a reverse form, with reference to criminal appeal courts after acquittals.[79]

The court requires a quorum of at least three judges but five judges often sit. Decisions are by a majority.

Leave to appeal

The House hears appeals on law from the civil division of the Court of Appeal. Because of the expense and time involved, it has been necessary to impose restrictions on these appeals, and an appeal requires leave either of the Court of Appeal[80] or of the House itself.[81]

In most cases a petition is made to the House for leave to appeal. These petitions are heard by a committee of three Law Lords.[82] An oral hearing follows if any one of them so wishes. Only in a very small proportion of cases tried in the Court of Appeal is leave to appeal to the House of Lords sought.[83] About three-fourths of the applications for leave are refused,[84] and only in half the appeals heard is the decision of the Court of Appeal reversed.[85]

Under the system of binding precedent the Court of Appeal is bound by its own decisions. This means that a litigant who wishes to appeal from a lower court knows that he cannot contest an unfavourable previous decision of the Court of Appeal but must generally appeal to the House of Lords.[86]

Procedure

A petition for leave to appeal must be lodged within one month, unless the Court of Appeal gave leave to appeal.[87] The petitioner serves a copy of his petition or application for leave to appeal on the respondent, stating the grounds of his appeal. Copies of the petition, the judgment of the Court of Appeal and the pleadings must be lodged in the Judicial Office for the use of the Appeals Committee. The parties and their counsel appear before this Committee, who decide whether the appellant may proceed.

---

[79] See *supra*, p. 157.
[80] This is occasionally given, *e.g. Pirelli General Cable Works* v. *Oscar Faber & Partners* (1982) 263 E.G. 879, where existing decisions were conflicting.
[81] Administration of Justice (Civil Appeals) Act 1934; The House disposed of 45 civil appeals in 1981.
[82] Act of 1934, s.1(2); [1976] 1 W.L.R. 638.
[83] 77 in 1981.
[84] 66 refused out of 75 in 1981.
[85] In 1981, 29 were affirmed, and 16 reversed.
[86] *e.g. Hill* v. *William Hill Ltd.* [1949] A.C. 530; *Williams* v. *Home Office* (No. 2) [1982] 2 All E.R. 564 (C.A.), but see *infra*. re leapfrog appeals.
[87] House of Lords Standing Orders (Judicial Business) (1971) II.

The appeal must be lodged within three months of the last judgment appealed from.[88] The appellant must give security for costs unless legally aided.[89] Documents and court orders, unless already in the Law Reports, must be printed or duplicated, with transcripts of evidence if needed, as an appendix to the appellant's petition. Each side must lodge a succinct document known as a "case on appeal," settled by counsel outlining their arguments for and against the decision of the Court of Appeal. Copies of the case and appendix must be lodged by the appellant within six weeks of the lodging of the appeal.[90] New points not raised in the lower courts will not generally be considered.[91]

The respondent must deliver his "case in reply" soon afterwards and the parties exchange copies of their cases. The appellants must apply to have the case set down for hearing. A volume is then bound, containing the papers relating to the appeal, the appendices and the combined cases of both parties.[92]

The Judicial Office must also be furnished with a full list of all cases and statutes intended to be referred to.

After notice of trial the House proceeds to hear oral argument, two counsel being permitted on each side.

The detailed opinions ("speeches") of the Lords of Appeal are delivered in writing.[93]

In case of need, fresh evidence may be admitted before the Lords.[94]

"Leapfrog" appeals

Where an important point of law arises on the interpretation of a statute or on a case where a Court of Appeal or House of Lords ruling already exists, provision is made to by-pass the Court of Appeal and proceed directly from the High Court to the House of Lords.[95] The High Court judge decides whether or not to issue a certificate for a direct appeal.[96] The House of Lords must then decide whether or not to give leave to appeal.[97] The applicant

---

[88] *Ibid.* I.
[89] *Practice Direction* July 30, 1981.
[90] *Ibid.* VII and *Directions as to Procedure* (1971) 15; *Yorke, M.V. Motors* v. *Edwards* [1982] 1 W.L.R. 444 (H.L.).
[91] *S. of Scotland Elec. Bd.* v. *British Oxygen Co.* [1956] 1 W.L.R. 1069.
[92] *Directions as to Procedure,* App.E.
[93] *Ibid.* Direction 35(11).
[94] *Murphy* v. *Stone Wallwork (Charlton)* [1969] 1 W.L.R. 1023; *Black-Clawson International* v. *Papierwerke Waldhof-Aschaffenburg* [1975] A.C. 591.
[95] Administration of Justice Act 1969. Pt. II, *O'Brien* v. *Robinson* (No. 2) [1973] 1 W.L.R. 515 (H.L.); *Vestey* v. *I.R.C.* [1980] A.C. 1148; *Supplementary Benefits Commission* v. *Jull* [1981] A.C. 1025; *Thompson* v. *Brown* [1981] 1 W.L.R. 744, (All H.L.). 4 cases were tried in 1981 in this way.
[96] *Ibid.* s.12; *I.R.C.* v. *Church Commissioners* [1974] 3 All E.R. 529, 552.
[97] *Ibid.* s.13, *Directions as to Procedure,* 3.

must present reasons for leave being granted.[98] In other respects the procedure followed in the House of Lords is identical with that followed in ordinary appeals.[99]

[98] *Practice Direction* [1970] 1 W.L.R. 97.
[99] Administration of Justice Act 1969, s.14; Supreme Court Act 1981, s.16.

CHAPTER 9

SPECIAL COURTS

ARBITRATION

Arbitration generally

Arbitration is a very ancient institution. The machinery of the courts of justice themselves probably originated in some form of arbitration, in a growing practice first of inducing and later of compelling submission of disputes to an impartial arbiter in place of resort to blood-feuds. During the Middle Ages arbitration became a common practice among merchants and was, for example, undertaken by the London City Guilds. Noblemen were also asked to settle land disputes amicably for their tenants and friends. Since medieval times the regular courts of justice recognised the validity of a condition in a bond providing for submission of disputes to arbitration, and enforced debts which originated in awards of arbitrators as to amounts owing by one contractor to another. They now allow arbitration clauses to be treated as valid conditions precedent to action in the courts, so as to prevent any action at law being brought over a dispute when the contract provides for the reference of such dispute to arbitration. The courts possess certain powers of control over arbitration but these exist in order to make arbitration itself fair and efficient, and not in order to restrict its usefulness.

The popularity of arbitration is due to several causes. Proceedings are private and informal. Expert arbitrators and assessors are used, with special knowledge of the problems of a particular trade. Personal feelings are less often exacerbated than in full-dress litigation in the courts. Expenses are generally but not invariably smaller.

As the law proceeds from the principle of unrestricted access to the ordinary courts, arbitration generally rests on contract.[1] This may take one of two main forms. The usual type is the arbitration clause, inserted into many commercial contracts and service contracts which provides in advance that any disputes which may

---

[1] Arbitration Act 1950, s.32; Relations with the courts are also regulated by the Arbitration Act 1979.

254

arise in relation to the contract shall be submitted to arbitration. The alternative type is an agreed reference to arbitration of a dispute which has already arisen, where the contract is silent on the point. In both cases the parties to the contract have agreed upon reference to arbitration.[2]

Arbitration is also sometimes provided for in the course of regular judicial proceedings, *e.g.* where a county court registrar is asked to decide a case by both parties or a High Court judge is appointed arbitrator. Some statutes provide for arbitration by special courts or other organisations. The nature of this process depends on the terms of the particular statute.

Clearly neither party to a contract containing an arbitration clause can revoke this clause without the consent of the other party. If either party starts proceedings in the courts the other party may apply to the court to stay the action.[3] This right is lost if the applicant has already taken what is technically known as a "step in the action." Not all steps in preparation for litigation are steps in this sense.[4] In any case, the court may prefer to let an action proceed, if satisfied that a lawsuit is more suitable than arbitration in the circumstances.[5]

The arbitrator

The law generally provides that the parties may agree to appoint one arbitrator, but they may make other arrangements by their contract. They often provide that each party shall appoint an arbitrator and that the two arbitrators shall proceed to appoint an umpire before they enter on the reference. The umpire is generally only called upon to decide the dispute if the arbitrators fail to agree.[6] If one of two arbitrators dies a second arbitrator must be appointed by the party empowered by the contract to do so.[7] If the

---

[2] But the two types of reference differ in "exclusion agreements" to exclude recourse to the courts; see p. 258, *infra* n. 35. An arbitration clause is effective even if the validity of the other parts of the contract is being questioned; *Govt. of Gibraltar* v. *Kenney* [1956] 2 Q.B. 41; *The Tradesman* [1962] 1 W.L.R. 6. This is illogical since the clause ought to stand or fall with the contract, but it is convenient and the courts can prevent abuse. But once the contract is terminated by both sides, the clause becomes ineffective; *F. J. Bloemen Pty.* v. *Council of the City of Gold Coast* [1972] 3 W.L.R. 43 (P.C.); the absence of a submission cannot be waived. *Altco* v. *Sutherland* [1971] 2 Lloyd's Rep. 515.

[3] Arbitration Act 1950, ss.4, 25(4), 25(2); Ord. 73, r. 3; *London Sack and Bag Co.* v. *Dixon and Lugton Ltd.* [1943] 2 All E.R. 763 (C.A.); *Re Phoenix Timber Co.* [1958] 2 Q.B. 1. Procedure is by summons before a master in the action brought by the other party.

[4] Act of 1950, s.4(1). The cases are numerous and complicated.

[5] *Oliver* v. *Hillier* [1959] 1 W.L.R. 551 (relevant statute referred to discretion of a court); *Finer* v. *Melgrave* [1959] C.L.Y. 2394 (court machinery to secure detailed partnership accounts superior to that available to arbitrator); *Taunton-Collins* v. *Cromie* [1964] 1 W.L.R. 633 (other joint defendant not bound by arbitration clause); *Radford* v. *Hair* [1971] Ch. 758; (charge of fraud made against plaintiff).

[6] Act of 1950, ss.6, 7, 8, 9; Act of 1979 s.6.

[7] *Marinos & Frangos* v. *Dulien Steel Products of Washington* [1961] 2 Lloyd's Rep. 192.

parties cannot agree on a single arbitrator, where that is the contractual arrangement, or the arbitrators cannot agree on an umpire, or a third party empowered to make an appointment fails to do so application may be made to the courts to make the necessary appointment.[8] To prevent hardship, the court may also extend the time-limit provided in the contract for the appointment of the arbitrator.[9] It may happen that a party discovers during the arbitration and before the award that the arbitrator is unfit to act or has been guilty of misconduct. Application may then be made to the courts to revoke the arbitrator's authority to act.[10] If misconduct is discovered after the award has been made, the party wronged should move to set aside the award.[11]

It is common in practice for the parties to appoint an independent body to act as arbitrator in their contract. An example is a submission to the Chartered Institute of Arbitrators' London Court of Arbitration, and this covers the validity of the original contract as well as questions arising out of the dispute.[12] There is a similar provision in the rules of the London Court of International Arbitration.[13]

These trade courts appoint arbitrators from special panels. The London Court of Arbitration has 38 expert panels to call on and the G.P.A.L. (General Produce Association of London) has similar panels.

Procedure

Arbitration is launched when a party files a claim, with a short statement of the nature of the dispute. The arbitration agreement must be appended to the claim. The other party is notified and files a defence.

Some arbitration rules provide for an oral hearing of the parties by the arbitrator, unless they agree to waive this right.[14] Other rules require express notice to be given by a party if he wishes to attend the hearing and adduce evidence.[15] Hearings are not open to the public.[16] Some rules allow either side to be represented by

---

[8] Arbitration Act 1950 s.10; amended by Arbitration Act 1979 s.6(4), procedure is by originating summons triable by a master in the Queen's Bench Division; R.S.C., Ord. 73, r. 3; *National Enterprises* v. *Racal Communications* [1975] Ch. 397 (C.A.).

[9] Arbitration Act 1950 s.27; *Watney, Combe, Reid & Co.* v. *Dower* [1956] C.L.Y. 338.

[10] *Ibid.* s.12. Procedure is by originating summons triable by a master.

[11] *Ibid.* s.23; Ord. 73, r. 2; *Birtley Dist. Co-op Society* v. *Windy Nook Co-op Society* [1960] 2 Q.B. 1.

[12] London Court of Arbitration Rules 1981, r. 1 and Sched. B.

[13] London Chartered Institute of Arbitration 1981 Rules, r. 1. See Arbitration Act 1975.

[14] Chartered Institute of Arbitration, r. 7(1), (2).

[15] General Produce Association of London Rules, r. 56.

[16] C.I.A. r. 7(2); G.P.A.L., r. 70.

solicitor or counsel, if they wish,[17] while others impose some conditions on this right.[18] These differences may be justified by the nature of the types of dispute which arise in particular trades. There is an impression among some commercial circles that lawyers incline to exaggerate the formal aspects of disputes. Where the arbitrator inspects goods some rules provide that the parties may accompany him and make observations, and insist on a hearing afterwards. The parties generally produce their own witnesses, if needed. The arbitrator does not subpoena witnesses but the parties can apply to the High Court to subpoena unwilling witnesses.[19] The parties or witnesses may be examined on oath if the arbitrator so wishes, but this is not always insisted on and evidence may be given by affidavit if the opposing party does not wish to cross-examine the deponent. Arbitration rules may exclude the ordinary law of evidence, *e.g.* by providing that "The arbitrators and umpire shall have power to obtain, receive and act upon such oral and documentary evidence or information (whether the same be strictly admissible as evidence or not) as they or he may consider necessary."[20] The arbitrator must not decide a reference on a point not raised by the parties unless they are given an opportunity to argue it.[21]

The arbitrator may, on application by the parties, give interlocutory relief, as by ordering discovery of relevant books and papers, and administration of interrogatories, after claim and before the hearing.[22]

The arbitrator can be asked by a defendant to dismiss a case for long delays by the plaintiff, but delays do not in themselves require abandonment of an arbitration.[23]

The award

The arbitrator proceeds to make his award after studying all the relevant facts and using his own particular experience. A general award is simply in the form of an award that X pay Y £x, with a title referring to the parties and their reference of the dispute to his arbitration. In such cases the arbitrator incidentally applies the law to the facts he finds. His decision may have been based on a choice

---

[17] C.I.A. r. 7(3), r. 26; *Hookway* v. *Isaacs* [1954] 1 Lloyd's Rep. 491.
[18] G.P.A.L., r. 72. Such a rule is not void as offending public policy. *Henry Bath & Son* v. *Birgby Products* (1962) 106 S.J. 288.
[19] Act of 1950, s.12(4), (6); Ord. 73, rr. 3, 4.
[20] G.P.A.L., r. 55, *Macpherson Train & Co.* v. *J. Milhem* [1955] 2 Lloyd's Rep. 59.
[21] *Sociéte Tunisienne D'Armement, Tunis* v. *Govt. of Ceylon* [1959] 1 W.L.R. 787.
[22] C.I.A. Sched. C. G.P.A.L., r. 59; *Crawford* v. *A.E.A. Prowting* (1971) 116 S.J. 195.
[23] *Paal Wilson & Co.* v. *Partenreederei Hannah Blumenthal* [1982] 3 W.L.R. 1149 (H.L.).

258 SPECIAL COURTS

between two versions of the facts or between two legal interpretations of the same facts.[24]

Some arbitration rules provide for special appeal committees to which appeals can be taken from awards of arbitrators.[25] The rules do not usually allow the original arbitrators or umpire to sit on such committees.[26]

The arbitrator may award interest.[27]

The position of the courts

It would be pointless to resort to arbitration if the unsuccessful party could appeal to the courts against the findings of fact in the award.[28] If the unsuccessful party fails to perform the award, he can be sued to recover the amount payable by him under it and will generally have no real defence in law at this stage. In order to expedite matters the successful party may apply to the court for leave to proceed to execution of judgment on the award without a fresh action.[29] This only applies where the award is for a sum certain, no further evidence of amount being needed.[30] If there appears to be any real ground in law to upset the award such leave will not be given and the party will be left to proceed by action in court.[31]

There is an appeal to a High Court judge on a point of law.[32] The court may require the arbitrator to give his reasons for this purpose.[33] Leave of the court is required and will only be given if the issue is very important.[34] The parties may agree to exclude appeals to the courts after commencing arbitration.[35]

Further appeals to the Court of Appeal and House of Lords require proof of special reasons, on the analogy of criminal appeals.[36]

---

[24] *Absalom Ltd.* v. *G.W. Garden Village Society* [1933] A.C. 592, 616.
[25] *e.g.* General Produce Association of London Rules (1981) rr. 74, 88, *Congimex S.à.r.l.* v. *Continental Grain Export Co.* [1979] 2 Lloyd's Rep. 346 (C.A.) (GAFTA).
[26] *London Export Corp.* v. *Jubilee Coffee Roasting Co.* [1958] 1 W.L.R. 561 (C.A.).
[27] *Techno-Impex* v. *Gebr. Van Weelde Scheepvaartkantoor B.V.* [1981] 1 Q.B. 648 (C.A.).
[28] *Tsakiroglou & Co.* v. *Noblee Thorl G.m.b.h.* [1962] A.C. 93, 119, 123, 129, 134.
[29] Arbitration Act 1950, s.26; Ord. 73, r. 3. Both parties appear before the master on originating summons. If leave is given the award becomes an order of the court.
[30] *Margulies Bros.* v. *Dafnis Thomaides & Co.* [1958] 1 Lloyd's Rep. 205.
[31] *Re Boks & Co. and Peters, Rushton & Co.* [1919] 1 K.B. 491 (C.A.). (new facts). Other grounds are want of jurisdiction, fraud by the arbitrator. Motions may also be made to set aside such awards; *supra.* p. 256.
[32] Arbitration Act 1979, s.11; Supreme Court Act 1981, s.148.
[33] *Ibid.* s.1(5).
[34] *e.g.* the position of shipping blocked by war, *International Sea Tankers of Liberia Inc.* v. *Hemisphere Shipping Co. of Hong Kong* [1982] 2 All E.R. 437 (C.A.).
[35] Arbitration Act 1979, s.3.
[36] *Ibid.* s.1(7).

An award may be remitted to the arbitrator, on motion in court, if it is obviously defective, incomplete or inconclusive, *e.g.* where there is no order as to payment of the costs.[37] Reconsideration may be ordered if fresh evidence comes to light.[38] A new arbitration may be ordered where the arbitrator did not consider the relevant materials.[39] If the arbitrator named in the contract is removed for misconduct either party may ask the court to appoint an arbitrator or to supersede the arbitration agreement and assume jurisdiction.[40] If there are means for appointing a substitute arbitrator in the contract, the parties may use these instead. If the arbitrator is appointed by some organisation to which the contract gives a power of appointing, that organisation may appoint a substitute.[41]

INTERNATIONAL ARBITRATION

These arbitrations are also held in private and need not observe the strict rules of evidence. Some allow the arbitrator to make his own enquiries,[42] to select which materials and witnesses he will consider[43] and to decide the language to be used.[44]

The judge as arbitrator

A High Court judge may now be appointed arbitrator in a commercial case if an arbitration agreement exists within the Arbitration Act 1950. His fees are regulated by law.[45] The judge and the Lord Chief Justice must decide whether he will accept.[46] The judge-arbitrator has more powers than other arbitrators, *e.g.* he can himself summon witnesses. He is supervised by the Court of Appeal.[47] An arbitration jurisdiction is exercised by County Court judges and registrars.[48]

---

[37] *Re Becker, Shillan & Co. and Barry Brothers* [1921] 1 K.B. 391; Act of 1950, s.18(4), provides for a special amending order to be applied for. See also *L.E. Cattan* v. *A. Michaelides & Co.* [1958] 1 W.L.R. 717.

[38] *Re Keighley, Maxsted & Co. and Durant & Co.* [1893] 1 Q.B. 405 (C.A.).

[39] *Walford, Baker & Co.* v. *Macfie & Sons* (1915) 84 L.J.K.B. 2221.

[40] Arbitration Act 1950, s.25(2).

[41] This appears to follow from the wording of s.25(2) and the general law of contract.

[42] London Court of International Arbitration Rules (1981) r. C.7.

[43] *Ibid.* r. C.6.

[44] *Ibid.* r. B.5.

[45] Administration of Justice Act 1970, s.4; on fees, s.4(3), Supreme Court Fees (Amendment) Order 1971.

[46] s.4(2).

[47] s.4(4) and Sched. III.

[48] In 1981, 110 awards were made by County Court judges; and 21,114 by County Court Registrars.

ADMINISTRATIVE TRIBUNALS

Modern statutes have created a number of bodies to discharge "quasi-judicial" functions, *i.e.* they have power by law to establish facts and apply legal rules without being constituted as parts of the regular judicial system or following the strict rules of procedure and evidence followed by courts. Most of these institutions form part of a larger administrative department which is not itself judicial, their jurisdiction is limited to very specific points set out in the constituent statute and their decisions sometimes embody reasons of policy as well as of law.

Although these tribunals are not uniform, considerable order was introduced into their operation by the Tribunals and Inquiries Act of 1958, now the consolidating Act of 1971, which sets up minimum standards for all such bodies, requires reasons to be given for every decision,[49] requires the chairman to be appointed by the Lord Chancellor and not by the head of the department, to ensure impartiality of procedure,[50] and allows an appeal on points of law to the High Court of Justice.[51] Representation by solicitor or counsel is usual but not invariable and there is often, but not always, an oral public hearing. A Council on Tribunals was set up, which intervenes on the basis of complaints and makes annual reports.[52]

A few examples may illustrate how some of these tribunals proceed:

Rent tribunals

These bodies determine the question of a fair rent under various statutes in the field of landlord and tenant. The chairman is usually a qualified lawyer and the two other members of the tribunal are experts on conditions in the locality appointed by the Secretary of State. Hearings may be oral or the parties may submit written representations. Legal representation is allowed, but strict rules of procedure are not prescribed.[53]

The Social Security Commissioner

At one time workmen had to prove the fault of their employer when injured in industrial accidents. Then legislation gave them

---

[49] Act of 1971, s.12; *Alexander Machinery (Dudley)* v. *Crabtree* [1974] 1 C.R. 120.
[50] s.7.
[51] s.13.
[52] See 23rd Annual Report.
[53] Rent Act 1977, ss.19, 76; as amended by the Housing Act 1980, s.72; now same members as Rent Assessment Committees, 1981 Rules.

wider rights where injured. But the machinery of the ordinary courts proved expensive and dilatory and there were frequent appeals to higher courts on matters of principle. In 1946 a basically social administrative machine was set up instead. This was amended in 1965 and rules made in 1967. This system has continued under the general Social Security Act 1980. Application is made to an insurance officer and there is an appeal from his decision to an appeal tribunal of three members, which sits in public. There is a further appeal to the Commissioner himself, a barrister, who holds a hearing on law on request, at which parties may be legally represented. Selected decisions of the Commissioner are published for the guidance of applicants.

The disciplinary jurisdiction over solicitors

Where a solicitor is claimed to have been guilty of conduct making him liable to be "struck off," the complaint is tried by a Solicitors' Disciplinary Tribunal appointed by the Master of the Rolls, consisting of at least three members for each hearing.[54] The hearing is private but the results are announced in public.[55] There is an appeal to the High Court.[56]

The Agricultural Land Tribunal

This body protects farm tenants from unjustified evictions. There is the equivalent of written pleadings, a public hearing with legal representation and a right of appeal on law to the High Court.[57]

Town and country planning inquiries

Land cannot be "developed" for new purposes without planning permission from the local planning authority under the Town and Country Planning Act of 1971. If planning permission is refused an appeal to the Secretary of State is possible. He can be required in such cases to send an inspector or other person to hold a local public inquiry which is governed by the Planning Inquiries (Attendance of Public) Act 1982 and the 1981 (Inquiries Procedure) Rules. The local planning authority, applicant and other interested parties are represented. The planning authority must submit a written statement of its arguments to the applicant, and

---

[54] Solicitors Act 1957, s.46, as amended by Solicitors Amendment Act 1974, s.11.
[55] Solicitors (Disciplinary Proceedings) Rules 1975, rr. 24, 34.
[56] Solicitors Act 1957, s.49 (as amended 1974 and 1981).
[57] Agricultural Holdings (Notices to Quit) Act 1977, ss.2, 12; Agricultural Land Tribunals (Rules) Order 1978, rr. 16, 20, 24, 33.

the applicant may be required to submit a written statement.[58] The actual order of proceedings at the inquiry is decided by the inspector, but the applicant makes the first and last statements.[59] Other government departments who are affected also state their views. Representation by solicitor or counsel is permitted.[60]

The inspector prepares a written report with his findings of fact and his recommendations as to the fate of the appeal.[61] The Secretary of State is not limited to the material in this report and need not follow the inspector's recommendations, but he must give his reasons if he decides to reject those recommendations.[62] There is generally no appeal to the courts, as this is a matter of implementing and interpreting policy and not strict law. The decisions are studied, however, as a kind of precedent in similar cases.

Employment Appeal Tribunals

Appeals from legal rulings by Industrial Tribunals in various fields lie to an Employment Appeal Tribunal.[63] This Tribunal draws on a panel of Supreme Court judges and other appointed members.[64] At least one judge and from two to four appointed members, representing employers and employees, sit on each occasion.[65]

MILITARY COURTS

Courts-martial have jurisdiction over service men and women under the Army Act of 1955 and similar Navy and Air Force legislation extendable until 1986 by Order in Council[66] as well as over civilians employed by the services, for offences committed while with the forces.[67] Civilians may also be compelled to appear as witnesses at courts-martial. These courts are held on military posts but are open to the public. Sentences are in line with those imposed in civil courts where the offences correspond. Treason,

---

[58] r. 6.
[59] *Ibid.* r. 11(2).
[60] *Ibid.* r. 8(3).
[61] *Ibid.* r. 13.
[62] *Ibid.* r. 14.
[63] Employment Protection Act 1978, s.135; Employment Act 1980, s.5(2). Industrial Tribunal (Rules of Procedure) Regulations 1980 r. 3; *Wass* v. *Binns* [1982] I.C.R. 486 (C.A.).
[64] Employment Protection Act 1978, s.135(2).
[65] *Ibid.* Sched. 11; Employment Appeal Tribunal Rules 1980; *Practice Direction* February 27, 1981: 682 cases were dealt with in 1981.
[66] Armed Forces Act 1981; Courts Martial Rules 1977.
[67] The Armed Forces Act 1976 set up Standing Civilian Courts for offences abroad by such civilians. Procedure is governed by the Standing Civilian Courts Order 1977.

murder and a few other very grave crimes may only be tried by the civil courts.

Much of the procedure is similar to that of civil courts, and there is an ultimate appeal to a Courts-Martial (Appeal) Court constituted by the same judges as the criminal division of the Court of Appeal, with further appeals, by leave, to the House of Lords in exceptional cases.[68]

The procedure, however, has peculiar features. In some cases depositions may be taken in the absence of the accused. Minor cases may be tried summarily by the commanding officer himself. Lay officers are appointed judges by the convening officer, and they are advised, but not bound, on legal points by a judge-advocate, a legal expert appointed by the Judge-Advocate-General. All convictions and sentences are subject to review by the convening officer and there is a further right to apply for a review to the Defence Council.

No jury is used in courts-martial, which are based on Roman law ideas. A formal written record of proceedings is prepared.

---

[68] Courts Martial Appeals Act 1968, ss.1–5, as amended by Supreme Court Act 1981, s.145.

CHAPTER 10

COSTS: LEGAL AID: THE LEGAL PROFESSION: EVIDENCE

COSTS

In Civil Cases

Queen's Bench Division

Costs payable by the unsuccessful party to the successful party comprise the latter's court fees,[1] solicitor's fees, counsel's fees and witness fees.[2] A plaintiff may be required by the master to give security for costs, as a condition of proceeding with an action, where he resides abroad and has no assets in England out of which to defray the defendant's costs if he is ultimately ordered to do so.[3]

A plaintiff who sues in the High Court and fails to recover £3,000, will only receive costs on the county court scale.[4] This may not apply if a point of importance is involved.[5] No costs are generally recoverable if less than £600 is awarded.[6] Legal aid will often make it possible for poor litigants to bring and defend actions.[7]

Cases are frequently terminated by payment of claims or by default of the debtor in appearing or defending. Here fixed scales of costs are recoverable.[8]

The court has a general jurisdiction to make orders as to costs.[9] This is regulated by rules of court.[10] Costs may be asked for at any stage of a case, but are generally dealt with at its conclusion.[11]

The successful party in a contested Queen's Bench action is generally awarded his costs "*as between party and party*" against

---

[1] See Supreme Court Fees (Amdt.) Order. 1975.
[2] An average action was taxed at £2,000 in 1981.
[3] R.S.C., Ord. 23. *Meijer* v. *John H. Taylor* [1981] F.S.R. 279.
[4] County Courts Act 1959, s.47; County Courts Jurisdiction Order 1981.
[5] Act of 1959, s.47(3), "sufficient reason" for trial in High Court.
[6] County Courts Act 1959, s.47; County Courts Jurisdiction Order 1981.
[7] *Infra.* p. 275.
[8] Ord. 62, App. 3. (1979).
[9] Supreme Court Act 1981, s.51.
[10] Ord. 62, r. 2(4); as to Admiralty cases see p. 268.
[11] r. 4 An injunction may be obtained to prevent disposal of assets to avoid payment of fixed costs, *Panton (Faith) Property Plan* v. *Hodgetts* [1981] 1 W.L.R. 927 (C.A.).

the loser, but this requires an exercise of the court's discretion.[12] The court may direct that any costs unnecessarily occasioned by a party be paid by that party.[13]

Taxation

The court may award a lump sum for costs. In any other case the successful party's solicitor draws up a bill of costs for all costs claimed against the other party.[14] If the opposing solicitor disputes the bill, taxation follows.[15]

The costs claimed are taxed by a taxing officer. Both sides attend, by appointment.[16] There is a right to a review of the taxation by a judge in chambers,[17] who may himself tax any item, or order taxation by a different officer. A number of fixed charges are laid down, *e.g.* for the issue and service of the writ, petition or notice of motion, the summons for directions, affidavits of documents, conferences with counsel, attending court, issuing of execution of judgment.[18] Some items are discretionary.[19] There is a further appeal from the judge to the Court of Appeal, usually with leave of the judge.[20]

The taxing officer disallows any expenses not strictly necessary or proper to establish the party's case or defence. Views often differ as to what is in fact necessary.[21] Hindsight may reveal that items of expenditure were unnecessary which foresight suggested to be necessary. In some cases very little is taxed off the bill, but since solicitors know what items will be allowed, this is inconclusive.[22] In very important cases where prominent leading counsel are engaged the gulf is often wider, or the judge may not certify a case for two counsel where two counsel in fact appeared.[23]

Total costs of prospective litigation are difficult to predict. Counsel's fees differ with the reputation and popularity of the individual. On taxation of costs the recognised scale of allowance

---

[12] r. 3.
[13] r. 7. Set-off sometimes results: r. 18.
[14] Ord. 62, r. 25. In personal injury cases a simplified bill is possible, *Practice Direction* [1979] 1 All E.R. 958.
[15] r. 21; *cf.* App. 1. Procedure is laid down in r. 21(5); *Practice Direction*, June 8, 1975.
[16] rr. 22, 26.
[17] rr. 12, 35. *cf. R.* v. *The Taxing officer ex. p., Bee Line Roadways International* (1982) 4 C.L. 322.
[18] Under r. 32 (1979) and App. Pt. I.
[19] Ord. 62, App. 2. Pt. X, shows how to exercise this discretion.
[20] Supreme Court Act 1981, s.18(1)(f).
[21] Evershed Committee Final Report, p. 232; *Atwell* v. *Ministry of Public Buildings and Works* [1969] 1 W.L.R. 1074.
[22] In 1981 about 80 per cent. of costs claimed in the Queen's Bench Division were allowed.
[23] *Gortin* v. *Odham's Press* [1958] 2 W.L.R. 314.

of counsel's fees depends on the nature of the case and not on the reputation of counsel. Solicitors' charges for preparation of cases for trial ("instructions for brief") also vary with the complexity and work involved.[24] The preparation of a bill of costs for taxation is a specialised art, and most firms of solicitors practising in the High Court employ a clerk who is wholly engaged in this work or farm it out to specialists. Expert witnesses' fees are a serious item, especially when witnesses are kept outside the court in anticipation of the case being reached on the list on a particular day. A volunteer witness, such as a medical expert, may be paid a high fee, whereas he could have been subpoenaed to appear, but might have resented such a step being taken.

A successful litigant is often deprived of certain items of costs. Thus the plaintiff may not get his costs or may have to pay the defendant's costs if he has exaggerated or multiplied his claims, especially where the other party might have satisfied him if the claim had been limited to the amount actually recovered. The same is true if the plaintiff delayed explaining the justification for his claim, when he may have to pay the defendant's costs incurred up to that time.[25]

Where costs are ordered by the court to be taxed on a "common fund" basis all reasonable expenses are generally recoverable.[26] The solicitor's bill to his client is then generally paid by the opponent in full.

A litigant in person may be allowed sums in respect of work done and expenses and losses incurred in connection with a case.[27]

Effect of tender on costs

Where a claim is made for a liquidated sum the defendant may, before any action is begun, tender the sum which he admits to be due. If the plaintiff insists on proceeding, he may lose his costs, and have to pay the defendant's costs after tender. On the other hand the defendant must pay the amount offered into court if he is going to plead "tender" and cannot use the offer as a bargaining point in trying to settle the action out of court. He must also tender the whole sum he admits to be due, as otherwise the plaintiff

---

[24] Ord. 62, App. 2, Pt. X; *Simpson's Motor Sales (London) Ltd.* v. *Hendon Corp.* [1965] 1 W.L.R. 112; *Re Eastwood* [1975] Ch. 112 (C.A.) (salaried solicitor).

[25] *Re Amory* [1951] 2 All E.R. 947, where a society claiming a gift failed to produce evidence of its identity with the society named in the will until late in the proceedings. Delay in suing is in itself liable to be reflected in denial of costs: *Taylor* v. *Taylor Garnett, Evans & Co.* [1954] C.L.Y. 2547.

[26] Ord. 62, r. 28; *Sammy* v. *Birkbeck College* (1964) 108 S.J. 897; the court retains wide powers to make other orders, Supreme Court Act 1981, s.51.

[27] *Cf.* Litigants in Person (Costs and Expenses) Act 1975.

would lose the balance or lose his costs if the balance was too small to justify a High Court action.[28]

Payment into court

A defendant may pay a sum of money with interest into court at any stage of any action, *e.g.* a claim for damages for libel or personal injuries. The plaintiff may accept it in full, within 21 days of notice of payment, and enter judgment for his costs already incurred.[29] The plaintiff will not get costs incurred after payment into court if he refuses to accept it and recovers no more in the result, and he may be liable for the defendant's costs.[30] He will recover his full costs if he recovers any larger sum, even if not much larger,[31] but not if the excess was due to a new claim raised at the trial.[32] If the plaintiff loses the action the money is repaid. The defendant cannot withdraw the money before the end of the case without leave of the court, even if the plaintiff declines to accept it in full satisfaction, but the plaintiff may take it out with leave of the court at any time.[33] The fact of a payment into court is not known to the judge or jury until after trial on the merits, as it might influence the assessment of damages or suggest an admission of liability by the defendant, so that the plaintiff would benefit by the payment without binding himself by accepting it.[34]

Chancery Division

In the Chancery Division the situation is somewhat different. Many Chancery suits are applications to the court to decide the correct interpretation and implementation of a will or settlement of property, or the proper steps to be taken in the administration of funds. *All reasonable costs* are treated as incurred for the benefit of the estate, whether incurred by the trustees or the beneficiaries, and the costs of all parties come out of the estate, so that the trust fund or the property left by will is to that extent reduced.[35]

This is not the case where there is hostile litigation between trustees or executors on the one hand, and beneficiaries or

---

[28] Ord. 18, r. 16.
[29] Ord. 22, rr. 1, 3.
[30] *Wagman* v. *Vare Motors Ltd.* [1959] 1 W.L.R. 853.
[31] *Read* v. *Smith* [1951] Ch. 439.
[32] *Cheeseman* v. *Bowaters U.K. Paper Mills* [1971] 1 W.L.R. 1773.
[33] *Practice Note* [1953] 1 W.L.R. 780; *Cumper* v. *Pothecary* [1941] 2 K.B. 58; but see *Gaskins* v. *British Aluminium Co.* [1976] Q.B. 524.
[34] Ord. 22, r. 7; *Findlay* v. *Ry. Executive* [1950] 2 All E.R. 969; *Beaumont* v. *British Uralite* [1973] C.L.Y. 2601.
[35] Ord. 62, r. 28; but see Supreme Court Act 1981, s.51; *E.M.I. Records* v. *Ian Cameron Wallace* [1982] 3 W.L.R. 245; in 1981 nearly 90 per cent. of costs claimed were allowed.

legatees on the other, or between beneficiaries. In such cases *party and party costs* are usually awarded on the same basis and for the same reasons as in the Queen's Bench Division. A trustee is generally entitled to be indemnified out of the trust estate to the extent of its assets for all his reasonable expenses of bringing or defending actions connected with the trust, whatever the result.[36] Decisions on costs are subject to review.[37] Probate costs follow the event.[38]

Family Division

Costs are in the discretion of the court but do not always follow the event in divorce cases. Costs must be claimed in the petition or by a notice from the respondent and asked for at the end of the trial.[39] Where the wife petitions and fails she pays the costs, if able.[40] If she succeeds as petitioner or respondent the husband is liable to pay her taxed costs and also any excess of expenditure over that, since it is regarded as expenditure for necessaries for which he is liable.[41] If the wife is the respondent she is not usually ordered to pay the petitioner's costs if he succeeds, unless her own means are sufficient.[42] A male co-respondent may be ordered to pay costs where a husband obtains a divorce, provided the husband asks for them. The woman cited in the petition may be ordered to pay costs, if guilty.[43]

The Admiralty Court (of the Q.B.D.)

Costs are in the discretion of the court.[44] They usually follow the event.[45] If neither ship or both ships are at fault costs are not generally awarded.[46]

Court of Appeal (Civil Division)

The winning party on the appeal usually obtains the costs of the trial and the appeal, though the court has a discretion.[47] If a new

---

[36] Ord. 62, r. 31; *Re Dargie* [1954] Ch. 16.
[37] *Practice Directions* [1960] 1 W.L.R. 1194; [1962] C.L.Y. 2387; no. 2 of 1982.
[38] R.S.C. Ord. 76; the former Probate Division Practice is followed.
[39] Matrimonial Causes Rules 1977, App. 2. para. 5, minimum and maximum amounts are laid down in the 1st column of the Appendix to the Matrimonial Causes (Costs) Rules 1979.
[40] *Gooday* v. *Gooday* [1969] P. 1.
[41] As to interlocutory proceedings, see [1958] 1 W.L.R. 492.
[42] *J.N. Nabarro* v. *Kennedy* [1955] 1 Q.B. 575.
[43] Matrimonial Causes Act 1973, s.49; 1977 Rules, r. 49(2).
[44] Supreme Court Act 1981, s.51. R.S.C., Ord. 62, r. 2; App. Pt. V. *The Modica* [1926] P. 72.
[45] *Ibid.* r. 3(2); *The Osprey* [1967] 1 Lloyd's Rep. 76.
[46] *The Lucille Bloomfield* [1966] 1 W.L.R. 1525.
[47] Supreme Court Act 1981, s.51. *Olivant* v. *Wright* (1875) 1 Ch.D. 41.

trial is ordered, the costs of all hearings follow the ultimate event, *i.e.* the fate of the later trial. An appellant may be refused costs if he succeeds on the appeal after being allowed to adduce fresh evidence or present new arguments not before the trial court, the theory being that by great diligence this could have been done before.

House of Lords

The successful respondent may be awarded costs in all courts including the House of Lords.[48] It is sometimes made a condition of giving leave to appeal that the appellant pay the costs of the appeal, even if he should win.[49]

Cases in county courts

The award of costs against a party is in the discretion of the court. The unsuccessful party is usually ordered to pay the costs of the successful party.[50]

The basic scheme is one of five scales of itemised costs varying with the amount of the plaintiff's judgment, if he wins, and the amount of his claim if he loses.[51] There is considerable elasticity within the limits of each scale, especially with regard to the preparation for trial by the solicitor. Costs may be fixed at various points between the maximum and minimum on a scale, according to the Registrar's view of the amount of work involved and the importance of the proceedings.[52] Costs may be allowed on a higher scale if the judge certifies that a difficult question of law or fact was involved.[53]

Counsel's fees are not allowed if the case is admitted or undefended.[54] In small contested cases the court must certify after the hearing that the case was "fit for counsel."[55]

Costs are limited in uncontested cases[56] and the amount of witness expenses at trials is also limited.[57]

---

[48] *Osenton & Co.* v. *Johnson* [1942] A.C. 130; *Practice Direction* [1977] 3 All E.R. 592; half his costs were awarded to the successful party in *Cassell* v. *Broome* (No. 2) [1972] A.C. 1136; as to the costs of a petition for leave to appeal see *Practice Direction* (H.L.) November 10, 1977.

[49] *Re Drake's Settlement* [1938] Ch. 133.

[50] County Court Rules, Ord. 47, r. 1: This may be on a solicitor and own client basis, *Greenhouse* v. *Hetherington* (1977) 122 S.J. 47 (C.A.).

[51] Ord. 47, r. 5.

[52] r. 16.

[53] r. 13.

[54] r. 20.

[55] r. 18.

[56] Ord. 11, rr. 1, 7, 8. The amount is stated on the summons.

[57] r. 29.

Where a divorce county court tries an undefended divorce, a special "divorce scale" is applied but the registrar may allow larger sums.[58]

The bill of costs is indorsed with the final amount of allowed or taxed costs (the "allocatur"). There is an appeal from the Registrar to the county court judge if either side is dissatisfied.[59]

The county court scales are applied in some High Court cases which ought properly to have been brought in the county court.[60] If a defendant transfers a small claim to the High Court[61] and the plaintiff succeeds, the plaintiff is not limited to county court costs, as the defendant chose the forum.[62]

Magistrates' courts

In civil proceedings in magistrates' courts the court may order the unsuccessful party to pay so much of the other party's costs as is just and reasonable.[63]

Arbitration

The arbitrator has a judicial discretion as to costs.[64] There must generally be a strong ground for refusing costs to the successful party.[65]

Administrative tribunals

Orders as to costs are not generally made in hearings by special tribunals or at local inquiries. The state is not a defendant and expenses are kept at a minimum. Representation by solicitor or counsel is usually optional and the party may conduct his own case, to save paying fees. The general operational costs of the system fall on public funds, but some statutes provide for liability for costs.[66] The Franks Committee recommended that the citizen should never be liable for costs,[67] and should be awarded a

---

[58] Matrimonal Causes (Costs) Rules 1979, r. 6.
[59] r. 42; Administration of Justice Act 1969, s.8.
[60] County Courts Act 1959, s.47; Administration of Justice Act 1969, s.4; County Courts Jurisdiction Order 1981; less than £3,000 recovered.
[61] County Courts Act 1959, s.75C.
[62] *Turner* v. *Jacaranda Club Ltd.* [1953] 1 W.L.R. 961.
[63] Magistrates' Courts Act 1980, s.64.
[64] Arbitration Act 1950, s.18; *Demolition & Construction Co.* v. *Kent River Board* [1963] 2 Lloyd's Rep. 7.
[65] *Lewis* v. *Haverfordwest R.D.C.* [1953] 1 W.L.R. 1486.
[66] *Re Jackman's Appn.* [1954] J.P.L. 458; Agriculture (Misc.Prov.) Act 1954, s.5; Solicitors' Act 1974, s.47(1)(*e*); Industrial Tribunals (Labour Relations) Reg. 1974; *Carr* v. *Allen-Bradley Electronics* [1980] I.C.R. 663 (E.A.T.).
[67] *Cf. R.* v. *Secretary of State for the Environment* (1971) 22 P. & C.R. 1022 (D.C.).

reasonable sum for expenses, irrespective of the result of the case.[68]

In Criminal Cases

Costs in summary proceedings

In summary cases the defendant, if convicted, may be ordered to pay some or all of the prosecution costs, and, on acquittal, the prosecution may be ordered to pay the costs of the defence, if just and reasonable to so order.[69] If an indictable offence is tried summarily, central funds may be used to pay the costs of the prosecution, and, if the case is dismissed, those of the defence.[70]

Costs in committal proceedings

Prosecution costs may be paid out of central funds, as may the defence costs if the magistrates do not commit the case for trial.[71] If the magistrates consider the charge was not made in good faith they may order the prosecution to pay the costs of the defence.[72]

Costs in the Crown Court

These are in the discretion of the court.[73]

The costs of the prosecution at a trial in the Crown Court may be paid out of central funds. Those of the accused will be so paid unless the accused is convicted on some count or won on a technicality or drew suspicion on himself.[74] Similar rules apply on committal to the Crown Court for sentence, to appeals to the Crown Court against conviction or sentence by magistrates and to cases stated to the Divisional Court by magistrates.[75]

If the accused is convicted he may be ordered to pay all or part of the prosecution costs at the trial and the committal proceedings.[76] The prosecution may correspondingly be ordered to pay the costs of the accused if acquitted.[77]

---

[68] (1957) Cmnd. 218, pp. 23, 70. See Cmnd. 2471.

[69] Costs in Criminal Cases Act 1973, s.2(1), (2) *R.* v. *Tottenham Justices ex. p. Joshi* [1982] 1 W.L.R. 631.

[70] *Ibid.* s.1(1), (2); see s.17 as to scale of payment and *Practice Note* [1982] 1 W.L.R. 1447. The Lord Chancellor is in charge of the system of criminal costs under the Transfer of Functions Order 1980.

[71] Costs in Criminal Cases Act 1973 s.1(1), (2).

[72] *Ibid.* s.2(4).

[73] Supreme Court Act 1981, s.52; *Practice Direction* (1980) 6 C.L. 57.

[74] Costs in Criminal Cases Act 1973 s.3(1)(*b*); *Practice Direction* [1981] 1 W.L.R. 1383 (C.A.).

[75] *Ibid.* ss.18, 3(2), 5.

[76] *Ibid.* s.4(1)(*a*); *R.* v. *Yoxall* (1972) 57 Cr.App.R. 263; *R.* v. *Smith* (1978) 67 Cr.App.R. 332 (C.A.). He may appeal to the Court of Appeal against the order, *R.* v. *Hayden* [1975] 1 W.L.R. 852.

[77] *Ibid.* s.4(1)(*b*).

Appeals in the Court of Appeal (Criminal Division)

Central funds may be used to pay the costs of the appellant if the appeal is allowed, and of the prosecution in any case.[78] If the appeal or an application for leave to appeal is dismissed, the court may order the appellant to pay all or part of the costs.[79]

Appeals in the House of Lords

Central funds may be used to pay the costs of either party.[80] The appellant, if unsuccessful, may be ordered to pay costs.[81]

Abandonment of charge

If a charge of an indictable offence is laid but not proceeded with, and the defence has incurred costs, the defence may be allowed the costs out of central funds.[82] The prosecution may be ordered to pay these costs.[83]

Witnesses' allowances

Witnesses are paid allowances out of central funds in a number of cases. This covers travel and subsistence and professional allowances.[84]

LEGAL AID

The provision of state aid to poor litigants or accused persons takes several distinct forms. It is based on the idea that the judicial machinery of redress or defence ought not to be denied on the grounds of financial need. The Lord Chancellor is responsible for Civil and Criminal aid legislation and regulations.[85]

Criminal Cases

Legal aid orders

Half a million applicants receive legal aid each year.

A legal aid order may be made by a magistrates' court in summary cases; in appeals from magistrates to the Crown Court it

[78] *Ibid.* s.7(1), (2); Costs in Criminal Cases (Central Funds) Appeal Regulations 1977.
[79] Costs in Criminal Cases Act 1973 s.9.
[80] *Ibid.* s.10.
[81] *Ibid.* s.11.
[82] Costs in Criminal Cases Act 1973 s.12(1).
[83] *Ibid.* s.12(3).
[84] *Ibid.* ss.1(3), (4), 3(3)(*b*), (4), (8); Costs in Criminal Cases (Allowances) Regulations 1975.
[85] Transfer of Functions Order, 1980

may be made either by the magistrates' court or by the Crown Court. The Crown Court may also make such an order where a person appears before it for trial or sentence or is committed to it for trial, although the examining magistrates may make an order including the Crown Court Trial. The criminal division of the Court of Appeal has similar powers where there is an appeal from a conviction by a Crown Court, and it may also make an order where there is a further appeal to the House of Lords.[86]

The court must be satisfied that the interests of justice would be served by such an order, but in murder cases and in cases where the prosecution appeal to the House of Lords, aid must be given.[87]

Application is made to the magistrates' clerk or to the appropriate officer of the Crown Court or to the Registrar of the Court of Appeal.[88]

The means test

The court must be satisfied that the applicant has insufficient means of his own to enable him to pay for his own defence.[89] The Secretary of State appoints an authorised officer to assess his means if the court so orders or the applicant requests it.[90] The applicant must supply a statement of his means.[91] A regulation provides that no applicant is to be refused aid if he has less than £70.[92]

The court making a legal aid order may require the assisted person to make such contribution towards the costs of his defence as is reasonable in view of his financial circumstances.[93] No contribution is required if the assisted person has less than £815 net income or joint incomes with a spouse of £1,319.[94] Net income is arrived at after various scheduled deductions from gross income, for reasonable rent, mortgage payments, income tax, and maintenance of dependants. In calculating net capital the applicant's interest in his home is not taken into account.[95]

If an order for costs is ultimately made in favour of the assisted person, that is charged with the amount of contribution due from

---

[86] Legal Aid Act 1974, s.28; Legal Aid Act 1982, s.2.
[87] Act of 1974, s.29.
[88] Legal Aid in Criminal Proceedings (General) Regulations 1968–1970 rr. 1–3.
[89] 1974 Act, s.29(2).
[90] s.33, Gen. Regs. (amended 1980) rr. 3, 17, Legal Aid (Assessment of Resources) Regs. 1980.
[91] Act of 1974, s.29(4).
[92] Legal Aid in Criminal Proceedings (Assessment of Resources) Regulations 1978, r. 6(4).
[93] 1974 Act, s.32; Legal Aid Act 1982, s.7. Only about £6m. contribution towards £97 expenditure was collected in 1981–82.
[94] Assessment of Resources Regulations, r. 7(2).
[95] r. 9(3).

him, if not paid, but only if he recovers more costs than his contribution.[96] He may also be sued for the amount of the contribution or his wages attached at the source.[97]

Scope of legal aid

This covers the fees and disbursements of solicitor and counsel, or solicitor, depending on the order.[98] Counsel are not provided in summary cases and only in difficult cases of indictable offences tried summarily.[99] Counsel may be provided in the Crown Court and for appeals.[1] In murder cases counsel must be ordered[2] and retainer of two counsel may be ordered.[3]

Regulations fix minimum and maximum amounts for lawyers' fees under legal aid.[4] The fees are worked out between these limits according to the length of time spent on the case and its difficulty or importance.[5] In exceptional cases the maximum may be exceeded.[6] Taxation may be reviewed and there is an appeal to the council of the Law Society.[7]

Choice of legal representative

In most cases the court itself assigns a practising solicitor or barrister, or both. There is no provision for a special panel.[8] Where proceedings are taking place in the Court of Appeal or House of Lords the wishes of the assisted person are, however, taken into account.[9] A lawyer may be excluded from being called on to undertake such defences if this is ordered by a special complaints tribunal set up by the Lord Chancellor.[10] Each court is accordingly supplied with a list of such excluded persons.[11] Complaints are made to the governing bodies of the two branches

---

[96] Act of 1974, s.36; Legal Aid Act 1982, s.13.
[97] Ibid. s.35.
[98] Ibid. s.30.
[99] Ibid. s.30(2); R. v. Guildhall Justices [1976] 1 W.L.R. 335; The 1982 Act. s.5 proposes that legal aid committees deal with representation by counsel before the magistrates.
[1] s.30; in 1981 nearly all applications in Crown Courts and the Court of Appeal were granted and most applications for summary trials of serious crimes.
[2] 1974 Act, s.29(1).
[3] Gen. Regs., r. 13 (as amended 1976).
[4] Ibid. r. 99, Sched. 3; Legal Aid in Criminal Proceedings (Costs) Amendment Reg. 1983.
[5] Ibid. Sched. 3, para. 3.
[6] Ibid. para. 4.
[7] Ibid. r. 99(2).
[8] 1974 Act, ss.30(1), 38.
[9] Gen. Regs., r. 11.
[10] 1974 Act, s.38(2)(ii).
[11] Gen. Regs. r. 7.

of the profession, who may pass them on to a special tribunal consisting of members of the branch nominated by such bodies.[12] The parties appear at the hearing but it is held in private. The decision of the tribunal is communicated to the parties and to the relevant bodies.[13] The tribunal may also reduce or cancel claims to remuneration or make the lawyers pay costs.[14] There is an appeal to the High Court.[15]

Financing of the scheme

The cost of the provision of legal aid in magistrates' courts falls on the legal aid funds maintained under the civil legal aid system.[16] In all other cases it is met by the Lord Chancellor's Department.[17]

Civil cases

Legal Aid has been applied to the Supreme Court, the Employment Appeals Tribunal, the Lands Tribunal, the House of Lords, the matrimonial jurisdiction of magistrates and county courts.[18] Appeals may only be aided if an area committee considers it necessary.[19]

The object of the scheme is to enable persons with small means to bring or defend actions without cost to themselves. Persons of limited means may be required to contribute towards the cost.[20]

Legal aid is available in all civil actions other than those for defamation.[21] Undefended divorce cases no longer qualify for legal aid.[22]

Legal aid extends to representation by solicitor and, where necessary, by counsel, in preparing claims or conducting litigation.[23]

Two parallel problems arise in legal aid, the question of whether the applicant is financially incapable of financing his claim or defence, and the question whether the projected litigation is justifiable, in view of the expense to the public.

---

[12] Legal Aid in Criminal Cases (Complaints Tribunals) Rules 1968, rr. 4, 2.
[13] Sched., paras. 5, 11, 12.
[14] Act of 1974, s.38(2)(iii).
[15] *Ibid.* s.138(4).
[16] *Ibid.* s.37(1)(*a*).
[17] See n. 85, *supra.*
[18] But not yet to Industrial or Rent Tribunals. Small county court claims do not qualify but go to arbitration.
[19] General Regs. 1971, s.3(1).
[20] General Regs. (1980) rr. 32, 44. About three-quarters of litigants pay no contribution. In 1981 the average contribution was about £150.
[21] Legal Aid Act 1974, Sched. I, Pt. II.
[22] Legal Aid (Matrimonial Proceedings) Regulations 1977.
[23] 1974 Act, s.7(4).

The means test

Financial assistance is provided with or without contribution if the applicant is a person[24] with a "disposable income" of less than £3,600 per annum and a "disposable capital" of less than £2,500.[25] An officer authorised by the Secretary of State, who may interview the applicant, decides if the applicant has such income or capital.[26] His decision is final, and there is no appeal, though he may reconsider the case in the event of a later change of circumstances.[27]

Detailed rules for assessment are laid down.[28] The assessment of a wage-earner's income is based on his wages for the preceding twelve months, less reasonable expenses connected with his employment.[29] From this is deducted full income tax for a year,[30] and any reasonable rent payable.[31] Allowance for maintenance of a spouse is made.[32]

In the computation of capital the value of a dwelling-house is ignored.[33] Capital repayments as well as mortgage interest are deductible from the income of a houseowner, and allowances for rates and repairs.[34]

If the applicant has more than £3,600 he must prove that he is unable to proceed without aid.[35] He is liable to contribute up to all his capital over £1,200. If his income exceeds £1,500 he may have to make a contribution of not more than one-third of the excess.[36]

The assessment officer fixes the maximum contribution possible and the general committee decides the actual amount.[37]

Aid will not be given if the applicant's expenses will be covered by insurance or if he is a member of some protective association which is willing to assist him.[38]

Reasonable grounds

Assuming the applicant is entitled to some legal aid, he must show he has reasonable grounds for taking, defending or being a

[24] *Ibid.* s.25.
[25] s.6, as amended by Legal Aid (Financial Conditions) Regulations 1979.
[26] General r. 3(6); Ministry of Social Security Act 1966, s.2; Social Security Act, 1975; Legal Aid (Assessment of Resources) Regs. 1980, rr. 4, 3.
[27] *Ibid.* r. 13.
[28] Legal Aid (Assessment of Resources) Regulations 1980, r. 5.
[29] *Ibid.* Sched. 2, para. 3.
[30] Sched. 2, para. 4.
[31] *Ibid.* para. 9.
[32] *Ibid.,* para. 11.
[33] *Ibid.* Sched. 3, para. 9.
[34] Sched. 2, para. 9(2).
[35] Act of 1974, s.6(1)(*b*), as amended 1976.
[36] Legal Aid Act 1974, s.9. Legal Aid (Financial Conditions) Regulations 1979.
[37] General Regs. (1980) rr. 17, 32.
[38] General Regulations 1980, r. 31.

party to proceedings,[39] that is to say, he must be able to establish some prima facie case or defence.[40] The decision as to whether he has done so is for the local general Committee appointed by the Area Committee.[41] The applicant must file forms which refer to his grounds for bringing or defending the action.[42] All information supplied by the applicant is confidential[43] and it is a summary offence to give false information.[44] Local committees have proved efficient in screening applications.[45] In many cases both parties are assisted, but these are cases where the solution of the case was not obvious. If a legal aid certificate is refused the local committee must give reasons.[46] The applicant may then appeal to the area committee whose decision is final.[47] A certificate may be revoked or discontinued if it is later discovered that the litigant ought no longer to be assisted.[48]

Operation of the scheme

The litigant who has obtained his legal aid certificate from the local committee selects any solicitor and counsel not excluded from acting under the scheme.[49] Counsel should only be instructed where really necessary.[50] Counsel's fees and solicitor's profit costs are not fixed in advance, but are 90 per cent. of the amount allowed by the taxing master in the Supreme Court after judgment.[51] Certain types of expenditure must be approved in advance by the general committee, such as the retention of two counsel.[52]

If an assisted party loses his case he must himself pay the opponent's costs if ordered to do so by the court, if the circumstances and his means warrant it[53]; his house and furniture are not computed as resources.[54] The order may be varied if the assisted party's circumstances change.[55]

---

[39] Legal Aid Act 1974, s.7(5).
[40] r. 29.
[41] Legal Aid Act 1982, s.5; Legal Aid Act 1974, s.15; Legal Aid (General) Regulations 1980, rr. 29, 3. About 80 per cent. of applications for legal aid succeeded in 1981–82.
[42] r. 11, 13. Emergency certificates may be granted in urgent cases without complying with formalities, rr. 19, 20.
[43] Legal Aid Act 1974, s.22.
[44] Ibid. s.23.
[45] Two-thirds of assisted claims in contested cases have succeeded.
[46] General Regulations 1980, r. 35.
[47] Ibid. r. 36 There are 13 areas; Scheme, Sched. I.
[48] Ibid. rr. 77, 78; Neill v. Glacier Metal Co. [1965] 1 Q.B. 16; Iverson v. Iverson [1967] P. 134.
[49] Act of 1974, s.12 (substituted by Administration of Justice Act 1977, s.1, Sched. 1, Pt. I).
[50] General Regulations 1980, r. 60.
[51] Act of 1974, s.10, Sched. 2.
[52] See n. 50.
[53] Act of 1974, s.8(1)(c), rr. 117, 122.
[54] s.8(4); r. 119.
[55] Legal Aid Act 1982, s.13. General Regs. (1980) rr. 53, 123.

If an assisted party wins his case any costs and damages recovered are used to defray the amount advanced to him by the Fund for his costs but certain sums recovered by wives and children are exempted.[56]

If an ordinary plaintiff would be deprived of his costs, though successful, the same will apply if he is legally aided. Hence if he recovers a lesser amount than the defendants have paid into court he will get no costs from the defendants and is liable to pay the defendant's costs if they exceed the damages awarded.[57] Any net damages such a plaintiff recovers will be used to recoup the costs advanced to him out of the Legal Aid Fund as these cannot be thrown on to the defendant.[58] An assisted person may be required to give security for costs where an unassisted person would.[59]

Payments for assisted persons are made out of the Legal Aid Fund.[60] Contributions by litigants and damages and costs recovered in the action are paid into this Fund.[61] It may also proceed to recover indemnities from any person which the assisted person could have recovered.[62] The Fund is running at a heavy loss.[63]

If an unassisted party wins a case and the assisted party is unable to pay the former's costs these may be paid out of the Legal Aid Fund but only if it is just and equitable to do so,[64] and, in the case of proceedings in a court of first instance where the unassisted party suffers serious financial hardship.[65]

Legal advice and assistance

A limited scheme existed under the 1949 Legal Aid Act but this was felt to be inadequate and, following a recommendation by the advisory committee on legal aid,[66] a new scheme was provided in 1972. This scheme covers non-litigious legal advice and advice preliminary to actual litigation being started. The limit is advice

---

[56] ss.8, 9; General Regs., rr, 88, 91, 96; *Law Society* v. *Rushman* [1955] 1 W.L.R. 681; *Wagg* v. *L.S.* [1957] Ch. 405.
[57] r. 127.
[58] *Kelly* v. *Thomas & Edge Ltd., The Times,* October 27, 1953 (C.A.).
[59] General Regs. r. 116.
[60] Set up under s.9 of 1949 Act, now Act of 1974, s.17.
[61] See n. 56, *supra.*
[62] Act of 1974, s.24(3).
[63] At present the annual deficit is £42m. (1981–2).
[64] Legal Aid Act 1974, s.13; Legal Aid (Costs of Successful Unassisted Parties) Regulations 1964; General Regs., r. 3, Sched. 4. *Saunders* v. *Anglia Building Society* [1971] A.C. 1039; *Davies* v. *Taylor (No.* 2) [1974]; *Millican* v. *Tucker* [1980] 1 W.L.R. 640 (C.A.). A.C. 225. £137,000 was paid out in 1981–82.
[65] *Gayways Linings* v. *Toczek* [1980] 124 S.J. 291; *Kelly* v. *London Transport Executive* [1982] 1 W.L.R. 1055 (large public corporation not so suffering); *Hanning* v. *Maitland (No.* 2) [1970] 1 Q.B. 580 (C.A.).
[66] Cmnd. 4249 (1970).

for which the sum of £40 is a reasonable fee, but the Area Committee may approve a larger sum.[67]

The client pays nothing if he does not have more than £40 "disposable income" weekly, but he contributes a graduated amount until his earnings reach £85, which is the upper limit of eligibility to benefit from the scheme.[68]

Any costs eventually received or property recovered may be charged with repayment of the amount advanced but this may be dispensed with.[69] The deficit falls on the legal aid fund and is borne by Parliament.[70]

Aid by representation

This is to some extent intermediate between full legal aid and legal advice.[71] It is applicable to various types of domestic proceedings concerned with children.[72] Application is made to the general legal aid committee.[73]

THE LEGAL PROFESSION

The legal profession in England is divided into two branches, the barristers, who plead cases in the superior courts and from whom the judges are selected, and the solicitors, who conduct legal negotiations for their clients, prepare cases for trial and draw up wills, conveyances on sale and other formal documents with legal effects. In some countries which apply English common law the legal profession is unified and lawyers do all types of legal work, being described as attorneys, barristers or counsellors. On the continent of Europe there are separate professions of judge, advocate, prosecutor, legal adviser and notary.

Historically the solicitor represents a person, not originally legally trained, who was authorised by a client to act in his name in carrying out a legal transaction, *e.g.* to appear in court in the formal stages of a lawsuit. The representative was called an "attorney" and became in time a professional man acting in cases

---

[67] Legal Aid Act 1974, ss.1–5; L.A.A. Regs. 1980, r. 15.
[68] 1980, Sched. 3; disposable capital must be less than £600, L.A.A. Regs. 1979 (No. 21).
[69] s.5; L.A.A. Regs., 1980, rr. 25, 26. Sched. 5 exempts dwelling-houses and some sums awarded in domestic proceedings.
[70] s.5, 12. The cost was £30m. in 1981–82.
[71] Legal Aid Act 1974, s.2A (added in Legal Aid Act 1979).
[72] L.A.A. Regs. 1980, Sched. 4.
[73] *Ibid.* rr. 16, 17.

in the common law courts. In the Chancery the term "solicitor" was used and has superseded "attorney" in English usage. The actual argument of a case before the court was often entrusted by a client to a learned or eloquent friend as his adviser or "counsel." In order to ensure expedition and efficiency the judges began to insist by the end of the thirteenth century on some minimum skill in this work and their right to examine and admit pleaders to practise. This led to the creation of the Bar and to the legal education of young barristers at the Inns of Court, taking part in moots, attending readings or lectures and attending court sessions and making notes. The client would then first consult his solicitor, often generally retained for all his legal work, and the solicitor would choose counsel for each case fought in the courts, preparing a brief on the case for the counsel he "instructed."

Solicitors

The solicitors' profession is regulated by modern statutes of 1957, 1965 and 1974. The solicitor has a right of audience in county courts and magistrates' courts and before masters and registrars of the High Court, and in certain appeals to the Crown Court from magistrates' courts. He may be authorised to appear in trials on indictment in certain Crown Courts. The Law Society regulate preparation for admission as a solicitor. The student must spend a preliminary period of practical training as a "clerk" in "articles" of apprenticeship to a practising solicitor. He often takes a university course for a law degree before embarking on articles, which are then reduced in length. A number of professional examinations must also be passed before admission as a solicitor.

Solicitors often form partnerships and each partner may specialise in some part of the work of the firm, e.g. litigation, conveyancing or commercial law. Solicitors may also be employed by firms or by local government authorities.

The solicitor must keep separate clients' accounts for his clients' money passing through his hands and must account for any interest received. These accounts are audited annually. His fees for many routine matters are fixed by law but for other types of work he may charge fees varying with the skill, time and trouble involved. A client who thinks a bill excessive may take proceedings to have it taxed. The solicitor is also liable to be sued for damages if he fails to use the reasonable care and skill generally expected of a competent solicitor, but can insure against such liability.

Most solicitors belong to the Law Society, an organisation which represents their interests and voluntarily satisfies clients with claims against insolvent solicitors out of a special contributory fund. A solicitor may be "struck off" the roll for misconduct, but may later apply for restoration to the roll. The Law Society drew up, and operates, the civil Legal Aid Scheme already referred to and may employ solicitors to operate the legal aid and legal advice schemes and assist local legal advice centres.

Solicitors often act as legal officers of cities and boroughs and as clerks to magistrates' courts and Crown Courts. They are eligible for appointment as stipendiary magistrates and Recorders. Time spent as a solicitor is counted towards the required term of standing at the Bar where a solicitor becomes a barrister and is later appointed to judicial office.

Barristers

Barristers have the monopoly of pleading before the higher courts: the High Court, Court of Appeal and House of Lords, and in most trials in criminal cases on indictment. The courts in the London area are open to all members of the Bar but in the provinces work is divided among the members of six circuits, which correspond to the seven old assize circuits, and it is unusual and generally impracticable to join more than one circuit.

The student barrister must join one of the four Inns of Court and pass two Bar examinations. University law graduates are exempted from the first of these. Students must "keep terms" by dining at their Inn during eight terms before call and four thereafter. After call the barrister who intends to practise in England and Wales must spend a year as a pupil in the chambers of a practising barrister, and may only practice himself after completing six months of his pupillage.

The governing body of each Inn of Court is composed of masters of the Bench (or "Benchers") who elect new masters from time to time. They are presided over by a Treasurer. Judges remain members of their inns and are usually appointed Benchers. There is also a senate representing all four inns.

After a number of years in practice a barrister may apply to the Lord Chancellor for the title of Queen's Counsel. If he obtains this distinction he enjoys certain privileges and is no longer entitled to take on certain types of work he could do while a junior barrister. This is known as "taking silk" because he will now wear a silk gown. All barristers wear traditional wigs and gowns in court except in magistrates' courts.

If a barrister is considered to have misconducted himself professionally he may be disciplined by the Benchers of his Inn, including the ultimate sanction of disbarment. All four Inns have similar regulations and policies. There is a right of appeal to a specially constituted court of judges.

Counsel may not seek clients directly and may not advertise, though he may list his special interests. He depends on solicitors approaching him through his clerk. The solicitor will also be present at interviews with clients and attend court while a case is being heard.

A barrister's fees vary with his reputation, being fixed by his clerk from time to time. He cannot sue a client to recover them; he may insist on payment in advance but this is unusual. Solicitors may sue clients for such fees as part of their disbursements and must pass them on to the barrister if they recover them.

Barristers are liable in damages for negligent opinions or preparation of cases (but not for advocacy in court) and insure against liability.

Fusion

The division of the legal profession has been criticised as accidental, illogical and irritating, though specialisation occurs even in countries where the profession is fused. Whether the total expense to the client is increased by paying two lawyers is a matter of dispute. There is in any case, easy movement from one branch of the profession to the other. On the other hand professional standards could no doubt be maintained by a single fused profession.

THE LAW OF EVIDENCE

Every court must confine its attention to matters which have a direct bearing on the case before it, *i.e.* which are "relevant" or "material" to the facts in dispute, as they appear from the pleadings or the criminal charge. Proof of facts is made by offering some type of evidence, such as the testimony of witnesses or the examination of documents or objects. If direct proof is unobtainable circumstantial evidence may be offered, *i.e.* proof of a number of facts from which the fact in dispute can reasonably be deduced.

There are also certain presumptions, which require a court to assume certain facts unless and until the contrary is proved, thus favouring the party who would otherwise have to prove those facts, *e.g.* that a couple living together are married. In some cases the court will dispense with the need to offer evidence, if the fact is so obvious that it would waste time to prove it, *e.g.* that Queen Elizabeth II is the Queen of England or that it is hotter in summer than winter. This is called "taking judicial notice" of a circumstance. A judge will not take notice of anything really debatable even if he happens to know it is true; the right course would be for him to offer himself as a witness in such a case and have the dispute tried by another judge.

Witnesses answer questions on facts only and do not give opinions or conclusions. There is an exception in the case of matters requiring expert knowledge, *e.g.* to determine the causes of death. The expert testifies in such cases to his opinion, giving his grounds for forming that opinion, and is subject to cross-examination by the other side in an endeavour to shake his conclusions.

Evidence in criminal proceedings

It is characteristic of the English court system that differing rules have grown up in many instances in criminal and civil cases. Serious crimes are tried by a jury of laymen and our judges have therefore built up a body of rules of admissibility of evidence, applied by the judge, designed to prevent a jury hearing or being shown any evidence which might unduly prejudice them against an accused person, even though such evidence would otherwise be relevant to their decision of the case. Typical of these is the confession. In ordinary life we should normally accept a confession as very good proof of the facts confessed, and admissions are readily accepted by civil courts if made against the party's interest, it being assumed that people will not normally fabricate evidence against themselves. However, there is a danger in criminal cases that confessions may be misunderstood or used as a pretext for omitting to offer other proof of guilt. Hence, and possibly also because of a traditional dislike of making people convict themselves, no confession may be put in evidence unless it is first established that it was freely offered without threats or inducements having been made by the police or prosecution. Even in such cases the court may exclude a confession from evidence if made without a previous caution to the party that he need not make any statement. Curiously enough, however, any other evidence discovered as a result of an inadmissible confession (*e.g.* where a weapon is hidden) is admissible in itself. No party or witness is required to answer any question if to do so would expose him to criminal charges, *e.g.* questions about other crimes, but the accused, if he decides to testify, can be cross-examined about the crime with which he is charged.

Trials are directed to prove facts by evidence and not mere inference or surmise, and the accused man is being tried for a specific crime and not required to justify his whole life. Hence evidence is inadmissible which would reveal to a jury the fact that he is of generally bad reputation or has been convicted of similar crimes. Such circumstances are not without some relevance but they do not directly prove the crime charged and prejudice a jury disproportionately to their possible relevance. There are some important exceptions to these rules, however. Thus, if a man is clearly proved to have insured his bride and been in a house where she drowned in the bath under violent circumstances on the day of the wedding, evidence would be admissible to show that this had happened to several previous brides of his, to prove "method" or design on his part. Our law also allows the previous convictions of the accused to be read to the jury if the accused has gone beyond a mere denial of the prosecution testimony and attacked the prosecution witnesses, e.g. charged them with perjury, or accused fellow prisoners. This exception is justified as discrediting the accused and rehabilitating the testimony of the witnesses whom he had tried to discredit, thus making his character relevant to deciding who is telling the truth. The court has a discretion whether or not to subject the accused to this.

The accused need not testify and be cross-examined unless he wishes. His wife may not testify against him unless he is charged with an offence affecting her personally. Other witnesses are competent if old enough to understand their duty to speak the truth. Relationship or the like does not disqualify a witness but is a circumstance to consider in weighing their evidence. The opposing counsel is entitled to ask questions, of witnesses designed to show that they are biased against his side, e.g. that they have something to gain by a verdict one way or the other, or have expressed an opinion about the guilt of the accused.

Testimony of accomplices raises many legal problems. It is obviously in the interest of an alleged accomplice to throw blame onto a fellow-accused in order to "save his own skin." On the other hand such testimony may be a valuable way of proving the case for the prosecution. One solution is to eliminate any possible trial of the accomplice by first trying him or allowing him to turn Crown evidence, so that he has nothing further to gain or lose from a verdict against the principal accused. If the defence allege that a prosecution witness was an accomplice the jury must decide whether he was or not. If they decide that he was they must be warned not to convict on his evidence unless corroborated by other evidence; the jury themselves decide what is to be regarded as corroboration, after direction by the judge as to what may be so regarded. In any case the jury must be reminded that a proved accomplice to a crime is not a very credible witness and warned to treat his evidence with care.

Hearsay evidence is not acceptable in criminal trials, with a few exceptions, because the person making the statement is not subject to cross-examination.

Tape recordings and radar recordings are now admissible under safeguards and computer printouts will be admissible.

Evidence in civil proceedings

Juries are seldom used in civil proceedings today and the law of evidence is far less elaborate. Sworn affidavits are often used in Chancery cases without examining the deponents in court, and the Civil Evidence Act 1968 made hearsay evidence admissible generally, subject to certain safeguards, such as a right by the opponent to have the person appear in court if he wishes to cross-examine him.

Two questions which often arise are "privilege" and "secondary evidence." Privilege is a claim to exclude evidence from being used in proceedings, e.g. correspondence which is marked "without prejudice" and consists of attempts to reach a settlement by making offers or admissions conditional on a settlement out of court being reached but not otherwise. Communications, oral or written, between a party and his legal adviser are also privileged. Our law does not privilege communications with medical advisers or, though this is less clearly settled, with religious confidants. The need to do justice is regarded as so important as to override any considerations of confidence or privacy, except where the public interest requires confidentiality to be maintained.

Secondary evidence of the contents of documents is not admissible unless some law provides that a certified copy shall be accepted or unless it would be unreasonable or impossible to produce the original document, e.g. it is very bulky or cannot be traced. If a party has an original document and refuses to produce it (and it is not privileged) the opponent can give other evidence as to its contents.

INDEX